Arnold F. Silva
(954) 213-2248

"If you want to better understand the foundations of your faith, deepen the theological root systems of what you believe, and find out how to apply the key teachings of God's Word to your everyday life and problems, this monumental work needs to be in your library. I have thousands of books in my library, and most of them just sit on the shelf, but this is a resource I'll be using on a regular basis. If you buy this book, I can promise you that it won't just sit on your shelf!"

—DR. GARY OLIVER, ThM, PhD,
executive director, The Center for Relationship Enrichment;
professor of psychology and practical theology, John Brown University;
author of *Mad About Us*

"Many dictionaries of theology are overly dense, terse, and a bit stuffy, all of which severely limit their usefulness. So, within the genre of theological dictionaries, the *Dictionary of Everyday Theology and Culture* is a burst of fresh air. The entries are well chosen, are written in an accessible manner, and would serve as helpful supplements to more detailed teaching. I dare say that the careful study of this book alone would provide a decent theological education."

—STEVE L. PORTER, PhD, professor of theology and philosophy,
Institute for Spiritual Formation, Talbot School of Theology/Biola University;
managing editor, *Journal for Spiritual Formation and Soul Care*

"Finally we have a book on theology that you don't have to be a brain surgeon to understand. I love the clarity of presentation of deep theological concepts and the practical guidelines on how to implement the great truths of the faith in your daily life."

—GARY D. VANDERARK, MD, professor of neurosurgery,
University of Colorado, Denver

"For those who have ever asked 'So what?' after reading a theological tome, this resource provides welcome relief. The collection of insightful summaries from esteemed scholars explains key Christian doctrines with a view to our historic faith and then applies those truths in the context of our current world. *Dictionary of Everyday Theology and Culture* is a treasure trove of sound doctrine and practical insight into daily application. I look forward to using it regularly."

—RICK CORNISH, DMin, president, Teaching Truth International;
author of *5 Minute Theologian*, *5 Minute Apologist*, and *5 Minute Church Historian*

"Many of the issues we face today are so complex that Christians often despair of ever knowing how to respond. This resource provides thoughtful Christians a solid start in what Scripture teaches, the church has affirmed, and conscientious disciples should keep in mind as they frame their own answers. The entries covered are accessible yet substantial. Anyone wanting to understand the core concepts of his or her faith (baptism, atonement, prayer) or the pressing issues of this day (abortion, racism, relativism) could easily build on the foundation offered here. A rich resource for any bookshelf."

—DR. JOHN ANDERSON, DMin, pastor,
Trinity Presbyterian Church, Arvada, Colorado

THE NAVIGATORS REFERENCE LIBRARY

DICTIONARY OF EVERYDAY THEOLOGY AND CULTURE

BRUCE DEMAREST AND KEITH J. MATTHEWS,
GENERAL EDITORS

NAVPRESS

NavPress is the publishing ministry of The Navigators, an international Christian organization and leader in personal spiritual development. NavPress is committed to helping people grow spiritually and enjoy lives of meaning and hope through personal and group resources that are biblically rooted, culturally relevant, and highly practical.

For a free catalog go to www.NavPress.com
or call 1.800.366.7788 in the United States or 1.800.839.4769 in Canada.

Library of Congress Cataloging-in-Publication Data

The dictionary of everyday theology and culture / Bruce Demarest and Keith J. Matthews, general editors.
    p. cm. -- (The Navigators reference library)
Includes bibliographical references.
    ISBN 978-1-60006-192-9
    1. Christianity and culture--Dictionaries. 2. Christian ethics--Dictionaries. 3. Theology, Doctrinal--Popular works--Dictionaries. 4. Christian life--Dictionaries. I. Demarest, Bruce A. II. Matthews, Keith J.
    BR115.C8D535 2009
    261.03--dc22
                                        2009037815

Printed in the United States of America

2 3 4 5 6 7 8 / 13 12 11 10

INTRODUCTION

Dictionary of Everyday Theology and Culture is an easy-to-use book about theology and culture for ordinary people living in the everyday world. In particular, it's a practical guide to Christian theology and to key social and cultural issues in the contemporary world. The focus of the *Dictionary* is practical: understanding core Christian truths that provide the framework of the Christian worldview and applying these truths to the task of everyday life and service as followers of Jesus.

The word *theology* means reflection or discourse about God and his relationship to the world. Because we build our faith on correct understanding about God, theology also means knowing God, loving him, and serving his kingdom in our needy world. The ultimate end of theology is to reflect and extend the glory of God in every dimension of life.

The term theology doesn't appear in Scripture. However, the word doctrine—a near synonym—is found several times in the New Testament. The apostle Paul commanded us as Christians to uphold "sound doctrine" (1 Timothy 1:10; Titus 1:9; 2:1) and to renounce every appearance of false doctrine (1 Timothy 1:3). Paul urged the critical importance of holding fast to faithful doctrine with the command, "Watch your life and doctrine closely" (1 Timothy 4:16).

Each article in the *Dictionary* is divided into two main parts: "Everyday Definition" and "Everyday Application." Approximately equal attention is given to defining the meaning of each term and to applying the meaning of the term to our lives and service in the world.

Because we must first gain a clear understanding of a doctrine or a cultural issue before living out its implications as good servants in daily practice, the Everyday Definition attempts to explain each term in nontechnical, everyday language. If we want to be solidly grounded in the faith, to develop spiritually, and to serve effectively, we need clear understanding of core Christian truths. A sound theology—drawn primarily from authoritative Scripture, as well as from the reflections of trusted Christians from both church history and the current church—is basic to every aspect of our lives as Christian disciples.

Of course, Scripture realistically asserts that this side of heaven "we know in part" (1 Corinthians 13:9) and we "see only a reflection as in a mirror" (verse 12, TNIV). So while thorough and detailed, the Everyday Definitions in the *Dictionary* remain inherently incomplete. We will only attain certain and complete knowledge on all points of doctrine in the life to come when, ushered into Christ's presence (1 Corinthians 13:12), we will see all things clearly.

Theology isn't simply an intellectual exercise of reflecting on God's existence and works. Unfortunately, in some periods of church history, theology morphed into a largely intellectual undertaking where applications to real life were never made clear. Thus, the goal of the *Dictionary* isn't merely to produce correct definitions of theological and cultural terms. After all, it's possible to be knowledgeable in these areas yet remain spiritually dull and practically ineffective. So the *Dictionary* intentionally addresses the relevance and application of each term to godly living and Christian service with the Everyday Application. This section highlights how each term affects and applies to our relationship with God, self, others, and the surrounding world. So, while the *Dictionary* doesn't neglect formal truths, it's intentionally practical — or life related — because it emphasizes the relevance of theology for Christian living and service in today's complex cultural setting.

To this end, the *Dictionary* is written for informed everyday Christians. However, pastors, other ministry leaders, and seminary and Bible college students will also find its explanations and life applications informative, enriching, and helpful.

The creative team behind the *Dictionary* believes its practical focus will make it uniquely useful. After all, if we want to be effective disciples of Jesus Christ, we must know the truth with our minds, feel the truth with our hearts, and obey the truth with our entire lives. Professor and author Dallas Willard wisely unites these two goals of understanding and application: "Every Christian must strive to arrive at beliefs about God that faithfully reflect the realities of his or her life and experience, so that each may know how to live effectively before him in his world. That's theology!"[1]

What's more, the *Dictionary* also brings attention to issues of importance and relevance in the world of today. While fundamental

---

1.   Dallas Willard, *The Spirit of the Disciplines* (HarperSanFrancisco, 1988), 26.

truths of theology remain unchanged from God's perspective, biblical, historical, and theological studies have brought to light new insights that enhance our understanding and facilitate our service for the kingdom. Christian theology isn't static. Because theology means knowing God, loving him, and serving his kingdom in our world, our conversations about theological issues must reengage with every new generation. Each age presents new issues and poses revolutionary questions.

The editors and contributors pray that this *Dictionary* will enhance your understanding of essential topics of theology and important issues of contemporary society and at the same time enable you to live virtuously and fruitfully for the glory of God and for the good of the church.

ABORTION

EVERYDAY DEFINITION

Abortion means the termination of fetal life in a uterus prior to birth. Some abortions are natural, such as when a pregnancy miscarries due to illness. Currently, the term "abortion" more often refers to induced abortions, involving human intention and intervention.

Especially since 1973, when the United States Supreme Court ruled it unnecessary to protect those who aren't "persons in the whole sense," abortion has become a matter of concern for Christians. We face the issue in personal decisions, in pastoral care, in political responsibilities, and in our response to culture in general.

The issue of abortion raises some important questions: What is "human" life? When does "personhood" begin? Is it ever appropriate to terminate a human life? What rights do human beings have? Some people argue that induced abortion should rarely be allowed. Others argue that abortion is rarely immoral. Still others fall somewhere between these two positions, identifying various cases where abortion might or might not be acceptable. A full treatment of this issue requires wrestling with medical, psychological, political, legal, philosophical, biblical, theological, and practical wisdom.

As Christians, we must consider key biblical and theological issues that inform our definition and practice of "life." Simply put, the Bible presents no explicit teaching regarding abortion. Ancient Assyrian law condemned a woman who "has a miscarriage by her own act," but the Israelites had no such law. Greek and Roman writings included a range of views on abortion, but the New Testament is silent on the issue. However, soon after the writing of the New Testament, early Christians condemned abortion along with magic and infanticide (see *Didache* 2:2; *Epistle of Barnabas* 19:5).

Ultimately, we must take a biblical approach to abortion by looking at Scripture's more general teaching about such themes as life, human nature, and sexuality. God is the giver of life, breathing into humans "the breath of life" (Genesis 2:7). Because we're stewards of life, not creators, when we terminate a fetus we take into our own hands the life and death of a being who belongs to God and whose times belong to God.

In addition, the human life that God creates is precious. Above all living things, God declared human beings to be "very good" (Genesis 1:31). Because human beings are created in God's image, they are of special value to him (Genesis 1:27-28; 9:6; Psalm 8:3-8). Human beings form a microcosm of God's full creation, participating bodily in the earthly realm and participating spiritually in the heavenly realm. God also gave humans a distinct role as partners with him in caring for creation (Genesis 1:28; 2:15).

Some cultures recognize an unborn fetus as a human life, condemning induced abortion while at the same time permitting the abandonment of deformed or unwanted children. Early Christians, however, rejected both abandonment and abortion, choosing instead to care sacrificially for those formed in the image of God. The Scriptures give no explicit answer to the issue of when human life begins, although we find clear hints that God acknowledges and honors life within the womb (Exodus 21:22-25; Psalm 139:13-16; Luke 1:44).

Our spirit/body nature and our role as caretakers of God's creation combine in a single act. Through intercourse, we contribute with God in creating new life (Genesis 4:1). Consequently, marriage and intercourse are sacred to God, a holy and life-giving institution. The Scriptures urge God's people to live lives that recognize the sacredness of human sexuality (1 Thessalonians 4:3-8; Hebrews 13:4). Human sexuality is the means through which we cocreate life with God.

In conclusion, while Scripture doesn't provide explicit instruction about induced abortions, the biblical teachings about life, human nature, and sexuality lead us toward a deep regard for all innocent human life.

EVERYDAY APPLICATION

The issue of abortion is first of all—as it was for early Christians—an issue the Christian community must wrestle with. Our current context of permissive abortion laws necessitates that the church form disciples intellectually, morally, and spiritually who are capable of honoring human life at every level. Within our own communities, we must be willing to provide—as in earlier centuries—the care necessary to heal and embrace those suffering among us, both unborn children and struggling parents.

Second, we must transcend the contemporary rhetoric around this issue to see the broader meaning of abortion. Human sexuality isn't simply about women, but about the relationships between men and women. Until men comprehend the sacred nature of intercourse, until the "hearts of the fathers" are turned "to their children" (Malachi 4:6), the casual sexual relationships that lie behind some abortions will continue. As cocreators of life and caretakers of creation, Christians are obliged to avoid sexual sin. In this way, culture is positively influenced through the model of the Christian community.

Third, as those who live in an increasingly advanced medical environment, we must learn to think through the complexities of abortion ethics. When does human life begin? At conception? At implantation? At viability? At birth? What kinds of factors are most central in understanding our personhood (physical, psychological, social)? With increased technology, we can predict the difficulties of a deformed embryo. Should this knowledge influence our decisions regarding abortions? We must learn to evaluate new questions in light of the fundamental themes of Scripture.

Finally, as Christians, we must also deal with abortion as a public policy issue. What is the responsibility of a mixed Christian/non-Christian republic toward the unborn child or toward its parents? How involved should Christians be in shaping public policy? What strategies should be used or avoided?

To honor the gospel of life means becoming a life-giving community, caring for unborn children and broken parents, honoring proper sexual relationships, and serving as salt and light in the world. Through these thoughts and actions, we can foster the life that comes from God.

FOR FURTHER READING

Paul B. Fowler, *Abortion: Toward an Evangelical Consensus.* Multnomah, 1987.

Richard B. Hays, "Abortion," in *The Moral Vision of the New Testament—Community, Cross, New Creation: A Contemporary Introduction to New Testament Ethics.* HarperSanFrancisco, 1996.

— EVAN B. HOWARD

ANGELS

EVERYDAY DEFINITION

Angels, like other beings, were created by God to be his cooperative coworkers, agents, and messengers. The Bible describes the number of angels as enormous: "ten thousands" (Deuteronomy 33:2; Psalm 68:17); "thousands upon thousands" (Hebrews 12:22); "ten thousand times ten thousand" (Revelation 5:11). Although they don't have physical bodies, angels are still personal beings. A part of the unseen world, they occasionally appear to humans, announcing the will of God, strengthening God's people, protecting, and guiding. Angels do sometimes take on human-like form. When angels appear to people, they act as instruments of God's plan, making known to our eyes and ears the unseen — yet real — world.

Both the Hebrew and Greek words for angel mean *messenger*. Angels are enormously powerful when they appear in Scripture — so powerful that they often frighten people. As a result, ancient art and various kinds of contemporary media give them exaggerated physical features. While an angel sighting would be dramatic — it isn't every day that we get a glimpse into the invisible world — the occasion would probably be functional.

In terms of function, angels are ambassadors of God who act from positions of power and prestige from within the heavenly court. While some angels rebelled against God, the angels who stayed true to God don't seem to struggle with a sin-nature as do God's human servants. They don't appear to be tempted with disobedience, so they are especially trustworthy servants of God. Angels act on God's behalf; they are representatives of God, carrying out his will. As his spokesmen, angels declare or witness to the words of God. As emissaries of God's government, angels execute the work of God. As ministering spirits, they strengthen and sustain God's people. Interestingly, as powerful and magnificent as angels are, God's people — as the renewed humanity — will ultimately judge them (1 Corinthians 6:3).

Some form of order or hierarchy seems to exist among the angels. For example, Michael is called an archangel (Daniel 12:1; Revelation 12:7). Gabriel, singled out by being named, might also have prominence. The designation "The angel of the LORD" (Judges 13:2ff and Luke 2:9) is thought to sometimes to be an appearance of Jesus Christ himself. At a minimum, The Angel of the Lord speaks with an unusual authority, perhaps from the precise connection of the message to The Messenger.

Other types of angels or distinct spiritual beings might exist as well. The biblical story mentions Cherubim, Seraphim, and "The Living Creatures." These beings guarded access to Eden (Genesis 3:24); continually worship God (Isaiah 6:2-7); and surround God's throne (Revelation 4:6-8).

Throughout church history, people have debated about the exact role of angels. Some have believed in *guardian* angels. Among these beliefs, the precise connection of angels to humanity differs. Some conclude that each believer has a personal guardian angel (Psalm 91:11-12; Matthew 18:10; Acts 12:15; Hebrews 1:14). In the book of Acts, angels are active among the first followers of Jesus. For example, an angel directed Phillip, guided Cornelius, moved Peter to action, and gave a promise to Paul (Acts 8:26; 10:3-6; 12:6-11; 27:23-24). The Bible describes a group of angels watching over all God's people (Psalm 34:7). Some Jewish traditions see angels watching over nations (Daniel 10:13,21). The New Testament depicts angels over churches (Revelation 1-3; 1 Corinthians 11:10), caring for children (Matthew 18:10), and ministering to believers at death (Luke 16:22).

Whatever work angels might be sent to do, they clearly play frequent and significant roles in God's story. Angels represent to us the view of heaven regarding things on earth. To note just a few instances, angels predicted to Abraham the birth of Isaac, to Manoah the birth of Samson, and to Abraham the annihilation of Sodom. God sent an angel to bring Israel out of Egypt, lead them to the Promised Land, and destroy their enemies (Exodus 23:20; Numbers 20:16). An angel brought Elijah meat and drink (1 Kings 19:5). There are also combative angels. In one night, The Angel of the Lord destroyed the entire Assyrian army of 185,000 men (2 Kings 19:35). Angels are notable at the birth (Luke 2:9), resurrection (Luke 24:4), ascension (Acts 1:10), and return in glory of Jesus Christ (Matthew 24:31).

EVERYDAY APPLICATION

As followers of Jesus, we should expect that in a myriad of unseen ways, and rarely even in a visible way, that angels act on our behalf as we act on God's behalf. Angels work alongside us, reinforcing and supporting our human role as ambassadors of God's kingdom. Essential to Christian discipleship is an ongoing, beneficial, and real interactive relationship with the unseen world. Clearly, our conversation is meant to be primarily with God the Father, the Son, and the Holy Spirit. Yet God, as a part of his means of grace for humanity, has also given angels to minister to and with his people.

The unseen world that angels are a part of is real. The Nicene Creed says we believe that God is the creator of things *seen and unseen*. This isn't merely theoretical knowledge; it's crucial to functional and practical discipleship. When Elisha was surrounded and about to be captured, he saw into the invisible world; he saw chariots of fire (2 Kings 6:17). Jesus in the garden, facing arrest, told his overzealous friend that he could call on God's angels at any time (Matthew 26:53). As Christians, we come to terms, in a practical sense, with this immaterial aspect of Christian life. God does actually watch over us—often through the agency of angels. Their consistent lives of devotion to God and their conformity to the story, the plan, and the intention of God is a great inspiration for us in our lives as followers of Jesus.

Although interaction with angels is a part of God's plan for humanity, we should exercise some cautions:

- We need to be cautious about believing things that purportedly come from angels but that are contrary to Scripture (1 Kings 13:18; Galatians 1:8; 2 Corinthians 11:14).
- We shouldn't have an over-exuberant interest in angels. The Holy Spirit is the primary leader of churches and the people of the church.
- No Scripture encourages us to pray to angels; we pray only to God.
- We shouldn't worship angels or even seek appearances from them. The scriptural pattern is that angels appear unsolicited.

Asking God to use angels in our lives according to his design for them is in alignment with the purposes of God and a life of faith. While the church now has the canon of Scripture, a great deal of historically agreed upon theology and practice, and the Holy Spirit directly at work among us, it doesn't follow that we no longer need the guidance, protection, and ministry of angels.

FOR FURTHER READING
J. I. Packer, *Concise Theology*. Tyndale, 1993.
Wayne Grudem, *Systematic Theology*. Zondervan, 1994.
Billy Graham, *Angels: God's Secret Agents*. A Crossings, 1994.

— TODD HUNTER

APOSTASY

EVERYDAY DEFINITION
Apostasy constitutes a serious turning away and repudiation of core Christian beliefs and practices. The Greek verb, *aphistēmi* (Luke 8:13; 1 Timothy 4:1; Hebrews 3:12) means "to fall away" or "become apostate." An apostate is a professing Christian who renounces Christian faith previously held and who often opposes and assaults the faith. Someone who professes Christianity but who then turns aside from the faith commits apostasy, or in the words of Jesus, commits "blasphemy against the Spirit" (Matthew 12:31). An apostate (unbeliever) can't be said to fall from grace because he never was truly in a state of grace.

The apostle Paul taught that "in later times some will abandon the faith and follow deceiving spirits and things taught by demons" (1 Timothy 4:1). He added, "Some have in fact already turned away to follow Satan (1 Timothy 5:15). The apostle Peter acknowledged in his day that false prophets and teachers "secretly introduce destructive heresies, even denying the sovereign Lord who bought them" (2 Peter 2:1). These false teachers claimed to know the way of righteousness, but they turned their backs on Christ and returned to the fallen world order where they belong. Peter characterized the false teachers and those influenced by them as blasphemers (verse 12), "springs without water" (verse 17), and "slaves of depravity" (verse 19). Peter described apostates via two sayings: "'A dog returns to its vomit,' and 'A sow that is washed returns to her wallowing in the mud'" (verse 22, TNIV). Peter repeatedly stated that God has reserved the blackness of everlasting punishment for those who repudiate sound faith (2 Peter 2:1,3,12,17). Jude also warned against apostate teachers, highlighting their depraved character and announcing their coming doom (Jude 4,8,10-13,16,18-19).

Apostasy shouldn't be confused with backsliding, which is understood as a temporary weakening of trust in Christ. Biblical examples of backsliding include believers in Israel who turned away from Yahweh to serve idols (Isaiah 1:4); David, as seen in his acts of adultery and murder (2 Samuel 11:1-17); Solomon, whose many wives turned his heart away from the Lord (1 Kings 11:4,9,10); Peter, who three times denied Christ (Mark 14:66-72); and Demas, a coworker of Paul who abandoned discipleship (2 Timothy 4:10). Regrettably, true Christians for a time can become weak in faith, love, and zeal for Christ.

EVERYDAY APPLICATION

A child who spurns the love and favor of his parents grieves and saddens their hearts. Similarly, God, who graciously offers the gift of eternal life, is grieved and angered when those he created for fellowship forsake him and serve other gods (Deuteronomy 32:16). Because he is righteous and just, God will bring judgment on those who break covenant and practice idolatry (Isaiah 65:11-12; John 15:6). For those of us who profess to be Christians, we must examine our hearts to determine if we truly belong to the Savior and if we harbor any hostility toward Christ and the gospel. We also need to be alert to the peril of backsliding, becoming indifferent to Christ and the practice of discipleship.

People who profess to be Christians who then spurn the Savior, abandon faith, and deny God's grace seriously damage the testimony of Christ in the world. Those who are weak and unsettled spiritually might look to the ways of apostates and be tempted to abandon faith and discipleship. The damaging consequences that rejecting Christ has on the spiritual welfare of others who bear the name "Christian" are enormous.

Even entire societies enjoy God's blessing and prosper by virtue of faithfulness to Christ and the gospel. As was the case with Israel, forsaking the true and living God in favor of idols weakens and destabilizes societies at their core. Ultimately, if departure from Christian faith and practice remains unchecked, societies disintegrate from within and eventually become unjust, oppressive, and inhuman. The stability and integrity of societies worldwide requires determination not to commit apostasy and to remain faithful to the gospel of Jesus Christ.

Professing Christians who threaten to renounce Christ and the gospel need to examine the meaning of apostasy as set forth in God's Word. They face perilous consequences for denying Jesus, who alone is "the way and the truth and the life" (John 14:6). Those threatening to commit apostasy should also understand the fatal outcomes of rejecting the gospel, which alone embodies the promise of eternal salvation. As Christians, we can pray that God will restore these potential apostates to the path of truth so they don't they commit the "sin that leads to death" (1 John 5:16).

FOR FURTHER READING

O. S. Hawkins, *In Sheep's Clothing: Jude's Urgent Warning About Apostasy in the Church*. Loizeaux, 1994.

David G. Bromiley, *Falling from the Faith: Causes and Consequences of Religious Apostasy*. Sage Publications, 1988.

— BRUCE DEMAREST

ASCENSION

EVERYDAY DEFINITION

The ascension refers to the crucified and resurrected departure of Jesus Christ from earth and return to his original exalted status and place in heaven with God the Father and God the Holy Spirit.

Preceding the ascension, the divine Son of God "descended" to the world of salvation-needing human beings (Ephesians 4:9), humbling himself in the incarnation by taking on real and fully human nature (Philippians 2:6-8; Hebrews 2:14-18). After living in the world for approximately thirty years, and ministering for three years, the God-man was put to death through crucifixion and buried in a tomb (Matthew 27). Three days later, he rose from the dead (Matthew 28:1-15) and appeared to his disciples for forty days (Acts 1:3; John 20:17). As he was blessing them, the ascension occurred: "He was taken up before their very eyes, and a cloud hid him from their sight" (Acts 1:9; Luke 24:50-51). Jesus Christ ascended into heaven, where he then sat down at the right hand of God (Ephesians 1:20; Colossians 3:1; Romans 8:34; 1 Peter 3:22).

Because of this event, great honor and glory were bestowed on the ascended Jesus, different from the majesty that had been his prior to his incarnation. Though glorified with the Father and the Holy Spirit from eternity past (John 6:62; 17:5), the Son is now highly honored with them as the crucified, resurrected, and ascended God-man (Philippians 2:9; 1 Timothy 3:16). He is now seated in heaven, indicating that his work of salvation on behalf of sinful people is completed (Hebrews 1:3) and sufficient to rescue all who embrace him as Savior and Lord.

Additionally, "exalted to the right hand of God, he has received from the Father the promised Holy Spirit" (Acts 2:33). On the Day of Pentecost, the ascended Jesus Christ poured out the Holy Spirit, launching him on his new covenant ministry (2 Corinthians 3) by which the church came into existence (Acts 2). Further, as the exalted Lord, Jesus "gave gifts" to humanity (Ephesians 4:8; Psalm 68:18), specifically equipping his followers to be apostles, prophets, evangelists, and pastor-teachers (Ephesians 4:11). People exercise these gifts for the building of Christ's church toward maturity (Ephesians 4:12-16).

Jesus Christ is the head of the church by means of the ascension. At that event, the Father exalted him above all heavenly and earthly powers, present and future, and "placed all things under his feet and appointed him to be head over everything for the church, which is his body" (Ephesians 1:22-23; 1 Peter 3:22). The fullness of the exalted Lord "fills everything in every way" (Ephesians 1:23), not bodily but by his Holy Spirit who is at work in and through the church.

EVERYDAY APPLICATION
As Christians, the ascension of Jesus Christ should encourage us to recognize the many benefits that flow to us as a result of Christ's enthronement at the right hand of God the Father in heaven. Those benefits include:

- The exalted "Lord and Christ" (Acts 2:36) now rules the entire universe from heaven. All angels, all demons and their leader Satan, and all other heavenly beings exist and function under the sovereign direction of the ascended Christ. Additionally, all human authorities—presidents, kings, dictators, and all lesser human rulers—live and exercise their roles under the sovereign control of the exalted Christ. Because he possesses "all authority in heaven and on earth," Jesus Christ decisively commissioned his church before his ascension with these words: "Therefore go and make disciples of all nations" (Matthew 28:18-20). This Great Commission is given to us as the divinely called and divinely sent people living under the sovereign rule of our majestic head. As Christians, we rejoice that our ascended Lord has been "exalted . . . to the highest place" and given "the name that is above every name" (Philippians 2:9).

- Our "life is now hidden with Christ in God" (Colossians 3:3), which means that our identity as Christians is fully associated with the ascended Christ. This identification means that we are "seated . . . with him in the heavenly realms" (Ephesians 2:6), and that we are to set our hearts and minds "on things above, not on earthly things" (Colossians 3:2). When we do this, we decisively break from "sexual immorality, impurity, lust, evil desires and greed . . . anger, rage, malice, slander, and filthy language" (Colossians 3:5,8). Although Christians are *in* this world and are *for* this world, we are *not of* this world and we refuse to participate in its evil deeds. This identification also signals our ultimate victory over sin and death. We experience the Lord's authoritative power now so as to struggle "not against flesh and blood, but . . . against the spiritual forces of evil in the heavenly realms" (Ephesians 6:12). Through the ascended Christ's authority and power, we achieve partial victory now over temptation, sin, and evil as we also look forward to his ultimate triumph over all enemies (Hebrews 10:12-14).

- The exalted Christ is actively engaging on our behalf. As the great High Priest (Hebrews 4:14; 8:1), he intercedes for us (Hebrews 7:24-25; Romans 8:34). He prays for our persevering obedience and faithfulness, and is the advocate before the Father on our behalf, pleading his blood as the atoning sacrifice for our sins (1 John 2:1-2). Further, Christ prepares a place for his disciples until he returns (John 14:1-3). Concerning his coming return, we eagerly await this next event: The ascended Lord will return physically (Acts 1:11), appearing "a second time, not to bear sin, but to bring salvation to those who are waiting for him" (Hebrews 9:28; Philippians 3:20-21).

FOR FURTHER READING

Gerrit Scott Dawson, *Jesus Ascended: The Meaning of Christ's Continuing Incarnation*. P & R, 2004.

Douglas Farrow, *Ascension and Ecclesia*. T & T Clark, 1999.

Michael Horton, *People and Place: A Covenant Ecclesiology*. Westminster John Knox, 2008.

— GREGG ALLISON

ATHEISM

EVERYDAY DEFINITION

Atheism is the philosophical position asserting that all forms of theism are false. Atheists believe there is no personal, Creator God that transcends the universe (monotheism or deism), no impersonal God that is one with the universe (pantheism), no utterly transcendent God who exists apart from evil matter (gnosticism or dualism), or no collection of finite gods (polytheism). Put positively, atheists are naturalists who believe that everything that exists can be understood in terms of physics, chemistry, and biology. Atheism is distinguished from agnosticism, which claims that one can't *know* whether or not God exists. Atheists claim they know God doesn't exist.

More specifically, in opposing Christianity, atheists assert that the universe wasn't created, but rather popped into existence at the "big bang" or has always been in existence in some form. Humans aren't made in God's image, but have evolved from lower life forms due to the combination of chance and natural laws. They claim that there is no soul, no supernatural salvation, no angels, no demons, and no afterlife. The Bible can't be divinely inspired, because there is no divine Author. Instead, these books are merely collections of prescientific superstition — groundless speculations that are refuted by the discoveries of science.

Atheists have been a distinct minority throughout history, but they can be found beginning with some of the pre-Socratic philosophers. In the West, atheism gained ground in the Enlightenment, as thinkers declared their autonomy from received religious traditions and attempted to rethink philosophy and culture apart from divine revelation. For many, Darwin's theory of natural selection was a kind of declaration of independence from divine design, since it could explain the development (but not the origin) of life through mindless processes. Following in this train, much of modern science (particularly biology) has excluded any theistic understanding of nature from its theories. In the twentieth century, the communist regimes of the USSR (1917-1981) and Red China imposed atheism on entire civilizations. Although the United States Constitution guarantees freedom of religion, public education in the United States is taught at all levels according to the demands of naturalism. God is omitted as a meaningful explanation for anything in the curriculum.

Atheism promotes itself as enlightened, liberating, and free of superstition. With the publication of *The End of Faith* (2004), Sam Harris initiated a movement called "the new atheism," which took a militant stand against belief in God and all religion. Richard Dawkins, Christopher Hitchens, and others jumped on the bandwagon with a scorched earth (or heaven) approach that declared belief in God to be not only false but dangerous.

EVERYDAY APPLICATION

Christians must recognize the need to challenge atheist claims by demonstrating in practical ways that atheism is an illogical and unlivable worldview and that good and sufficient reasons exist for believing in the existence of the Christian God. Some ways we can do that are as follows:

- We must show that atheism provides no moral meaning for life. As Friedrich Nietzsche (1844-1900) realized, the so-called death of God brings the death of any objective moral order. If matter is all that exists, we can make no appeal to any transcendent standard for conduct. We're left only with instincts and changing social situations.
- We must communicate that if God is dead, so is human uniqueness. Atheists would argue that humans don't bear the divine image, all forms of life have equal value. However, no animals are trying to protect humans from extinction. Given our rationality, creativity, and morality, we transcend the animal realm in ways that atheism cannot explain.
- We need to point out that moral responsibility makes no sense in a world without God, a world of mere matter in mindless motion. If humans are "meat machines," who are part of a

larger cosmic machine, they cannot be held accountable for their actions. One well-known atheist claimed that when we do science, we deny humans free will; but when we think of law and morality, we must "play that game." Christians must recognize this as double-think of the highest order.

- We must articulate sound reasons for belief in the existence of God. Several powerful lines of evidence have convinced many scientists and philosophers that the universe came into existence out of nothing a finite time ago. This "big bang" perspective denies the eternality of the universe and forces the atheist to claim that everything came from nothing without a cause and for no reason. But God as the universe-Maker is a far more rational explanation. In addition, scientists have found that dozens of factors about the universe must be just so in order for life to exist. If any of these "cosmic constants" or other variables—such as the expansion rate of the universe—were off by even a fraction, no life would exist. Atheists must claim this is sheer chance or that some unknown natural law explains it all. Yet, the idea that a Mind fine-tuned all of these elements is a far better explanation. Lastly, at the microscopic level of the inner workings of the cell, scientists have discovered extremely complex molecular machines and information-rich systems that can't be explained on the basis of mindless matter and chance. Christians must argue the point that a designing Intelligence is the best explanation for observable phenomena.

Although atheism poses a significant and well-funded challenge to the Christian worldview, it is propped up more by ideology than by evidence. Given the strength of the arguments available against atheism and for God, we need to gain courage and acquire the needed knowledge to out-argue atheism in all areas of life.

FOR FURTHER READING
Lee Strobel, *The Case for a Creator.* Zondervan, 2004.
Anthony Flew, *There Is a God: How the World's Most Notorious Atheist Changed His Mind.* HarperOne, 2007.

— DOUGLAS GROOTHUIS

ATONEMENT

EVERYDAY DEFINITION

Atonement generally refers to the way that the life, death, and resurrection of Jesus has forever changed the human situation. The atonement is considered to be the heart of the Christian story: the restoration and redemption of humanity.

However, the word itself is a relatively recent theological innovation. In his popular translation of the English Bible in 1526, William Tyndale substituted the Latin word *reconciliatio*, "reconciliation," with his own creation, "atonement." By combining two words, "at" and "onement," he hoped to capture the deeper significance of the work of Christ and avoid any historically limiting terminology. Although the word "atonement" isn't native to the biblical tradition, the notion of the atoning work of Jesus Christ is pervasive and represented by five distinct models: sacrifice, redemption, victory over the powers of evil, reconciliation, and revelation.

Sacrifice. The most influential biblical model of atonement revolves around the sacrificial death of Jesus on the cross. The language of sacrifice can be found throughout the New Testament, but most especially in the book of Hebrews, where the Crucifixion is framed in light of the most important of Jewish festivals, *Yom Kippur*, the "Day of Atonement" (Hebrews 9:1-14). This solemn festival was a day of spiritual accounting when the sins of Israel would be judged and forgiven.

Redemption. This second model emerges from the tradition of "redeeming" slaves or prisoners of war by paying the necessary price for their release. The Jewish people understood their liberation from Egypt in the book of Exodus as an act of redemption from slavery. In a similar vein, the gospel of Mark describes the death of Jesus as a "ransom for many" (Mark 10:45), an act liberating all of humanity from slavery to our own brokenness.

Victory over the powers of evil. The classic biblical support for this third model is found in the apostle Paul's letter to the church at Colossae: "And when you were dead in trespasses and the uncircumcision of your flesh, God made you alive together with him, when he forgave us all our trespasses, erasing the record that stood against us with its legal demands. He set this aside, nailing it to the cross. He disarmed the rulers and authorities and made a public example of them, triumphing over them in it" (Colossians 2:13-15, NRSV). The world is caught in the middle of a cosmic battle between the powers of good and evil; Satan has held humanity captive, but through Jesus Christ, God has defeated Satan and his kingdom forever.

Reconciliation. This fourth model describes atonement in a uniquely personal way; the relationship between God and humanity was broken but now has been restored. Although this isn't a common view, Paul clearly articulates this perspective in his letter to the church in Rome: "For if while we were enemies, we were reconciled to God through the death of his Son, much more surely, having been reconciled, will we be saved by his life" (Romans 5:10, NRSV).

Revelation. The fifth model is almost exclusively found in the gospel of John. The human situation is characterized by ignorance and darkness; Jesus brings light to dark places, revealing the true glory of God. "And this is the judgment, that the light has come into the world, and people loved darkness rather than light because their deeds were evil. For all who do evil hate the light and do not come to the light, so that their deeds may not be exposed. But those who do what is true come to the light, so that it may be clearly seen that their deeds have been done in God" (John 3:19-21, NRSV).

EVERYDAY APPLICATION

At first glance, the variety of biblical models that represent the atoning work of Jesus Christ might seem disorienting. However, the beauty of the scriptural witness regarding atonement lies in the kaleidoscopic reality it reveals:

- Divine justice requires both personal and corporate responsibility.
- The human predicament is such that divine intervention is necessary.
- Evil has been defeated and goodness reigns.
- Creation has been restored to the Creator.
- Light has come to the world and the dark places have been undone.

Brokenness is an ever-present and immeasurably diverse reality of the human experience. The world is filled with suffering and despair to such an extent that the prospect of hope might seem fleeting and illusory. But the person of Jesus Christ is a divine proclamation that the human drama is beginning anew. The cross and Christ's work of atonement is a sign of a changed world—that which was broken is being made whole again.

FOR FURTHER READING

Joel B. Green and Mark D. Baker, *Recovering the Scandal of the Cross: Atonement in New Testament and Contemporary Contexts.* InterVarsity, 2000.

Martin Hengel, *The Atonement: The Origin of the Doctrine in the New Testament*, translated by John Bowden. Fortress, 1981.

I. Howard Marshall, *The Work of Christ.* Zondervan, 1969.

—MATT HAUGE

BAPTISM

EVERYDAY DEFINITION

Baptism is the initiation rite into the Christian community. The physical rite involves washing with water and is a sign of purification from sin. Along with communion, it is one of two rites considered sacraments by most Christians. The author of Hebrews described baptism as one of the foundational doctrines of the church (Hebrews 6:1-2).

Some significant differences exist among Christians about how the ritual of baptism should be performed. Eastern Orthodox, Oriental Orthodox, and some Protestant groups baptize only by immersion in water, while Roman Catholics and other Protestant groups allow pouring or sprinkling as well. Some Protestant groups do not baptize infants, while Roman Catholic, the Orthodox, and other Protestant churches do. Baptism is performed "in the name of the Father, the Son, and the Holy Spirit" by almost all Christians, but a few baptize "in the name of Jesus."

Although baptism as an initiation rite isn't mentioned in the Old Testament, by the time of Jesus it was a requirement for Gentiles who wanted to convert to Judaism (in addition to circumcision for males who wanted to become Jews). John the Baptist also demanded Jews to repent and be baptized for the forgiveness of sins (Mark 1:4). We see the coming importance of baptism for Christians when Jesus submitted himself to be baptized by John the Baptist before beginning his ministry. At this event, the Holy Spirit descended upon Jesus in the form of a dove and God proclaimed, "This is My beloved Son, in whom I am well-pleased" (Matthew 3:17, NASB; Mark 1:11; Luke 3:22).

Jesus showed the necessity of baptism for salvation by telling Nicodemus, "Unless one is born of water and the Spirit he cannot enter into the kingdom of God" (John 3:5, NASB). Later, Jesus commanded his disciples, "Go therefore and make disciples of all the nations, baptizing them in the name of the Father and the Son and the Holy Spirit" (Matthew 28:19, NASB).

After his resurrection, Jesus promised his disciples, "John baptized with water, but you will be baptized with the Holy Spirit not many days from now" (Acts 1:5, NASB). The New Testament church began on the Day of Pentecost with the coming of the Holy Spirit. On that day, the apostle Peter told the crowd who had become convicted of their sins, "Repent, and each of you be baptized in the name of Jesus Christ for the forgiveness of sins; and you will receive the gift of the Holy Spirit" (Acts 2:38, NASB). Three thousand people were baptized that day, and baptism has been a central part of all missionary activity of the church ever since.

EVERYDAY APPLICATION

Christian baptism is a sign of the most important event in salvation history: the death, burial, and resurrection of Jesus Christ. Baptism serves as a sign that we've been purified from our sins. The apostle Paul wrote, "Do you not know that all of us who have been baptized into Christ Jesus have been baptized into His death? Therefore we have been buried with Him through baptism into death, so that as Christ was raised from the dead through the glory of the Father, even so we too might walk in newness of life. For if we have become united with Him in the likeness of His death, certainly we shall also be in the likeness of His resurrection" (Romans 6:3-5, NASB; Colossians 2:12).

Baptism represents a new beginning. When we're baptized, we put on Christ (Galatians 3:27). This means that we no longer serve sin but are servants of Christ.

In addition, we are baptized into one body, the church of all believers. As the church, no distinction exists between Jew and Gentile, slave and free, male and female; we are all one in Christ (Galatians 3:28). Through baptism we are joined to Christ and to all believers.

FOR FURTHER READING

G. R. Beasley-Murray, *Baptism in the New Testament.* Macmillan, 1962.
J. H. Crehan, *Early Christian Baptism and the Creed: A Study in Ante-Nicene Theology.* Burns, Oates & Washbourne, 1950.
J. Jeremias, *Infant Baptism in the First Four Centuries.* Westminster, 1962.

— TIM FINLAY

BIBLE, AUTHORITY OF THE

EVERYDAY DEFINITION

The Bible is the very Word of God. Most Christians agree that it has no error concerning not only matters of faith and salvation but also science, geology, history, archaeology, and other matters. The Bible has no error because all the books of the Bible, both Old and New Testaments, were supernaturally inspired by the Holy Spirit. The whole Bible is God-breathed and a product of God's direct involvement. "And how from infancy you have known the Holy Scriptures, which are able to make you wise for salvation through faith in Christ Jesus. All Scripture is God-breathed and is useful for teaching, rebuking, correcting and training in righteousness, so that all God's people may be thoroughly equipped for every good work" (2 Timothy 3:15-17, TNIV). The Holy Spirit's inspiration makes the Scriptures both inerrant and authoritative. Divine inspiration entails divine authority. Because the Bible has divine authority, it provides the absolute standard for good and evil as well as the true and the false. When the Bible speaks, God speaks. The words of the Bible are the authoritative words of God.

Jesus repeatedly affirmed the supreme authority of the Bible. He identified the Scriptures (during his earthly life, the Old Testament) as the Word of the Father. When Jesus said, "It is written," he meant, "God says." Jesus answered, "It is written: 'People do not live on bread alone, but on every word that comes from the mouth of God'" (Matthew 4:4,

TNIV). As a person of the triune God, he is the author of the entire Bible. However, as the only mediator between God and sinners, he submitted himself completely to the authority of the Bible. Jesus obeyed the Bible thoroughly. He submitted himself to the demands and the commands of the Bible. He identified his submission to the Bible with his obedience to God the Father. He said that he came to fulfill the law and prophets (the writings of the Old Testament). "Do not think that I have come to abolish the Law or the Prophets; I have not come to abolish them but to fulfill them. Truly I tell you, until heaven and earth disappear, not the smallest letter, not the least stroke of a pen, will by any means disappear from the Law until everything is accomplished" (Matthew 5:17-18, TNIV).

God has spoken in the past and continues to speak in the present through authoritative Scripture. According to John Calvin, the sixteenth-century French reformer, when we read the Bible we encounter God who personally speaks in and through the Scriptures through the Holy Spirit. Although the Bible is the Word of God, apart from the Spirit's illumination we cannot understand the message of the Bible. The same Holy Spirit who originally inspired the Bible and its writers enables and empowers us to understand the Word of God.

EVERYDAY APPLICATION

As Christians, we should understand and live out the following truths about the Bible and its authority:

- The Scriptures have absolute and final authority over all matters of our faith. If we want to know who God is, we must listen to the Bible. If we want to know what God does, we should pay attention to the Bible. If we want to know what God demands of us, we should understand the teachings of the Bible. If we want to understand God's purposes for our life, we should read the Bible. If we want to have true faith in God, we should study the Bible.
- The Bible possesses divine authority over matters of our salvation. The Bible teaches that everyone is under sin and its curse. Scripture proclaims that "the heart is deceitful above all things and beyond cure" (Jeremiah 17:9). The Bible also teaches us the way of salvation. It proclaims that Jesus

Christ is the only Savior and Lord of sinners. By shedding his blood on the cross, Jesus paid in full the wages of sin. By being resurrected from the dead, he completed the work of redemption so that sinners can be saved from the power of sin and death. When a sinner puts personal trust in the person of Jesus Christ and what he has accomplished for our salvation, that person is saved forever. Faith in Jesus Christ as revealed in the Bible is the only way of salvation.

- The Bible possesses divine authority over all matters of our moral and ethical lives. If we want to know how to live as faithful disciples of Jesus, we must listen to the Bible. The Bible provides us with profound insights into what kind of life we should lead as holy children of God. The goal of the Christian life lies in imitating Christ. In order to live a moral life, the Bible affirms the importance of imitating God and Jesus: "Follow God's example, therefore, as dearly loved children and walk in the way of love, just as Christ loved us and gave himself up for us as a fragrant offering and sacrifice to God" (Ephesians 5:1-2, TNIV).

In order to lead a life solidly grounded in the authoritative Word of God, we must regularly practice several important spiritual disciplines that relate to Scripture:

- We should read the Bible on a regular basis so as to hear the written Word and gain personal encounter with the living Word.
- We should attend to the formal proclamation of the Scriptures. When we hear God's Word being taught, we understand God's will and grow spiritually.
- We should make every effort to study the Word of God, which becomes for us spiritual food. Without studying the Bible, we can't learn how to apply biblical teachings to the situations of our lives.
- We should meditate and ponder the Word of God on a daily basis. The psalmist wrote, "Blessed are those who do not walk in step with the wicked or stand in the way that sinners take or sit in the company of mockers, but who delight in the law

of the LORD and meditate on his law day and night" (Psalm 1:1-2, TNIV).

- We should memorize as much Scripture as possible. Jesus set a great example for us, for when he was tempted by Satan and attacked by Jewish religious leaders, he refuted them with Bible verses that he had memorized from his youth. The Holy Spirit uses Scripture when we are tempted, attacked, and in despair. The Word of God gives us spiritual power to fight the power of darkness. Thus, the apostle Paul exhorted us to "Take . . . the sword of the Spirit, which is the word of God" (Ephesians 6:17).

By reading, listening to, studying, mediating upon, and memorizing the Bible, we are equipped to be faithful disciples of Jesus Christ.

FOR FURTHER READING
John R. W. Stott, *Understanding the Bible*. Baker, 2001.
Gordon D. Fee and Douglas Stuart, *How to Read the Bible for All Its Worth*. Zondervan, 2003.

— SUNG WOOK CHUNG

BIBLE, INSPIRATION OF THE

EVERYDAY DEFINITION
Inspiration can be defined as the supernatural action of the Holy Spirit upon the writers of the Bible such that what they wrote was the infallible and authoritative Word of God — the truth that God intended to be written. This special revelation was given to prophets and apostles, was recorded in Scripture, and is preserved for all generations.

In the Old Testament, the stone tablets containing the Ten Commandments were written by the very "finger of God" (Exodus 31:18; 32:16). At Sinai, Moses wrote the book of the covenant by the command of God (Exodus 34:27). Elsewhere, God ordered chosen prophets, including Isaiah (8:1; 34:16), Jeremiah (30:2), and Habakkuk (2:2), to write down his words in scrolls.

Jesus upheld the entire Old Testament as the infallible word of God (Matthew 5:17-19) down to the "least stroke of a pen" (Luke 16:17). He asserted the truthfulness of inspired Scripture with the petition, "Sanctify them by the truth; your word is truth" (John 17:17). Jesus certified the inspiration and authority of the Old Testament by sentences such as "it is written" (Mark 1:2; 9:13), "Have you never read?" (Mark 2:25; Luke 6:3), and "This is what is written" (Luke 24:46). The apostle Paul wrote in similar terms with equal conviction (Romans 1:17; 1 Corinthians 1:19; Galatians 3:10).

Paul's words, "All Scripture is God-breathed" (2 Timothy 3:16) asserts that the whole of Scripture originates by inspiration of God (see Psalm 33:6). What is divinely breathed out and written by prophets and apostles is the very Word of God. The apostle Peter wrote, "No prophecy of Scripture came about by the prophet's own interpretation of things. For prophecy never had its origin in the human will, but prophets, though human, spoke from God as they were carried along by the Holy Spirit" (2 Peter 1:20-21, TNIV). The Greek word for "carried along" is used elsewhere to describe a sailing ship propelled by a strong wind.

Regarding the inspiration of the New Testament, Paul identified his writings as "the Lord's command" (1 Corinthians 14:37). Peter testified that Paul wrote "with the wisdom that God gave him" and placed Paul's letters on a par with the "other Scriptures" of the Old Testament (2 Peter 3:15-16).

Historically, the church has upheld the belief that the entirety of Scripture is God-breathed. Christian tradition also affirms verbal inspiration, meaning that the Holy Spirit guided the biblical writers so directly that the words they wrote were the words God intended to be written.

Because Scripture is the inspired Word of God, it is truthful in all it teaches. The term infallibility indicates that written Scripture fulfills the purposes God intended. Inerrancy means that the Bible is free from errors in all that it affirms, consistent with the standards of accuracy prevailing at the time. And because Scripture was inspired by the Holy Spirit, it possesses the authority of God himself.

Just as Jesus Christ, the living Word, was both human and divine, the written word of Scripture is both a divine and human document. Evidences of the Bible's humanness include the following: the biblical writers engaged in historical research (Luke 1:3), utilized oral tradition and historical archives (1 Kings 14:29; 1 Chronicles 29:29), and pursued their own unique styles of writing. Emotional outbursts reflected in some of the Psalms (Psalm 69; 79; 109; 137) also testify to the Bible's humanity.

Under the guidance of the Holy Spirit, early church councils certified the canon of inspired Scripture as containing thirty-nine books of the Old Testament and twenty-seven books of the New Testament.

EVERYDAY APPLICATION

As Christians, abundant evidence leads us to believe that the Bible is completely truthful and dependable for all people of all times and cultures. Psalm 119 testifies to the excellencies of God's Word, reminding us that Scripture in its entirety is "righteous" (119:7,62), "good" (119:39), "trustworthy" (119:86,138), "right" (119:128,137), and "true" (119:142,151). Jesus urged us to not be like those he chided as "foolish" for being "slow to believe all that the prophets have spoken" (Luke 24:25, TNIV).

We search the pages of the inspired written Word to learn about the living Word, Jesus Christ. He is the central theme of all Scripture. From the inspired Word, we learn of his coming to earth, love for sinners, death on the cross, triumphant resurrection, and coming return to earth with glory and power to receive us, his followers, to himself.

We study inspired Scripture to gain a true portrayal of humanity. The Bible answers fundamental questions of human experience: "Who am I?" "Why are humans morally and spiritually flawed?" "How do we receive a new nature, realize our identity in Christ, and achieve our final destiny?" The inspired Scriptures, wrote Paul, "are able to make you wise for salvation through faith in Christ Jesus" (2 Timothy 3:15).

Further, inspired Scripture fortifies us to grow spiritually and serve fruitfully. The inspired Word, illumined by the Spirit, blesses and comforts the heart (Psalm 1:1-2; 119:52), revives the soul (Psalm 19:7), guards against sin (Psalm 119:11), defends against the wiles of the devil (Ephesians 6:1), and guides our steps (Psalm 119:105). As followers of Jesus, we must be eager to study (Psalm 1:2), memorize (Psalm 119:11), preach (2 Timothy 4:2), and teach (Deuteronomy 11:19) God's Word. Inspired Scripture is "useful for teaching, rebuking, correcting and training in righteousness, so that all God's people may be thoroughly equipped for every good work" (2 Timothy 3:16-17, TNIV).

FOR FURTHER READING
D. A. Carson and John D. Woodbridge, *Scripture and Truth.* Zondervan, 1983.

I. Howard Marshall, *Biblical Inspiration.* Eerdmans, 1983.

Benjamin Breckenridge Warfield, *The Inspiration and Authority of the Bible.* Presbyterian and Reformed Publishing, 1948.

— BRUCE DEMAREST

BIOETHICS

EVERYDAY DEFINITION
Bioethics literally means "life ethics." Sometimes it's used as a synonym for medical ethics, but it's increasingly common to see the scope of bioethics as larger than medical ethics, including topics such as environmental ethics, the assumptions and uses of research methodologies, the application of various technologies to any living entity, and public policy. Still, much of the subject matter for bioethics originates in the medical setting, encompassing questions such as abortion, euthanasia, distribution of resources within medical practices, genetic screening and engineering, patient confidentiality and autonomy, and others.

Of course, ethical concerns about life, medical treatment, and death have been with us for centuries, and to this extent, bioethics has existed as long as human beings have had to make ethical decisions on these matters. Several reasons exist for the development of bioethics as a unique and specific discipline existing under the broader umbrella of ethics. Without doubt, a main impulse for bioethics has been the rapid development and application of new technologies within the medical profession. New advances broaden the scope of concern, raising the potential for extending life through technological means, genetically engineering the characteristics of an unborn child, using fetal stem cells in developing potential life-saving drugs, cloning, and a host of other possibilities for biological interventions.

Another reason for the development of bioethics as a distinct discipline is the potential for abuse in treatment or research, prompting the need for public policy about use of humans in medical experiments, informed consent and confidentiality, and application (or denial) of new technologies and treatments. In short, bioethics came into being in large part because of a growing recognition of the tension between what we are able to do and what we should do.

EVERYDAY APPLICATION

While most of us will never be involved directly in policy development or advising patients on bioethical matters, the entire field provides some important areas for Christians to think through.

First, we will be confronted with bioethical issues on a personal level. Questions concerning advance directives outlining our desires for resuscitation if our heartbeat or breathing stops or becoming an organ donor at death bring us directly into the realm of bioethics. We might have to make decisions about whether to terminate a pregnancy because significant defects have been identified within a fetus. Or we might struggle with decisions to hasten our own terminal condition by euthanasia or to remove a relative from life-support. These are just a few examples of how the questions of bioethics challenge us on an individual level.

Second, bioethics represents a unique challenge for Christians because it deals with issues not specifically addressed in Scripture. For obvious reasons, we won't find anything in the Bible about mapping the human genome, cloning, development of herbicide-resistant plant hybrids, or a broad array of other bioethical topics. At the same time, it seems clear that Christians should work out thoughtful positions on such questions. Although we can't outline a complete method for how Christians address issues not addressed directly in Scripture, an important place to begin is a set of basic convictions about God, human nature, and the purpose of human existence that we can apply to bioethical decisions. For example, Scripture tells us from the beginning that "God created human beings in his own image" (Genesis 1:27, TNIV) and that God created the first human "from the dust of the ground and breathed into his nostrils the breath of life" (Genesis 2:7). Such passages tell us that human beings have a unique place within the created order and remind us that we are dependent on God for our existence. These and other pivotal passages help us build the foundations of a biblically informed worldview about the nature and treatment of persons. This, in turn, provides a foundation for decision making on matters where Scripture offers no specific directives.

In addition, bioethics provides an important opportunity for

Christians to think carefully about how their faith relates to science in general. Unfortunately, Christians have sometimes staked out a hostile stance toward science, and those in science have frequently held the same opinion of Christianity. However, if Christians want to take positions on bioethical issues (and it's hard to imagine how we cannot), we should acquaint ourselves with the science behind those issues. Otherwise, we will make uninformed pronouncements and simply expose Christianity to increased marginalization from both the scientific community as well as the policy-making processes that surround bioethical matters.

Finally, bioethics creates the opportunity to think through our faith in the area of public policy. As a society, we can't avoid making decisions about whether we should make use of certain technologies to preserve, enhance, or end human life. Rules, regulations, and guidelines will be written and will provide a legal framework for our life. Christians have a duty to be involved in this process. However, American society is pluralistic, and many citizens don't begin from Christian ethical assumptions. This raises the broader challenge to Christians about how we enter into public debates where our convictions aren't shared by all who are affected by decisions we must make as a society.

FOR FURTHER READING
Gilbert Meilander, *Bioethics: A Primer for Christians*. Eerdmans, 2004.

— STEVE WILKENS

BLESSING

EVERYDAY DEFINITION
The Hebrew root (*b-r-k*) for bless or blessings also serves as the basis for the verb "to kneel." The Greek word (*eulogein*) and its derivatives carry similar meanings. In the Bible, the giving of blessings means imparting good wishes, health, prosperity, thanksgiving, and power, from one party to another, in an established positive relationship.

In the Bible, blessings are uttered in three types of contexts:

1. A blessing may be pronounced by God on humans as an act of goodwill, benefaction, or favor (Genesis 1:22; Luke 24:50-51).

2. Humans may bless God as an expression of private or communal praise, thanksgiving, or worship (Psalm 115:18; 145:1-2).
3. Individuals may utter blessings upon each other as signs of salutation (1 Samuel 13:10). This might occur during the transfer of family blessings from one generation to another (Genesis 27:27-29), in worship ceremonies where a ruler blesses the congregation (Numbers 6:24-26), or as wishes of fertility (1 Samuel 2:20-21). Blessings can be accompanied by symbolic acts such as the laying on of hands (Genesis 48:14; Mark 10:16) or the sharing of a meal (Genesis 14:18-20).

In several passages of Scripture, a list of blessings is set alongside a list of curses. As noted in the covenant with Moses, the fulfillment of God's blessings is conditional upon obedience to the covenant stipulations (Deuteronomy 28:2), while the execution of curses results from disobedience to God's instructions (Deuteronomy 28:15). A partial list of blessings and curses similar to that found in the book of Deuteronomy also appears in the so-called Holiness Code (Leviticus 26:14-39). In the New Testament, Jesus echoes the Old Testament paradigm of blessings and curses in Luke's gospel, where he counterbalances his four "blessed are you" statements with four "woe to you" readings (Luke 6:20-26).

EVERYDAY APPLICATION
Throughout Scripture, God promises to bless his people with provisions (Psalm 104:27-28; 111:5), protection (Psalm 18:30-36; 144:2), favor (Psalm 5:12; 2 Corinthians 6:1-2), and inner peace (Isaiah 26:3; Philippians 4:7). Although the Bible emphasizes God's blessing of those who turn their hearts toward him, Scripture reveals that, in his great love and mercy, God blesses even those who have turned away from him (Hosea 2:21-23). This model of divine grace should compel us to love the unlovely and to extend kindness and benevolence to those who don't deserve it. Scripture instructs us to bless not only those who bless us but also to bless those who persecute us (Luke 6:27-28; Romans 12:14-21). Our natural tendency is to withhold blessings and kindnesses from those who hinder and persecute us; but with Jesus as our example we know that it's more blessed to give to those in need than to receive (Acts 20:35) and to love our enemies than to hate them (Luke 6:27-35).

In contemporary culture, divine blessing is often linked with material abundance and the absence of sickness, distress, and adversity. Yet a close examination of Scripture reveals that suffering comes to all individuals, even to those who love and serve God without reproach (Job 1:21-22). Throughout history, God has been willing and faithful to pour his blessings on all of humankind.

FOR FURTHER READING

Claus Westermann, *Blessing in the Bible and the Life of the Church.* Fortress, 1978.

— HÉLÈNE DALLAIRE

BLOOD

EVERYDAY DEFINITION

Blood is a metaphor for life in Scripture (Deuteronomy 12:23; Leviticus 3:17). The shedding of blood is a symbol of life lost, whether through an act of sacrifice or murder (Hebrews 9:22).

Because God declared human life to be sacred, the Bible admonishes against the shedding of blood (Genesis 9:5; 4:10). The primary use of the word *blood* focuses around issues related to atonement (Leviticus 17:11). Because the theme of redemptive sacrifice weaves throughout Scripture, this symbol is crucial and prominent throughout the biblical story as well as in Christian experience. The metaphor of blood invokes the declaration that Christ died on the cross in order to restore a relationship between God and humanity (1 Peter 1:2; 1 John 1:7; Hebrews 9:14). This follows the themes of sacrifice found in the Old Testament and the Jewish religion.

Blood is a difficult metaphor, because it is both graphic and poignant. Some of Jesus' own followers walked away when Jesus used graphic language to speak about his death on the cross. "Jesus said to them, 'Very truly, I tell you, unless you eat the flesh of the Son of Man and drink his blood, you have no life in you'" (John 6:53, NRSV).

Jesus used the image of bread and wine in the Passover feast, which becomes the Lord's Supper, to illustrate his broken body and shed blood on the cross. The apostle Paul wrote, "For I received from the Lord what

I also passed on to you: The Lord Jesus, on the night he was betrayed, took bread, and when he had given thanks, he broke it and said, 'This is my body, which is for you; do this in remembrance of me.' In the same way, after supper he took the cup, saying, 'This cup is the new covenant in my blood; do this, whenever you drink it, in remembrance of me.' For whenever you eat this bread and drink this cup, you proclaim the Lord's death until he comes" (1 Corinthians 11:23-26).

EVERYDAY APPLICATION

Because the term *blood* richly proclaims the work of Jesus on the cross, the church has produced a variety of music revolving around the theme of blood. This music sometimes has a jarring quality, but it also demonstrates the importance of the cross for the Christian faith. Just among Christian hymns, this music includes: "Alas! And Did My Savior Bleed?" "Are You Washed in the Blood?" "Nothing But the Blood," "The Blood Will Never Lose Its Power," "There Is a Fountain," and "There Is Power in the Blood." Christians rejoice in the sacrifice of Jesus for our sins. His sacrifice, symbolized by blood, becomes an example for us as we extend ourselves to others (1 John 3:16).

FOR FURTHER READING

Scott McKnight, *A Community Called Atonement*. Abingdon, 2007.
James Beilby and Paul R. Eddy, *The Nature of the Atonement*. InterVarsity, 2006.

— KURT FREDRICKSON

CALLING

EVERYDAY DEFINITION

Calling in Scripture involves a God-given summons to salvation. Most Christians distinguish between a general, external call and a special, internal call of the Spirit for salvation. Explicit evidence for the two callings is found in Jesus' parable of the wedding banquet (Matthew 22:1-14). Those initially invited refused to attend. But when the king's servants "gathered all the people they could find . . . the wedding hall was filled with guests" (Matthew 22:10). The story ends with Jesus' words of explanation: "Many are invited, but few are chosen" (Matthew 22:14).

The general call explains the gospel and invites an individual to repent of sins and trust Christ. The general call represents a legitimate invitation to "whosoever will" respond and be saved, but often it is met with indifference or rejection (Isaiah 65:2; Jeremiah 7:13). During his time of ministry on earth, Jesus extended a legitimate, general call to salvation (Matthew 11:28). But because of hardened hearts, few responded positively to his invitations (John 5:39-40).

Because of the debilitating effects of sin on the mind and heart (1 Corinthians 2:14; Ephesians 4:18), the universal, external call alone proves ineffectual. Jesus taught, "No one can come to me unless the Father who sent me draws them" (John 6:44, TNIV). In his own time and way, God graciously issues the internal, effectual call to those he wills to be saved through a secret wooing of the Spirit (1 Corinthians 1:9,26). The Spirit's internal operation illumines the darkened mind, softens the stubborn will, and inclines the reluctant heart to seek God. According to the Baptist preacher, C. H. Spurgeon, "There is a fountain filled with blood, but there may be none who will ever wash in it unless divine purpose and power shall constrain them to come."[1] In other words, the internal call of the Spirit opens the sinner's heart, giving that individual both the desire and the ability to repent of sins and trust Christ.

The Spirit's special call is seen in the dramatic conversion of Saul of Tarsus on the road to Damascus (Acts 9:1-9) and the opening of Lydia's heart at Corinth (Acts 16:14). The dominant view of the church since the Reformation is that God draws sinners to Christ through both the general call of the gospel and the special drawing power of the Spirit. This twofold calling explains why many who hear only the general call fail to trust Christ, but that all who are drawn by the Spirit's inner call believe and are saved (see John 6:44-45).

EVERYDAY APPLICATION

When the Spirit extends the invitation to salvation, we must immediately respond to that gentle call before the day of opportunity has passed. Once we make that decision, we must understand why the Spirit has called us to himself: "We know that in all things God works for the good of those

---

1. *Metropolitan Tabernacle Pulpit: Sermons Preached and Revised by C. H. Spurgeon*, 1877. 8:185.

who love him, who have been called according to his purpose" (Romans 8:28). God's call to vocation in the world follows his call to salvation. In addition, believers are called into intimate relationship with Jesus: "[God] has called you into fellowship with his Son, Jesus Christ our Lord" (1 Corinthians 1:9, TNIV). In this new relationship we receive a new identity in him, for we have been "called to belong to Jesus Christ" (Romans 1:6). As a result of this new relationship, we're "called children of God!" (1 John 3:1). Believers are called to holiness of life, that is, "called to be saints" (Romans 1:7). In a time when some professing Christians discredit the gospel by unworthy behavior, God calls us to live a blameless life. "God did not call us to be impure, but to live a holy life" (1 Thessalonians 4:7). Finally, Christians also are called to peace. In our high-pressured and anxiety-ridden world, we must appropriate the peace that Jesus gives to those he calls: "Let the peace of Christ rule in your hearts, since as members of one body you were called to peace" (Colossians 3:15).

Christ commanded his followers to issue the general call of the gospel to all. The apostle Peter declared, "You are a chosen people . . . that you may declare the praises of him who called you out of darkness into his wonderful light" (1 Peter 2:9). Called and redeemed people faithfully proclaim the gospel to the lost and dying, while trusting the effectual call to the wise and loving Holy Spirit. The Spirit's effectual call assures Christian witnesses that their ministry will not be in vain—that the full harvest God intends will be brought in. God himself promised, "My word that goes out from my mouth . . . will not return to me empty, but will accomplish what I desire and achieve the purpose for which I sent it" (Isaiah 55:11).

Apprentices of Jesus must live intentional, disciplined, and God-centered lives while proclaiming the Word in season and out of season. Paul wrote, "I press on toward the goal to win the prize for which God has called me heavenward in Christ Jesus" (Philippians 3:14). Believers fulfill their calling by living Christ-honoring lives before a watching and hurting, and often skeptical, world.

FOR FURTHER READING

Wayne Grudem, *Systematic Theology*. Zondervan, 2000.

— BRUCE DEMAREST

CAPITAL PUNISHMENT

EVERYDAY DEFINITION

Capital punishment refers to a state's execution of an individual for a crime, following a legal judicial process. Capital punishment has a long history, being used by nearly every society as the penalty for offenses deemed serious. Prior to the twentieth century, almost every nation practiced capital punishment, although crimes that carried the death penalty varied from one society to another. Virtually every society classified murder and treason as crimes punishable by death. However, other transgressions also brought the death penalty, including political dissent, adultery, homosexuality, theft, mutiny or military desertion, rape, and religious crimes like apostasy or heresy.

In recent decades, many nations have abolished capital punishment. Most of the countries of Europe, South America, and Oceania have done so, while the majority of Asian and African countries retain it. In the United States, individual states determine whether to levy the death penalty, and about two-thirds of the states have retained it as an option for punishment. Even though a significant number of countries maintain the death penalty as an option among other forms of punishment, its frequency of use has dropped dramatically. In addition, while earlier stages of history often used quite gruesome means for carrying out the death penalty, the trend has been toward more humane methods of execution.

As within the general population, Christians don't unanimously agree in their opinions about capital punishment. In the United States, Protestants are more likely than Americans in general to favor capital punishment, but even within Protestant circles death penalty support has dropped in recent years. Roman Catholics are less inclined than Protestants to support the death penalty. Indeed, the Catechism of the Roman Catholic Church finds capital punishment justifiable only in cases when no other means can safeguard innocent life. This broad and deep-seated diversity of opinion makes it impossible to speak of *the* Christian position on the topic.

EVERYDAY APPLICATION

We might question why capital punishment remains a hot-button issue given that relatively few death penalties are carried out annually

(42 United States executions in 2007). The prominence of the debate can be explained by its connection with two broader issues: the value of life and the nature of justice. The disagreements about capital punishment come, not in the validity of the principles about life's value and the importance of justice, but in how these principles should be properly applied.

Those favoring capital punishment argue that when one individual intentionally and unlawfully takes the life of another, both justice and respect for life require the death of the guilty party, provided guilt has been established by the proper judicial process. Death penalty advocates point to Genesis 9:6, which states, "Whoever sheds human blood, by human beings shall their blood be shed; for in the image of God has God made humankind" (TNIV). By grounding the worth of human life in "the image of God," supporters of capital punishment argue that failure to impose this penalty devalues the life of the victim and places the lives of other innocent individuals at risk. In addition, proponents say that if the death penalty isn't in place, we send a message to potential murderers that society doesn't value life. In essence, capital punishment is the social equivalent to the principle of self-defense. Further, the entire concept of justice implies that punishment should equal the crime committed, so proponents of capital punishment argue that termination of a murderer's life is the only equivalent retribution for the crime committed.

Capital punishment opponents draw on the same principles, but employ them in different ways. Many Christian abolitionists argue that it is morally and logically inconsistent to be pro-life on topics such as abortion and euthanasia while supporting the death penalty. They hold that human life, regardless of circumstances, should be preserved as a gift from God until God, not humans, allows death. Closely related to this is the argument that the death penalty forecloses on any future opportunity for repentance and rehabilitation by the criminal; concerns for the spiritual state of a murderer require preservation of life in pursuit of repentance for that individual's wrongs.

Opponents of capital punishment also argue that we can't count on imperfect human beings to administer justice perfectly. Biases creep into decisions, and minorities are more likely, proportionally, to receive death sentences. The justice system has made mistakes and innocent people have been executed. Because of the finality of execution, opponents argue that the death penalty should be abolished.

We also find disagreements within the Christian community concerning the proper interpretation or application of Scripture's teaching. Death penalty opponents, for example, note that Jesus' teaching for his followers to "turn to them the other cheek" (Matthew 5:39, TNIV) when wronged establishes a new standard for response to crimes. Jesus' response to those who tested him about stoning (a form of capital punishment in that era) a woman caught in adultery (John 8:3-11) is also viewed as an illustration of an ethics of forgiveness. Finally, while many abolitionists acknowledge that the Old Testament does call for the death penalty in a number of passages, this punishment extends to a broad variety of crimes (such as adultery, witchcraft, cursing parents, false prophecy, and others) that no one wants to place under this sanction today. As a result, death penalty opponents argue that it's inconsistent to argue for the validity of the punishment for only one or two categories of crime today and to apply a lesser penalty (or no penalty) to other offenses.

Supporters of capital punishment note that the Old Testament explicitly prescribes the death penalty in several places (see Genesis 9:6; Exodus 21:12-17; Numbers 35:16-21; Leviticus 20:1-16; Deuteronomy 18:20; 19:21). While they recognize that the New Testament doesn't specifically mention capital punishment, the apostle Paul did note that civil governments are ordained by God to execute punishment (Romans 13:1-4). Citizens who live peacefully have no reason to fear government authorities, "but if you do wrong, be afraid, for rulers do not bear the sword for no reason. They are God's servants, agents of wrath to bring punishment on the wrongdoer" (verse 4, TNIV). While this includes no explicit reference to the death penalty, the statement that rulers "bear the sword" strongly implies it. Also, when Pilate asked Jesus, "Don't you realize I have power either to free you or to crucify you?" Jesus responds, "You would have no power over me if it were not given to you from above" (John 19:10-11). Supporters argue this indicates that secular governments, while flawed, do have authority from God to carry out this penalty.

Of course, Christians offer many other pro and con arguments on this matter. Yet this brief discussion demonstrates why the question of capital punishment promises to remain a thorny issue within the Christian community for some time to come. Discussions like this stand as an example of just one area where Christians share strong agreement on fundamental moral principles and the authority of Scripture but continue to have equally strong disagreement about the application of these principles and proper biblical interpretation.

FOR FURTHER READING

H. Wayne House and John Howard Yoder, *The Death Penalty Debate: Two Opposing Views of Capital Punishment*. W Publishing, 1991.

— STEVE WILKENS

CELIBACY

EVERYDAY DEFINITION

The Christian doctrine of celibacy is rooted in a proper understanding of sex, because sexual intercourse isn't merely a physical act, but a relational, emotional, and spiritual one. Genesis 2 sets forth the foundation for marriage: the man and the woman know each other in all ways and seek a fruitful life through various forms of intimacy. Sexual intercourse is a normal expectation within marriage as a way to grow in relational connection (1 Corinthians 7:2-4), as well as to produce children. Within marriage, sexual intercourse is God's intention for a man and a woman when they have committed before God to become one flesh.

In God's holy plan, the unmarried should remain celibate, because they haven't entered into a state where sexual intercourse creates one flesh. Rather, it would merely be a physical act. The apostle Paul's teaching regarding both virgins (those who had never been married) and widows affirms this (1 Corinthians 7). The Bible never views sexual intercourse itself as sinful, but rather as God's good gift to create greater intimacy between a husband and wife. The practice of sexual intercourse outside of marriage — taking on the form of intimacy without the commitment of vows — makes God's gift an act of idolatry and therefore sinful.

We can easily become confused by Paul's statements (1 Corinthians 7) that it's better for an unmarried and celibate man or woman to remain this way rather than to marry. Paul says it's better to remain unmarried, but if one burns with passion it is better to be married. Paul is speaking of celibacy as a spiritual gift. If someone has the gift of celibacy—meaning that person is dedicated full-time to God's work and not to a spouse—then that individual should live in the celibate state. The advantage is that in the midst of severe trials, a celibate and unmarried individual doesn't have to witness the sufferings of loved ones (see Jeremiah 16). Still, marriage is as honored a calling as singleness is. What distinguishes the two states is the will of God.

EVERYDAY APPLICATION

We usually associate celibacy with priests, monks, and nuns of the Roman Catholic and Eastern Orthodox churches—a practice that began as early as the second century and is rooted both in Jesus' celibate life and in Paul's words recorded in 1 Corinthians 7. First-century pagan culture was much like ours today—highly sexualized and consumed with immediate gratification of physical urges. In those days, as in ours, celibacy speaks to the deeper meaning of sexual intercourse as something directed toward the spouse, not self, and being only a part of life, not the whole.

Today, Christians who have never been married and those who have lost a spouse through death or divorce have the opportunity to speak about what satisfies their true needs—to be known, to know God, and to know our neighbor. When entering into marriage, we commit at a deep level to being known by our spouse for a lifetime. Celibacy isn't merely an act of the will; it's an act of dedication to the deeper meaning of sex and to the higher calling that a married couple becomes one flesh. Celibacy is not a higher calling than marriage, but it's a calling that works alongside marriage to make both sexual intercourse and marriage reflect their lofty intentions.

According to many statistics, a growing number of young Christians are unable to find a mate who is maturing in Christ and dedicated to serving him. Paul encourages these individuals to welcome the opportunity to focus more devotedly on Christ and the unique calling available to single people.

For both the married and unmarried, we need to keep in mind that marriage doesn't "complete" us. Only the presence of Christ and our participation in whatever he calls us to can offer that grace.

FOR FURTHER READING

Randy C. Alcorn, *Sexual Temptation*. InterVarsity, 1989.

Tim Stafford, *Sexual Chaos*. InterVarsity, 1993.

— CHRISTOPHER MORTON

CHRIST, DEITY OF

EVERYDAY DEFINITION

Christianity is all about Christ, the second person of the Trinity and the divine Son of God. The word "Christ" comes from the Greek, meaning "the anointed one," which points to Jesus as the divine Messiah. The Bible and Christian authorities through the centuries overwhelmingly assert that Jesus Christ is not only human but that he shares in the being and perfections of God as truly God. Only one who is God can save humanity from their sins, reconcile sinners to the Father, and bestow eternal life. The Apostles' Creed succinctly confesses faith in "Jesus Christ, His [God's] only Son, our Lord."

The case for the deity of Jesus Christ is highly compelling, as the following evidence shows. The gospel accounts of Jesus' life testify to divine *qualities* he possessed. Christ is eternally unchangeable, or immutable (Hebrews 13:8).

- Throughout his earthly ministry, Jesus possessed superhuman knowledge (omniscience). Jesus knew in advance that Judas would betray him (Matthew 26:21-25) and that Peter would deny him three times (26:34). Christ's disciples stated, "Now we can see that you know all things" (John 16:30), and his apostles acknowledged, "Lord, you know everyone's heart" (Acts 1:24).
- Christ exercised superhuman powers (omnipotence) during his ministry. By his powerful word, he quieted the stormy sea (Mark 4:39), fed five thousand people (Mark 6:39-44), cast out demons (Mark 7:25-30), and brought the dead back to life (Mark 5:35-42).
- Scripture designates Christ as "the Almighty" (Revelation 1:8). Jesus Christ attributed absolute eternality to himself by affirming, "before Abraham was born, I am!" (John 8:58).

John also ascribed self-existence to Christ: "For as the Father has life in himself, so he has granted the Son also to have life in himself" (John 5:26, TNIV; 1 John 1:2).

The Gospels record Jesus' supernatural *works* that could not be performed by humans. Christ forgave people's sins (Mark 2:1-12) even as the scribes and Pharisees grumbled among themselves, "Who can forgive sins but God alone?" (Mark 2:7). Christ's work of forgiving sins was widely preached by the apostles (Acts 5:31; 10:43).

- Jesus Christ is portrayed as the divine creator (Colossians 1:16; Hebrews 1:2), the divine sustainer (Colossians 1:17; Hebrews 1:3), and the divine providential ruler (1 Corinthians 10:1-10) of the cosmos. He is also the agent of redemption, rescuing all who believe in him from sin and Satan (Ephesians 1:7) and reconciling us to the Father (Romans 5:11). Only one who is God could rise from the dead, destroy death, and open wide the gates of heaven (2 Timothy 1:10).
- At the end of the age, Christ will judge the world, casting the unrighteous into hell and rewarding the righteous with the eternal kingdom (Matthew 13:41-43; 25:31-41). As the early Christian preachers proclaimed, God "has set a day when he will judge the world with justice by the man he has appointed" (Acts 17:31).

Christ's deity is also established by the astonishing *claims* he made.

- He claimed authority over the sacred Jewish law (Matthew 5:21-22,27-28,31-34).
- He claimed that the new covenant established with his own blood would supersede the old covenant inaugurated through Moses (Matthew 26:28).
- Christ professed authority over the Old Testament Sabbath (Mark 2:28).
- He made the claim that he was the true bread from heaven that gives life to the world (John 6:32-33,48).
- Jesus claimed to be the only way to God (John 14:6). More

than that, he claimed to be truly God, saying, "I and the Father are one" (John 10:30). The Jews sought to stone him, understanding these words to be a claim to deity (verses 31-33).

- Christ claimed he would raise all the dead at the end of the age (John 5:25; 6:39). His own resurrection from the dead authenticated his claims and validated his deity (Romans 1:4). For other claims to deity see Mathew 4:7; John 10:38; and John 17:5.

Christ's deity is further established by the *prerogatives* attributed to him.

- People called upon Christ's name in prayer and worship: Stephen (Acts 7:59-60), Saul (Acts 9:5), and hosts of other repentant sinners (Acts 9:21).
- Thoughtful men and women risked their very lives for him, as recorded in the New Testament (Acts 15:26) and throughout centuries of church history. Jesus demanded absolute loyalty and allegiance from his followers. They were to obey him unconditionally and worship him alone (Matthew 14:33; 28:9-10). Christ asserted his unqualified authority in Matthew 28:18: "All authority in heaven and on earth has been given to me." Saul, who met Christ in a life-changing encounter enroute to Damascus, testified that Jesus the Messiah "is God over all, forever praised!" (Romans 9:5). John asserted that the "Word" (*logos*) "was with God . . . in the beginning" and, indeed, "was God" (John 1:1). When the Word became flesh at the Incarnation, his glory was manifested, "the glory of the one and only [Son]" (verse 14, TNIV).

Christ understood himself to be God's only Son and promised Messiah. Jesus commended Peter for his truthful confession, granted by the heavenly Father, of his divine personhood (Matthew 16:16). When arraigned before the Sanhedrin and charged by Caiaphas to state publicly whether he was the Messiah and Son of God, Jesus replied forthrightly, "I am" (Mark 14:62). As the hour of his crucifixion approached, Christ openly acknowledged before the authorities his divine identity and messianic vocation. Christ's self-understanding as the divine Son of God and second person of the Trinity was fully validated by his extraordinary life and teaching.

EVERYDAY APPLICATION

Each of us must make a prayerfully informed decision about whether Jesus Christ is the divine Son of God as he claimed. Do we accept the truthfulness of his words, "the Father is in me, and I in the Father" (John 10:38)? Do we acknowledge his claim, "I am the way and the truth and the life. No one comes to the Father except through me" (John 14:6)? The late Christian apologist, C. S. Lewis, challenged us to judge whether Jesus Christ was a good man, a liar, a lunatic, or the Lord of all. If Jesus isn't the divine Lord, as he claimed, he is hardly worth emulating. Our eternal destiny lies on this decision of following the Son of God as his disciples. May we say with the Roman centurion guarding Christ as he hung on the cross, "Surely he was the Son of God!" (Matthew 27:54). And may we confess with Simon Peter, "You are the Messiah, the Son of the living God" (Matthew 16:16, TNIV).

Further, if we believe that Jesus Christ is the divine Son of God with all the perfections of the Godhead, we must go beyond acknowledging his deity to yielding him our wholehearted allegiance. We must bow the knee before "both Lord and Messiah" (Acts 2:36, TNIV). We value Jesus Christ above everything in the universe. In total surrender we offer our "bodies as living sacrifices, holy and pleasing to God" (Romans 12:1). We detach our minds from fleeting earthly things and fix them "on things above, where Christ is seated at the right hand of God" (Colossians 3:1). We relish the thrill of intimate relationship with the Lover and Redeemer of our souls. Our goal is that the divine Christ should become the supreme object of our love and devotion. We long to commend the divine Lord to those who do not know him.

We also will recognize the three appointed offices that Christ holds as prophet, priest, and king:

1. During his earthly life, Jesus was widely recognized as a prophet (see Matthew 21:11; Luke 7:16; John 4:19). As a prophet he preached and taught with truth and authority that which he saw and heard from his heavenly Father. As a prophet he revealed the Father (John 17:6). He also accurately predicted events that

would come to pass in the future, particularly in the end times (Mark 13:1-31). The writer of Hebrews declared, "In the past God spoke to our ancestors through the prophets . . . , but in these last days he has spoken to us by his Son" (Hebrews 1:1, TNIV). We must attend to and obey Christ's prophetic teaching concerning spiritual matters, for as he said, "Heaven and earth will pass away, but my words will never pass away" (Mark 13:31).

2. We must also value Jesus Christ as our great high priest who offered himself once for all as the final sacrifice for sins (Hebrews 7:27). As our high priest, he empathizes with our weaknesses (Hebrews 4:15). We can take great comfort in knowing that we're not alone in our trials and suffering, but that the divine Lord is present to sustain us. As our high priest, Christ also prays for us continually before the Father (Hebrews 7:25). By virtue of his high priesthood we have the right to enter the Holy of Holies on his merits apart from any human intermediaries. As God's blood-bought children we can directly "approach God's throne of grace with confidence, so that we may receive mercy and find grace to help us in our time of need" (Hebrews 4:16, TNIV).

3. Jesus Christ is also the promised King descended from David, although his kingdom "is not of this world" (John 18:36). As our King, Christ wisely and powerfully rules the universe, the world, and our individual lives in every detail. Christ the King faithfully safeguards and shelters us by his might and grace. As his people, we have nothing to fear because he is the omnipotent Sovereign over all principalities and powers. We have the privilege and joy of trusting, worshipping, obeying, and adoring Christ, the Son of God, Messiah, and King.

FOR FURTHER READING

Bruce Demarest, *Who Is Jesus: Revisiting Jesus Christ the God-Man.* Kregel, 2006.

John MacArthur, *The Superiority of Christ.* Moody, 1986.

Peter Toon, *Jesus Christ is Lord.* Judson Press, 1979.

— BRUCE DEMAREST

CHRIST, EXALTATION OF

EVERYDAY DEFINITION

In the Christian tradition, theologians have spoken of two states of Jesus Christ—humiliation and exaltation. The first refers to Jesus humbling himself by taking on a human body and nature with its earthly limitations. The ultimate humiliation of his life was the Crucifixion. Christ's second state is his exaltation as a result of his finished work on earth. In the exalted state Christ is glorified as the Savior of sinners and the Lord of the universe before whom "every knee should bow, in heaven and on earth and under the earth, and every tongue acknowledge that Jesus Christ is Lord" (Philippians 2:10-11, TNIV). There are four aspects to this exalted state of Christ as the glorious God-man: his resurrection, ascension, being seated at the Father's right hand, and his future triumphant return to earth.

1. The resurrection of Christ was the climax of his redemptive work as he was declared with power to be the Son of God (Romans 1:4). God the Father raised him from the dead according to Old Testament promises (see Acts 13:30-37). While Christ's resurrected body is still flesh and bones (Luke 24:39), it has now shed its earthly limitations and been raised as a new glorified body (Philippians 3:21) or "spiritual body" (1 Corinthians 15:44). It is this glorified body that believers will share (1 Corinthians 15:20-23; 1 John 3:2) when Christ returns.

2. Christ ascended back into heaven in his new resurrected body, partaking again of the glory he had shared with the Father before creation (Acts 1:9-11; John 17:4-5). When he ascended, he sent the Holy Spirit to his disciples (John 16:7; Acts 2:33) as he had promised. Christ's physical departure from the disciples also began his work of preparing a place for them in his Father's house (John 14:2-3) until the time when the latter will restore all things as he promised (Acts 3:21).

3. When Christ ascended into heaven he sat down on God's right hand, the seat of authority and influence (Hebrews 1:3-13). From his exalted position, the sovereign Christ intercedes for his people on earth as a priest who made the once for all

sacrifice of himself on their behalf (Romans 8:34; Hebrews 7:25-27). Christ will continue to reign from the Father's right hand until all his enemies have been subdued (Psalm 110:1; Matthew 22:44).

4. The final stage of Christ's exaltation will be "the appearing of the glory of our great God and Savior, Jesus Christ" (Titus 2:13, TNIV) just as he promised (John 14:3; Acts 1:11). The saints will marvel at the glory of the Son when he returns (2 Thessalonians 1:9-10). Christ will separate believers from non-believers (both the living and the dead), and those who have rejected him will be judged (Matthew 25:31-46). When all his enemies, including death, are subdued, Christ will hand over the kingdom to his Father (1 Corinthians 15:24-28).

EVERYDAY APPLICATION

The humility and exaltation of Jesus Christ were central themes of the preaching of the apostles and early Christian worship, even appearing in a New Testament hymn to Christ (1 Timothy 3:16). The Apostles' Creed mentions all four stages of Christ's exaltation: "On the third day he rose from the dead; he ascended into heaven and sits on the right hand of God the Father Almighty; from there he shall come to judge the living and the dead." As vital elements of Christian faith, the great truths of Christ's exaltation are relevant to our everyday life. We can find that relevance in the same four aspects of the exalted state of Christ.

1. Christ's resurrection is a promise that, as his followers, our bodies will also be "raised imperishable," shedding earthly weakness; we each will receive a "heavenly" body (1 Corinthians 15:40-42). Christ's resurrection is described as the "firstfruits" of those who will be raised with him when he returns (Romans 8:23). Our physical sufferings in this world are temporary as we await the redemption of the body. In a world full of sickness and death, this promise is a priceless treasure for us as followers of Christ.

2. After his departure into heaven, Christ sent the Spirit at Pentecost to empower his people on earth. The ascension of Christ means that as believers and disciples, we've received

the precious gift of the Holy Spirit (Acts 2:33; 1 Corinthians 12:12-13). Through the Spirit, Christ has given special gifts to the church to equip his people for service (Ephesians 4:7-13). As his disciples, we possess the indwelling strength of the Spirit for our unique calling to serve in the church and the world in Jesus' name.

3. Christ sitting at God's right hand means that we have an advocate in heaven with the Father (1 John 2:1-2). As great high priest, Jesus Christ daily lives to intercede for us (Romans 8:34) — which is to say that his sacrificial death assures our forgiveness before the Father. In Christ's resurrected body, now ascended into heaven, the bodily wounds from his earthly suffering still plead our case before God the Father.

4. Just as Christ is seated at the right hand of the Father, there's a sense in which his followers have already been raised with Christ (Colossians 3:1) and are presently seated with him in heavenly places (Ephesians 2:6). The spiritual reality of our identity with Christ means that we now participate in the promised resurrection and heavenly joy through union with the exalted Christ. The fullness of this union will be experienced at Christ's glorious appearing, which is the blessed promise to all of Christ's disciples (Titus 2:13).

Each aspect of Christ's exaltation reveals something about the beauty of the second person of the Trinity, who as eternal God continues to share in our humanity in the heavenly realm. As Christ willingly received worship from the disciples in his state of humility, so the exalted Christ is worthy of all worship and praise, both now and forever (Psalm 27:4).

FOR FURTHER READING

Gerritt Scott Dawson. *Jesus Ascended: The Meaning of Christ's Continuing Incarnation.* P & R Publishing, 2004.

— DON FORTSON

CHRIST, HUMANITY OF

EVERYDAY DEFINITION

The person of Jesus Christ is the very heart of Christian faith and life. His death on the cross atoned for sins and reconciled to God those who believe in Jesus. Because Jesus Christ is God among us in human flesh, knowing Jesus amounts to knowing the triune God.

Scripture plainly teaches that Jesus Christ was fully human. Biologically, Jesus was born of Mary in a humble stable in Bethlehem. The Gospels record that Jesus experienced all the phases of human growth and development. He grew weary, hungered, thirsted, suffered pain, and died (see John 4:6; 19:28,30). Matthew's gospel traces Jesus' genealogy from Abraham through the royal line of Israel to his mother, Mary (1:1-17). In reverse order, Luke's gospel traces Jesus' ancestry through David and Abraham back to Adam, the first man (Luke 3:23-38). Luke, who was a physician, certified that Jesus experienced perfectly normal physical, moral, and social development (Luke 1:80). "And the child grew and became strong" (Luke 2:40).

- Intellectually, Jesus advanced in knowledge and wisdom while on earth (Luke 2:40,52). Yet his knowledge on occasion was limited (Mark 5:30-33; 9:21; 13:32)—a consequence of his voluntary laying aside at the Incarnation the independent use of his divine attributes.
- Emotionally, Jesus felt the full range of feelings that all humans do: compassion, sorrow, pity, joy, anxiety, righteous anger against injustice, etc. Jesus wept at the death of Lazarus, a dear friend (John 11:35).
- Spiritually, Jesus was circumcised on the eighth day according to Jewish tradition (Luke 2:21), was baptized by John in the Jordan (Luke 3:21-22), throughout his life communed with his heavenly Father in prayer (Mark 1:35; Luke 6:12), and worshipped in the synagogue (Luke 4:16). Socially, Jesus enjoyed the companionship of family and friends (Luke 10:38-42). He celebrated a wedding in Cana of Galilee with other guests (John 2:1-11).
- Vocationally, Jesus learned the skill of woodworking, laboring with his hands at a carpenter's bench (Mark 6:3).

Toward the end of his life when nailed to a wooden cross, Jesus suffered excruciating pain. Fluid flowed from a spear wound in his side, and he breathed his last. Early Christian apostles acknowledged Jesus' descent from David (Acts 2:30), his childhood in Nazareth (2:22), and his identity as a man whom the Jewish leaders killed by cruel crucifixion (4:10; 5:30). The apostle Paul certified that Jesus was born of the seed of Abraham (Galatians 3:16), was a descendant of David (2 Timothy 2:8), and was born under the law to Mary (Galatians 4:4). At least three times (Romans 5:15,17,19) Paul stated that Jesus was properly a "man."

Reformer Martin Luther wrote that God the Son nursed at Mary's breast, slept in a cradle, suffered, was crucified, and died.[2] Theologian John Calvin observed that since the punishment due us sinners must be born by a man, Jesus Christ must be perfectly human with a human body and soul. "God's natural Son fashioned for himself a body from our body, flesh from our flesh, bones from our bones, that he might be one with us"[3]

Jesus also was fully tempted in every way: psychologically, sexually, spiritually, ethically, and behaviorally. "For we do not have a high priest who is unable to sympathize with our weaknesses, but we have one who has been tempted in every way, just as we are" (Hebrews 4:15). Following his baptism by John, Jesus was tempted by Satan in the wilderness (Matthew 4:1-11). He experienced the full force of Satan's enticements to use his divine powers in ways contrary to the Father's will. Jesus was also tempted in the Garden of Gethsemane while contemplating the cross (Mark 14:32-42), becoming "deeply distressed and troubled" (verse 33). With his three closest disciples, he shared his soul's anguish: "My soul is overwhelmed with sorrow to the point of death" (verse 34). Luke recorded that the agony of Jesus' temptation was so intense that sweat fell from his body like drops of blood (Luke 22:44). As a human, Jesus longed to avoid the physical and emotional suffering on a cross (Mark 14:35-36). Yet ultimately he insisted not on his own will but on the Father's loving purpose for him (verse 36).

Although tempted, Jesus never succumbed to sin. Throughout his life, he remained a fully sinless person; there were no deficiencies, eccentricities, or sinful flaws in his character as a human. Jesus

---

2. *Luther's Works*, vol. 5, 352, 492-94.
3. *Institutes*, II.12.2.

had no faults or sins to confess to a priest or to God. Scripture is replete with testimony that Jesus never succumbed to sin but remained perfectly holy in thought, word, and deed (see John 8:46; Acts 3:14; 2 Corinthians 5:21; Hebrews 4:15; 7:26; 1 Peter 2:22; 1 John 3:5). By remaining perfectly holy, Jesus could serve as the spotless sacrifice for our sins. Because his life on earth was entirely sinless, he had authority to forgive sins (Mark 2:5).

Many philosophies and ideologies have denied Jesus' authentic humanity. One of the earliest Christian heresies (Docetism, from the Greek verb *dokeo*, "to appear") denied that Jesus was human, asserting rather that Christ was some sort of a heavenly phantom and only appeared to be human. The Docetists further alleged that Jesus' sufferings on the cross were an illusion. This widespread heresy in the Greek world was roundly refuted by the apostle John (1 John 1:1-4; 4:2-3; 2 John 7). Docetism was also opposed by second-century apologists Ignatius and Justin Martyr, by the Apostles' Creed, and by the Council of Nicea (325) that drafted the Nicene Creed.

EVERYDAY APPLICATION

As Christians, we must be careful not to deny or devalue Jesus Christ's genuine humanity. The value of his saving work depends on the authenticity of his humanity as well as his deity. We must heed the warnings of the New Testament writers against devaluing Jesus' complete humanity. As expressed by the apostle John, "Every spirit that acknowledges that Jesus Christ has come in the flesh is from God, but every spirit that does not acknowledge Jesus is not from God. This is the spirit of the antichrist, which you have heard is coming and even now is already in the world" (1 John 4:2-3).

As Christian disciples we must model Jesus in every aspect of our lives. Jesus instructed his followers to "Take my yoke upon you and learn from me" (Matthew 11:29), adding "You must follow me" (John 21:22). The apostle Paul was passionate about copying Christ. He wrote, "Be imitators of me, just as I also am of Christ" (1 Corinthians 11:1, NASB). Paul's word for "imitator" literally means one who "mimics." Peter likewise commanded Christians to imitate, or "follow," the example of Christ (1 Peter 2:21). In what ways, by God's grace, should we follow the example of Jesus' life?

- Intellectually, we must think Jesus' thoughts after him by patterning our lives according to all that he taught.
- Volitionally, we must commit wholeheartedly to doing his will. Not only must we choose those kingdom goals that please him, but we must adopt strategies, or means, for achieving these ends.
- Emotionally, we imitate Jesus by allowing the Spirit to refine and shape our emotions like those of Christ himself, including empathy, compassion, and joy.
- Morally, our characters should become more like Jesus in righteousness, holiness, and truth. Our consciences, or moral barometers, ought to grow more sensitive to unrighteousness, becoming more discerning of God's moral expectations. We realize, however, that we never attain complete perfection this side of heaven.
- Relationally, we follow Jesus' example by interacting or relating more openly, honestly, and authentically to ourselves, to others, and to God himself. With barriers of sin dismantled, we will walk closely with the Lord and enjoy precious communion with him.
- Behaviorally, we will live with uprightness and integrity in all our ways. We will serve God's providential purposes as stewards of the earth's resources. We will also serve faithfully God's redemptive purposes of evangelism and kingdom building. We will invest our talents, energies, and resources wisely for his glory.

By God's grace, in all these respects, we'll strive to grow more fully into the image of Jesus of Nazareth.

FOR FURTHER READING

John Knox, *The Man Christ Jesus*. Willett, Clark & Company, 1942.
T. E. Pollard, *Fullness of Humanity: Christ's Humanness and Ours*. Almond Press, 1982.
Clifford Pond, *The Beauty of Jesus: A Portrait of the Perfect Human Character of Jesus Christ*. Grace Publications Trust, 1994.

— BRUCE DEMAREST

CHRIST, INCARNATION OF

EVERYDAY DEFINITION

Incarnation means embodied in flesh, and for Christians, the Incarnation refers to Jesus, as God, becoming a human being. John 1:14 is perhaps one of the most recited verses of the New Testament, largely due to its radical declaration: "And the Word became flesh, and dwelt among us, and we saw His glory, glory as of the only begotten from the Father, full of grace and truth" (NASB). In other words, Jesus became "enfleshed."

Of course, the idea of God being embodied in flesh raises the question, "If God is truly divine, how could he become flesh without tainting his flawless nature?" Yet, that is the profound truth found in the incarnate Word.

Why is it important that Jesus became fully human? On a temporal, here-and-now level, Jesus' incarnation translates into an understanding of having lived enfleshed. He lived the full human experience, including growing up, encountering temptations, feeling hunger, and experiencing the range of human emotions. Hebrews 4:15 declares, "For we do not have a high priest who cannot sympathize with our weaknesses, but One who has been tempted in all things as we are, yet without sin" (NASB). The Gospels provide a written record of Jesus' life and ministry, including his words and actions. As a result, we have a model of what it means to walk in total obedience with God. By taking on our level of existence, Jesus provided a tangible example of what it means to live a life in relationship with God.

On an eternal level, the very act of incarnation demonstrates the nature of God. At the very core of God's being is his desire to reconcile with humans. This nature of God as Reconciler creates the need for the Incarnation. God's movement toward us through the Incarnation reveals his desire to reconcile with us. Jesus' full humanity was required in order to function as our high priest. Hebrews 2:14,17 declare that "Since the children have flesh and blood, he too shared in their humanity so that by his death he might destroy him who holds the power of death—that is, the devil. . . . For this reason he had to be made like his brothers in every way, in order that he might become a merciful and faithful high priest in service to God."

EVERYDAY APPLICATION

The Incarnation provides us with a deeper understanding of who God is and who we are called to be as his followers. As we grasp a better understanding of the nature of God as reconciler, it prompts us not only to love God more deeply but also to pursue reconciliation in our own relationships. If reconciliation is truly core to God's being, perhaps we as his children should move in that same direction.

The Incarnation also demonstrates the reality of God's presence among us. In turn, we're called to be the presence of God among those around us, through the power of the Holy Spirit. How do we do that? By following Jesus' lead: "Then the King will say to those on his right, 'Come, you who are blessed by my Father; take your inheritance, the kingdom prepared for you since the creation of the world. For I was hungry and you gave me something to eat, I was thirsty and you gave me something to drink, I was a stranger and you invited me in, I needed clothes and you clothed me, I was sick and you looked after me, I was in prison and you came to visit me.' Then the righteous will answer him, 'Lord, when did we see you hungry and feed you, or thirsty and give you something to drink? When did we see you a stranger and invite you in, or needing clothes and clothe you? When did we see you sick or in prison and go to visit you?' The King will reply, 'I tell you the truth, whatever you did for one of the least of these brothers of mine, you did for me'" (Matthew 25:34-40).

FOR FURTHER READING

Dietrich Bonhoeffer, *Ethics*. Simon & Schuster, 1995.

James D. G. Dunn, "Incarnation," in *The Anchor Bible Dictionary*. Doubleday, 1992.

Stanley J. Grenz, *Theology for the Community of God*. Eerdmans, 1994.

— CHERYL CRAWFORD

CHRIST, LORDSHIP OF

EVERYDAY DEFINITION

Embracing Jesus as Lord is at the center of what it means to be a Christian. But what does it mean to confess that "Jesus is Lord" and to live our lives with Jesus as Lord?

The word used for "Lord" in the New Testament is the Greek word *kyrios*. In the Greco-Roman world, *kyrios* had a wide range of meanings. As a term used to address someone, it could simply mean "sir" and many of those who met Jesus and called him *kyrios* probably used it in this way. However, *kyrios* often meant much more. The *kyrios* was master with complete authority over his house, his wife, and his slaves. *Kyrios* was used in the Septuagint, the Greek translation of the Old Testament, to translate the Hebrew word *Adonai*, which meant "lord, master" (reflecting that God was lord over creation and his people), and the Hebrew word *Yahweh*, the covenant name for God.

Jesus didn't often refer to himself as "Lord." One important exception occurred when Jesus quoted Psalm 110 (Mark 12:35-37; Matthew 22:41-46; Luke 20:41-44). When Jesus asked the crowd, "How can the Christ be David's son and his lord?" he was suggesting that the Christ was more than merely a human descendent of David. Jesus was clearly referring to himself as the "lord" who was also David's master. Jesus was implying that, as Lord, he was more than human as heir to David's throne.

Soon after the resurrection of Christ, the apostles began to call Jesus "Lord." In his sermon to the crowd in Jerusalem on the Day of Pentecost, the apostle Peter declared that Jesus' resurrection and exaltation was God's public certification and proclamation that he was "Lord and Christ" (Acts 2:36). The apostle Paul quoted one of the earliest Christian statements of belief in Jesus, using the word "Maranatha," meaning "The Lord comes" or "is at hand" (1 Corinthians 16:22, NASB, KJV).

These instances show that the earliest Christians recognized that Jesus was coming as judge and king, so they called him "Lord." Many of these early followers of Jesus knew the Old Testament teaching that the Lord (*Yahweh*) was the coming judge and king, and that this Lord would save those who called out to him for rescue from the coming judgment (Joel 2:28-32). Paul quoted a verse from Joel (Romans 10:13) to show that the only way for all people, Jew or Gentile, to be saved from the coming judgment and receive God's salvation blessings is to call out to God to save him in *his* way—by trusting in God's finished, saving work in Jesus. When Paul called Jesus "Lord" (Romans 10:9,13), he meant that Jesus as the coming Judge is the only one who can also save from that judgment. According to Paul, trusting in Jesus as Lord in this sense is the defining mark of a Christian.

Only through the work of the Holy Spirit in an individual's life can that person acknowledge Jesus as Lord (1 Corinthians 12:3). Pagans might have many lords and masters, but Christians are unique because Jesus is their only Lord (1 Corinthians 8:5-6). Eventually, everyone in creation will acknowledge that Jesus is this divine Lord (Philippians 2:10-11), but only those who trust in Jesus as their Saving-Lord-from-the-Coming-Judgment will be saved (Romans 10:9-10).

EVERYDAY APPLICATION

Christians are those who have acknowledged Jesus as Lord. This means recognizing that Jesus is *Yahweh*, the God of the Old Testament. We can't call ourselves Christians without recognizing Jesus as God. However, confessing that "Jesus is Lord" means more than mentally affirming Jesus' deity. If Jesus is God, then we can't call ourselves Christians unless we actively seek to honor him as God in our lives. The lordship of Christ demands that we treat him as our master, our Lord, the one we will obey. We should seek to know what he commands and obey him.

Some have said that "if Jesus is not Lord of all, he's not Lord at all," meaning that if a person knowingly disobeys Christ's commands or refuses to give a part of his or her life over to Jesus, then this person is not a true believer. Others have felt that this seems to make salvation conditioned on obedience and good works, rather than the free grace of the gospel. However, we don't need to fall into either of these extremes in our response to the lordship of Christ.

People who truly trust someone will follow that person's instructions. For example, when a doctor says we are sick and must take a certain kind of medicine to get well, if we truly trust the doctor, we'll follow the doctor's instructions and take the medicine. Similarly, all who recognize their need for a Savior and truly trust in Jesus as the only one who can save from God's coming judgment will have a desire to submit their lives to him and follow his commands. Yet we know that the very sinfulness that drives us to acknowledge our need for Jesus' salvation will repeatedly lure us to deny Jesus' lordship and make ourselves lord of our own lives (Romans 7:14-25). As believers, we acknowledge Jesus' rightful role as our divine master, even when we sometimes fail to treat him as we know we should.

Submitting to Jesus' lordship in our lives is a gradual process of allowing the Holy Spirit to control us (Ephesians 5:18; Romans 8:9-14) and seeking to become more like Jesus by obeying him in every area of our lives (Romans 6:12-23). Submitting to Jesus' lordship means we commit to bringing our decisions and emotions under *his* control, we recognize that *he* is the owner of all our time and possessions, we allow *him* to direct our relationships, and we use our gifts and abilities for *him* (Matthew 25:14-30; Romans 12:1-2; Ephesians 4:17–6:9). The result of honoring Jesus as Lord is that our lives will increasingly display the fruit of the Holy Spirit, which is the evidence of the Spirit's control of our lives, and that we'll *not* display the actions that characterize nonbelievers (Galatians 5:16-26). Our faith in Jesus will continually lead to obedience as we come to know him better and become more like him (2 Peter 1:3-11).

FOR FURTHER READING

I. Howard Marshall, *The Origins of New Testament Christology*, InterVarsity, 1990.

Jerry White, *Choosing Plan A in a Plan B World: Living out the Lordship of Christ*, InterVarsity, 1987.

— STEVE STRAUSS

CHRIST, PERFECTION OF

EVERYDAY DEFINITION

The perfection of Christ has multiple meanings, including the following:

- Christ is perfect as God. At least eight New Testament passages, including John 1:1, proclaim that Jesus Christ is God. Jesus Christ has perfect divine qualities and attributes. As God, Christ is omnipotent, omniscient, and omnipresent. Christ is absolutely sovereign, holy, righteous, merciful, and loving.
- Christ is perfect as the Son of God in relation to the other persons of the Trinity. Christ enjoys a perfect unity with the Father and the Holy Spirit. Christ also enjoys perfect personal fellowship and communion with the Father and the Holy Spirit.
- Christ is perfect as God incarnate. The Bible teaches that in his

incarnation, Jesus Christ was fully God and fully man. In his
one person, divine and human natures were united perfectly
without division, separation, mixture, and confusion.

- Christ as the Son of Man gave perfect obedience to God
  the Father. Christ fulfilled the law of God perfectly; Christ
  loved God with all his heart, mind, strength, and will. In
  obedience to God, Christ died on the cross. Christ also loved
  his neighbors perfectly, dying for all sinners, demonstrating his
  perfect agape love for all people.
- Christ is perfect in his three offices. Christ is the King of kings
  and the Lord of lords. Christ is the High Priest for his people.
  Christ is the Prophet of prophets who reveals God to us and
  conveys God's Word to us.
- Christ accomplished redemption perfectly. He offered himself
  as the perfect sacrifice for our sins. He died for and instead of
  us as our perfect substitute.

EVERYDAY APPLICATION

As Christians, we apply the above truths to our everyday lives in various
ways, including the following:

- As Christians, we believe that Jesus Christ is God in his
  original nature. This means that we worship Jesus Christ as
  our God who deserves our praise and adoration. This helps us
  defend the Christian truth claims against various heresies that
  deny Christ's deity.
- We pursue a personally intimate relationship and fellowship
  with Jesus Christ. We learn how to deepen our personal
  relationship with Christ. This personal relationship can be
  characterized by our dependence upon and trust in him. This
  personal relationship is characterized by mutuality, as well. We
  talk to Christ in prayer and we listen to his voice in reading of
  and meditation upon the Word of Christ.
- We imitate Christ as our model of true humanity. As a true
  human being, Christ perfectly loved God and his neighbors.
  In loving God and our neighbors, we desire to be conformed
  to the image of Christ. In particular, we should practice the

love of agape toward our fellow Christians and the least of these people.

- We give praise and thanksgiving to Christ for his atoning death and glorious resurrection. By dying on the cross and shedding his blood, Christ has forgiven our sins, saved us, and given us eternal life.
- We preach Christ and share the good news of Christ's grace with others. The best gift we can give others is the gospel of grace and eternal life. Sharing the gospel with others is a way to obey Christ and a way to express our love for him.

FOR FURTHER READING

Sung Wook Chug, *Christ the One and Only: A Global Affirmation of the Uniqueness of Jesus Christ.* Baker, 2005.

John R. W. Stott, *The Incomparable Christ.* InterVarsity, 2004.

— SUNG WOOK CHUNG

CHRIST, WORK OF

EVERYDAY DEFINITION

The work of Christ typically refers to all that Christ did for us and our salvation when he was born, lived, died, and was resurrected. The term "work of Christ" can also include the work he presently does on our behalf at the right hand of God and in his return in glory. This definition focuses on the birth, life, death, and resurrection of Christ as his "work."

In classical theology, a division is often made between "the person of Christ" (Christology) and "the work of Christ" (soteriology); this reflects the distinction between who Christ *is* and what he *does*. Some theologians see this distinction as unhelpful except for reasons of presentation. Others suggest that the categories of Christ's Person and Work remain conceptually distinguishable and therefore useful.

The alienated relationship between humanity and God can only be healed by a person with an identity grounded in both divinity and humanity. As result, classic theologians typically began their reflection on the distinctive identity of Christ as truly human and truly God and then proceeded to discuss the work of Christ as the mediator between God and humanity.

Jesus said, "I am the way and the truth and the life" (John 14:6). Christ as teacher makes known a new way of life and imparts true knowledge about God, man, and human destiny. This was an important theme, especially as Christianity encountered various pagan cultures. Christ imparted true knowledge of God, death and the life after, the meaning of the good life, and how to enter into this good life—topics where paganism offered little illumination or insight. Jesus' illuminating work isn't limited to doctrine or answers to life's questions; his life also illuminates a way of life. Jesus as the Way represents a way of living in trusting obedience to God the Father, and patiently and confidently waiting on the direction of the Spirit of God. Jesus not only models our way to God, but he also becomes God's way to us.

Historically, theologians have used a "shorthand" way of summarizing the work of Christ in terms of Prophet, Priest, and King. These follow the sequence of Christ's ministry: Jesus first emerges as a teacher in the prophetic office; then as high priest in his suffering and death; and finally by his resurrection received his kingdom and actively governs his creation.

Jesus' prayer as recorded by the apostle John (John 17:1-11) provides a glimpse into the transition of the work of Christ from his prophetic ministry (where he revealed himself to the world) to his priestly ministry (where he offers himself as sacrifice, he intercedes for his followers, and he bestows blessing). In the high-priestly prayer, Jesus declares that as the Son, he is given authority by the Father to give eternal life. Near the end of his prayer, Jesus asks God to protect his disciples and those who would believe in him through the witness of the apostles.

In the high-priestly prayer and his prayer in the Garden of Gethsemane, Jesus voluntarily accepts the mission of the Father by offering himself as a sacrifice to atone for the sins of the world, dying once for all. In his sacrificial death on the cross, he liberates humanity from the sin, death, and bondage to evil. He prays for those he loves. He prays for their protection, sanctification, and incorporation into the loving life of God. He blesses humanity by offering the hope of reconciliation, protection, and the promise of eternal life.

After his resurrection, Jesus continues his work of intercession with the Father and offers blessing through the promised Holy Spirit. His authority to give eternal life is now recognized in his resurrection (Matthew 28:18-19) and in his ascension (Hebrews 10:12). The risen Lord continues to guide his community by his Word and protect and empower his people by the Holy Spirit. He orders, directs, and preserves the church. He promises that he will love, protect, and guard those he loves until the day of their salvation.

EVERYDAY APPLICATION

Most of us alive today find it hard to imagine life before the invention of the refrigerator. We take for granted that meats and dairy products we store in our refrigerators will be safe to eat. And most of us have personally experienced the sickness that results from consuming spoiled food, which can make an otherwise healthy body sick.

In the ancient world, as it is today, the only proper option for spoiled food was to throw it away. Now think of humanity and creation as spoiled by sin, becoming corrupted to the point that it was no longer of any use or able to produce life. What happens when we become corrupted by sin? What hope do we have? Are we to be thrown away like rotten food?

As a result of his work, Jesus completely identified with us in order to reunite God's love with his corrupted creation. Jesus' obedience unto death removed the corruption ingrained in our very being, knocking down the barrier that our contamination had erected. The life that Jesus gave through his work — the greatest of all gifts — involved trading the life of God for the life of the world. But through this work, he overcame the degradation, brought health back to humanity, and restored the relationship between God and humanity.

FURTHER READING

Alister McGrath, *Christian Theology: An Introduction*. Blackwell
    Publishers, 2001.
Thomas Oden, *Systematic Theology*. Hendrickson Publishers, 2006.

— MIKE GLERUP

CHRISTIAN

EVERYDAY DEFINITION

From its earliest of meanings, the word *Christian* has had an obscure rendering. This term, which has only three occurrences in the New Testament (Acts 11:26; 26:28; 1 Peter 4:16), was originally more of a sarcastic descriptive term for Christ followers rather than something the community of faith originated or owned. According to the book of Acts, "The disciples were first called Christians in Antioch" (Acts 11:26, NASB). Antioch was a pagan city which first recognized Christians other than just a Jewish sect. However, Antioch was notorious for its sarcastic name-calling and joking even of their emperor. So the word Christian was a derisive military term that most likely meant "soldiers of Christ."

The Christian community redeemed the term and then owned it, as if to say, "Yes, we are soldiers of Christ!" As a result, the people described by this ironic term changed the world! The term became not only a positive one, but has identified millions upon millions of followers of Christ all over the world and throughout history who identify with their Lord, Jesus Christ.

EVERYDAY APPLICATION

Interestingly, time has a way of giving words different meanings. In the early church, the radical nature of the Christian faith provoked a term fitting of their embodied calling, "soldiers of Christ." Today, the word Christian can mean a wide range of options. For some, the term is synonymous with being an American, or having a certain set of values with no religious meaning. Others match it to their denominational holdings. Still others take it to mean a deeply held brand of faith.

Perhaps we can agree that the word Christian has lost its moorings. The negative term that early Christians redeemed and embraced must now be "re-redeemed" and defined for new generations. If this term came as a result of what others witnessed as a community of faith, then what does our witness today look like? Often the negative caricatures of Christ result from many who call themselves Christians. Some outsiders who reflect on the Christian community say that Christians are judgmental, angry, hypocritical, etc. How does this reflect the person of Jesus?

Perhaps the time is right to rethink the radical nature of the original word that was so tied to Jesus Christ himself. As Christians in contemporary culture, we can embrace and embody Christ's likeness through radical love of others, kind acts of service to strangers, and caring, authentic communities of all kinds of people. This kind of living can redeem the word Christian for the next generation, with Jesus himself helping us to become true "soldiers of Christ."

FOR FURTHER READING
N. T. Wright, *Simply Christian*. HarperSanFrancisco, 2006.
David Kinnaman, *UNChristian*. Baker, 2007.
C. S. Lewis, *Mere Christianity*. Macmillan, 1943.

— KEITH MATTHEWS

CHRISTIAN MIND

EVERYDAY DEFINITION
The term "Christian mind" was first popularized by educator and author Harry Blamires in a book of the same title first published in 1963. The concept Blamires defended and promoted is deeply biblical and practical for all of life. Jesus said the greatest commandment was to love God with all our heart, soul, and *mind* (Matthew 22:37). Blamires defined a Christian mind as "a mind trained, informed, equipped to handle data of secular controversy within a framework of reference which is constructed of Christian presuppositions. The Christian mind is the prerequisite of Christian thinking" (p. 43). Blamires also lamented in the first sentence of the book that, "There is no longer a Christian mind," and wrote the book to remedy the situation in which Christians' thinking had "succumbed to secularization" (p. 3). That is, Christians had become worldly in their approach to the Bible and to knowledge outside the Bible. As Paul warned, they had become "captive through hollow and deceptive philosophy" (Colossians 2:8) and had been "conformed to this world" rather than "transformed by the renewing of [their] minds" (Romans 12:2, NASB).

Since Blamires' groundbreaking book, the term "Christian mind" has become fairly more commonly used to mean a mind obedient to the objective and absolute truths of biblical revelation. Evangelist and apologist Francis Schaeffer's first book, *The God Who Is There* (1968), articulated the importance of developing a Christian mind—which he referred to as a "Christian worldview"—that was both fully biblical and proficient to handle the great intellectual and social issues of the day. Schaeffer's many books and widespread personal ministry inspired a whole generation of Christians to out-think the world for Christ (see 2 Corinthians 10:3-5).

More specifically, a Christian mind strives to approach all of life according to the perspective of the Bible. Schaeffer stressed the lordship of Christ over the totality of life (see Matthew 28:18-20; Colossians 1:12-19). In other words, Christians should understand the world, not in terms of secularism or according to the assumptions of a false religion, but according to the knowledge given in Scripture. Schaeffer, as well as Wheaton College philosophy professor Arthur Holmes, also stressed that "all truth is God's truth." God has revealed truth in both nature (Psalm 19:1-4; Romans 1:22) and Scripture (2 Timothy 3:15-17), and these truths will not conflict. In his book *All Truth Is God's Truth* (1977), Holmes powerfully argued that the Christian shouldn't allow for any division between the secular (politics, art, business, etc.) and the sacred (the church, evangelism, etc.). All of life should be lived unto the triune God and be understood in Christian terms, whether that be theology, philosophy, politics, law, art, or anything else.

The basic structure of a Christian mind can be summed up in the themes of creation, fall, and redemption, as recently articulated by Nancy Pearcey in *Total Truth* (2004). The triune God created the universe as good and people as "very good" and equipped for harmonious relationships (Genesis 1–2). But humans turned away from God and became estranged from God, themselves, nature, and each other (Genesis 3; Romans 3:9-23). Still, God didn't abandon a rebellious creation, but pursued sinful humans through his providential events in history, the sending of the prophets, and supremely through the life and death of Jesus Christ, God incarnate (Hebrews 1; John 14:1-6). Christians should understand the world through the creation/fall/redemption model, in order to refute false philosophies, commend the gospel (1 Peter 3:15-16; Jude 3), and seek to redeem as much of an errant world as possible before God's final act of judgment and redemption.

Everyday Application

There are as many applications of the Christian mind as there are legitimate spheres of life under the lordship of Jesus Christ. But consider the following three pressing areas of engagement:

1. As Christians, we must deeply understand the teachings of the Bible in order to possess a mindset that honors God. God's people perish from a lack of knowledge (Hosea 4:6). Studies disclose that Christians are ignorant about even basic biblical truths. In 2003, a widely cited Barna poll claimed that only a small percentage of evangelicals possessed a biblical worldview. This unawareness must be countered by repentance from worldly ways that keep people from immersing themselves in Scripture. This means forsaking overindulgence in worldly influences that hinder us from knowing biblical truth. The church should redouble its efforts to teach the whole will of God and exhort Christians to grow in the knowledge of God, creation, history, and culture (Acts 20:27; 2 Timothy 2:15).

2. As Christians, we should make the reading of thoughtful books a higher priority. We can't develop a Christian mind in isolation from the significant intellectual issues of the day. The National Endowment for the Humanities' research in 2004 and 2007 noted a disturbing drop in reading among the general population, likely not excluding Christians. As Francis Schaeffer noted, "Americans don't read enough (that's true) and Americans read too much (that's true too). . . . Many don't read enough material to really be informed, and yet they read too much because what they do read they often do not stop to assimilate and think through. . . . I urge you, with all my soul, in such a day as ours to really, truly learn to read."[4]

3. To develop a proper Christian mind, we must apply ourselves to the defense of the Christian worldview as true, reasonable, wise, and pertinent to all of life. This is the perennial responsibility and opportunity of apologetics, which means "speaking in defense" (1 Peter 3:15-16). Without a strong

---

4. Francis A. Schaeffer, *Back to Freedom and Dignity* (Downers Grove, IL: InterVarsity, 1972), 18.

defense of our faith before the watching world, our Christian witness languishes and our Christian mind will remain undeveloped. Like Paul throughout Acts, we must dialogue and reason with unbelievers, demonstrating that Jesus is the Christ (Acts 17:16-34).

FOR FURTHER READING

Harry Blamires, *The Christian Mind: How Should a Christian Think?* Servant, 1978.

J. P. Moreland, *Love Your God With All Your Mind.* NavPress, 1997.

Francis A. Schaeffer, *Back to Freedom and Dignity.* InterVarsity, 1972.

— DOUGLAS GROOTHUIS

CHURCH

EVERYDAY DEFINITION

When contemporary inhabitants of Western culture hear the word "church," one of two very disparate images probably comes to mind. For some, the term evokes pleasant thoughts of a particular group of people who regularly gather together to worship God at a specific location. For others, the word invokes notions of a repressive institution that has too often tried to impose particular religious and moral beliefs on its members and at times even those outside the community. While the first perspective represents an incomplete perception held by many Christians, the second view is the result of specific encounters people have had over the years with individuals or communities claiming some sort of affiliation with a church.

With these two very different views in mind, we can gain a deeper understanding by examining how the biblical writers and other early Christians understood the nature of this community and how their insights might constructively shape our contemporary perceptions.

Writers of the New Testament use numerous terms and images in their effort to address the church and describe its nature. Some of the more familiar ones include the "bride of Christ" (Ephesians 5:22-27), a "royal priesthood" (1 Peter 2:9), or "the temple of God" (2 Corinthians

6:16). However, the word *church* actually originates from the Greek word *ekklesia*. In the New Testament, this word sometimes refers to a local community of believers living in a particular place at a particular time (Acts 5:11; 11:22; 12:5; 1 Corinthians 1:2; Galatians 1:2). At other times, it alludes to the whole people of God no matter where they live or gather (1 Corinthians 10:32; 12:28). Finally, some writers used it to describe a community of believers who were trying to live out the dimensions of their new life in Christ (1 Thessalonians 1).

Paul employed another important image of the church when he described the Christian community as "the body of Christ" (1 Corinthians 12:12-27). By using this imagery, he acknowledged that all Christians everywhere are part of one body that comes under the headship of Christ. Additionally, this imagery points to an understanding of the church as a dynamic and living organism that grows and requires all of its members to carry out their proper function in order to ensure the optimum operation of the body. While these represent just a few of the ways New Testament authors described the church, early Christian theologians echoed some of these same sentiments.

The Nicene Creed represents an early declaration about the nature of the church still deeply valued in many traditions today. The members of this Council affirmed their commitment to "four marks" of the true church. They described the church as "one holy catholic and apostolic." Each of these descriptors reveals a significant way in which early Christians perceived the nature of their community.

- "One" reiterates Paul's contention that all Christians are a part of a single body (Romans 12:5; 1 Corinthians 12:13; Ephesians 4:4-6).
- "Holy" reflects not only a description of the church's character as a result of God's saving work in Christ (Ephesians 5:25-27), it also resounds a call to live corporately and individually in a particular fashion (1 Peter 1:14-16).
- The term "catholic" often arouses some confusion among Christians because many instinctively relate it to a particular branch of Christianity identified as the Roman Catholic Church. However, the word is meant to convey a belief that the Christian community should be inclusive of all believers.

As the disciples learned very early, the community was never intended to be exclusive, but to include believers from all races (Acts 8:26-40; 10:23-48; 15:1-21), languages (Acts 2:6), and genders (Acts 2:17-21; Galatians 3:26-29).

- "Apostolic" refers to the way these early Christians expressed the importance of maintaining continuity with the earliest apostles' teaching.

EVERYDAY APPLICATION

As Christians in today's culture, we can learn much from these sources about the nature and purposes of the church.

To begin, we need to recognize the local yet universal character of the church. While Christians will always be involved in particular communities, we must acknowledge the importance of regularly engaging in dialogue with Christians from other cultures and lands. When we truly grasp that the Christian church is universal, we'll open hearts and minds to how Christians from other cultures can assist us in understanding the Christian faith and life in fruitful ways.

We must also commit to pursuing the oneness or unity under Christ emphasized in these early declarations. The history of the church is wrought with disunity and divisiveness over personal, political, and theological issues. We've often emphasized the matters that divide us rather than valuing those issues we share in common. Although we'll never agree on every point of doctrine, we can begin to set aside our differences and seek out values that Christ would have us rally around.

Paul's use of the "body of Christ" imagery also provides important insight into our responsibilities as individual members of the church. Sadly, Christians sometimes find it difficult to overcome their tendency toward consumerism when thinking about involvement in church. We often choose churches and regulate our participation based on how it benefits us. If we don't sense that we're getting what we expect from a church or our participation, we'll simply shop elsewhere for a community that better meets our needs. In contrast, the image of the body that Paul provided implies that when we join the church, we have certain responsibilities to employ our gifts in order to facilitate the proper functioning of the body of Christ. So we should be investing more time into weighing how our gifts and talents benefit our local communities, and less time thinking about how our communities will benefit us.

Finally, we need to rediscover the idea that the Christian community is a tangible representation of God's continuing mission in this world. The negative perception that many people have about the church is a result of their very real interactions with Christians who have lost sight of this truth. By allowing ourselves to be defined by our impassioned stances about certain issues rather than being committed to embodying the commands Jesus defined as the greatest, we've often cast a vision of God's character and mission that is inadequate or inaccurate. Therefore, we should rededicate ourselves—individually and corporately—to being the type of community that provides a clear alternative by acting justly, loving mercy, and walking humbly with our God (Micah 6:8).

For Further Reading

Neil Cole, *Organic Church: Growing Faith Where Life Happens.* Jossey Bass, 2005.

Richard J. Foster, *Streams of Living Water: Celebrating the Great Traditions of Christian Faith.* HarperCollins, 2001.

Eddie Gibbs, *ChurchNext: Quantum Changes in How We Do Ministry.* InterVarsity, 2000.

Howard A. Snyder, *Decoding the Church: Mapping the DNA of Christ's Body.* Baker, 2002.

— Matt Elofson

CIRCUMCISION

Everyday Definition

Circumcision is the act of removing the foreskin of an infant male. The word comes from Latin *circum* (around) and *cædere* (to cut).

In the Bible, God called for Jews to practice the rite of circumcision when he issued the covenant with Abram, changing him from being merely a "great father" to Abraham, the "father of many nations" (Genesis 17:4-5). This rite acted as both a sign of the covenant and as a seal of the promise of God.

Circumcision was common in the nations surrounding Israel (although it was not practiced by the Philistines), but the practice of circumcising infants on the eighth day (see Leviticus 12) rather than adolescents, and the rite's connection to the promises of God make the Jewish practice distinct. The children of the people of God were seen both as a fulfillment of the covenant God made with Abraham and a promise of its continuance for another generation. As the story of Abraham's physical descendents proceeds through the books of Genesis and Exodus, we see living proof of God's promise to make Abraham a father of many nations. When the children of Israel go into the desert following God's miraculous rescue of them from the hand of Egypt, every male, including servants bound to a family and alien peoples who joined them, entered the Exodus having undergone the rite of circumcision.

Circumcision also served as a powerful statement of recommitment to God by the Jewish people. In Joshua 5 we find the nation of Israel halting on the edge of the Promised Land to undergo circumcision as a statement that they would not be like their fathers who died in the wilderness for unfaithfulness. Circumcision thus served not only as a symbol and sign of God's covenant but also as a national marker symbolizing an outward commitment to the lordship of God.

During his reign over the Jews, the foreign King Antiochus Epiphanes attempted to end circumcision in order to break Jewish national identity, even murdering those who had practiced it. Circumcision was so vital to the Jewish understanding of the covenant with God, however, that it helped lead to the revolt against Epiphanes that ended with Jewish victory.

In the Old Testament, the word *uncircumcised*, with its connection to the vile practices of the Philistines, became a byword for those who were godless, wicked, and ultimately disloyal to God. When used by the prophet Jeremiah to confront Israel (9:26), it is a particularly direct attack, as Israel itself is accused of being as disloyal to God and as outside of the covenant as pagan nations. Stephen used this same charge in Acts 7, again as a sign that those who claimed to be followers of God were in fact disloyal, wicked, and outside of the covenant. This final charge—where Stephen called the Jews uncircumcised because of their rejection of Jesus—was such an insult to their national and religious pride that it triggered Stephen's stoning.

In the New Testament, the issue of whether circumcision is required of non-Jewish believers became a major issue. The council of Acts 15 decided that circumcision is not required of Gentiles. Their decision confirmed that salvation is found in Christ alone, and no believer can add to the work of Christ (Galatians 2:3; 5:6).

EVERYDAY APPLICATION

The apostle Paul used the language of circumcision as a synonym for "the Law," meaning the Old Covenant (see especially Romans 3). For Paul, as is true in the rest of the New Testament, the emphasis should not be on whether a follower of Christ is externally circumcised, but whether the internal person, represented by the "heart," is. Paul used the phrase "circumcision of the heart" (Romans 2:29) by the Holy Spirit to speak of those who are truly of God, connecting this true circumcision with God's great promise of the new covenant (Jeremiah 31:33). In place of the external mark of circumcision, the seal of the new covenant is the Holy Spirit. So, while we still desire external marks of our faith — sources that we can look to as "proof" of our faith — the key is still whether our hearts bear the mark of circumcision. This mark on our hearts represents the work and presence of the Holy Spirit, which can never be a source of pride for ourselves, but rather gratefulness as God's promise to us and to all generations of those who hear his voice and give themselves to him.

FOR FURTHER READING

Lelan Ryken, Jim Wilhoit, Tremper Longman, Colin Duriez, Douglas Penney, Daniel G. Reid, "Circumcision" in *Dictionary of Biblical Imagery*. Electronic edition. InterVarsity, 2000.

Gerald F. Hawthorne, Ralph P. Martin, Daniel G. Reid, "Circumcision" in *Dictionary of Paul and His Letters*. InterVarsity, 1993.

— CHRISTOPHER MORTON

COMMUNION

EVERYDAY DEFINITION

Holy Communion, also known as the Lord's Supper or Eucharist (Greek "thanksgiving"), was established on the night Jesus was betrayed (see 1 Corinthians 11:23). Jesus instructed his disciples—and by extension his followers through the centuries—that whenever they share the elements of communion, to remember him (Luke 22:14-20; Matthew 26:26-29; Mark 14:22-25).

Repeated reference by the apostles to the Lord's Supper in their New Testament writings secured the place of communion in the worship life of the church. However, the meaning of Jesus' words "this *is* my body" remain contested. For the most part these debates concerned the *what* and the *how*.

Priest and theologian Thomas Aquinas (1225-1274) explained the *how* by suggesting that a miracle occurs at the table, and the bread and wine are *transformed* into the body and blood of Christ. The bread and wine actually change into the body and blood, yet keep the qualities of bread and wine. Martin Luther found this explanation of *how* inadequate. Luther believed that communion elements became the body and blood of Christ but the *how*—because it was the result of a promise—remained a mystery. For Luther, what was important was not the explanation but the trust in the promise of Christ that the bread was his "body" and the wine was his "blood." Calvin differed from both of these positions, because they suggested Christ was *physically* present at the celebration of Communion. He argued that Christ was indeed present but only spiritually, through the work of the Holy Spirit. Calvin differed with Luther on the physical presence of Christ at the table on the basis of the scriptural testimony that Christ was now at the "right hand of the Father." How could Christ be both physically present in heaven and in the elements? For Christ to be physically present in a variety of places at once would undermine the reality of Christ's incarnation and humanity.

In the early church, the issue of *how* wasn't the central concern about Communion. The question focused more on what Holy Communion represented. Justin the Martyr provided one of the earliest descriptions of Christian worship and the celebration of Holy Communion. He wrote, "When we have finished the prayer, bread is brought forth, and wine and water, and the presiding minister offers up prayers and thanksgiving to the best of his ability, and the people assent, saying the Amen; after this the consecrated elements are distributed and received by each one. Then a deacon brings a portion to those who are absent."

Justin not only described the service but he also offered an explanation. He wrote, "This food we call Eucharist of which no one is allowed to partake except one who believes that the things we teach are true, and has received [baptism], and who lives as Christ taught us. For we do not receive these things as common bread or common drink but as Jesus Christ who became incarnate by God's word and took flesh and blood for our salvation. So we have been taught that the food consecrated [made holy] by the word of prayer which comes from him, from which our flesh and blood is nourished by being renewed, is the flesh and blood of that incarnate." These believers stressed that Holy Communion was most importantly a meal of thanksgiving for what God has done in Jesus Christ. It wasn't a meal for everyone; only those baptized or immersed into the reality of Christ. And it wasn't just a memorial meal but the real presence of Christ. Further, it was a source for nourishment and for renewal.

For many Christians today, the most pressing question surrounding Communion is *why*? Why do we celebrate Holy Communion? Why is it important? This question becomes more pressing for Christians who prefer to call Communion an ordinance. As an ordinance, Communion is a practice (like baptism) ordained by Christ to be continually performed in the church until Christ's return. Communion, for them, is a memorial meal that focuses the attention of participants on the death of Jesus Christ for sins. As a result, Communion becomes a devotional reflection. However, most Christians consider Holy Communion a sacrament. This means that Communion is more than a meal; it's a means to grace for strengthening their faith and nourishing their spiritual life. As a result, they would argue that there is some *real presence* of Christ in Communion, although they differ on *how* the bread and wine become the body and blood of Christ.

EVERYDAY APPLICATION

To understand and apply what God wants us to gain from Communion, consider this experience of a college student who experienced Communion in a very personal way:

> My experience of Holy Communion came as a challenge to what
> I was taught. Like many of my contemporaries, I wondered why

Communion was celebrated regularly. I felt that the same thing that happened in Communion could just as easily occur through hearing an entertaining sermon or singing an emotionally driven praise song. It wasn't until I was invited by one of my professors to a weekly Eucharist service at the campus chapel that I changed my understanding of Communion. Slowly, over a year I began to sense an inner renewal of my heart. My devotional and prayer life began to become more passionate. My service to others was driven by a desire to serve and not necessarily obligation. As I pondered these changes, I realized the only external change in my religious life was my attendance at this weekly service. I broke down the various elements of the service to see if I could locate a possible source of inner renewal.

The sermons were substantive but not very entertaining.

The songs were usually pre-twentieth-century hymns alternatively sung in English and Korean, so not emotionally charged with meaning.

The only realistic explanation was the weekly celebration of Holy Communion. Yet, every week the Scripture readings, prayers, and thanksgiving offered before and after Communion were the same. No moving appeals to my emotions to see the meaning in the table; only an invitation to come with the eyes of faith and feed my heart with thanksgiving on the nourishing body and blood of Jesus Christ.

As I reflect, I now see that my resistance to the real presence of Christ stemmed from my aversion to dependence. For this to be true I had to depend on God to show up. I preferred the other alternatives because if worship wasn't working for me, I could always go in search of a church with a better preacher or a bigger praise band. But at the table I had to give up my independence and wait in patient expectation. What I experienced at the table was grace, a pure gift of the Holy Spirit. What I experienced at the table was the power of God that nourished my spirit as I learned to trust in Christ's promise "this is my body . . . this is my blood."

FOR FURTHER READING

Leonard Vander Zee, *Christ, Baptism and the Lord's Supper: Recovering the Sacraments for Evangelical Worship.* InterVarsity, 2004.

John P. Burgess, *After Baptism: Shaping the Christian Life.* Westminster John Knox Press, 2007.

— MIKE GLERUP

COMMUNITY

EVERYDAY DEFINITION

To understand community, we need to go back to the word's roots. In Latin, *communitas* means "the same." That evolved into *communis,* which means "common; shared by all."

Modern sociologists differentiate between "community" and "society." While society implies a looser connection between people, community tends to mean that people are more closely joined, such as in families or churches. In other words, community tends to mean that the people within that closely joined group share something significant in common, like a blood-relation or a belief system. While what people share in common varies from community to community, it's the sharing of things *in common* that marks a community.

In the early days of Christianity, for example, sharing material possessions in common was one of the markers of the church. Directly after his report on Pentecost, Luke wrote that the early believers "were together and had everything in common. Selling their possessions and goods, they gave to anyone as he had need. Every day they continued to meet together in the temple courts. They broke bread in their homes and ate together with glad and sincere hearts, praising God and enjoying the favor of all the people. And the Lord added to their number daily those who were being saved" (Acts 2:44-47).

The Old Testament records the history of Israel, a people who very much marked themselves as a community. The male mark of circumcision was the indicator of a man's inclusion in the nation of Israel and, consequently, in the covenant between Abram's descendents and God (see Genesis 17). The community of Israel also had a shared set of laws ("Torah"), scriptures, and practices. While the Israelites didn't always have their own land, they had these other markers that set them, as a community, apart from their neighbors.

Throughout much of the last 2,000 years, the church has served a civic function as much as a spiritual one. However, with the advent of globalization and pluralization of society in the late-twentieth century, the church seemed to lose much of its civic prominence. As a result, many church leaders began calling for the church to once again become a community, much as it had been in the first century. This quest for community in Christianity can be seen in the number of churches that have named or renamed themselves "Community Church." This meshes with what sociologists acknowledge: Many of the institutions that once formed community in our culture no longer do, so people are looking for community in other places.

EVERYDAY APPLICATION

The entire Bible was written to people living in community. The Old Testament was recorded for the nation of Israel, while the New Testament was written for different iterations of the early church. With God's inspired Word written for communities, it follows that Christianity is fundamentally a communal faith, intended for individuals who are living together and working their faith out together.

This raises some valid questions about the church today, including "How has the church historically failed at being the community that Jesus envisioned?" and "How can the church succeed at being that community in the future?" This means that even when we become frustrated at the church's reception by the world as being hypocritical, judgmental, or overly political, the appropriate response to these criticisms is not to abandon the church, but to correct it so it becomes the community Jesus intended all along.

Toward the end of John's gospel, Jesus gives an extended sermon to his disciples, challenging them to love one another and to face down the persecution of the world. He ends with a poignant prayer: "I pray also for those who will believe in me through their message, that all of them may be one, Father, just as you are in me and I am in you. May they also be in us so that the world may believe that you have sent me" (John 17:20-21). The very culmination of Jesus' message is that the Christians of the world would be one and form a community.

FOR FURTHER READING

Robert Putnam, *Bowling Alone.* Simon & Schuster, 2001.

Stephen E. Fowl and L. Gregory Jones, *Reading in Communion.* Wipf & Stock Publishers, 1998.

Dietrich Bonhoeffer, *Life Together: The Classic Exploration of Faith in Community.* HarperOne, 1978.

— TONY JONES

CONDEMNATION

EVERYDAY DEFINITION

To understand the biblical meaning of condemnation, we first need to recognize the social context of the rule of law and the nature of justice. When someone is accused of a crime, a legal process begins to determine what law, if any, has been broken. When finished, a verdict of either innocent or guilty is handed down by the court. If declared guilty, the individual is legally condemned and usually subject to some sort of punishment; if declared innocent, that person is set free. The result, in theory at least, is that justice is served and the rule of law is upheld.

The word condemnation can be used in both a cultural and spiritual manner. When people are negatively designated by their peers or community, they have been condemned, regardless of whether or not it was just (1 Corinthians 5:4-5; Luke 4:28). And if people are convicted by their conscience of inappropriate attitudes, thoughts, or actions, the Bible calls that spiritual condemnation (Romans 2:14).

As Creator, Lawgiver, and Savior, God is the merciful judge of all humanity. Divine judgment is necessary because Adam and Eve sinned against God (Genesis 3), which led to spiritual alienation, relational breakdown, and death for all humanity. Although this rebellion has continued with each generation in human history, God lovingly instituted his plan of redemption through Jesus (Romans 5:12-21). His heart is not to condemn but to graciously woo back to himself every prodigal son and daughter of our fallen race (Luke 15).

God took upon himself the necessary action to accomplish this purpose. By condemning sin in the sinless Jesus, the Father justifies those who trust in Christ, freeing them from condemnation (Romans 3:25;

2 Corinthians 5:21). This is the good news of the gospel. However, those who refuse to repent and accept God's gracious gift of eternal life in Christ are already condemned and face eternal punishment at the Last Judgment (John 3:16-18; Revelation 20:11-14).

EVERYDAY APPLICATION

As Christians, we've been freed from condemnation by the grace of God. Given this blessing, we are called to live in a manner that reflects our spiritual freedom (Galatians 5:14). Living this way includes the following:

- We'll be motivated to give our lives to the Savior in worship. Gathering with other believers on a regular basis and individually submitting ourselves to God's will are some specific ways this can be done (Hebrews 10:26-27; Romans 12:1-2).
- Our walk with Christ calls us to regular self-examination so as to grow in faith, hope, and love (1 Corinthians 11-13). Specifically, this means consistently evaluating our character development and relational skills, as well as being good stewards of our time, talents, and treasures (Galatians 5:22; Matthew 25:14-30).
- When we do sin, we will repent, confess, and seek healing (James 5:15-16). A clear conscience rooted in God's grace and his calling makes for both godly living and effective ministry (1 Timothy 1:18-19; 2 Timothy 1:3).
- We'll be compelled to pray for and then share the good news with those who have yet to embrace the Savior. Compassion for the lost and the needy is a visible characteristic of all those who have been freed from the oppressive condemnation of sin and its destructive tendencies (Matthew 25:31-46). This means that we will live to serve others and share Christ with people outside the faith whenever and wherever we can (Acts 20:31).

FOR FURTHER READING

John Ortberg, *The Life You've Always Wanted*. Zondervan, 1995.
Bruce Demarest, *The Cross and Salvation*. Crossway, 1997.

John Stott, *The Cross of Christ*. InterVarsity, 1986.

—Scott Wenig

CONFESSION

EVERYDAY DEFINITION

Confession refers to the admission of sin and exploring the roots of the sin in order to move forward to restoration and wholeness: "Therefore confess your sins to each other and pray for each other so that you may be healed" (James 5:16). Confession stems from healthy guilt that we have acted in a manner contrary to what we believe is right. It flows from godly sorrow and repentance "that leads to salvation and leaves no regret" (2 Corinthians 7:10). Confession involves an understanding that God can work in us and change us.

Confessing our sins has numerous benefits. It can bring release from a pattern of sin and help us move toward Christlikeness. Without confession, we're more likely to get stuck in the same old behaviors, feeling there is no way out. Unacknowledged sins then eat away at us as we hide them (Psalm 32:3). When we confess our sins, the forgiveness of God becomes a healing balm and the result is spiritual growth. Confession of sin can also result in intimacy with God because willingness to confess reveals an understanding of God's character. When we experience his forgiveness, we see that God is loving, not cynically disappointed in every mistake we make. We understand that God is patient as we take our "next steps," not annoyed at our imperfections. We learn that God is willing to work with us in our transformation, not just irritated that we aren't instantly renewed (1 Corinthians 13:4-5). A lifestyle of confession helps us embrace the character of God.

Some Christians question whether confession is necessary given that God already knows our sins. But life with God is about relationship, which requires vulnerable disclosure of ourselves. Confession builds that intimate relationship.

EVERYDAY APPLICATION

Sometimes we neglect to confess our sins because we don't exactly know how to approach God. While there's no mystical formula we need to follow to confess our sins, it can be helpful to have a general pattern in order to restore an intimate and growing relationship with God. So consider these biblically based steps for confession:

1. Confession begins with a blunt statement of the sins we've committed. For example, Psalm 51 begins with the statement of David's sin. "When the prophet Nathan came to him after David had committed adultery with Bathsheba" (verse 1), David made his confession without excuses: "Against you, you only, have I sinned and done what is evil in your sight" (verse 4).

2. Next, we state the thoughts and feelings behind the sin. This takes some inward-focused investigation because the heart is wily and deceitful (Jeremiah 17:9). The motives behind our sin often stem from pride or fear or determination to get what we want. When we simply say, "God, I'm sorry. Please forgive me," we skip this exploratory step and don't discern all that we need forgiveness and healing for. So stating thoughts and feelings often involves being specific: "I lied at dinner last night to our guest because I wanted to impress him. In fact, I struggle with wanting people's approval. I'm not secure in your approval alone, O God."

3. Then we're ready to ask God for forgiveness and to soak in that forgiveness: "Wash me, and I will be whiter than snow. Let me hear joy and gladness; let the bones you have crushed rejoice. Hide your face from my sins and blot out all my iniquity" (Psalm 51:7-9). If we struggle to *feel* forgiven, it can help to write down or confess the sin aloud (perhaps with someone else). Then we can take comfort in these words: "If we confess our sins, he is faithful and just and will forgive us our sins and purify us from all unrighteousness" (1 John 1:9).

4. Finally, we ask God for help to plan a next step. Some of David's next steps were: teaching rebels God's ways, singing anthems to God's life-giving ways, and singing out God's praise (Psalm 51:13-15). It's wise to ask God for a doable step. This might be a form of restitution (restoration or compensation; see Exodus 22:3-12; Luke 19:8) or it might be concerted effort to change the thought patterns that led to the

sin. While we might not know the next step, at this point we ask God to show us the way forward.

Confessing sins directly to those we've sinned against can be a powerful healer. The sinned-against person hears the full contrition of heart and the sinner comes to a deeper realization of the sin by repeating it to the individual offended. Of course, we need to approach this prayerfully with the goal of doing good, not of defending ourselves or making ourselves feel better. Occasionally such a confession could do more harm than good, and in that case confessing to a third person is more helpful. God guides us in these decisions when we ask. When choosing a neutral person to confess to, we need to choose someone who adequately grasps the grace of God. An advice-giver or armchair psychologist might not be helpful. Tell the other person exactly what you need: to say your sin aloud and to hear God's forgiveness in a human voice.

FOR FURTHER READING
Jan Johnson, *Spiritual Disciplines Bible Studies Reflection and Confession*. InterVarsity, 2002.
Richard Foster, *Celebration of Discipline*, chapter 10. HarperSanFrancisco, 1998.

— JAN JOHNSON

CONSCIENCE

EVERYDAY DEFINITION
The moral faculty of conscience enables people to discern between good and evil, right and wrong. The Greek word for conscience (*syneidēsis*) literally means "co-knowing." Conscience is the moral faculty that dialogues between a person's thoughts and actions and God's law implanted on the heart (Romans 2:14-15) and revealed in Scripture (Psalm 19:7-12). Proverbs 20:27 describes the conscience within the human spirit as a lamp that illumines the human individual's moral center.

Scripture affords numerous examples of the conscience at work. After Adam and Eve disobeyed God by heeding the serpent, their consciences testified to their guilt, expressed as spiritual nakedness

(Genesis 3:8-13). They then wrapped themselves in leaves in an attempt to ease their guilty consciences. Also, "David was conscience-stricken after he had counted the fighting men, and he said to the LORD, 'I have sinned greatly in what I have done'" (2 Samuel 24:10). And concerning his love for his Jewish friends in the flesh, the apostle Paul testified, "I am not lying, my conscience confirms it through the Holy Spirit" (Romans 9:1, TNIV).

When we follow the precepts of God's law by righteous living, our consciences confirm a sense of well-being or peace. The title of the well-known hymn, "It Is Well with My Soul," testifies to the peaceful outcomes of a clear conscience. But when we break God's law (as we all do), our consciences testify to our wrongdoing, resulting in restlessness and anxiety (Isaiah 57:20-21), self-hatred and shame (Ezekiel 20:43), psychosomatic symptoms (Psalm 38:5-10), and in extreme cases, suicide (so Judas, Acts 1:18). The point is that sin results in a guilty, self-accusing conscience (Hebrews 9:9,14; 10:2) with painful and potentially disastrous consequences.

EVERYDAY APPLICATION
Conscience assures us that there is an inviolable moral standard in the universe. As followers of Jesus, we obey God's righteous laws in order to keep our consciences clear before the holy God. Because a guilty conscience dims the light of God's presence, we strive to keep our consciences clean. As Paul put it, "I strive always to keep my conscience clear before God and all people" (Acts 24:16, TNIV; 23:1). We can resolve to follow this pattern of the apostle, resisting enticing attractions from the world, the flesh, and the devil that defile conscience and disturb our peace.

When we persistently sin, we establish a destructive moral pattern that causes our conscience to become "weak" and "defiled" (1 Corinthians 8:7), "corrupted" (Titus 1:15), and "seared" (1 Timothy 4:2). The result is progressive loss of moral discrimination between good and evil, and right and wrong (Ephesians 4:19). If we compromise our moral compass, our faith becomes shipwrecked (1 Timothy 1:9). On the other hand, when we renounce sin and live righteously, we possess a conscience at peace with God and ourselves, expressed as a "good conscience" (Acts 23:1; 1 Timothy 1:19) and a "clear conscience"

(1 Peter 3:16). A pure conscience is particularly needful in Christian leaders (1 Timothy 3:9).

When fellow Christians are ensnared in sin, we rightly appeal to their God-given conscience to bring about repentance (2 Corinthians 4:2). This allows God's Spirit to function as the erring person's teacher and facilitator of repentance. The moral faculty of conscience ensures that erring believers are aware of their disobedient way of life and need to deal with it before God.

In matters not specifically addressed by the Word of God — such as eating certain foods or observing special days of religious observance (Romans 14) — we must respect the convictions of fellow Christians whose consciences point them in other directions. As for the matter of eating food sacrificed to idols, Paul honored the consciences of weak or immature believers who found this practice to be a stumbling block (1 Corinthians 8; 10:25-31). Even though *our* consciences might be clear with respect to a particular action, our love should motivate us to respect other Christians whose consciences might condemn them on such matters.

Conscience, then, is a useful, God-created moral compass that helps us differentiate right from wrong and good from evil. Given this, we resolve with Job, "I will maintain my innocence and never let go of it; my conscience will not reproach me as long as I live" (Job 27:6, TNIV). We recognize the fact that in a fallen world, God's infallible Word stands above our fallible human consciences (1 Corinthians 4:4-5).

FOR FURTHER READING

James R. Beck and Bruce Demarest, *The Human Person in Theology and Psychology.* Kregel, 2005.

John MacArthur, *The Vanishing Conscience.* Word, 1994.

Steve Shores, *False Guilt: Breaking the Tyranny of an Overactive Conscience.* NavPress, 1993.

— BRUCE DEMAREST

COVENANT

EVERYDAY DEFINITION

A covenant is a formal contract between two or more parties where one or all the parties involved are bound by the promises and/or obligations outlined in the agreement. In Scripture, a covenant (Hebrew *berith*, Greek *diathëkë*) was typically ratified through ritual acts or oaths (see Genesis 15; Matthew 26:26-28), and was sometimes conditional (for example, covenant with Moses) or promissory (such as covenants with Noah and Abraham).

The promissory covenant with Noah (Genesis 9:8-16), ratified after the catastrophic flood, served mainly to guarantee the future of the fallen human race. After Noah offered the appropriate sweet-smelling sacrifice, God provided a rainbow as a sign of the covenant (Genesis 9:12-16), and he promised that he would never again destroy all living things (Genesis 9:15-16).

The covenant with Abraham, ratified by God through a sacrificial ritual (Genesis 15), included two major elements: a *land* and an *offspring* that would produce a nation more numerous than the stars of the heavens (Genesis 12:1-3; 17:1-21). As a sign of the covenant, God instructed Abraham to circumcise all males eight days old—an obligation that was to be performed during his day and for all generations to come (Genesis 17:10-13; Acts 7:8). This act of shedding of blood symbolized the future shed blood of Jesus Christ. The covenant with Abraham was renewed through Isaac (Genesis 26:1-5) and then Jacob (Genesis 28:12-16).

The covenant with Moses at Sinai is the most prominent of the Old Testament covenants (Exodus 20-24). It spelled out in detail the behavioral and moral obligations of the Israelites in their special relationship with Yahweh. Unlike the covenants with Noah and Abraham, the covenant with Moses was conditional, promising blessings and preservation of life through obedience to the divine decrees, and listing curses for disobedience (Deuteronomy 28–29). Ratification of the covenant involved the sprinkling of blood on the altar and the offering of sacrifices—two rituals seen earlier in the ratification ceremonies of the covenants with Noah and Abraham (Exodus 24:1-8). Included with the Mosaic covenant were the Ten Commandments (Exodus 20:2-17; Deuteronomy 5:7-21).

Like the covenants with Noah and Abraham, the covenant with David belonged to the category of a *promissory* (unconditional) agreement. Echoing the covenant with Abraham, the covenant with David included the promise of *land* and a *seed* through which the people of God would flourish and multiply (2 Samuel 7; 1 Chronicles 17). In Scripture, where God established a promissory covenant, expressions of approval and admiration often appear. For example, Abraham walked before God (Genesis 24:40; 48:15) and obeyed him and kept his decrees (Genesis 26:5). Similar praises were sung of King David. According to Scripture, David was faithful, righteous, and upright in heart (1 Kings 3:6); he kept God's commands and followed him with all his heart, doing only what was right in his eyes (1 Kings 14:8); and he followed the LORD completely (1 Kings 11:6). Similar commendations appear in texts of the Ancient Near East, where kings praised individuals whose character and conduct distinguished them from the rest of the community. These individuals received gifts from the king and were praised for their uprightness and integrity.

The writings of the biblical prophets serve as a bridge between the Old Testament covenants and the New Covenant. While exposing the failure of the Israelites to observe the law received at Sinai, biblical prophets point toward a better future when the Messiah would come to deliver his people and establish a new and everlasting covenant, where God's law would be written on their hearts (Jeremiah 31:31-34; Ezekiel 16:59-63). Jesus frequently used covenant language when referring to his shed blood and his broken body (Mark 14:24; Matthew 26:28), and when revealing the purpose of his first coming (Matthew 5:17). The writer of Hebrews revealed the shortcomings of the old covenant (Hebrews 8:7-8) and testified that Jesus came to mediate a new and eternal covenant through his own shed blood (Hebrews 9:15-26).

EVERYDAY APPLICATION

Covenants play a major role in our understanding of biblical theology. Scripture clearly shows that God is the initiator and designer of the covenants made with Noah, Abraham, Moses, David, as well as the New Covenant. In addition, Scripture maintains that God's purpose for establishing and preserving these relationships is for the ultimate redemption of humankind.

Only when we as Christians truly understand the covenantal nature of God's relationship with us, can we appreciate the eternal bond of love that exists between God and humans. Although first established in ancient times, the God-initiated covenants are still extremely significant in that they provide behavioral, ethical, and moral principles to guide the way we should live today as believers. God's covenants were gracious gifts freely given to us. They were designed as guiding principles in order to help us live honorable and righteous lives. They were meant to protect us from harm and to teach us how to live in socially healthy communities.

Scripture often speaks of God's covenants in terms of a marriage relationship between a bride and a groom, where the union requires faithfulness, respect, commitment, and the highest level of devotion (Isaiah 62:5; Song of Songs). Throughout history, God as husband has remained faithful to his bride, both Israel and the church (Isaiah 54:5). Unfortunately, God's people often transgressed the marriage covenant by committing spiritual adultery, prostituting herself with foreign gods, and forsaking the commandments given to them (Jeremiah 3:20). As a faithful Husband, God forgives our offenses, pursues us, and restores our broken relationship with him through his abounding love (Hosea 2:16).

The New Testament records the most important of all the biblical covenants. Through Jesus Christ, God established an eternal covenant with all those who believe in the name of his Son (Hebrews 13:20). The new covenant was permanently sealed through the blood of Jesus. At the Last Supper, Jesus took the cup of wine, blessed it, and declared that it represented his shed blood that he would pour out as an offering for the forgiveness of sins (Matthew 26:28; Mark 14:24). Through his shed blood, Jesus became the mediator of a new and better covenant, one that finally brings us freedom from sin (Hebrews 9:14-15).

FOR FURTHER READING

Paul R. Williamson, *Sealed with an Oath: Covenant in God's Unfolding Purpose*. InterVarsity, 2007.

— HÉLÈNE DALLAIRE

CREATION

Everyday Definition

Creation refers to the account of making the heavens and earth as recorded in the first two chapters of Genesis. For Christians, this means that God is the Creator and this creating activity is his gracious gift.

The first words of the Bible give the starting point: "In the beginning God created the heavens and the earth" (Genesis 1:1; Hebrews 11:3; Revelation 4:11). The Apostles' Creed affirms: "I believe in God the Father Almighty, maker of heaven and earth." This is our primary declaration. All of our discussions about creation must emerge from this central teaching.

For some, it might be tempting to restrict our conversation about creation to the issues of science versus faith. Such questions can occupy our thinking without resolution. Another more fruitful direction simply proclaims that the Bible declares *who* made everything that exists: God spoke, and everything came into existence. The rest of the discussion will always include elements of speculation. Still, this does not end our discussion. The very fact that God is the Creator has profound implications for the way we think and live.

God created. This means that God is majestic and powerful. However creation was accomplished, we look at the vast scope of creation and we marvel, "The heavens declare the glory of God" (Psalm 19:1; Psalm 8). Look at the wonders of our world through microscopes, binoculars, and telescopes. They tell the story of a wonderful, powerful, and uncontainable God. God created, but God is not the creation. So we resist any thinking that merges creation and the Creator. And we resist any tendency to worship the created. Nothing is to usurp God.

God created, and God said that it was good. God saw what he made and blessed it. God takes delight in what he has made. Although the world has now been tainted and smudged by the actions of humanity, and we face troubles and fears, still, God looks at his creation and affirms its value. We see this value through God's ongoing interaction in the world. God isn't a cosmic watchmaker who created the world, wound it up, and then let it just wind down on its own. God remains involved in his creation: "The earth is the LORD's and the fullness thereof" (Psalm 24:1, KJV). No division exists between the sacred and the secular. God created all that exists and he values it.

God created, and he created humanity in his image (Genesis 1:26). This concept of *imago Dei* stretches beyond our comprehension. God cares about all of his creation, but most about humanity (Matthew 6). Humanity is created just "a little lower than the angels" (Psalm 8:5, KJV). We see the ultimate demonstration of the value of human creation in the incarnation of Jesus. John 1:14 reminds us that the Word, Jesus Christ, became flesh and dwelt among us, becoming a human being so that humanity might have a restored relationship with God. We see that God views creation as good since God is willing to enter into creation and become a human being. Humanity more than any other part of creation is created for relationship with God and with others (1 John 1:3).

EVERYDAY APPLICATION

Because we are created *imago Dei* and because God desires to be in relationship with his creation, particularly humanity, God has engaged in the mission of redemption. God comes to us in the action of creation, through Israel, and ultimately through Jesus Christ, drawing humanity back toward God. Creation and redemption flow together. The people of God participate in the missionary activity of the creating and redeeming God.

Culture is what humans do with creation. In this sense we are co-creators, taking the raw materials that God has placed in this world and in humanity. From these materials we craft human cultures full of artifacts reflecting our creativity. In our working and creating, we find echoes of the work of the God the Creator.

God created humanity in his own image, meaning that humans have a responsibility in this world. God blessed humanity and said, "Be fruitful and increase in number; fill the earth and subdue it. Rule over the fish in the sea and the birds in the sky and over every living creature that moves on the ground" (Genesis1:28, TNIV). God made humanity stewards over the world he created. We're responsible to care for it, to maintain it, and to nurture it.

Creation that now exists in the world's state of brokenness yearns toward a restoration of God's created order. The Bible tells us that creation groans (Romans 8:19ff). This groaning points to the promise of a new heaven and a new earth. Marred by sin, creation looks forward to the redemptive acts of God that make all things new.

FOR FURTHER READING

Tony Compolo, *How to Rescue the Earth Without Worshipping Nature.* Thomas Nelson, 1993.

Brian McLaren, *Everything Must Change.* Thomas Nelson, 2007.

— KURT FREDRICKSON

CREEDS

EVERYDAY DEFINITION

In the early centuries of Christianity, church leaders wrote summaries of faith for believers. These statements of belief became known as "creeds" from the Latin *credo*, meaning "I believe." A series of Councils in the early church produced numerous creedal statements. Two of the ancient creeds are universally recognized by Roman Catholics, Orthodox, and Protestants—the Apostles' Creed and the Nicene Creed.

The New Testament includes a number of poignant declarations concerning Christ that appear to be primitive hymns or creed-like affirmations (1 Corinthians 15:3-7; 2 Corinthians 13:14; 1 Timothy 3:16; 1 John 4:2). Second-century church fathers (Ignatius, Justin Martyr, Irenaeus, Tertullian) gave us primitive summaries of fundamental teachings about Christ, sometimes referred to as a "rule of faith." In the following centuries, a standardized form of these early confessions was used throughout the church in what became known as the "Apostles' Creed." While not written directly by the apostles, the creed reflects first-century gospel preaching, and therefore the title was appropriate.

The Apostles' Creed had several functions within the community of believers: instruction in the faith, defense against heresy, and liturgical use (worship). The apostle Paul had warned the church about false teachers (2 Corinthians 11:13; 1 Timothy 6:3; 2 Timothy 4:3-4) urging believers to "stand firm and hold fast to the teachings we passed on to you" (2 Thessalonians 2:15, TNIV). To safeguard the church against second-century Gnostic sects who denied God the Father as creator and dismissed Christ's real humanity, the creed emphasized "God the

Father Almighty, creator of heaven and earth" and affirmed the true earthly life, death, and resurrection of Christ.

When converts entered the early church, they were instructed in essential doctrines before being baptized and invited to the Lord's Supper as full church members. The creed was sometimes memorized by new believers and used as an affirmation of faith at baptism. Both the creed and the baptismal formula emphasized the Trinity of God, confessing faith in the name of Father, Son, and Spirit. The Protestant Reformers accepted the Apostles' Creed as an excellent summary of biblical teaching. Martin Luther used the creed as an outline for Christian teaching in his *Catechism* (1529); John Calvin included it in the new Protestant worship service in Geneva.

One of the key themes of the New Testament is the divinity of Jesus Christ (John 1; Colossians 1; Hebrews 1). At the beginning of the fourth century, the church faced a crisis when a church leader in Alexandria named Arius began to publicly challenge the accepted teaching of the Trinity. Arius taught that there is only one uncreated, all-powerful being of God; therefore, the Son was a created being and not eternal like God the Father. The Holy Spirit, according to Arius, is an even lesser deity, subordinate to the Son. These views spread throughout the eastern part of the empire, and tension became so great that the emperor Constantine called for a general council of bishops to settle the dispute. In 325, two hundred and twenty bishops met in Nicaea with the emperor presiding.

The bishops rejected the views of Arius, but debated over the language that would be included in the creedal statement produced by the bishops. The bishops decided that a Greek word meaning "one substance" could be used to clarify that the Son and Father shared the same essence, or are equal in deity. After much discussion, the Creed of Nicaea (the basis of the Nicene Creed, 381) was written, and Arius was denounced. The original Creed of Nicaea (325) described the Son as "God of God, Light of Light, True God of True God, begotten not made, of one substance [Greek *Homoousion*] with the Father." The Nicene Creed was affirmed by sixteenth century Protestant groups as a necessary defense against heresy.

EVERYDAY APPLICATION

Some believers have declared simplistically that "there is no creed but Christ." These well-meaning people forget that core creeds have safeguarded biblical teaching about Christ for many centuries. Non-Christian cults have twisted the Bible to justify many forms of aberrant teachings about the person of Christ and his redemptive work on the cross. Historic Christianity has consistently embraced biblically faithful creeds as legitimate boundary markers for genuine Christian teaching.

The ancient creeds mean that as Christians, we are part of something bigger than ourselves—that we belong to a family of faith that spans the centuries. When we recite the Apostles' Creed during private or corporate worship or as part of a baptismal service, we connect with the faith held dear by millions of believers past and present. The creeds have helped to ensure that the essence of Christian faith has remained constant through history. The creeds align us as disciples of Jesus with the bedrock truth of Christianity that the true Savior, Jesus Christ, is "the same yesterday and today and forever" (Hebrews 13:8).

The creeds remind us today—many centuries later—of the universality of the faith. The saving truth about Christ unites God's diverse people across time, nationalities, and cultures. As the apostle Paul declared, "There is . . . one Lord, one faith, one baptism" (Ephesians 4:4-5). Despite great diversity in the body of Christ, certain core doctrines define the essence of Christianity, and these truths are faithfully preserved in the Apostles' Creed and the Nicene Creed.

As Christians, we might consider employing these creeds more frequently in worship, because thoughtful recitation of the creeds can be a great blessing. The creeds remind us that faith in Christ is not built on ever-changing novelty or senseless superstition but on biblical truths and ancient faith that has stood the test of time. As we meditate on the meaning of each phrase in these creeds, we strengthen our faith and foster faithfulness to God. The truth about Christ nourishes and establishes the soul as we commune with the authentic Lord described in the creeds. Although not Spirit-inspired, as Scripture is, the creeds provide many positive benefits to the church and the lives of followers of Jesus Christ.

FOR FURTHER READING
John Leith, *Creeds of the Churches*. John Knox, 1973.
Philip Schaff, *Creeds of Christendom*. Baker, 1993.

— DON FORTSON

CROSS

EVERYDAY DEFINITION

The cross has long represented the most recognizable symbol of Christianity. It refers to the instrument of execution by which Jesus Christ was crucified. As such, the cross is doubly meaningful. On one hand, it represents the humble sacrifice of Jesus, who voluntarily died as a substitute on behalf of sinful humanity. On the other hand, the cross represents the triumph of Jesus over sin and death through his resurrection.

The cross is foreshadowed in the Old Testament, but not until the New Testament does the cross become a central focus. Jesus predicted his death on the cross several times, and all four Gospels recount the story of his crucifixion (Matthew 27:33-50; Mark 15:22-37; Luke 23:33-46; John 19:16-30). Being crucified on a cross was considered a curse, and Jesus' experience was a humiliation as well as execution.

Early Christian preaching emphasized the cross (1 Corinthians 1:17-23). Paul said, "For I resolved to know nothing while I was with you except Jesus Christ and him crucified" (1 Corinthians 2:2). In other words, Christians preached the life, death, and resurrection of Jesus, focusing on the cross as representative of all Jesus accomplished on behalf of people for their salvation. These early believers used the cross to describe redemption from the curse of the law upon people for their disobedience against God (Galatians 3:13). The cross was seen as destroying the power of Satan (Colossians 2:13-15) and proclaiming people's justification and reconciliation with God (Romans 4:25; 5:10). These characterizations of the cross convey the ways Jesus unites people with God (Romans 6:4-7).

The cross also signified the importance of Christian discipleship and sanctification. Christians are called upon to take up their crosses daily in order to live Christlike lives of obedience and expectation of spiritual growth (Matthew 16:24; Luke 9:23). Although the cross emphasizes how Christians are to offer themselves as living sacrifices to God (Romans 12:1-2), they are graciously aided by God's Holy Spirit.

Christians didn't initially use the cross to identify themselves, using other symbols such as the *ichthus* (Greek, "fish"), which signifies an acronym for "Jesus, Christ, God, Son, Savior." Once Christianity became culturally acceptable in the Roman Empire, the cross increasingly became a focus of Christian understanding and self-identification.

Theologically, the cross reminds Christians of the doctrine of the atonement. Atonement means "at-one-ment" between God and people, which occurred because of Jesus' life, death, and resurrection. Most beliefs about the atonement emphasize what Jesus objectively accomplished on behalf of Christians on the cross. He was a substitute in place of sinful humanity, and people are saved because of Jesus' victory over sin and death.

Visually, the cross inspires Christians individually as well as collectively. Throughout church history, many styles of crosses were produced. Crosses appear on countless pieces of artwork, architecture, clothing, jewelry, and even weaponry. Christian cathedrals, for example, are often built in the shape of a cross. In addition, Christians — laity as well as clergy — commonly wear crosses as a public testimony. However, they've become so common in contemporary society that people sometimes wear crosses without any religious meaning.

EVERYDAY APPLICATION

Crosses represent a continuous reminder to us of the gift of salvation, provided by Jesus through his life, death, and resurrection. Displaying crosses at home or meditating on them devotionally can be an encouragement as well as inspiration for spiritual growth.

Although the cross initially signifies the death of Jesus, it immediately brings to mind his resurrection. The cross by itself is never the end of the story, so its meaning should be multidimensional and hopeful. Whenever we see a cross, we should rejoice for the blessed promise we have for resurrection and for eternal life with God in heaven.

Jesus used the cross as a way to exhort people to live Christlike lives (Matthew 10:38). People are saved by grace, but God wants to work in and through their lives both for the sake of God's will and for the restoration of people, who are created in God's image (Genesis 1:26-27). Paul says that people should offer their lives as living sacrifices, holy and acceptable to God (Romans 12:1-2). The result is that by the power of God's Holy Spirit, people are transformed by restoring the image of God (Romans 12:2; 1 Thessalonians 5:23-24).

Wearing a cross is an opportunity to display our faith publicly. Not all will feel the need to wear crosses for either personal or cultural reasons. But the public display of crosses or other religious symbols can be a helpful witness to others.

Some people today question the appropriateness of the cross as the best symbol for Christianity. Their concerns include a possible over-emphasis on passivity, submissiveness, and defeat associated with the cross without an appropriate biblical balance of obedience, leadership, and victory. Certainly every symbolic representation of Christianity needs to be understood and used wisely.

FOR FURTHER READING

Andreas Andreopoulos. *The Sign of the Cross: The Gesture, the Mystery, the History.* Paraclete Press, 2006.

John R.W. Stott. *The Cross of Christ.* InterVarsity, 1986.

Richard Viladesau. *The Beauty of the Cross: The Passion of Christ in Theology and the Arts from the Catacombs to the Eve of the Renaissance.* Oxford University Press, 2005.

— DON THORSEN

CROSS-CULTURAL THEOLOGIES

EVERYDAY DEFINITION

How can theology be "cultural"? Isn't theology a summary of the absolute and unchanging truth of God's Word? If so, how can there be different "theologies" originating from different cultures?

Theology is our understanding and expression of what God has revealed about himself and his relation to the world, primarily from the Bible. Although theology is an attempt to express the universal truth that God has revealed, it is never identical to God's revelation itself. All theology is human, shaped by the personal circumstances and the culture of the theologian who is speaking or writing. All theology is "contextual" in that it reflects local ways of thinking and expression. It should respond to local questions, challenge local assumptions, and resonate with the local culture. Cross-cultural theology is a comparison of the different ways in which believers from different cultural contexts express God's truth.

The Bible gives different examples of God's people expressing their theology based on the culture or circumstances of the listeners. The apostle Paul presented the gospel in different ways, depending on the background of his listeners (see Acts 13; 14; 17). The three synoptic gospels are complementary, but not contradictory, presentations of Jesus' life and ministry, each shaped to address the specific needs of a different community of first-century Christians. Old Testament passages of Scripture are cited in different, but not contradictory, ways in the New Testament; for example, Habakkuk 2:4 is used with a slightly different nuance in Galatians 3:11, Romans 1:17, and Hebrews 10:38-39. As a result of the Jerusalem Council (Acts 15), the gospel was specifically disconnected from the Jewish culture, allowing Gentiles to come to Christ and still remain Gentiles culturally.

Theologian Millard Erickson identifies two basic approaches to cross-cultural theology: transformers and translators.[5]

1. *Transformers* are those who see the source of theology in culture or current political, economic, or sociological situations. Most transformers have a more liberal view of the Bible, seeing it as one of many sources for belief and practice. Many transformers see the Bible as only a "casebook" of how others responded to God, and not the primary source of God's revelation to all people of all time. Liberation theology is an example of a cross-cultural theology rooted in a political and economic situation. Liberation theologians find the starting point of their theology in the economic inequalities in society.

2. *Translators* are those who understand the source of all theology to be in the revelation of God, primarily in the Bible. They seek to express their theology in ways that are appropriate to each

---

5. Millard Erickson, *Christian Theology* (Ada, MI: Baker Academic, 1983), 112-120.

culture and situation, but they recognize that the Bible is their final authority and source of theology. Translators recognize that God wrote the Bible in such a way that its basic message could be understood and applied by people of all cultures and times (2 Timothy 3:14-17; see examples in Nehemiah 8:7-8; 1 Timothy 5:17-18; Hebrews 3:7–4:3). They recognize that God has created people with sufficient commonality so that they could share the essential message of the Bible. But they also recognize that the context of those who read the Bible will affect the way they read the text. Because individuals come to Scripture with different questions in mind and a different worldview, they will be more aware of some aspects of the text and less aware of others. For example, Christians in contexts of persecution may be more aware of aspects of the biblical text that speak of suffering than believers who live in situations of peace and affluence. Context will shape the way they understand and apply the text. Christians of different cultures will express their theologies based on the language, stories, proverbs, and customs of their own culture and will address issues that especially concern their own cultural context.

EVERYDAY APPLICATION

As Christians, all of us have blind spots in the way we read Scripture and live out our Christian lives. We can easily read the Bible and only see it confirming what we already believe and the life we're already living. One of the best ways to remove these blind spots is to look at Scripture and our Christian lives through the eyes of believers from other cultures. They might see truths in Scripture that we've overlooked because we've fallen into a "rut" of only seeing what we have always seen. Others might see sin and hypocrisy in our lives that we don't see because Christians in our own particular culture have always accepted a particular practice.

One way to look at the Scriptures through the eyes of believers in other cultures is to get to know them and talk about God and his Word with them. Believers should take every opportunity to make friends and spend time with Christians from other cultures. Another way to learn from other Christians is to read some of the books and articles they've written. These are increasingly available from Christian publishers. Christians from our culture have much to learn about prayer, spiritual warfare, hospitality, economic justice, dependence on God, wealth and poverty, suffering and persecution, and living with people of other faiths from fellow Christians in different cultures.

The idea of cross-cultural theology shouldn't disturb our confidence in the inspired and authoritative Bible. God in wisdom breathed forth his Word for all cultures at all times. Scripture's message can be understood and applied by believers around the world and throughout history. We can read our Bibles with the confidence that God's will can be known clearly. But we should also read the Scriptures humbly and in conversation with fellow Christians from around the world.

FOR FURTHER READING

William Dyrness, *Learning About Theology from the Third World*. Zondervan, 1990.

Paul-Gordon Chandler, *God's Global Mosaic: What We Can Learn from Christians Around the World*. InterVarsity, 2000.

Dean Fleming, *Contextualization in the New Testament: Patterns for Theology and Mission*. InterVarsity, 2005.

— STEVE STRAUSS

CULTURE

EVERYDAY DEFINITION

Culture is what human beings do with nature. A forest is nature; a log cabin is culture. A beach is nature; a sand castle is culture. Culture is the realm where human beings influence the world in a multitude of ways: through architecture, agriculture, law, politics, art, dress, language, writing, education, medicine, business, transportation, and more. Culture is created by human beings, who, because they bear the image and likeness of God (Genesis 1:26), shape God's creation in manifold ways. Adam and Eve (and all humans descended from them) were created for, and charged with, the responsibility of developing and cultivating the earth under the authority of the Creator (Genesis 1–2; Psalm 8). This is known as the creation or *cultural* mandate. God made the world good, but it was unfinished. The pinnacle of creation—humanity, which was "very good"—was given the charge of bringing more good out of creation through their personal involvement.

Human culture takes in a great wealth of forms globally and through time, from African drumming to American jazz to Italian opera to Chinese calligraphy. These forms all flow from humans manifesting the divine image. But God's very good creatures, his culture-creators, have gone radically wrong because of sin. When Adam and Eve heeded the lie of the serpent and turned away from God and toward themselves, sin entered and fractured the creation, thus staining every aspect of human culture ever since (Genesis 3; Romans 8:19-23). Because of this fall, human cultural activity is marred by alienation from God, from ourselves, from others, and from nature. In the wake of these broken relationships, all culture is a mixture of what honors God (righteousness) and what does not (sinfulness).

Still, the Creator didn't abandon his erring creation. Despite the brokenness of cultures, God worked through them, continuing to reveal himself in manifold ways, making covenantal promises, sending his prophets, calling a special nation for himself, and finally sending his Son, Jesus Christ, for the salvation of persons and the ultimate healing of the earth and the nations (Hebrews 1; Revelation 21–22). We know this because God inspired the Holy Scriptures as a record of these realities (2 Timothy 3:16; 2 Peter 1:20-21). The Bible itself bears the imprint of two main languages (Hebrew and Greek), rooted in two quite different cultures.

During the time of God's theocratic nation of Israel, God's people were given very specific instructions covering every aspect of culture—agriculture, economics, law, warfare, and family relations—that they might be a holy people under a holy God. With the coming of Jesus and the New Covenant, this arrangement was superseded so that the church could extend as salt and light throughout every culture on earth, preaching the gospel and applying all of Jesus' teachings until he comes again (Matthew 5:16-18; 28:18-20). Christians pray, "Your kingdom come, your will be done *on earth* as it is in heaven" (Matthew 6:10, emphasis added). This requires cultural involvement on every level.

EVERYDAY APPLICATION

How should we as Christians relate to the cultures where we find ourselves?

- We can seek to understand the three great biblical themes that come together in cultural engagement: the creation mandate, the Great Commandment, and the Great Commission. Despite the fact that we humans will never create heaven on earth through our efforts, we're still summoned to care for and develop nature under God. We should do this by heeding the great command to love God with all our being and to love our neighbor as ourselves (Matthew 22:37-40). Part of the task of being human for the glory of God also involves the responsibility and privilege of evangelism, or fulfilling the Great Commission (Matthew 28:18-20; Acts 1:8).
- We can seek to gain wisdom in cultural endeavors by comprehending and applying the biblical worldview to all we do (Romans 12:1-2). This can be summarized by three themes: creation, fall, and redemption.

  1. *Creation*: Life and work on earth is part of God's good intention for his creatures.
  2. *Fall*: Since the world is fallen, some things must be shunned as hurtful to creation and an offense to God.
  3. *Redemption*: Still, God is redeeming humans and aspects of cultures as his kingdom is manifested throughout history and will be concluded at the end of this age.

- We should wholeheartedly but judiciously participate in every area of life—except, of course, those specifically prohibited by God. Our work should be done to the glory of God (1 Corinthians 10:31; Colossians 3:17). There is nothing less spiritual about being a lawyer or a physician than being a pastor or an evangelist, because each domain can contribute to the unfolding of the kingdom of God under the lordship of Jesus Christ. Christians, however, need to remain morally and spiritually pure in their cultural endeavors and not succumb to worldliness (James 1:27; 1 John 2:15-17). If someone is a lawyer or a physician, that individual should work out these vocations according to Christian principles.

- While we should attempt to redeem areas of culture not specifically condemned by Scripture, we need to realize that much of contemporary culture marches to the beat of the world, the flesh, and the devil (Luke 16:15). As such, we need to evaluate the effects of culture on our souls, asking God to guide us into wholesome and redemptive activities (Philippians 4:6-7). For example, a violent video game might be popular, but it's not a redemptive activity that can be engaged for the glory of God.

FOR FURTHER READING

Kenneth Myers, *All God's Children and Blue Suede Shoes: Christians and Popular Culture.* Crossway, 1989.

Richard Mouw, *When the Kings Come Marching In: Isaiah and the New Jerusalem*, rev. ed. Eerdmans, 2002.

—DOUGLAS GROOTHUIS

DAY OF THE LORD

EVERYDAY DEFINITION

The expression "day of the Lord" is most often found in the writings of the Old Testament prophets. The phrase refers to a period of time when God will execute his judgment upon the earth. In Scripture, the Hebrew word for "day" (*yom*) may refer to a literal twenty-four hour day (1 Samuel 31:8), to a year (Isaiah 34:8; 63:4), to a thousand years (Psalm 90:4), to an unspecified period of time (Deuteronomy 5:10), or in idiomatic expressions meaning "year after year" (1 Samuel 1:3).

In some cases, announcement of the day of judgment is directed toward foreign nations (such as Egypt, Babylon, Damascus, Moab). In other cases, God promises to punish his very own people for their transgressions of the covenant and for their syncretistic practices (Amos 5:18-27). In addition, God promises that on "the day of the Lord," he will execute judgment on his creation, specifically on heavenly and earthly powers (Isaiah 24:21-22).

In the Old Testament, the "day of the Lord" is described primarily in negative terms as the day of God's wrath (Psalm 110:5-6), a "cruel day" (Isaiah 13:9), "the day of his burning anger" (Isaiah 13:13), "a day of vengeance" (Jeremiah 46:10), "the day of his fierce anger" (Lamentations 1:12), "a day of darkness and gloom, a day of clouds and blackness" (Joel 2:2), a "dreadful" day (Joel 2:11), and a day of "disaster" (Obadiah 1:13). The announcement of this catastrophic event is often accompanied by a sense of urgency expressed by the phrase "the day of the LORD is near" (Joel 1:15; 3:14), and by a somber call to repentance (Joel 2:12-17).

The New Testament paints both a negative and a positive picture of the day of the Lord. It describes the event as "the great and glorious day of the Lord" (Acts 2:20), "the day of our Lord Jesus Christ" (1 Corinthians 1:8), "the day of judgment" (2 Peter 2:9), and "the day of judgment and destruction of the ungodly" (2 Peter 3:7, TNIV), echoing the sense of urgency and accountability found in the Old Testament writings.

EVERYDAY APPLICATION

The Bible depicts God as the great Judge of all the earth, whose commitment to righteousness is reflected by his judgment upon sin and its agelong effects upon mankind (Genesis 18:25; Psalm 9:8). God isn't just some distant magistrate who executes blessing and judgment from afar. On the contrary, he is omnipresent and near to us and to all who call on him in truth (Psalm 119:151; 145:18). He promises to judge the earth with righteousness and justice (Psalm 9:7-8). Although his final judgment will be carried out swiftly and completely, in the meantime God is patient and gracious toward his creation, not willing that any should perish but that all would repent and trust Christ for life and salvation (2 Peter 3:9).

Until the great day of the Lord comes, God has provided the necessary paradigm of justice for us through Scripture (Psalm 111:7-8). Without this biblical model, we'd be left to our own partial devices, and we would cause inequity, injustice, and chaos to prevail on the earth. While we await Christ's return, we're commanded to execute justice for the poor (Exodus 23:6), the fatherless (Deuteronomy 24:17), the widow (Deuteronomy 24:19), the innocent (Proverbs 18:5), and the oppressed (Isaiah 10:1).

God has appointed a time when the living and the dead will be judged. This day of judgment only needs to be feared by those who refuse to submit to God's order and who resist the call to turn and repent from their wicked ways. Throughout history, God has called us as individuals and communities to repent and to live holy lives before him (Leviticus 19:2; 2 Peter 3:11-14). Those of us who adhere to this call can look forward to the day when sin will be annihilated and the kingdom of righteousness will be established by the just Judge of all the earth (2 Peter 3:11-14).

FOR FURTHER READING

Steven J. Keillor, *God's Judgments: Interpreting History and the Christian Faith.* InterVarsity, 2007.
Donald G. Bloesch, *The Last Things: Resurrection, Judgment, Glory.* InterVarsity, 2004.

—HÉLÈNE DALLAIRE

DEATH

EVERYDAY DEFINITION

The Bible speaks of death in several senses.

In a biological sense, the term refers to the end of life in every sort of living entity—plant, animal, or human. "Surely the fate of human beings is like that of the animals; the same fate awaits them both: As one dies, so dies the other. All have the same breath" (Ecclesiastes 3:19, TNIV). Physical death is the fate of all living entities.

Scripture also uses death to refer to the absence of spiritual vitality. Jesus told his listeners that "whoever hears my word and believes him who sent me has eternal life and will not be judged but has crossed over from death to life" (John 5:24, TNIV). This speaks of the event when someone who is biologically alive but spiritually dead crosses over into spiritual vitality and responsiveness.

"Death" can also specify a spiritual death subsequent to physical death. In the latter case, it refers to a state of damnation, a "second death" (Revelation 20:6,14; 21:8).

The Bible doesn't view death as simply the end of a biological cycle of birth, life, and death. Instead, it frequently links both biological and spiritual death with sin. Roman 6:23 states, "For the wages of sin is death, but the gift of God is eternal life in Christ Jesus our Lord." This might be the most well-known reference to this connection, but it occurs in other places as well. The relationship between sin and death is also found in passages where death is personified as a power under the control of Satan that opposes and seeks to hold us captive (Acts 2:24; Hebrews 2:14-15). Slavery to power of death is not simply the fate of humanity, but encompasses all creation, which awaits liberation from its "bondage to decay" (Romans 8:21).

Many references to death in the New Testament speak of Jesus' death as the means by which believers are made alive spiritually. At the heart of the gospel, the apostle Paul says, is the fact that "Christ died for our sins" (1 Corinthians 15:3; Romans 4:25; Colossians 1:22). Christ's death "for us" repeals our own spiritual death penalty so that "we may live together with him" (1 Thessalonians 5:10). In an ironic reversal, the death that Jesus endures is the antidote for our spiritual deadness. In addition to spiritual revitalization, Jesus' death and resurrection is promised as the means allowing our own resurrection to occur. Just as all humanity shares in Adam's death, those who are united with Christ will be resurrected: "But in this order: Christ, the firstfruits; then, when he comes, those who belong to him" (1 Corinthians 15:23, TNIV). With our resurrection comes a new status where "the perishable has been clothed with the imperishable, and the mortal with immortality" (1 Corinthians 15:54). The culmination of this process isn't simply the defeat of our death. Death itself will be "swallowed up in victory" (1 Corinthians 15:54) or, as Revelation puts it, "Death and Hades were thrown into the lake of fire" (Revelation 20:14).

EVERYDAY APPLICATION

The close connection between death and sin or separation from God helps us make sense of our intuition that something is deeply tragic about death. If death is nothing more than the natural end of our existence, why would we view it differently than other natural phenomena such as the effect of gravity or the speed of light? However, Scripture constantly reminds us that death can't be fully understood apart from our broken relationship with God. Death is a symptom of the rupture that separates us from the very source of life itself.

Humans are not unique as a result of our mortality; all living entities will die. However, we are unique in the sense that we are conscious of the fact we will die, and reflect on what that means. Theologically, death stands as the most vivid reminder that we are not God, "who alone is immortal" (1 Timothy 6:16). Despite all our efforts to avoid death and find salvation on our own terms, only God can overturn the fate that all mortals must endure. As the God who is the source of all life, our immortality is dependent solely on him.

FOR FURTHER READING
Peter J. Kreeft, *Love Is Stronger Than Death*. Ignatius Press, 1992.

— STEVE WILKENS

DEMONS

EVERYDAY DEFINITION
Demons are evil and malevolent spiritual beings (Matthew 8:16; 10:1; 12:43-45) who work under the dominion of Satan to undermine the will and activity of God. Sometimes called unclean or evil spirits, the Bible also refers to demons as fallen angels—those angels initially created by God to be his servant-partners, but who rebelled against God along with Lucifer the archangel, who became the devil (Isaiah 14:12-14). Many scholars agree that one third of the angels also fell with Lucifer into sin and became demons (Revelation 12:3-4).

Because demons were created, they have limited power (James 2:19; Revelation 16:14). For example, they recognize that as the Son of God, Jesus is superior to them (Matthew 8:20; Luke 4:41). Still, because of their previous revolt, they spitefully oppose the purposes and the people of God. They're aligned with Satan, the leader of all evil powers, the ruler of this world (John 12:31) and the prince of the power of the air (Ephesians 2.2). Demons are the personal forces behind the "principalities" and "powers" that the apostle Paul said is our real battle (Ephesians 6:12, KJV).

In scriptural accounts, demons oppose all people—both those in and outside the people of God. They afflict with disease and various other forms of trouble including psychological, intellectual, ethical, and bodily torment of various kinds (Luke 9:42-43). They deceive and seek to turn believers away from God and God's will. Demons tempt God's servants (Matthew 4:1-11). They sometimes make people ill (Matthew 17:14-18; Luke 13:11-16). But not all illness has its roots in demonic activity. This is evident in the ministry of Jesus: Most times Jesus simply healed, but occasionally to affect healing he cast out a demon (Matthew 12:22; 17:18; Luke 9:42).

The Old Testament mentions evil spirits (Leviticus 16:10; 1 Samuel 16:14-16; Isaiah 34:14), but does not provide a great deal of detail as to their origin or how to combat them. The closest thing to a demonic expulsion mentioned in the Old Testament concerns David's ministry to Saul (1 Samuel 16:23).

In the New Testament, acting as God's agents and serving through the power and authority of God, both Jesus and his early followers cast out demons. These demon expulsions were simultaneously an act of healing and restoration of God's creation and a sign to onlookers that the kingdom of God was at hand. This in-breaking of the kingdom of God (Mark 1:14-15,27) demonstrates the rule and reign of God, which will one day produce a new heaven and new earth where all evil and evil spirits are banished (Matthew 25:41; 2 Peter 2:4; Jude 6; Revelation 12:9).

Both the Old and New Testament writers and church leaders throughout history forbid divination and "magic arts" such as astrology, Tarot reading, Ouija Boards, etc. (Deuteronomy 18:9-11; Isaiah 8:19-20; Acts 13:6-12; 19:19), as they are ways to search for information outside of a personal relationship with God. While often nothing much happens, this kind of seeking can actually put someone in contact with unseen evil powers.

EVERYDAY APPLICATION

As Christians, perhaps the most important understanding we can have about demons is that while they are potent with evil, they're not all-powerful. If even Satan only operates under the watchful and purposeful eye of God, then demons also can only go as far as God allows them. Like all creation, demons are under God's sovereign purview. As Christians, we can resist demons (James 4:7). Sometimes, this is a part of repentance and cooperating with God's grace to bring transformation to our life. Demons are restricted by the ultimate purposes and completion of God's story. While they work now, they only work in ways that God is able to redeem for his final purpose. Satan and his demons are real and active, but we don't need to have an undue fear of them, "because greater is he that is in you, than he that is in the world" (1 John 4:4, KJV).

The coming of Jesus revealed what has been true since the rebellion of Satan: There are two kingdoms in conflict—the kingdom of God and the kingdom of Satan. But Scripture puts the matter in clear contrast. The apostle Peter depicted the battle: "The devil prowls around like a roaring lion looking for someone to devour" (1 Peter 5.8) while the apostle John revealed the ultimate victory: "The reason the Son of God appeared was to destroy the devil's work" (1 John 3:8). Acting on his mission to defeat evil and the Evil One, Jesus cast out demons with his simple, but ultimately authoritative word (Matthew17:18).

As Jesus' followers, we stand in his linage against evil—both personal and systemic. We are ambassadors of his kingdom (2 Corinthians 5:20). We have been given a role to work with the resurrected Christ through the power of the Holy Spirit. This includes driving out demons when necessary.

Jesus gave authority to the twelve (Matthew 10:8) and the seventy (Luke 10:17) to cast out demons. This authority also worked through others in the early church (Acts 8:7; 16:18; James 4:7; 1 Peter 5:8-9). Understanding that all Christians can minister to the demonized is crucial. To act in cooperation with God as his agents of healing requires that Christians relieve the suffering of those tormented by demons.

However, demons don't merely work against God and others. Sometimes they work against Christians. For example, unrelenting temptation and habitual sin can be signs of demonic oppression. This doesn't mean we can claim "the devil made me do it" as if we have no free will. It means that demons are alive and well, doing their normal work trying to get us to live lives that are out of alignment with God's plans and purposes for us. Demons seem to operate most frequently using deception, discouragement, and spiritual despair. For example, when some of Jesus' first hearers stood against him, he said they were doing so because they were following "your father, the devil, . . . the father of lies" (John 8:44).

Even thoughtful Christians have disagreed about whether a Christian can be demon possessed. Actually, the term "demon possessed" does not occur in the New Testament. The biblical words indicate a condition more accurately translated "to have a demon" or to be suffering from "demonic influence." These words sometimes describe someone who has lost most or all capacity to exercise willpower or to defend against the demon(s). But, it's clear that not all cases of demonic intrusion lead to this level of influence. While there is clearly a range of demonic activity in a person (Matthew 16:23), those who are new creatures in Christ are not left subject to levels of demonic activity to which they have no power to resist.

Though the devil and his hierarchy of demons are present and active, they can be resisted. The Bible promises that God will never let us be tempted beyond that which we can bear (1 Corinthians 10:13). The death of Jesus has given ultimate victory over demons (Hebrews 2:14). We cooperate with this victory by not doing things that give the devil opportunity to harass us (Ephesians 4:27). We best resist demonic activity through confession of faith, repentance from sin, and accepting the freeing, liberating grace and power of Jesus.

FOR FURTHER READING

Wayne Grudem, *Systematic Theology*. Zondervan, 1994.

Clinton E. Arnold, *Three Crucial Questions About Spiritual Warfare*. Baker, 1997.

Thomas B. White, *The Believers Guide to Spiritual Warfare: Wising Up to Satan's Influence in Your World*. Regal, 1990.

Neil T. Anderson, *Victory over Darkness*. Regal, 2000.

— Todd Hunter

DEPRAVITY

EVERYDAY DEFINITION

Scripture plainly teaches that Adam and Eve's disobedience to God in the Garden brought upon themselves and the entire human race guilt, depravity, and the sentence of condemnation. Depravity refers to the corruption of human nature and all its capacities by virtue of God's righteous judgment as a consequence of the fall of Adam and Eve.

Biblical teaching on depravity is extensive. Following the sad story of human rebellion and wickedness recorded in the early chapters of Genesis, God concluded that "every inclination of the human heart is evil from childhood" (Genesis 8:21, TNIV). The book of Job describes "mortals" as "vile and corrupt, who drink up evil like water!" (Job 15:16, TNIV). Concerning those who reject God, the psalmist David wrote: "Everyone has turned away, all have become corrupt; there is no one who does good, not even one" (Psalm 53:3, also see 14:1-3). The prophet Jeremiah concluded, "The heart is deceitful [crooked] above all things and beyond cure [sick]. Who can understand it?" (Jeremiah 17:9). Jesus said, "Evil people bring evil things out of the evil stored up in them" (Matthew 12:35, TNIV). The apostle Paul wrote of this "warped and crooked generation" (Philippians 2:15, TNIV).

Paul employed as a synonym for human depravity the word "flesh" (*sarx*)—consistently translated in the NIV and TNIV as "sinful nature" (for example, Romans 7–8; Galatians 5:16-17). Rather than affirming that depravity is "total" (suggesting that the unsaved are as bad as possibly can be conceived), it is preferable to state that depravity is "holistic," in the sense that it extends to each capacity of human nature, as follows.

- Scripture asserts the *mind* of sinners is depraved (Romans 1:28) and unreceptive to spiritual truths (1 Corinthians 2:14; 2 Corinthians 4:4).
- The *will* of the unregenerate is held captive to sinful motives and choices. The will is hardened (Hebrews 3:8,15), opposed to God (Romans 8:7), and enslaved to sin (Proverbs 5:22; John 8:34) and Satan (2 Timothy 2:26).
- Sinners' *emotions* are disordered (Psalm 38:5-10), their affections yearning for things of the world rather than desiring God and loving him. Their psychological world is characterized by crippling inner conflicts resulting in lack of peace (Isaiah 57:20-21) and fear of death (Hebrews 2:15).
- *Relationally,* the unregenerate are alienated in measure from themselves, often from other people, and chiefly from God (Isaiah 59:2; Ephesians 4:18). Loving fellowship and communion with God are broken.

- *Behaviorally,* sinners live out their depraved natures in the form of debased actions: corrupt speech, drunkenness, fornication, homosexual acts, murder, drug trafficking, rape, white collar crimes, acts of terrorism, etc. (see Romans 1:29-32).
- *Socially,* humans oppress their neighbors, exploit the poor, and mistreat foreigners (Micah 3:1-3).
- *Religiously,* the unregenerate are prone to idolatry (Galatians 4:8) and to the practice of false religions (Romans 1:23; 2 Peter 2:15).

In spite of this dark picture, most Christians hold that the image of God isn't destroyed, but that it is seriously spoiled and corrupted (James 3:9). Indeed, given God's common grace—his goodness and beneficence to all—sinners aren't as evil as they could possibly be. Still, apart from God's saving grace, the unregenerate are incapable of altering their dispositions (Jeremiah 13:23) or justifying themselves before God.

EVERYDAY APPLICATION

Anyone who isn't a follower of Jesus must recognize that the only way to eliminate the distressing depravity of the heart is to turn to him in repentance, faith, and surrender of life. Only Jesus can deliver individuals from the baneful effects of sin, cleanse the heart, and set them on the renewing road of holiness and love of God.

In order that our hearts might beat more fully with God's compassionate heart, we Christians must "feel" the dreadful and destructive effects of sin and depravity. Only as we grasp depravity's degrading and dehumanizing effects on the people around us will we be motivated to come to their aid with practical assistance and the life-saving message of salvation. As we reflect on lustful impulses and violent behaviors in the unsaved without being compromised ourselves, we'll learn to despise evil more intensely. As the psalmist put it, "Let those who love the LORD hate evil" (Psalm 97:10; Proverbs 8:13). A righteous hatred of evil is a first necessary step for the overcoming of evil.

As followers of Jesus, we must respect sinners as individuals who are uniquely created in God's image and highly valued by him. Although defiled by a sinful heart and corrupt behaviors, the unsaved deserve our respect and concern as well. While not loving someone's degraded behavior, we must love the sinner, even as God does. Recall that Jesus socialized with unbelievers and bore the reputation of being "a friend of tax collectors and 'sinners'" (Matthew 11:19).

The notion that non-Christians are guiltworthy and liable to condemnation is highly unpopular in the postmodern world. But if we're committed to a biblical understanding of human depravity and the judgment to come, we followers of Jesus must share the good news with those who are bound in sin. As did the apostle Paul in Athens, we deliver the message: "In the past God overlooked such ignorance, but now he commands all people everywhere to repent. For he has set a day when he will judge the world with justice by the man he has appointed" (Acts 17:30-31). The eternal life Christ offers is the only antidote to pervasive human depravity.

Given the serious sins committed by biblical saints—including Noah, Moses, David, and Peter—we Christians must prayerfully put to death the power of the sinful flesh remaining in us. We must fight temptations that play on our sinful nature or "flesh." Yielding to temptations of pride, materialism, sexual gratification, and others only violates our sacred covenant relation with the Lord. The solution to residual depravity is the prayerful pursuit of sanctification, or godliness.

FOR FURTHER READING

Augustine, *Against Julian*. Fathers of the Church, 1957.

Thomas Goodwin, *Man's Guiltiness Before God*. Sovereign Grace Publishers, 1960.

Arthur W. Pink, *Gleanings from the Scriptures: Man's Total Depravity*. Moody, 1972.

—BRUCE DEMAREST

DISCIPLE

EVERYDAY DEFINITION

The Greek term disciple (*mathetes*) means learner, student, or apprentice. It is the most common term found in the New Testament describing a follower of Jesus. The word appears more than 260 times in the New Testament and is the "entry level" descriptor of all who follow Jesus.

A disciple as a student or apprentice is attached to a rabbi or teacher.

This designated relationship is clearly what Jesus had in mind when he called the twelve to himself. In Jesus' day, when we read of his calling of the twelve disciples (Mark 1:16-19), we witness a common apprenticeship education model taking place with Jesus, the Rabbi, assembling his students. His teaching, of course, was less about the "law and the prophets," and more about revealing, manifesting, and teaching them about life in the "kingdom of God" (a fulfillment of the "Law and the Prophets" Romans 3:21).

This apprenticeship model of rabbi to student is an ongoing status throughout life. In other words, as disciples of Jesus, we're always learning from him how to live our lives as he would live if he were us. At the heart of all disciples is the desire to be like their teacher in character and action, in all things (Colossians 3:17). In order for this to occur, disciples must arrange their lives for this type of training. This arrangement is what we call discipleship. The disciple of Jesus constantly seeks to be in the presence of Jesus to be guided, instructed, and helped by him in every aspect of life.

In John 8:31-32 Jesus says, "If you continue in my word, you are truly my disciples; and you will know the truth, and the truth will make you free" (NRSV). So, the mark of a disciple is to be with Jesus, to look like him, and "abide in" him (John 15:4, NRSV). We should see discipleship as an adventure, not a burden. It's the "easy yoke" that Christ promised (Matthew 11:28-30). It's the life that sets us free!

EVERYDAY APPLICATION

The richness of seeing ourselves as disciples of Jesus is the understanding that Jesus himself will daily teach us how to become like him in word and action. Our role is to daily enlist and submit to his wise and gentle leadership and apprentice ourselves to him, "training" for the eternal kind of life we are being fitted for.

Becoming a disciple is more about "training" than about "trying." Trying to be like Christ is almost sure to fail, and it's prone to guilt and discouragement. However, training under Christ's guidance and love is sure to produce a new person who looks and acts as Jesus would if he were in our shoes. So as disciples of Christ, we can wake up each day filled with the faith and knowledge that the living Jesus is ready to guide, lead, and teach us how to become like him for the redemption of the world.

FOR FURTHER READING

Dallas Willard, *The Divine Conspiracy.* HarperSanFransico, 1998.

Dallas Willard, *The Great Omission.* HarperSanFrancisco, 2006.

— KEITH MATTHEWS

DISCIPLESHIP

EVERYDAY DEFINITION

The word "discipleship" comes from the challenge that Jesus himself made, for us all to become disciples. The Greek word that the English word *disciple* comes from means, in its most basic sense, "a learner." However, from his usage of this word, Jesus clearly meant more than just getting smarter intellectually. In his Great Commission, he called those with him to go to all nations and make disciples, baptizing and teaching them to keep all the things Jesus commanded.

The concept of discipleship wasn't unique to Jesus. In the ancient world, all sorts of religious leaders had a form of discipleship. The focus of discipleship was on the students of a master learning to emulate and model their behavior and lives on that of the master. So, the Bible's usage of this word to describe what the followers of Jesus should be means keeping some of that same concept. However, Jesus also placed more expectations on what discipleship should look like. The Scriptures reveal the following expectations about discipleship to Jesus:

- *Giving total allegiance to Jesus.* In the call of Matthew 28, baptism is part of the life of a disciple. While baptism has a large and diverse meaning in the Bible, it symbolizes a transformation of an individual from one family into another. So discipleship involves a transformation of a Christian's family relationship from the family of origin to Jesus and his family. This places discipleship to Jesus at a higher level of importance and allegiance than a Christian's own family, ethnicity, gender, or social status. In part, this is why Jesus' message was so difficult to hear in a society that highly valued all these things. It remains so difficult today for these same reasons. Jesus called people to discipleship who were

Samaritans, Romans, slaves, women, and sinners. While these external forms of identity continued to be part of life, the connection and allegiance to Jesus becomes the identity of his disciples.

- *Being willing to pay any cost.* At times, Jesus seemed completely uninterested in followers who merely "believe" in him (John 5; 8). His desire is discipleship, not just belief. Mere belief won't bear the costs of following Jesus our Master. Jesus tells us that those who want to follow him will pick up their cross daily (Mark 8:34), that they must be willing to lose their life (Mark 8:35), and that they will have no guarantee of a place to even lay their heads and must be willing to abandon all to follow after him (Luke 9:57-62). He promises that those who follow after him will experience persecution, lies, and hatred, all because of his name (John 15:18-20). Throughout the Gospels, we see crowds that are interested in Jesus. Yet the call to discipleship is more than interest; it's a call to endure what must be endured for his name and kingdom's sake. Discipleship is not a fainthearted calling.

- *Bearing the message of Jesus and his good news to all peoples.* Even in the discipleship of the first disciples, we see the importance of the message in discipleship (Matthew 28; Acts 1). Later, the apostle Peter called all those who have received faith to be ready to give account for the hope we have in Christ Jesus. Discipleship is rooted in the willingness to bear witness to Jesus' life, ministry, death, resurrection, and coming kingdom.

EVERYDAY DEFINITION

As Christians, we don't seem to have any option except to be the disciples of Jesus. Nowhere in Scripture do we see a calling for people to be converted but not to be disciples. Jesus' parable of the Sheep and the Goats (Matthew 25:31-46) reminds us that all true followers of Jesus are engaged in the life of discipleship, faithfully carrying out the calling of the Father on our lives where he places us, just as Jesus modeled for us.

One of the primary ways we grow as disciples of Jesus takes place as we model our lives after him. This includes modeling Jesus' practices, such as fasting, praying, worship. But it also means modeling his way of life: offering grace to sinners, serving as he served, and seeking the will of the Father. Discipleship means being like Jesus by growing in stature and in favor with God and men (Luke 2:52).

Discipleship is a lifelong process, one without a graduation that sets you up as master to be followed. Christian discipleship is always discipleship of Jesus and his kingdom.

FOR FURTHER READING

Michael Wilkins, *Following the Master.* Zondervan, 1992.

Michael Wilkins, *In His Image: Reflecting Christ in Everyday Life.* NavPress, 1997.

Joel B. Green, Scot McKnight, I. Howard Scot Marshall, "Discipleship" in *Dictionary of Jesus and the Gospels.* InterVarsity, 1992.

Lelan Ryken, Jim Wilhoit, Tremper Longman, Colin Duriez, Douglas Penney, Daniel G. Reid, "The Meaning of Discipleship" in *Dictionary of Biblical Imagery.* electronic edition, InterVarsity, 2000.

— CHRISTOPHER MORTON

DIVORCE

EVERYDAY DEFINITION

Divorce is the disunion of husband and wife, the legal dissolution of a marriage. To divorce is to admit that two people in a marriage have failed. There is no such thing as a "no-fault divorce," except as a legal contrivance. Divorce is a manifestation of hardness of heart. While marriage is a covenant of commitment, divorce is a disavowal, a breach of promised faithfulness. To divorce is to declare an unwillingness to be reconciled.

In Jesus' day, there were two main schools of rabbinic thought regarding divorce. Both lines of thought were based on Deuteronomy 24:1, "When a man takes a wife and marries her, and it happens that she [*'erwat dabar*] . . . he writes her a certificate of divorce" (NASB). The first-century school of Shammai, to begin with, interpreted the Hebrew phrase *'erwat dabar* as a "matter of nakedness," meaning that a man could divorce his wife if she was adulterous. The school of Hillel (60 BC–AD 20), by contrast, interpreted *'erwat dabar* more generally as "something indecent or displeasing," meaning that a man could divorce his wife for almost any reason at all.

When the Pharisees tested Jesus by asking, "Is it lawful for a man to divorce his wife for any reason at all?" he answered with a counter-question, "Have you not read that He who created them from the beginning made them male and female?" (Matthew 19:3-4, NASB). Jesus didn't appeal primarily to Deuteronomy 24:1 in his teaching on divorce. Jesus pointed instead to Genesis 1–2. Jesus looked back to the very beginning to God's original plan for marriage.

Jesus redirected their attention to God's intention. God did not intend for married couples to divorce. The Bible says, "I [God] hate divorce" (Malachi 2:16). Jesus said, "For this reason a man shall leave his father and mother and be joined to his wife, and the two shall become one flesh" (Matthew 19:5, NASB). The "cause" for which a man shall leave his parents is the union of male and female. In other words, it's precisely because God "made them male and female" that a man shall "leave father and mother" and "cleave to his wife" (Matthew 19:4-5, KJV).

Jesus' commentary on Genesis reveals that marriage is a reunion of human flesh. Eve's flesh was Adam's flesh already—because Eve was created from Adam's side. Upon meeting Eve, Adam said, "This is now . . . flesh of my flesh." Yet he did *not* say that "flesh of my flesh" shall be called "Wife." He said, "She shall be called Woman, because she was taken out of Man" (Genesis 2:23, NASB). Eve didn't become Adam's wife until their same flesh became "one flesh" in marriage. What's particularly striking about Jesus' teaching is that Jesus told the Pharisees that the husband is supposed to "cleave" to his wife, not divorce her.

To divorce is to "put asunder" what God has joined together (Matthew 19:6, KJV). To divorce is to rupture the "one flesh" marital union of husband and wife (Mark 10:8). The mystery of marriage is that the husband and wife form a head and body union that reflects the spiritual union of Christ and the church (Ephesians 5:32). As Christ is the Head of the church, so the husband is the head of his wife (Ephesians 5:23). As the church is the body of Christ, so the wife is the body of the husband. The metaphorical picture of a head and body union of husband and wife vividly shows the mystery of the two becoming "one flesh" (Genesis 2:24; Ephesians 5:31).

Divorce is tragic because it finalizes the division of a head and body union. A divorce is a decapitation of a head from its own body, the amputation of a body from its head. That's why divorce is so painful. A body is not meant to be amputated wholly from its head. A head is not designed to be severed from its body.

In Old Testament times, divorce was a viable option, but only for men. Wives lived at the mercy of their husbands. Jesus revised Old Testament law by raising the standard back to God's original plan for couples to stay married. What Jesus also showed is that adultery is inexcusable for both women and men. In Jewish law, adultery was seen as a property violation, a form of stealing from a man. Since women were forbidden to own property, adultery by definition could not be committed against a woman (because no man was her sexual property). Jesus revolutionized Jewish law and tradition by explaining that even if a wife divorces her husband, "she is committing adultery" (Mark 10:12, NASB; see also 1 Corinthians 7:4).

Biblically speaking, divorce can be legitimate, but only in two cases:

1. When there is *porneia,* a summary term for sexual sins in Leviticus 18 (Matthew 5:32).
2. When an unbelieving spouse deserts a believing spouse by leaving the relationship altogether (1 Corinthian 7:15).

Divorce, then, is a concession given by God due to hardness of heart (Matthew 19:8). Divorce should not be viewed as a safety net for Christians who no longer want to be married to their spouse.

EVERYDAY APPLICATION

The subject of divorce raises many other questions, including:

- What should be the freedoms and limitations of divorced people in the Christian community?
- Is it acceptable for divorcees to remarry?

Before addressing these questions, it's important to emphasize the Christian community's responsibility to "bear one another's burdens" (Galatians 6:2, NASB), including the painful burden of divorce. No divorcee in the church should ever be labeled as a "worse sinner than the rest" strictly on account of a failed marriage. Rather, the community of believers should work to "restore" the ones who are divorced "in a spirit of gentleness" (Galatians 6:1, NASB), bearing in mind that some who are divorced do not want to be divorced and had little choice in the matter. Yet since no divorced person is purely innocent, the body of believers should also be intentional about helping divorcees to identify the patterns of sin in their life that might keep them from being restored to a soft-hearted state of earnestly seeking to imitate the character of Christ (2 Timothy 4:2).

With regard to what freedoms and limitations divorced people should have in the Christian community, the answer is debated among Christians. Certainly, people who are divorced should be invited to participate fully and freely in the fellowship and worship of the church. Whether or not divorcees should serve as leaders in the community is a more difficult question. Biblically, some Christians see warrant for prohibiting a divorcee from serving as an elder (1 Timothy 3:2, NASB: "An overseer, then, must be . . . the husband of one wife"). Of course, this could also mean that an elder of the church must be married. Because such an interpretation leads to the unlikely conclusion that neither Jesus nor Paul (who were both unmarried men) were qualified to be elders, there is also biblical warrant for understanding the author's intent to be saying that elders, if married, are not to be polygamists, but rather the partners of just one spouse. If a divorcee participates in a healthy process of restoration (Galatians 6:1), makes amends with the family members they hurt (Matthew 5:24), remains humble and candid about their broken wedding vows (James 5:16), and is appropriately gifted and developed for the position, then he or she could be ready to serve as ministry leader.

As for the topic of remarriage, there is no broad consensus about it, especially with regard to the remarriage of a person whose spouse violated the marriage with *porneia*. However, most Christians agree that Jesus raised the standard for divorce and remarriage by removing the Jewish rule that made divorce obligatory for any man whose wife committed adultery. The ongoing challenge is to discern Jesus' saying, "And I say to you, whoever divorces his wife, except for immorality [*porneia*], and marries another woman commits adultery" (Matthew 19:9, NASB). Was Jesus saying that it's actually okay for a person to remarry if their spouse broke covenant by having sexual intercourse with someone else? Or was he merely saying that the sin of *porneia* legitimizes divorce for the jilted spouse? Because the exception clause, "except for immorality [*porneia*]," occurs only in Matthew, there is some debate about its application given that writers such as Mark, Luke, and Paul don't include it.

For believers who are deserted by their unbelieving spouse, no line in Scripture legitimizes the option of remarriage. On the contrary, Jesus' words indicate the opposite (Mark 10:11-12). Paul's words further underscore the point: "Do not be bound together with unbelievers; for what . . . fellowship has light with darkness? Or what harmony has Christ with Belial?" (2 Corinthians 6:14-15, NASB). Apparently, the risk taken in marrying a nonbeliever entails the risk of being deserted without having God's permission to remarry.

FOR FURTHER READING

David Gushee, *Getting Marriage Right*. Baker, 2004.

Richard Hays, "Divorce and Remarriage" in *The Moral Vision of the New Testament: A Contemporary Introduction to New Testament Ethics*. Harper, 1996.

Jim and Sarah Sumner, *Just How Married Do You Want to Be? Practicing Oneness in Marriage*. InterVarsity, 2008.

— SARAH SUMNER

ECOLOGY

EVERYDAY DEFINITION

Literally, "the study [*logos*] of the household [*oikos*]," the word *ecology* was first used in 1866 to mean, "the comprehensive science of the relationship of the organism to the environment." Today, the term is used both to refer to the study of organisms and their environments and, more broadly and loosely, to connote ideas that are environmentally friendly or "green."

The most significant aspect of the study of ecology is examining the relationships that organisms have with one another, as well as the relationships that organisms have with their environment. For example, scientists have long studied ways that animals relate to one another, developing ideas like the "food chain," in which predators eat prey up the chain.

More recently, scientists have turned their attention to the environments that sustain animal populations and studied the ways that changes in these environments affect animal populations. For example, studies on the culling of Amazon rainforests have fueled scientific debates about the ways that the human population affects the Earth's environment. These debates often center on whether human activity is directly responsible for changes in the global environment or if these changes would have naturally taken place.

One recent example is the hole in the ozone layer, a layer in the Earth's atmosphere that absorbs and deflects more than 90 percent of the sun's harmful ultraviolet rays. In 1985, scientists discovered a hole in this layer above the South Pole, and they attributed this hole to the human use of CFC-producing aerosol spray cans. If allowed to continue, the depletion of the ozone layer could have significantly altered the Earth's environment and its habitability by humans and many other species. In 1987, a treaty was signed banning such sprays, and by 2007, 191 of the world's 196 countries had signed the treaty. As a result, scientists have seen a significant reversal in the depletion of the ozone layer.

Christians have long considered their relationship to the rest of creation, especially in light of the creation account in Genesis where God declares, "Let us make man in our image, in our likeness, and let them rule over the fish of the sea and the birds of the air, over the livestock, over all the earth, and over all the creatures that move along the ground," and "Be fruitful and increase in number; fill the earth and subdue it. Rule over the fish of the sea and the birds of the air and over every living creature that moves on the ground" (Genesis 1:26,28). For many centuries, some Christians took these verses to imply that human beings were to dominate the rest of creation. But more recently, many Christians have viewed these verses as meaning that humans are to be caretakers of the Earth and its inhabitants.

EVERYDAY APPLICATION

In Genesis, God directs Adam to name the "the birds of the air and all the beasts of the field" (Genesis 2:20). This seems to indicate that God wanted humans to have more of a caretaker role in creation. Genesis also explains why Adam is placed in the Garden: "The LORD God took the man and put him in the Garden of Eden to work it and take care of it" (Genesis 2:15).

Currently, the world's population stands at 6.5 billion people—that's ten times more than just three centuries ago. And the human population continues to grow at more than 1 percent annually. Our species continues to expand and use the limited resources of this planet to fuel our expansion. As Christians, we need to reflect on our relationship to creation.

Many Christians today advocate for limited use of the Earth's resources and for alternate sources of energy. Churches, Christian colleges, and seminaries are using "green" building techniques and curbing their energy use. However, other Christians think that these efforts are misguided. Some believe that the Bible predicts an inevitable degradation of the natural environment prior to Christ's Second Coming; others believe that the environmental agenda of the scientific community is at odds with the spiritual agenda of the church.

In the end, each of us needs to decide where we as human beings stand in relationship to the rest of God's creation. If we are, indeed, God's appointed caretakers, then we must work to ensure that his creation will be sustained for future generations.

FOR FURTHER READING

Steven Bouma-Prediger, *For the Beauty of the Earth: A Christian Vision for Creation Care.* Baker Academic, 2001.

Fred Van Dyke, David C. Mahan, Joseph K. Sheldon, Raymond H. Brand, *Redeeming Creation: The Biblical Basis for Environmental Stewardship.* InterVarsity, 1996.

Wendell Berry, *The Unsettling of America: Culture & Agriculture.* Sierra Book Clubs, 2004.

— TONY JONES

ELECTRONIC MEDIA

EVERYDAY DEFINITION
Electronic media—such as radio, telephone, television, and the Internet—are communication technologies that humans create and use in light of their environments. These activities stem from our

intellectual and creative endowments as creatures made in God's image (Genesis 1:26; 9:6; Psalm 8). These abilities should be employed for God's glory (1 Corinthians 10:31). Media technologies differ from previous forms of media, such as books, magazines, and letters, by virtue of being part of an electronic system. They differ from nonelectronic media in the following ways:

- Electronic media are *animated* in that they are active. Radio transmits voice, sounds, and music. Television broadcasts moving images as well as sounds. A book, on the other hand, doesn't make sounds or move on its own; it is inactive, and the reader discerns meaning by the activity of reading.
- Electronic media possess unique powers of *distribution*. There may be a million copies of one book. But the content of an online book can be read by anyone who has an Internet connection. The information can be distributed without the information being lodged in any physical book.
- Electronic media are *disembodied*. Television, the Internet, telephones, and so on mediate communication without the physical presence of another person. We can see the president on television, but he is not physically present in the room with us.

EVERYDAY APPLICATION

Christians should investigate how any electronic medium — given its animation, distribution, and disembodiment — affects both the message it carries and the soul that receives the message, whether for good or for ill (see 1 John 2:15-17; Romans 12:1-2). Marshall McLuhan, whose work is considered the cornerstone of media theory, said that "the medium is the message." Although he knew nothing about electronic media in the first century, the apostle John realized that each medium has its strengths and weakness: "I have much to write to you, but I do not want to use paper and ink. Instead, I hope to visit you and talk with you face to face, so that our joy may be complete" (2 John 12; see also 3 John 13). Watching a sermon on television isn't the same experience as hearing it in person. Taking a course online isn't equivalent to being in the classroom. Electronic media can extend the reach of information, but it often diminishes the depth of experience, because interaction is mediated through impersonal technology.

Electronic media might inhibit real community (see Psalm 133). A pastor's sermon can be broadcast to several locations, but much is lost by the pastor's physical absence. How many family get-togethers are diminished by people talking on cell phones or playing video games instead of speaking and listening to each other face-to-face?

Ecclesiastes says, "There is a time for . . . every activity under heaven" (3:1). As Christians, there is a time to embrace electronic media and a time to refrain from it (verse 5). Knowing the difference requires wisdom and guidance from God (James 1:5).

FOR FURTHER READING

Douglas Groothuis, *The Soul in Cyberspace*. Wipf & Stock, 1999.
Quentin Schultz, *Habits of the High Tech Heart*. Eerdmans, 2002.

— DOUGLAS GROOTHUIS

ESCHATOLOGY

EVERYDAY DEFINITION

Eschatology is a theological term that many Christians might not be familiar with, but probably have encountered its ideas and formed distinctive opinions about the topics it addresses. The word derives from the Greek word *eschata*, which means "last things." So when theologians or pastors speak about eschatology, they're referring to the study of last things.

Christians often limit the scope of this area of theology to speculation about when Christ will return and how the world will end. However, eschatology actually refers to a broader field of study, with the overall theme of how God brings about his purposes in all of creation.

The roots of Christian eschatology can be found in certain statements by prophets as recorded in the Old Testament. Traditionally, the prophets of Israel were concerned with appealing to that nation and its leaders to honor the covenant God had established with them. As the nation experienced military defeats and exile, prophets began calling the people of Israel to look to the future for a ruler who God would raise up to govern with peace and justice in a restored kingdom. Originally, these declarations weren't interpreted as involving the end of the world, but as God acting through history to fulfill his purposes by re-establishing the kingdom of Israel among the nations. As centuries passed without any perceivable indication that God was acting to restore the nation to its former glory, some began to interpret these prophecies as the foretelling of God breaking into human history in a way that would bring this world to an end so that a new one could be created. The Old Testament passages that promote these themes of eschatology are called "apocalyptic" literature. The last six chapters of the book of Daniel are the most prominent example (Daniel 7–12), while portions of Isaiah (Isaiah 56–66), Ezekiel (Ezekiel 37–48), and Zechariah (Zechariah 9–14) are also classified in this manner.

During his earthly ministry, Jesus embodied and articulated his own apocalyptic vision of the future in a cultural context familiar with these diverse perceptions of the nature and purposes of the coming Messiah. Because many of the Israelites expected a military or political leader who would dramatically change their plight as a nation, they were unable to recognize Jesus as their Messiah because his mission involved the establishment of the "kingdom of God," which included his death and resurrection. When Jesus' disciples questioned him about the signs of his return, the establishment of his kingdom, and the end of the age, Jesus revealed his own assessment of future events (Matthew 24). Jesus created a menacing picture of events that will foreshadow his return, including wars (verse 6), natural disasters (verse 7), persecution (verse 9), increasing wickedness (verse 12), and an abundance of false prophets and people who claim to be the Messiah (verses 23-24). He then encouraged his disciples to keep watch for these signs so they won't be caught by surprise by his imminent return (verses 32-35,42-44).

After Jesus' death and resurrection, the disciples were attentive to the signs all around them and already believed they were living in the last days that Jesus spoke of (Acts 2:17-21; Hebrews 1:2; 1 Peter 4:7; 1 John 18; 19). Ever since, Christians of every generation have seen current events as signs of the return of Christ and the establishment of his kingdom.

Although most Christians agree that Jesus will return and each of us face impending judgment (Matthew 12:36; Romans 14:10; 2 Peter 2:9; 1 John 4:17), a lot of debate exists about the timing of this return.

These views primarily arise from how we interpret the millennium John wrote about in Revelation 20:1-6. Most Christians take one of the following three views:

1. *Postmillennialism* suggests that the return of Christ will occur after an extended period of time when Christian values and beliefs have spread throughout the world creating a type of Christian "golden age." At the end of this period, Satan will again attempt to deceive many people, but Christ will return to stop the rebellion and establish his kingdom on earth.

2. *Amillennialism* maintains that the thousand years John referred to was symbolic of something other than the reign of Christ on earth. They believe that the world will grow more evil over time and that the second coming of Christ will reveal his power over evil and mark the beginning of his eternal kingdom.

3. *Premillennialism* advocates the physical return of Jesus to earth prior to the millennium so he can establish his rule for that period. Then Satan will lead a final futile rebellion against God after which everyone will be judged. Premillennialism is divided into two camps based specifically on differing understandings of a seven-year period occurring before the millennium called the "Tribulation." Historic premillennialists believe a seven-year period of intense persecution against Christians will precede the triumphant return of Christ. Dispensational premillennialists contend that the return of Christ will occur in two stages. He will return prior to the tribulation to remove Christians from the world in what is known as the "Rapture." Then he will return again at the end of the seven-year period in which God has poured out his wrath upon the earth to establish his reign.

Each of these views has been popular among certain groups of Christians throughout the history of the church.

EVERYDAY APPLICATION

As Christians, despite the differing opinions we hold regarding the details of Christ's return and how the world will end, our eschatological beliefs should influence our daily lives in a number of ways. While the imminent return of Christ shouldn't be represented as something scary, Christians can definitely express it as a great promise, that one day God will fulfill his purposes in our lives and our world. This hope in Christ's setting all things right serves as a calming reality in our lives even in the midst of the most trying circumstances because we know these events aren't the end of the story.

We must also recognize that God has been working from the beginning of time to make his kingdom known and fulfill his purposes in history. Part of the reason the disciples were so convinced that they were living in the last days is because Jesus claimed that part of his mission was to initiate the kingdom of God in their day (Matthew 12:28; Mark 1:15; 9:1; Luke 9:1-2). They didn't fully grasp that God's kingdom involved both a present reality and a future culmination. However, we can pay attention to how God is working in history to further reveal the purposes and nature of his kingdom in our world today, even as we seek to understand what that means for the future.

If we believe that God will eventually make his kingdom known, we should also be working to integrate the values of his kingdom into our lives and world. As a result, we should always evaluate how our motives and actions as individuals and communities align with the values of this coming kingdom, as opposed to those championed by the cultural context in which we live. If our actions and behaviors don't reflect values such as love, reconciliation, justice, and peace, then we need to work to align our values more closely with the values we know characterize God's present and future kingdom.

FOR FURTHER READING

Paul Boyer, *When Time Shall Be No More: Prophecy Belief in Modern American Culture.* Harvard University Press, 1992.

Millard J. Erickson, *A Basic Guide to Eschatology: Making Sense of the Millennium.* Baker, 1998.

Stanley Grenz, *The Millennial Maze: Sorting Out Evangelical Options.* InterVarsity, 1992.

Eugene Peterson, *Reversed Thunder: The Revelation of John and the Praying Imagination.* HarperCollins, 1991.

N. T. Wright, *Surprised by Hope: Rethinking Heaven, the Resurrection, and the Mission of the Church*. HarperCollins, 2008.

— MATT ELOFSON

ETERNAL LIFE

EVERYDAY DEFINITION

Many people view eternal life as existence that starts when you die and never ends. In reality, eternal (*aionios*) life doesn't simply banish death. It begins now. Eternal life also refers not just to *length* of life, but also to *quality* of life and our experience of wholeness and union with God. In eternal life, we experience now something of the splendor, joy, and peace that are characteristic of the life of God.

Jesus defined eternal life this way: "Now this is eternal life: that they may know you, the only true God, and Jesus Christ, whom you have sent" (John 17:3). To know Christ is not to simply know about Christ or to believe certain things about him. The concept of knowledge moves beyond acquaintance with facts and intellectual acceptance and toward interactive relationship, a complete devotion of life in harmony with God's will, and an intimate fellowship with Jesus.

In the present stage of eternal life, our trust in Christ grows so that our character is progressively transformed into Christlikeness. Such trust changes us radically: "We know that we have passed from death to life, because we love our brothers" (1 John 3:14). We become purposeful, patient, and kind because we're abiding in Christ and his eternal life fills ours. This character transformation helps us partner with God to do God's work here on earth.

In the future stage of eternal life, we'll have "priestly work" to do as we "reign with Christ" (2 Timothy 2:12; Revelation 1:5; 5:10; 20:6; 22:5). Such work will astound and fascinate us because Jesus described it as entering "into the joy of [our] Lord" (Matthew 25:21, KJV).

EVERYDAY APPLICATION

Striving to live an eternal kind of life now comes as we seek a life of abiding in Christ, which Jesus himself described as, "Remain in me, and I will remain in you" (John 15:4). This mutual indwelling provides us with the juices to bear fruit such as love, joy, and peace (John 15:5). Without such nourishment, we as branches wither and die (John 15:6). Abiding in Christ's love, however, creates obedience (John 15:9-10) because deep devotion for Jesus gives us the desire to obey and sustains us when we might otherwise have second thoughts.

As we abide in Christ, we find ourselves more and more able to live in the power of the invisible kingdom of God. Inwardly, we become transformed people who outwardly:

- Live with joy and gratefulness.
- Bless enemies (difficult people).
- Don't hold grudges.
- Are not resentful.
- Care deeply about others.
- Don't run off at the mouth, but offer caring words.
- Go the extra mile.
- Live with purposeful intentionality.
- Are humble (letting go of pride, not grabbing the credit or engaging in power struggles).
- Never judge (that's God's job).

FOR FURTHER READING:
Dallas Willard, *The Divine Conspiracy.* HarperSanFrancisco, 1998.
Jan Johnson, *Invitation to the Jesus Life.* NavPress, 2008.

— JAN JOHNSON

EVANGELISM

EVERYDAY DEFINITION
Evangelism is the act of sharing the good news of Jesus Christ with those who don't yet believe, in an effort to see them come to faith and, therefore, to personal salvation. This activity is rooted in the initiative of God himself. John 3:16 notes, "For God so loved the world that he gave his one and only Son, that whoever believes in him shall not perish but have eternal life."

Evangelism is a foundational aspect of the advance of God's kingdom, which Jesus himself proclaimed and inaugurated (Matthew

4:23-24). Following his death for sin and his resurrection from the dead, Jesus commissioned his disciples to share this good news of God's grace with all they encountered. Because God has acted for the salvation of humanity in Christ, the church was given an evangelistic mission from its inception (Matthew 28:18-20; Acts 1:8). The apostle Peter noted that God does not want anyone to perish, but everyone to come to repentance (2 Peter 3:9). This means that God expects his people to act as his ambassadors in sharing the good news with those who don't yet know him.

The word evangelism comes from the Greek verb *euangelizesthai*, which means "to announce the good news." This word is found fifty-two times in the New Testament, indicating that evangelism is a fundamental aspect of the Christian faith. The noun *euangelion* means "good news" and occurs seventy-two times, mostly in the writings of the apostle Paul. As Paul noted in one of his more prominent uses of the word, the gospel (*euangelion*) is the power of God for the salvation of everyone who believes (Romans 1:16). God's righteousness in Jesus Christ is revealed in the gospel and is to be received by faith (Romans 1:17). The word *euangelistes*, which is translated "evangelist," is only used three times in the New Testament. It refers either to a spiritual gift (Ephesians 4:11), to someone who possesses and exercises that gift (Philip the Evangelist; Acts 21:8), or to a specific responsibility of ministry (2 Timothy 4:5).

The New Testament doesn't advocate any particular methodology for sharing the good news of Jesus. Paul addressed the issue of motive in a surprising sort of way. While he stressed the importance of sharing the gospel with purity of heart (2 Corinthians 2:17; 4:2), he was far more concerned that the good news be proclaimed regardless of motive (Philippians 1:15-18). He emphasized that Christ should always be preached, recognizing that some will come to faith while others will reject him due to spiritual blindness (2 Corinthians 4:3-4). This indicates that evangelism shouldn't be defined by numerical results; "success" is measured only in terms of obedient action by the followers of Jesus.

In recent years, various groups have stressed a close connection of evangelism with observable events. Some believe that unless churches are formed, no real evangelistic endeavor has taken place. Others emphasize the necessity of preaching the good news in the context of social action, such as feeding the poor. Still others argue that genuine gospel proclamation will always be accompanied by signs and wonders as a demonstration of Satan's defeat. However, as Christians, we can rest in the confidence of the New Testament's teaching that the results of evangelism are determined by the Holy Spirit alone.

EVERYDAY APPLICATION

Like Jesus' examples of a shepherd who searches for a lost sheep, a woman who searches for a lost coin, and a father who waits for the return of his lost son (Luke 15), we are to evangelize because lost people matter to God. Because no specific methodology is given in Scripture, we are free to do anything short of sin to see people come to Christ (1 Corinthians 9:24-27). Sharing the gospel with others one on one, starting "seeker services," inaugurating an evangelistic campaign, or giving others a cup of cold water in Jesus' name are just a few of the many acceptable approaches for telling others about the love of Christ. Whatever our method, it should always be based in love and rooted in personal integrity.

As we seek to evangelize, we must be clear about our message. We should address the problem of human sin (Romans 3), stress the love of God for people in Christ, and communicate his desire for reconciliation with those who are lost (2 Corinthians 5). Jesus' atoning death for sin must always be central in our efforts, as well as the promise of eternal life he offers by his resurrection from the dead. In addition, we must emphasize that receiving Jesus by faith results in the forgiveness of sins, the eradication of moral guilt, and the hope of a transformed life.

All our individual and corporate efforts at evangelism should reveal a sincere desire to reflect Christ and recognize his saving power. This means keeping these crucial thoughts in mind:

- We should "devote [ourselves] to prayer, being watchful and thankful" (Colossians 4:2). Only the Holy Spirit causes people to be born again (John 3:5-8), not even our best human efforts.
- We should engage others in a positive and winsome way. As the apostle Paul noted, this means being "wise in the way [we] act toward outsiders" (Colossians 4:5-6) and living "peaceful and quiet lives in all godliness and holiness" (1 Timothy 2:2).

When we base our evangelistic endeavors on prayer and godly living, the Holy Spirit will use us to reach the lost. As we do so, we will glorify our Father in heaven and fulfill our part in completing the Great Commission.

FOR FURTHER READING
Paul Little, *How to Give Away Your Faith*. InterVarsity, 1988.
Brad J. Kallenberg, *Live to Tell: Evangelism in a Postmodern World*. Brazos Press, 2002.
Rick Richardson, *Evangelism Outside the Box: New Ways to Help People Experience the Good News*. InterVarsity, 2000.

—SCOTT A. WENIG

EVIL

EVERYDAY DEFINITION
Evil is anything that opposes the character of God and the goodness of God's creation. Goodness is the prime reality of existence — the eternal and incorruptible goodness of God's own being. Evil is not the rotten twin of goodness; it is not on an equal level of reality. Evil, rather, is a defection from the good, or good gone wrong. The Bible does not teach dualism, that good and evil are equal and opposite powers. Rather, evil is a usurper, a parasite, an interloper.

People can both be affected by and be instruments of evil. Movements, such as Nazism, Fascism, and the Ku Klux Klan, can be evil in their essential principles and goals. Human institutions, such as slavery and prostitution, can be evil as well, because they debase human beings.

The origins of evil aren't laid out in great detail in Scripture, but the broad outline is clear enough. One of God's angels, known as Lucifer or Satan, fell from grace by somehow opposing God and took two-thirds of the angelic hosts with him (Jude 6; 2 Peter 2:4; Revelation 12:4). After God's creation of the universe and the first man and woman, the serpent, animated by Satan, successfully tempted the couple (Genesis 3; Revelation 12:9). Their disobedience to God's command thrust sin and evil into the world. Because of this rebellion, human life is now fragmented, and every originally good relationship is out of sync with God's original pattern of creation (Romans 8:19-23).

Humans find themselves in a rather maddening matrix of good

and evil. They find evil both within themselves and confronting them in the outside world. While humans retain the image of God after the Fall (this defines who they are), every aspect of human personality has been infected by sin, thus making people capable of various evils (Mark 7:21-23; Romans 3:9-20).

However, humans aren't garbage. Rather, they are the objects of God's free offer of forgiveness, restoration, and eternal life through the work of Jesus Christ. In addition, the Bible insists that Christ has triumphed over the powers of darkness through his perfect life, crucifixion, and resurrection (Colossians 2:14-15; 1 John 3:8). While the ultimate destiny of the universe is the vindication of God and his people (Revelation 21–22), the time between Christ's resurrection and the end of the age is marked by spiritual warfare between the forces of good and evil. The apostle Paul tells the Ephesian Christians—who resided in an occult stronghold—to put on the whole armor of God, taking their stand against evil (Ephesians 6:10-18). Paul also employed the language of warfare for his own struggles: "The weapons we fight with are not the weapons of the world. On the contrary, they have divine power to demolish strongholds. We demolish arguments and every pretension that sets itself up against the knowledge of God, and we take captive every thought to make it obedient to Christ" (2 Corinthians 10:4-5).

EVERYDAY APPLICATION

As Christians, we have a worldview available to us that makes sense of good and evil. We also receive power through the Holy Spirit to recognize and combat evil for the glory of God and the good of God's creation (Acts 1:8). This worldview helps us understand the following:

- Because Christ has risen from the dead, we have sufficient historical evidence that God will bring all things to justice and restoration in the end (1 Corinthians 15). This is true, in spite of unbelievers who claim that evil in the world is incompatible with the existence of an all-good and all-powerful God. We can communicate that without God, no objective and transcendent standard exists for morality. In addition, without God, there is no hope that good will triumph over evil in the end.

- Given the Bible's understanding of the Fall, we can oppose evil—such as abortion on demand, poverty, racism, and terrorism—without opposing God himself. Jesus himself was both grieved and revolted by the death of his friend Lazarus, because death is an intruder in God's world (John 11:33-35). The world, in a sense, is abnormal because of the entrance of evil. But because of God's revelation in Christ and the Bible, we have a standard for evaluating matters of good and evil (Hebrews 5:11-14). Christians also can find guidance and inspiration through the Holy Spirit (Luke 11:13; Acts 13:9) and gain strength for life's spiritual and moral battles through consistent prayer (Ephesians 6:18; 1 Thessalonians 5:17).

- Knowing that the world has been scarred by evil and tragedy, we can lament this fact without losing our faith. We can weep in faith and comfort those who weep. To lament means to recognize the existence of deep evil, to mourn over it, and to call out to God for both comfort and justice. The Bible is filled with lamentation, including an entire book (Lamentations) and many Psalms (22; 38; 80; and 88). Paul lamented the unbelief of his Jewish brethren (Romans 9:1-3). Jesus uttered the most profound and pained lament of all, crying out on the cross, "My God, my God, why have you forsaken me?" (Matthew 27:46). Yet this lament was heard and answered by God the Father, who received Christ's offering and later raised him from the dead, declaring him to be the Son of God with power (Romans 1:4).

As Christians, the Holy Spirit helps us understand the basic meaning of evil. This allows us to successfully stand against it, shedding holy tears over the brokenness of God's world while anticipating its final redemption.

FOR FURTHER READING

Nicholas Wolterstorff, *Lament for a Son*. Eerdmans, 1987.
D. A. Carson, *How Long, O Lord? Reflections on Suffering and Evil*. Baker, 2006.

— DOUGLAS GROOTHUIS

EVOLUTION

EVERYDAY DEFINITION

Evolution is an ambiguous concept. Although it generally refers to any gradual development over time, it can also mean anything from an uncontroversial statement about the way bacteria evolve when resisting antibiotics to the grand metaphysical claim that the universe and life naturally evolved by the meaningless forces of chance. And while evolution most often refers to biological evolution, no broad consensus exists about what that means. For example, microevolution refers to the mutation-selection mechanism that causes small-scale changes in organisms and occurs only within fixed boundaries of any given form of life, while macroevolution presupposes that organisms can morph in large-scale ways beyond perceived boundaries, allowing one living species to transform into another.

A great number of definitions of evolution are naturalistic, meaning that they rest on an assumption that the universe is closed to supernatural intervention. Naturalistic versions of the idea of evolution have been disseminated widely since the publication of Charles Darwin's *Origin of Species* (1859). Darwin's big idea was that nature could do alone what had previously been attributed to God. Rather than believing that God had orchestrated the development of life, Darwin suggested that single-celled life had gradually developed into multicellular life, and eventually into human life by means of evolution.

From his detailed observations, Darwin concluded that the species aren't immutable, and that new species had arisen from old ones. Darwin then reasoned that if newer forms of life had derived from older ones, it could be possible for all living things to be physically connected by virtue of a common ancestry. Darwin also believed the phrase, "the survival of the fittest," which explained how over the span of billions of years a bacterial cell could turn into a human. For Darwin it made sense to think that evolution had been guided, not by God, but rather by natural selection, the process of nature honoring the fittest.

The scandal of Darwin's idea wasn't that he believed that life-forms can adapt and be improved over periods of time. The problem with Darwin's proposal was that Darwin could not produce any illustration to confirm his hypothesis that human life evolved from lower life-forms, except by way of an analogy that logically proves to be false. Darwin's analogy said that natural selection can be likened to the art of breeding. It's scientifically proven that breeding does produce superior life-forms. Darwin's idea, however, was to propose hypothetically that nature itself—without intelligence—can make superior life-forms by natural selection—that is, the breeding of the fittest. Darwin wasn't saying that nature could take two of the fittest dogs and breed a better dog from them. Instead, he was saying that by means of natural selection, nature could gradually convert an amoeba into a tree or a human.

Darwin couldn't confirm his analogy scientifically. Nothing in the fossil record conclusively shows one species becoming another. But more to the point, Darwin's analogy breaks down logically from the start, because it's not a fair comparison to say that natural selection is like breeding. Breeding involves intention and intelligence. The scandal of Darwin's notion of natural selection was precisely that it excluded any element of intention or intelligence.

In more recent years, evolution has been shown to be un-Darwinian. The facts show that the fittest are not the ones who always survive. For this reason among others, evolution is being defined in the contemporary scientific community as a process that is essentially random. Counter to Darwin's claim that the process of evolution was actually guided by natural selection, a common claim made today is that evolution was unguided altogether. Also, evolution is often understood —even by some scientists—as including the possibility of God. This is also un-Darwinian.

Those who hold to a belief in both macroevolution and God identify themselves as theistic evolutionists. A theistic evolutionist says that God somehow directed the natural process of evolution. While it's rational to say that the process of evolution was partially, if not completely, guided by God, such an assertion implies a nuanced definition of *evolution* that counters naturalistic assumptions.

Theologically speaking, it doesn't make sense for a theist to affirm a naturalistic definition of evolution, because saying that an undirected random natural process was somehow guided by God is a contradictory statement. Logic prohibits a process that is guided and yet genuinely random. Unless evolution is defined as something different from an "undirected random natural process," a theistic evolutionist has to concede that God did not create the universe after all. Unless evolution is redefined, the term "theistic evolutionist" turns out to be an oxymoron.

So, it's difficult to believe in evolution while also believing in God—unless the word evolution is redefined. Naturalistic evolutionists reject the idea of defining evolution as an apparently undirected random natural process that conceivably could have been guided by a humble hidden God. Christians need to know that the default definition of evolution is naturalistic; it excludes the very notion of the existence of God precisely because it claims that evolution is an undirected random natural process.

EVERYDAY APPLICATION

The real crux of the debate on evolution hinges on how evolution is defined. The stakes of this debate are very high, because whatever we believe about evolution shapes our worldview. The converse might be even truer: Our worldview will decide our definition of evolution. This is important because basic questions about our existence, such as, "Who am I? What's my purpose? What's the meaning of life?" will be answered very differently by those who believe they purposelessly evolved from lower life-forms and those who believe they were specially created by God.

The implications of adopting any worldview are far too many to list. Necessarily, our worldview has a significant impact on our sense of self, our sense of destiny, and our understanding of the value of every life. The most important aspect of our worldview is our view of God. No people group has ever arisen above their idea of God. The world has not yet seen what an unmixed society of naturalistic evolutionists would become.

Regardless of the fact that some atheists seem wise and altruistic, those who see the universe as a closed mechanistic system that randomly evolved are far more vulnerable to despair. Only those who believe in God can hope for miracles. Christians believe in three great miracles: the creation of the world (Genesis 1), the incarnation of God (John 1:1,14), and the resurrection of Jesus Christ (Mark 16:6-7).

Since the Bible presents the universe as God's creation, Christians know that nature is not God (Genesis 1:1). Creation is the art of God —something God designed that can be studied without fear of it being spooked. The Scriptures reveal that nature displays God's glory (Psalm 119). Because nature is a gift from God, science should be conducted in gratitude and with fear and respect of the Lord. From a biblical point of view, nature is to be stewarded, not exploited. The peril of naturalistic evolutionists is that their belief in evolution runs counter to the Word of God (Genesis 1–2); the truth of Jesus Christ, who created all things (John 1:4); and the revelation of God in nature (Romans 1:20).

FOR FURTHER READING
Francis Collins, *The Language of God: A Scientist Presents Evidence for Belief.* Free Press, 2007.
Stephen Jay Gould, *Wonderful Life: The Burgess Shale and the Nature of History.* W. W. Norton, 1990.
Nancy Pearcey, *Total Truth: Liberating Christianity From Its Cultural Captivity.* Crossway, 2004.

—SARAH SUMNER

FAITH

EVERYDAY DEFINITION
Faith is a fundamental and necessary step to becoming a Christian, receiving eternal salvation (Acts 16:30-31), and living the Christian life. Faith and repentance represent the two sides of the transaction known as conversion of life (Acts 20:21; James 5:20). Because saving faith is a multifaceted reality, we need to understand the dimensions of faith that make it "saving faith":

- Faith first involves knowledge of Christ and the gospel (John 20:31). The gospel we embrace is anything but a message devoid of rational basis and truth. The term that best captures this aspect is "belief." Mere knowledge of the good news, however, doesn't save. For example, early in Jesus' ministry "many people saw the signs he was performing and believed in his name. But Jesus would not entrust himself to them, for he knew all people" (John 2:23-24, TNIV).
- Saving faith also requires personal assent to the truths of the

gospel (Luke 24:25; 2 Thessalonians 2:13). We must not only understand the truth; we must also agree to the truth without reserve from the heart. This includes assent to Jesus' deity (John 1:1), sacrificial death on the cross (1 Corinthians 15:3), and resurrection from the dead (Romans 10:9).

- The faith that saves includes wholehearted trust in and commitment to Jesus Christ as personal Savior (2 Timothy 1:12). As those who profess Christ, we must count the cost of discipleship, put our hands to the plough, and never look back. The evidence of this faith is obedience (Romans 1:5) and good works (1 Thessalonians 1:3) that bless others and glorify God.

We have many accounts of saving faith in the Bible. Early in Scripture, when God entered into covenant with Abram, we read that "Abram believed the LORD, and he [God] credited it to him as righteousness" (Genesis 15:6). The form of the Hebrew verb here means to "believe in" or "trust." During Israel's wilderness wandering God instructed Moses to fashion a bronze snake and place it upon a pole. When someone bitten by a serpent looked at the bronze snake, that person lived (Numbers 21:8-9). This typology anticipated faith in Christ that leads to eternal life (John 3:14-15). Righteous people in the Old Testament "trusted in the LORD, the God of Israel" (2 Kings 18:5) in the sense of "have faith in" or "rely upon." Through inspired spokespersons, God constantly called all who would hear to place their trust in him. "Trust in the LORD with all your heart and lean not on your own understanding" (Proverbs 3:5).

Jesus began his public ministry with a call to faith: "Repent and believe the good news!" (Mark 1:15). This paradigm of simple and unconditional faith, according to Jesus, is the uncomplicated trust of a little child (Matthew 18:3). Faith was a central feature of the apostle Paul's teaching—the noun "faith" and the verb "believe" appear 142 and 54 times respectively in the apostle's writings. In the New Testament, the object of saving faith is not only the body of gospel truth (Acts 6:7), but also the person of Jesus Christ (Acts 16:31). Listing the faith of Old Testament figures (Enoch, Noah, Abraham, etc.), the writer of Hebrews put forth faith as the confidence that God will fulfill his promises and uphold his people in their trials (Hebrews 11:11). The apostle James insisted that authentic faith is publicly validated by compassionate deeds (James 2:17,20-26).

EVERYDAY APPLICATION

Each of us as humans needs to do a reality check to ensure that we're not relying on matters such as noble parentage, superior education, good works, church membership, or rites of baptism or holy communion as means of salvation. Because God demands perfect compliance with his holy law for fellowship with himself, the best we have to offer contributes nothing to our salvation. To gain eternal life, we must simply receive the free gift of Christ's finished work on the cross. As Paul testified to the Philippian jailor, "Believe in the Lord Jesus, and you will be saved—you and your household" (Acts 16:31). We need to follow Paul's exhortation to "examine yourselves to see whether you are in the faith; test yourselves" (2 Corinthians 13:5).

Like the early Christians who acknowledged Jesus as Lord (Acts 2:21,36), we must also accept Jesus for who he is: the crucified, risen, ascended, and reigning Lord of heaven and earth. We must not only believe the tenets of the gospel, but we must embrace to the best of our knowledge and ability Jesus as Savior, Master, and Lord (John 20:28). By faith we own him as Lord because, as Jesus himself stated, no one rightfully can embrace two masters (Matthew 6:24).

This means that to truly realize God's best for our lives, we must commit all that we are—our lives, relationships, dreams, and plans—to Jesus in a decisive act of faith and commitment. The prophet Jeremiah affirmed, "Blessed are those who trust in the LORD, whose confidence is in him" (Jeremiah 17:7, TNIV). We come to salvation through Christ by faith, and we live our lives day by day to the glory of God by the same exercise of faith (2 Corinthians 5:7). In other words, the life of the Christian is a persistent life of faith, trust, and commitment to the triune God. At the same time we realize that faith is not a work or the outcome of human effort, but is the gift of God's grace (Ephesians 2:8; Philippians 1:9).

As mortal beings living in the flesh and in a fallen environment, we understandably harbor legitimate doubts (see Matthew 28:17). Doubt has been defined as "a state of mind in suspension *between* faith and unbelief."[6] The reality is that the faith and trust of every believer will be tested at some time or another—often many times. Our responsible course of action when troubled by doubt is prayerfully to follow all available lines of evidence—particularly the teaching of God's Word—to their logical conclusion. This occurs when we follow the example of the first-century Berean Christians, who "examined the Scriptures every day to see if what Paul said was true" (Acts 17:11). We can also share our doubts about matters of faith with a pastor or a knowledgeable and trusted fellow-believer.

We must be alert not to believe all the voices or spirits that present themselves, however attractive they might appear. Disguising himself as an angel of light, the Evil One breeds a host of lies and distortions that threaten true faith. So we must guard against being among those who exchange true faith for the devil's deceptions. As the apostle John wrote, "Dear friends, do not believe every spirit, but test the spirits to see whether they are from God" (1 John 4:1). May our life's prayer be, "Lord, 'increase our faith!'" (Luke 17:5).

FOR FURTHER READING

Os Guinness, *The Journey: Our Quest for Faith and Meaning*. NavPress, 2001.

Philip Yancey, *Soul Survivor: How My Faith Survived the Church*. Doubleday, 2001.

— BRUCE DEMAREST

FALL

EVERYDAY DEFINITION

The fall of humanity refers to the tragic disobedience and moral declension of Adam and Eve, and, by extension, the experience of each person who comes into the world.

While some regard the Genesis account as saga or myth, Scripture itself states that Adam (Romans 5:14; 1 Corinthians 5:22,45; 1 Timothy 2:13-14), the serpent (2 Corinthians 11:13; Revelation 12:9), and the Fall (1 Timothy 2:14) are factual, historical realities.

---

6. Os Guinness, *In Two Minds* (Downers Grove, IL: InterVarsity, 1976), 27.

God placed Adam and Eve in a pristine environment in the Garden of Eden where their every need—physical, social, and spiritual—was abundantly supplied. In the center of the Garden, God placed two trees: the tree of life and the tree of the knowledge of good and evil (see Genesis 2:9). The first tree served the purpose of preserving human life. The second tree, which God instructed Adam and Eve not to eat (Genesis 2:17), symbolized the full range of ethical knowledge the partaker would come to experience. God commanded Adam and Eve not to eat the fruit of the tree of the knowledge of good and evil as a test of their resolve either to trust him fully or to pursue their own self-will. The issue of submission and obedience to God—the author, provider, and sustainer of life—was at stake.

In a pivotal moment of history, Satan (in the form of a serpent), issued a threefold temptation to Adam and Eve:

1. To doubt God's word (Genesis 3:1-4).
2. To believe that God had selfishly barred them from eating the fruit because he didn't want Adam and Eve to become like him (verse 5).
3. To perceive in the forbidden fruit what was good for food, pleasing to the eye, and "desirable for gaining wisdom" (verse 6).

The Fall occurred when Adam and Eve willfully disobeyed God by partaking of the forbidden fruit: Eve "took some and ate it. She also gave some to her husband . . . and he ate it" (verse 6).

The remainder of Genesis 3 unfolds the ruinous effects of the historic Fall on Adam and Eve:

- They were afflicted with a profound sense of objective guilt (verse 7).
- They experienced estrangement from God, or spiritual death (verses 8-10). Previously, they knew friendship and communion with God in the Garden; now they instinctively hid themselves from God's presence.
- They experienced a fallen or depraved heart, evidenced by the evasive answers they gave to God (verses 10-13).
- They were punished with physical death by being banished

from the Garden to prevent them from eating of the tree of life (verses 22-24).

As a result of the Fall, God cursed the serpent Satan used as his mouthpiece (verses 14), punished the woman with the pain of child-bearing (verse 16), cursed the ground that man must work (verses 17-18), and condemned the couple to physical death (verse 19). However, even in the midst of this dark scene, God graciously gave the promise of the coming Redeemer, who would be crushed by the serpent, yet who would "strike his heel" (verse 15).

The effects of the historic Fall quickly passed down to the human family in the form of persistent evil behavior (Genesis 6:5,11-12; 8:21; etc.), prompting the judgment of the flood. Later, David testified, "Surely I was sinful at birth, sinful from the time my mother conceived me" (Psalm 51:5; see also 58:3). The prophet Isaiah confirmed this judgment: "We all, like sheep, have gone astray, each of us has turned to our own way" (Isaiah 53:6). The apostle Paul clearly taught the passing on of Adam's sin and guilt to the entire human family in what theologians call "original sin." The apostle wrote, "sin entered the world through one man, and death through sin, and in this way death came to all people, because all sinned" (Romans 5:12, TNIV); "the many died by the trespass of the one man" (verse 15); "by the trespass of the one man, death reigned through that one man" (verse 17); "one trespass resulted in condemnation for all people" (verse 18, TNIV). Paul made the same point to the Christians in Corinth, stating that sin and death came upon the entire human family as a consequence of Adam's defection from God in the Garden: "in Adam all die" (1 Corinthians 15:22).

Theologians have used two principal theories to explain how Adam's guilt and punishment extend to all humans. The "federal head-ship theory" states that by divine appointment Adam served as the covenant head of the race, while the "natural headship theory" states that corruption of nature passed from generation to generation by natu-ral propagation (see John 3:6; Hebrews 7:4-10).

EVERYDAY APPLICATION

As Christians, we understand that the fundamental human predica-ment is not caused by faulty cultural evolution, bad karma, childhood traumas, inadequate educational systems, or psychological maladjustment. We know that our sinful nature as humans was caused by sinful rebellion against, and alienation from, our Creator. Morally and spiritually, we humans are not what we were created to be. We fail to live up to our God-given potential because of the damaging effects of the fall of our first parents in the Garden of Eden. Our understanding of this fallen nature is vital because faulty and naïve assessments of the human condition will lead to inadequate solutions.

Biblical teaching concerning the Fall should lead us to hold realistic expectations of ourselves and our communities. As believers, we are born from above, yet we live in a world far removed from that pristine environment. As individuals—and even as communities and churches—we remain tainted by the Fall. For this reason, we fall short of God's ideal. This means we should have realistic expectations about perfection this side of glory. The biblical call to perfection (Matthew 5:48) summons us to wholeness or maturity, not to flawlessness. As we lay aside perfectionist ideals (in this life), we can be as gentle and forbearing about our shortcomings as God is.

The doctrine of the Fall teaches that the world is under the control of powerful and hostile forces—namely, Satan and evil spirits (Colossians 1:13). We live in the midst of a spiritual battlefield involving a fierce struggle between the kingdom of God and the kingdom of evil (Ephesians 6:12). The world's political, economic, and social systems are also fallen, and because of their fallen nature, they give way to abuse and oppression. Because of the Fall, ungodly political leaders are often corrupt and even tyrannical, depriving citizens of fundamental human rights and oppressing the poor and the helpless. Driven by lust for power and control, many world rulers are adamantly opposed to the Lord and his cause (Psalm 2:2). As Christians, we understand that the fall of humanity long ago provides the answer to the psalmist's question: "Why do the heathen rage, and the people imagine a vain thing?" (Psalm 2:1, KJV).

The fall of humanity into a state of guilt and condemnation means that we humans can't justify ourselves before God. Even with our noblest efforts, we can't live up to God's law or measure up to his standard of righteousness. Pouring money into new social and educational programs—however good they might be—will never solve our entrenched problems and yield a social utopia. Our most desperate need isn't self-help, but personal and social transformation as we return to God and receive his free grace. Otherwise, we languish under the judgment by a holy and righteous God.

FOR FURTHER READING

William T. Bruner, *Children of the Devil: A Fresh Interpretation of the Fall of Man and Original Sin*. Philosophical Library, 1966.
John Murray, *The Imputation of Adam's Sin*. Eerdmans, 1959.
Marguerite Shuster, *The Fall and Sin: What We Have Become as Sinners*. Eerdmans, 2004.

— BRUCE DEMAREST

FAMILY

EVERYDAY DEFINITION

The family is a communion of people related by blood or by vows, and it represents the closest of all human relationships. An earthly family reflects the communal nature of the triune God, copying the perfect communion of God the Father, Jesus Christ the Son, and the Holy Spirit. Families typically copy the configuration of Adam and Eve, with a marriage vow between a man and a woman. This unites two families and might eventually include the birth of children. Family bonds are also formed by vows, such as the adoption of children and spiritual adoption of (adult) children, parents, grandparents, brothers or sisters, and aunts or uncles (1 Timothy 1:2; Titus 1:4). In this way, individuals of any birth or marital status experience Christ's love and example in family life.

In Christian families, family unity is grounded in the love of God in Christ, which is self-giving and selfless. Because a family is a nearly lifelong relationship, family relationships test character and provide the primary laboratory of learning to love and to forgive. This learning occurs as individuals faithfully care for obstinate or grumpy relatives (often in stages of transition or disconnection, such as "terrible-two" toddlers, rebellious teens, and/or ailing grandparents). Because family members stand by each other "for better or for worse," resilience and compassion are essential qualities in family life. To refuse to "provide for his relatives, and especially for his immediate family," is to deny the faith for those who understand family obligations (1 Timothy 5:8).

Family life is so central that it serves as God's metaphor for the church—the family of God (1 Peter 4:17). Caring family relationships provide the standard for how Christians treat one another: "Do not rebuke an older man harshly, but exhort him as if he were your father. Treat younger men as brothers, older women as mothers, and younger women as sisters, with absolute purity" (1 Timothy 5:1-2). In Christ, even those who have wronged each other can become brothers and sisters "in the Lord" (Philemon 16). Managing a family well trains people to manage the church family well (1 Timothy 3:4). The table fellowship of a home prepares people for the table fellowship of communion in God's family. As families become the dwelling place of God, they enable the church to become that as well.

A family life of trust equips its members to live in the world, which isn't always trustworthy, and prepares its children to bond with a spouse if they choose to marry. As children witness family members loving and respecting each other in the midst of differences, they learn to live agreeably with others without insisting on their own way. Family is so essential that God provides substitutes when our families fail us (Psalm 27:10), especially within the church (2 Timothy 1:2; Titus 1:4).

Family provides for not only physical sustenance but also the nurture of emotional and relational needs and guidance for intellectual and spiritual needs, such as learning to love others and finding meaning in life. Ideally, parents teach children spiritual truths not only in words but also by living out reciprocal love and respect. While God commanded, "Children, obey your parents in the Lord, for this is right," he also commanded, "Fathers, do not exasperate your children; instead, bring them up in the training and instruction of the Lord" (Ephesians 6:1,4). As first authority figures for children, parents create early impressions of what God is like. If in later life children discern conflicts between their parents' will and God's will, they can respect parents even as they obey God. By this personal development of their spiritual life, grown children become friends to their parents without diminishing the respect due to their parents.

Family life is the first place of discipleship and spiritual formation. The Great Commission begins at home. Parents disciple their children to know God and to make disciples of others, becoming agents of God's grace in a broken and hurting world (Matthew 28:19-20). Families disciple their children by reaching out together to help others—whether they help a neighbor or relative or formally volunteer together as a family. This helping others *together* also creates so-called "quality time" for family members.

Every parent-child activity becomes a vehicle for learning, both good and bad. Parents "teach" children all day long—in words and by modeling—such skills as developing sports abilities, practicing good hygiene, achieving academic excellence, and making choices about relaxation and the spending of money. In many of these areas, Christian families stand out against the culture's aims. For example, while the culture focuses on acquiring more money, pushing an individual's own agenda, or achieving at all costs, Christian families focus on spending resources to help others, meeting other people's needs, and living with integrity.

Because family life occurs out of the public eye, it might seem insignificant. However, it's worthy of the time spent, as exemplified in the thirty hidden years of Jesus' life in Nazareth. As the oldest son and possibly a replacement father-figure (if Joseph died as early as many suspect), Jesus worked hard day by day, ran the family business, probably taught in the village Sabbath school, and provided guidance and discipline for the family. The one who came to do the important work of redeeming and reconciling humanity and ushering in the kingdom of God didn't look down on routine family life, but spent most of his earthly life in obscurity doing this important work.

EVERYDAY APPLICATION

The hands-on classroom of family builds wisdom and inner strength in human beings as family members work through basic lessons of life: "What do I do when I fail?" "When I feel angry?" "When I'm disappointed?" "When I want what others have?"

Discipleship within the family occurs all day long as children notice how parents respond to both routine and difficult situations. Intentional discipleship might also occur in interactive family devotions and times of celebration (family nights, holidays, birthdays, spontaneous festivities over the first flower in a yard, or the sharing of a blessing). Through these routines, family members also notice each others' unrecognized spiritual gifts.

Family life finds its challenges in trials, driving its members to pray for guidance, for income, and (some days) for the grace not to scream. As family members move through transitions, they continue to ask God, "What does it look like to love this person *now*? At this unpleasant stage of their life?" "Courage and persistence—these then are elements of the sacrament of the care of others. It is persistence that keeps a person working at a life expressing love when the rewards of such a life no longer seem clear, and it is courage that dares such commitment."[7]

Another challenge is that family life is so ordinary and routine that character growth in other family members might be barely noticeable. This growth might seem insignificant compared to physical growth and academic and athletic achievement. Because of this, everyday family life needs to be celebrated as a spiritual journey made up of small incidents where the still, small voice of God permeates spilled milk incidents and wakeful nights. The family becomes a school for learning the "sacrament of the routine. Those caring for others will always come to know the hardship. The call here is for them to also learn to know the beauty."[8] As family members practice finding God in all situations, including the ordinary and routine (Colossians 3:17), they can live in the moment and say: "This is the day the LORD has made; let us rejoice and be glad in it" (Psalm 118:24).

Without such a focus, the daily tasks of caring for the young or the aged will seem oppressive rather than sacred. To move beyond drudgery and boredom requires continuing in God's strength when exhausted and speaking the truth in love when it would be natural to speak in harshness or to be silent in bitterness (Proverbs 3:5; Ephesians 4:15).

Before each task, such as repairing a toy, changing a diaper, or fixing a meal, it's wise to reflect on the companionship of God and how we might delight in God in these routines. We can repeat a short prayer as we work, such as those of Brother Lawrence as he worked in a monastery kitchen: "Give me grace to keep company with you; Lord, work with me; receive my work and possess all my affections."[9] After the task,

7. Ernest Boyer, *Finding God at Home* (New York: HarperCollins, 1988), 64.
8. Boyer, 81.
9. Brother Lawrence, *The Practice of the Presence of God,* 120.

we can thank God for help and ask God to use our efforts to help other family members in hidden ways. As we constantly share our thoughts and feelings with God, his presence becomes a reality that our families are always aware of.

FOR FURTHER READING

Ernest Boyer, *Finding God at Home: Family Life as a Spiritual Discipline*. HarperCollins, 1988.

Valerie Hess, *Habits of a Child's Heart: Raising Your Kids with the Spiritual Disciplines*. NavPress, 2004.

Jan Johnson, *Growing Compassionate Kids*. Upper Room Books, 1991.

—JAN JOHNSON

FATHER, THE NATURE OF

EVERYDAY DEFINITION

The Father is the first person of the Trinity.

The earliest Christians came up with a term to speak to the Father's nature. They said he was "unbegotten." If this sounds a bit unclear, it's because it describes what the Father is not. Of the Son, it is said he is "Begotten of the Father." And of the Spirit, it is said that he proceeds from the Father. Both the Son and Spirit have always been with God the Father (John 1), but the Son and the Spirit in some way come from the Father from and for all eternity.

Within the Trinity, there is mutual submission and mutual indwelling. This means that there exists not three beings, but one. The Father is the one who sends the Son and the Spirit. The Son and Spirit mutually submit to the will of the Father. The Son, and later the Spirit, act so that all of humanity might call God "Father." They glorify the Father and work to make his glory known on earth; the Father also glorifies the Son, by word (at his baptism and then again at the Transfiguration) and most powerfully in the Resurrection.

The Old Testament gives us many names for God, but in the case of describing God as Father, it relies more on images. While Father is applied explicitly to God only a few times in the Old Testament, we see God acting in ways that emphasize his Fatherhood. God is seen carrying, disciplining, pitying, adopting, and loving as a father would. The Israelites even incorporated the image into some of their names, like Joab (Jehovah Father), Abiel (God is my father), and Eliab (My God is Father). The idea of God as Father was already presented before we received the gift of the Son, who helps us to even better understand the nature of the Father.

Throughout the Gospels Jesus makes it clear that he is the only Son of the Father, and that his Father is the God to whom people should look. He uses the term Father 107 times in the gospel of John alone to address God. While the Old Testament affirms that all are children of God, Jesus' relationship to the Father is a unique form of Sonship that he alone possesses as the preexistent one. However, the work of the Son and the Spirit is to make us the Father's children, to bind us back to the Son's own Father, and to make us coheirs of the Father's kingdom. This is one of the key components of God the Father's nature. He is the one who provides our inheritance.

Jesus always points to the Father as the one who is truly righteous, who is worthy of praise and complete worship, and to whom even the glorified Son desires to return. While it is Jesus' kingdom, he gives the kingdom back to the Father. Because of the will of the Father, because of the work of the Son, and because of the indwelling of the Spirit, we are able to become children of God. This identity is given to us and can't be taken away (Romans 8).

EVERYDAY APPLICATION

We should celebrate that we have a Father in heaven, the one who willed for us to be and knows us by name. Our prayers are never addressed to an unknown god or to a god who might be disinterested in our lives, but to Our Dearest Father who knows our name. With various issues of fatherhood in modern culture, some have tried to distance themselves from calling God "Father." However, to do so not only detaches us from Jesus' own commands, it also diminishes the character of God, who identifies himself as Father. In addition, it eliminates the great promises of the Bible that we will be his children, receive an inheritance, and be part of the family of God for eternity. There is simply no room in the message of Jesus Christ to leave behind the name of Father from the God we worship. From the lips of Jesus Christ, we see Father as the proper and personal name of God. The person of the Trinity we call "our Father" isn't one of patriarchy or another cultural vestige. Rather the name Father is a true testimony to God's very nature.

FOR FURTHER READING

Christopher Wright, *Knowing God the Father in the Old Testament.* IVP Academic, 2007.

Marianne Meye Thompson, *The Promise of the Father: Jesus and God in the New Testament.* Westminster John Knox Press, 2000.

— CHRISTOPHER MORTON

FATHER, WORK OF

EVERYDAY DEFINITION

The term Father, in reference to God, is used sparingly in the Old Testament. Its use increases substantially in the Gospels. Jesus refers to God as his Father (Luke 2:49), he addresses God in prayer as Father (John 11:41), and he teaches his disciples to pray to "Our Father in heaven" (Matthew 6:9).

For some people, referring to God as Father presents a problem. In some cases, they've experienced their biological father as absent, unreliable, abusive, or unloving. Even in the cases of good father figures, many fathers are inadequate examples of fatherhood. So it's important that we let Jesus show us what *father* really means (John 14:8). According to Jesus, God the Father is rich in mercy and shows compassion to both those who do good and those who do evil (Matthew 5:45).

The work of God the Father, sometimes referred to as *opera Dei* (Latin), or the activity of God, is particularly important for Christian reflection because God is known through what he does. Only through God's self disclosure does he become known. The apostle Paul told the Athenians (Acts 17) that he would make known the God they worshipped as unknown, and that this "God who made the world and everything in it is the Lord of heaven and earth" (verse 24). First, then, the Father is the maker of heaven and earth. He is the maker of everything visible and invisible. This is a very important description of the activity of God in the Old Testament, as well as the specific activity of the God of Israel, known as *Adonai* (Lord, YHWH). As Father, God is the source of all that exists.

Speaking to the Athenians, Paul then said that God "himself gives all men life and breath and everything else" (verse 25). The Father is the giver of life or existence. As the Father of all people and all existence in the cosmos, God cares for humanity by freely governing creation according to his purposes. He acts according to the divine nature, which is Love (*agape*), seeking what's best for the universe he lovingly created. God's activity of ordering all events in history so that his purpose for creation is achieved is referred to as God's providence. Providence (Greek *pronoia* or Latin *pro-videre*) means to see ahead, to foresee, or to provide. Yet God's providence is more than simple foresight; it consists of God's active involvement in the midst of depravation, atrocities, and trying circumstances.

God providentially acts in creation by preserving, cooperating, and guiding:

- God unceasingly upholds creation and preserves life.
- God cooperates with natural and secondary processes to achieve good.
- God guides various agents and causes to achieve his good ends. God's mercy is manifested when he draws good from the various forms of evil in the world.

EVERYDAY APPLICATION

With the demise of older understandings of physics, some of us have set aside the traditional understanding of preservation, God's continuous sustaining of creation. Instead of a mere physical understanding of God's preservation, we might argue that God is the one who preserves us in the face of apparent meaninglessness of existence. However, God is the provider of all meaning as the source and goal (*telos*) of all creation. God preserves us in the face of the meaningless of seemingly random events by providing an integrative center and purpose.

Likewise, God's *cooperating* providence relevance lies beyond the purely physical. God's cooperating providence functions both negatively and positively. In a negative way, it answers the question that has plagued the faithful through the ages: "Will the wicked always prosper?" While it seems that those who act maliciously seem to carry on without any consequence, biblical faith responds that they will not. There's only one ultimate reality—a future free from the consequences of evil—that will come to consummation in the coming kingdom. And in a positive way, God's *cooperating* providence is evident in his care for the undeserving, as God provides for both those who do good and those who do evil (Matthew 5:45).

Finally, God's *guiding* providence emphasizes his greatness in the face of evil. God guides the world, directing it toward its goal of new creation by bringing good out of evil. The work of the Father can be simply summed up: love wins.

FOR FURTHER READING
Stanley Grenz, *Theology for the Community of God*. Eerdmans, 2000.
Christopher Wright, *Knowing God the Father Through the Old Testament*. IVP Academic, 2007.

— MIKE GLERUP

FLESH

EVERYDAY DEFINITION
The term "flesh" refers to several elements in Scripture.

- The flesh is the organ that covers the human body. This reference to skin (Genesis 2:21,23) is often found in contrast with "blood" (Ezekiel 39:17) or "bones" (Job 33:21).
- The flesh is the human body, the whole entity composed of skin, bones, and organs (Ezekiel 32:6).
- The flesh is the entirety of human nature, particular its physicality. Jesus took on the flesh in the Incarnation (John 1:14; 1 John 4:2).
- The flesh points to human beings in reference to their origin. For example, it can refer to our "flesh and blood" relatives (Genesis 37:27). Similarly, it can refer to ancestors, such as Jesus Christ "who as to his human nature was a descendant of David" (Romans 1:3).

- The flesh refers to human beings regarded outwardly, in terms of their abilities, gifts, achievements, and appearance. Genuine worshippers, for example, "put no confidence in the flesh" (Philippians 3:3).
- The flesh refers to sinful human nature (Romans 7:5,18), which is weak, deadly, hostile to God, and in opposition to living in the Spirit (Romans 8:3-13).

The complexity of this term means we should use caution when we come across it in the Bible. For example, if we think "the flesh" refers to sinful human nature when the context where it's used instead refers to the body, we could wrongly conclude that the body is inherently evil, an impediment to God's sanctifying work.

EVERYDAY APPLICATION
As we pay close attention to the various uses of this expression, several applications become evident.

As human beings, we are in "the flesh," or embodied creatures. God created us this way, so human embodiment is tied up with being made in the divine image (Genesis 1:26-27). The human body is an essential aspect of human beings during this earthly existence and, following Christ's return, in the age to come.

Further, in order to rescue human beings created in God's image yet fallen into sin, the Son of God became incarnate ("enfleshed"). The God-man took on "the flesh," or the whole of human nature, including a body, so as to become a real and fully human being for our salvation (Hebrews 2:14-18).

This salvation is experienced in part during this lifetime, which is also characterized by following after "the flesh." Scripture's instruction is to "not gratify the desires of the sinful nature" but instead to "live by the Spirit" (Galatians 5:16). The sinful nature prompts Christians to disobey God, but the Holy Spirit stimulates obedience. As Christians are "led by the Spirit," (verse 18) they will overcome the desires of the flesh and please God. Accordingly, they "put no confidence" in their own accomplishments but depend rather on God's mighty work in their lives.

FOR FURTHER READING
George Eldon Ladd, *A Theology of the New Testament*. Eerdmans, 1974.

— GREGG ALLISON

FOREKNOWLEDGE

EVERYDAY DEFINITION
Foreknowledge is a term that describes God's foresight and knowledge of future events. Three main Scriptures address God's foreknowledge:

1. Romans 8:29: "For those God foreknew he also predestined to be conformed to the image of his Son, that he might be the firstborn among many brothers and sisters (TNIV)." Most authorities agree that the verb "foreknow" (*proginōskō*) means not only to know the future but also to "choose beforehand."[10]
2. Romans 11:2: "God did not reject his people, whom he foreknew."
3. 1 Peter 1:1-2: "To God's elect, strangers in the world, . . . who have been chosen according to the foreknowledge of God the Father, through the sanctifying work of the Spirit, for obedience to Jesus Christ and sprinkling by his blood." The apostle Peter's use of the noun "foreknowledge" (*prognōsis*) signifies God's knowledge of those he will choose.

The common Hebrew verb, "to know" (*yāda'*), means more than knowing with the mind. It also signifies to love, to enter into a relationship with, and to choose. Many Scripture passages highlight this relational nature of knowing: Jeremiah 1:5; Hosea 13:5; Matthew 7:23; John 10:27; Galatians 4:9; 2 Timothy 2:19. Sometimes, this Hebrew verb "to know" is translated as "to choose": "You only have I chosen [literally known] among all the families of the earth" (Amos 3:2, NASB). Old Testament scholar Walter Kaiser concludes: "'To know' in this covenantal context had nothing to do with recognition or acknowledgment of one's deeds; it had to do with God's gift of choice — an unmerited choice as Deuteronomy 7:8 *passim* had made plain."[11]

---

10. *New International Dictionary of New Testament Theology*, vol. 1, 693.
11. *Toward an Old Testament Theology* (1978), p. 194.

Specifically, the verb *proginōskō* means to "know intimately" or to "forelove." Bible scholar F. F. Bruce comments on Romans 8:29: "The words 'whom he did foreknow' have the connotation of electing grace which is frequently implied by the verb 'to know' in the Old Testament. When God takes knowledge upon his people in this special way, he sets his choice upon them."[12] Significantly, the biblical word "foreknow" is always used of those who are already following Christ, not of sinners or their responses.

Christians in the Reformation tradition, emphasizing God's sovereignty and sinful human inability, interpret God's foreknowledge not just as his perfect knowledge of the future, but also as God graciously setting his love and favor on those he purposed to save. According to this view, foreknowledge takes on the sense of foreordination and predestination, which is the belief that God sovereignly chooses those he desires to be saved.

Many in the broadly Arminian tradition, emphasizing God's prevenient grace, Christ's death for all, and the freedom of the human will (a higher view of fallen human nature), interpret foreordination as God's foresight of those he knew would trust Christ and be saved. According to this view, salvation involves a cooperative venture between God and sinners.

The recent movement known as Open Theism claims that God knows not all, but only some, future events. They claim that if God knew all things future, then free human choices and the future itself would be determined, not open. In this case humans would no longer be free and, as a result, less than human.

Scripture, however, holds in tension God's complete foreknowledge of future events *and* free human choices. Texts such as Acts 2:23 support this position, which Bible scholars identify as "antimony" (an apparent contradiction between two opposing statements, each of which nevertheless is true).

EVERYDAY APPLICATION
As Christians, we experience great joy and confidence in being fully known by God. We receive great comfort as God's children, knowing

---

12. F. F. Bruce, *Romans* (1963), 176.

that although we deserve divine wrath because of our sins, we are both known and unconditionally loved as God's covenant people. As a result, when hardships and trials come our way, we can take heart and persevere because God knows and cares. We are fully reassured that from the foundation of the world we are embraced by God's powerful love.

Because we are fully known and unconditionally accepted by God, we can venture the risk of costly discipleship as we follow Jesus, serve the kingdom, and do battle against our spiritual enemies. The apostle Paul, for example—encouraged by God's loving knowledge of him and presence with him (Acts 18:9-11)—persevered courageously in his preaching and missionary ministry in the city of Corinth.

God knows everything about us and our circumstances and loves us all the same. So we have no need to hide anything from him. Rather, as children of the King, we can bring before him all our concerns, fears, and struggles, knowing that he can handle anything we present to him. The fact that he knows us completely motivates us, his children, to please him in all things. We have no greater incentive to please God than the fact that he totally knows and unconditionally loves us. This knowledge prompts us to bow before the sovereign Lord in gratitude, wonder, and praise.

FOR FURTHER READING
G. C. Berkouwer, *Divine Election*. Eerdmans, 1960.
J. I. Packer, *Knowing God*. InterVarsity, 1993.

— BRUCE DEMAREST

FORGIVENESS

EVERYDAY DEFINITION
Forgiveness is the pardoning and blotting out of offenses. God forgives humans for their sins and commands humans to forgive each other (Matthew 6:12,14; Mark 11:25). Yet forgiveness goes against human nature, which when wronged instinctively responds, "Pay back what you owe me!" (Matthew 18:28).

Forgiveness evidences the generous grace of God who doesn't begrudgingly forgive, but "as far as the east is from the west, so far has he removed our transgressions from us" (Psalm 103:12; see also Ephesians 1:7). Such sweeping and ever-abounding forgiveness is pictured in Jesus' parable about a father who ran down the trail to embrace his prodigal son who instead deserved to be disowned (Luke 15:20). God doesn't ask that humans atone for sins, because Christ has already done that. Rather God directs, "If we confess our sins, he is faithful and just and will forgive us our sins and purify us from all unrighteousness" (1 John 1:9).

Forgiving those who have sinned against us—even when they perhaps don't realize they've done so—is a practical implementation of Jesus' teaching to love enemies, because those who wound us become enemies in the sense that they are difficult to love.

How is such forgiveness humanly possible? The willingness and capacity to forgive others flows out of God's forgiveness of us: "Bear with each other and forgive whatever grievances you may have against one another. Forgive as the Lord forgave you" (Colossians 3:13; see also Matthew 6:12; Ephesians 4:32). Because forgiveness is such a radical and counterintuitive behavior, it must emanate from God's forgiveness of us and can't be done without God's help. It's God's gift, with which we cooperate. God has to do this through us.

To forgive another person is concrete evidence that we know we are created, forgiven, and sustained only by God's grace. This is what Jesus referred to when he said, "For if you forgive men when they sin against you, your heavenly Father will also forgive you. But if you do not forgive men their sins, your Father will not forgive your sins" (Matthew 6:14-15). It's not that we earn God's forgiveness by forgiving others or that God's character of love is dependent on our wavering character of love. To not forgive reveals that our rock-bottom belief is that we live by our own goodness, wits, and power and so should others. To forgive, however, reveals that we've experienced God's generous forgiveness of ourselves and now gladly live in it, passing it on to others.

Forgiveness is not the same as approving what another person has done or even being tolerant of others. It's not the same as excusing a wrong, ignoring it, trying to forget it, or pretending a wrong didn't occur. Instead, it's a choice to bless someone who has done us wrong when there appears to be no sensible reason to do so.

To refuse to forgive is a conscious choice even if it disguises itself as "forgetting" or "putting it out of my mind." Because no sin is too gross or is repeated too often so as to not be forgiven (Luke 17:4), an unforgiving spirit is a serious sin (Matthew 18:34-35). To choose *not to forgive* locks us out of abundant life, like the older brother in the prodigal son parable who chose not to join the party—which is life in the kingdom of God. To forgive is the "best form of self-interest since anger, resentment and revenge are corrosive" (*No Future without Forgiveness* Desmond Tutu, p. 35).

EVERYDAY APPLICATION

The more we have experienced and embraced generous forgiveness from God, the more easily we forgive others. This can happen in many ways, notably by meditating on passages about God's forgiveness, or by being generously forgiven by another human.

As humans, we often struggle to forgive ourselves because our inner judge is too harsh to let us off the hook. Yet, God forgives us so we must work to forgive ourselves. Otherwise we set up ourselves above God as judge. In forgiving self, it helps to be specific about our failure and what character flaw bred it and to find a trustworthy believer to confess to and to pray with for healing (James 5:16).

Forgiving others is usually not instantaneous but a continuing process that takes time. It's not unusual to think we've forgiven but to find more forgiveness work must be done. The work of processing hurt and forgiveness requires a safe sacred space such as talking with a friend or counselor or journaling. It's important to be truthful with the reality of the hurt, not denying the offense or minimizing it.

As we become ready to forgive, we need to ask for God's help as this prayer process suggests: Not denying the person's faults, we ask [1] that "the love of Christ come into us and [2] go on through us into this person, healing the [painful] memories and bringing forth all that is good and lovely in his nature. Then [3] we gave thanks . . . and . . . make in the mind a picture of that person transformed into the image of his real Christ-self and [4] we rejoice that this was so."[13] We might need to pray such a prayer daily.

Forgiving others doesn't force us to live without boundaries. We

---

13. Agnes Sanford, *The Healing Gifts of the Spirit* (New York: HarperOne, 1984), 68.

might still choose to limit access or participation with former offenders if their behavior is harmful, but we don't hold their offenses against them. In ideal situations, two estranged people come together in a restored relationship. But sometimes the other person is not willing or is deceased. Still the work of forgiveness can be done as we stand with the intention of loving that person. We can clean only our own side of the street and let the other side (the other person's conscience) be as that person chooses. Our goal is an honest release of the other person. When we forgive others, we wish them well and want God's best for them.

FOR FURTHER READING

Agnes Sanford, *The Healing Light, The Healing Gifts of the Spirit.* Ballantine, 1983.

Lewis Smedes, *Forgive and Forget.* Harper and Row, 1984.

Desmond Tutu, *No Future without Forgiveness.* Doubleday, 1999.

— JAN JOHNSON

FREEDOM

EVERYDAY DEFINITION

Freedom is one of the greatest blessings of life, as well as one of the great issues of today. In the Bible, freedom means to be liberated from captivity. The captivity can be physical or spiritual.

A great example of physical freedom is found in the book of Exodus. God promised to deliver his people from slavery in Egypt under Pharaoh (Exodus 6:6). Through Moses, he freed his people and provided a way out, leading them to the Promised Land. From then on, Israel was to live as God's covenant people and regularly to celebrate its freedom. In the year of Jubilee, after each seventh Sabbath year, a grand celebration took place. The leaders were to "proclaim liberty throughout the land to all its inhabitants" (Leviticus 25:10). Property was restored, servants were set free, and God's rest was proclaimed.

This physical liberty became a defining picture of a deeper spiritual liberty. The deeper captivity—a bondage to sin, fear, decay, and death—is revealed clearly in the New Testament. Jesus said he was sent to "proclaim freedom for the prisoners" (Luke 4:18), and "the truth will set you free" (John 8:32). He boldly declared that "everyone who sins is a slave to sin" (John 8:34), adding that "if the Son sets you free, you will be free indeed" (John 8:36). Therefore, because of Christ—through his truth and his atoning work on the cross—we are set free from sin. We are also set free for God, to live lives pleasing to him (Romans 6:22; Revelation 5:1).

EVERYDAY APPLICATION

Freedom might be one of the most misunderstood ideas of our time. The key to understanding freedom is found in how we define the term. Freedom isn't an absolute concept; it is always defined in relationship to something else. For example, there is liberty under God, where people seek to do right in the eyes of the Lord. And there is a sense of liberty apart from God, where "everyone did as they saw fit" (Judges 17:6, TNIV).

We can also consider another aspect of freedom. The blessings of liberty are always derived. When freedom becomes a first desire, and God is removed from the picture, freedom becomes an idol that ultimately enslaves. Indeed, some argue that liberty understood in this way has become the great golden calf of our time.

The political crisis in many countries of the world today is in large measure an argument about the definition of freedom. As Christians, we should be apologists for freedom as defined in the biblical sense—namely, an ordered liberty in, under, and for God.

Finding freedom's reference point is key. Someone said that the purpose of life is not to find your freedom, but to find your master. When we find the right master, we'll find freedom. In this sense, one of the best ways to share the gospel today is to present it in terms of true freedom.

FOR FURTHER READING

Richard Bauckham, *God and the Crisis of Freedom*. Westminster John Knox Press, 2002.

Benjamin Hart, *Faith and Freedom*. Here's Life, 1988.

J . I. Packer, *Freedom and Authority*. Regent, 2003.

—DONALD W. SWEETING

GOD, THE EXISTENCE OF

EVERYDAY DEFINITION

Christianity is a hopeless delusion if God doesn't exist. But if the God of the Bible does exist, this is the most important truth that anyone can know, because so much depends on how we respond to God's revelation to humanity found in nature, conscience, Scripture, and Christ. The debate over God's existence rages worldwide, at both the popular and academic levels. Christians who desire to defend their faith rationally should understand the essentials of this controversy and engage it wisely.

Some want to make religion and particularly belief in God a matter of private and relative opinion. However, the Bible claims that true faith is based on the objective existence and character of a knowable God, and that God matters for every aspect of life. God has attributes that distinguish him from creation. God is a personal and moral being, unlimited in goodness, power, and knowledge. Being unlimited or perfect makes God transcendent over his creation, which depends on God's existence for its origin and continuation (Genesis 1:1; John 1:1; Acts 17:25; Hebrew 1:3). At the same time, God is present at every point in creation (Psalm 139).

Christianity affirms that God is triune—one God (Deuteronomy 6:4) who exists eternally in three coequal persons: the Father, the Son, and the Holy Spirit (Matthew 3:13-17; 28:18-20). God revealed himself to humanity supremely through the life, death, and resurrection of Jesus Christ, who is God Incarnate (John 1:14,18; Hebrews 1). Of course, the idea of an Incarnation makes no sense if God doesn't exist. Therefore, Christians who desire to defend the gospel to nonbelievers should be able to present savvy arguments for God's existence.

EVERYDAY APPLICATION

We can know that God exists in many ways, including through creation. The psalmist proclaimed, "The heavens declare the glory of God; the skies proclaim the work of his hands" (Psalm 19:1). The apostle Paul further stated that all people are accountable to God, "since what may be known about God is plain to them, because God has made it plain to them. For since the creation of the world God's invisible qualities—his eternal power and divine nature—have been clearly seen, being understood from what has been made, so that people are without excuse" (Romans 1:19-20, TNIV). This means that belief in a Creator isn't a blind leap of faith, but that such faith rests on the evidence of creation itself. The universe doesn't explain itself; rather, it calls out for a divine Author to account for its existence and nature.

Various Christian thinkers have developed philosophical arguments for the existence of God. This endeavor is called natural theology, and it is one part of the discipline of apologetics, which labors to demonstrate that Christianity is true, rational, and pertinent (1 Peter 3:15-16). Natural theology doesn't use the Bible to argue for God's existence. Instead, it appeals to aspects of nature that point to God. Although natural theology fell out of favor during the Enlightenment, and was deemed a philosophical failure by many philosophers in the first half of the twentieth century, well-respected philosophers in recent decades have resurrected these arguments with impressive results. While these arguments can be complicated, we'll briefly look at three arguments for the existence of God.

1. Cosmological arguments appeal to the existence of the cosmos as evidence for a Creator. These arguments come in different forms, but all claim that the universe can't account for itself. Either the universe has always existed, it came into existence by chance, or it was created by God. Strong scientific evidence from Big Bang cosmology shows that the universe came into existence out of nothing a finite time ago. If so, then it hasn't always existed, and its origin needs to be explained. But trying to explain the creation of the universe by chance really explains nothing. Further, we can't assume that things pop into existence without causes. Therefore, the best explanation for the origin of the universe is God, a First Cause vastly greater than and outside of the universe.

2. Design arguments appeal to aspects of the universe that indicate a mind or designer. For example, in recent decades physicists and philosophers have noted that dozens and dozens of features of the universe (such as its proportions, constants, and laws) must be fine-tuned to a precise degree in order for life to exist. It's fantastically improbable that these features

would come about through chance. Further, no single natural law can account for all of these fine-tuned features. Therefore, the best explanation for this fine-tuning is God, who served as the Fine-Tuner or Designer.

3. Moral arguments for God don't appeal to aspects of the physical world, but to our internal sense of right and wrong, good and evil. If objective moral truths do exist—such as "racism is always wrong"—what makes them true? The best explanation is that moral truths are based on God's eternally good character. God designed us and knows what's best for us. God is the Law-giver and source of moral obligation. An atheistic universe lacks any such Law-giver, contains no objective moral meaning, and thus can't make any sense of objective moral truth.

The existence of God is a timeless and momentous question. Christians should give the best possible arguments for the existence of the God who both created and saved them, so that others may know this God as well.

FOR FURTHER READING
Lee Strobel, *The Case for a Creator*. Zondervan, 2004.
Anthony Flew, with Roy Varghese, *There is a God*. HarperOne, 2007.

—DOUGLAS GROOTHUIS

GOD, FAITHFULNESS OF

EVERYDAY DEFINITION
Our life experiences make us cautious when other people make us promises, when we need to sign contracts, and even when we must rely on others to come to our aid in difficult times. But this isn't the case with God, for he is faithful, reliable, trustworthy, and loyal (Psalm 33:4; 1 Corinthians 1:9; 1 Thessalonians 5:24). In addition, God remains faithful forever (Psalm 119:90; 146:6). So, despite our cautiousness in our human relationships, we can always count on God to keep his promises (Numbers 23:19; Hebrews 11:11).

Certainly, we can't dictate to God when he should fulfill a promise.

Yet we can freely ask him to fulfill the promises he has made (see Nehemiah 1:4-11). We can be assured that God will fulfill each of his promises at the right time and in the right way because the whole of God's Word is trustworthy (Psalm 119:30,86,138; Revelation 21:5), a reliable guide for living well (Psalm 1).

God's faithfulness is a common theme in the Old Testament (Deuteronomy 7:9; Psalm 33:4; Lamentations 3:22) as well as in the New Testament (1 Thessalonians 5:24; 2 Thessalonians 3:3; Hebrews 10:23). God's faithfulness is portrayed as a protective shield that dissipates fear (Psalm 91:4-5) and as a shining light that guides our pathway (Psalm 43:3). Jeremiah testified that God demonstrates his reliability every day: "Because of the LORD's great love we are not consumed, for his compassions never fail. They are new every morning; great is your faithfulness" (Lamentations 3:22-23).

In the Old Testament, God's faithfulness is associated with his covenant relationship with his people: "I will walk among you and be your God, and you will be my people" (Leviticus 26:12; see also Jeremiah 7:23; Joel 2:27; Revelation 21:3). God commits himself to remain faithful, even if his people prove unfaithful (2 Timothy 2:13). In fact, the term "lovingkindness/covenant love" (Hebrew *hesed*) is often used with "faithfulness" (Genesis 32:10; Psalm 40:10-11; 57:3; 85:10; 98:3; 138:2). This pairing appears three times among the eight occurrences of "faithfulness" in Psalm 89.

Moses connects God's covenant with his faithfulness: "Know therefore that the LORD your God is God; he is the faithful God, keeping his covenant of love to a thousand generations of those who love him and keep his commands" (Deuteronomy 7:9; see also Isaiah 61:8; Hosea 2:19-20). God always acts in faithfulness (Psalm 33:4; 111:7-8), even in the midst of our unfaithfulness (Nehemiah 9:33).

Specific activities identified with God's faithfulness include: God plans and executes his plan (Isaiah 25:1), he saves (Psalm 69:13), he afflicts his children (Psalm 119:75), he rewards his people (Isaiah 61:8), and he judges the world (Psalm 54:5; 96:13).

Through his incarnation, obedience, death, and resurrection, Jesus Christ became our faithful high priest (Hebrews 2:17). The Old Testament contains numerous promises about the coming Messiah's faithfulness (Isaiah 11:5; 16:5; 42:3). As the only mediator between humanity and God (1 Timothy 2:5-6), Jesus faithfully prays to the Father on our behalf (Romans 8:34; Hebrews 7:25). The book of Revelation speaks of Christ as the "faithful witness" (1:5; 3:14), whose very name is "Faithful" (19:11). Consistent with what was said about Yahweh in the Old Testament, the apostle Paul wrote of Christ: "if we are faithless, he remains faithful, for he cannot disown himself" (2 Timothy 2:13, TNIV).

EVERYDAY APPLICATION

Because of our experiences with untrustworthy people, we need to remind ourselves that God always remains faithful and that we can rely on him to keep his promises. The following are some practical ways to focus on God's faithfulness:

- We can meditate on Scripture passages (such as Psalm 89; 138) that remind us of God's constant faithfulness.
- Journaling our life experiences when God demonstrates his faithfulness nurtures our confidence in his faithfulness. Then, in times when God seems absent or distant or when we wait on God to answer our prayers, we can turn to our experiences and receive encouragement about his past faithfulness to us.
- We can sing a worship song, traditional or contemporary, that highlights God's dependability. The classic hymn "Great Is Thy Faithfulness" has reminded God's people of his faithfulness through many generations.
- We can pray God's promises back to him as Nehemiah (Nehemiah 1:4-11) and Daniel (Daniel 9:1-27) did in the Old Testament. Studying, meditating on, and praying God's promises can be rewarding spiritual disciplines. As children, we often asked our parents for something we wanted. Similarly, Jesus invites us to make our requests known to God, especially since our heavenly Father is ready to "give good gifts to those who ask him" (Matthew 7:11; see also Luke 11:13).
- We can recognize that God is a faithful Father who sometimes chooses to train us in righteousness through discipline and suffering (Hebrews 12:4-11). For the joy set before him, Jesus endured trials, chiefly death on the cross (12:1-2). Likewise, we

can be assured of receiving God's promises by persevering in difficult times (10:23,36). While suffering agony on the cross, Jesus expressed his complete confidence in the Father (see Luke 23:46; Psalm 31:5). The apostle Peter reminds us that even while suffering, we should commit ourselves to the "faithful Creator" (1 Peter 4:19, see also 1 Corinthians 10:13).

- We can mirror God's own faithfulness in our manner of life and in our ministry to others (1 Corinthians 4:2; 2 Timothy 2:2). The apostle Paul explicitly pointed out and commended Tychicus' faithfulness in service of the gospel (Ephesians 6:21; Colossians 4:7). Being faithful even in life's small tasks is a virtue that pleases our faithful God (Matthew 25:21,23; Luke 16:10-12).

- We can share our personal milestones of God's faithfulness with others (see Psalm 145:1-7). King David testified that he did not withhold from telling God's moments of deliverance in his life (Psalm 40:10-11). As parents, for example, we can share stories of God's faithfulness with our children (Isaiah 38:19). Hearing accounts of God's faithfulness reminds us that God actively cares for the needs of his people. Recalling Jesus' birth, life, death, and resurrection — the main events of God's redemptive plan — become occasions to affirm that God has been faithful to his promises. Many people in Scripture testified to God's faithfulness: Mary (Luke 1:46-55), Zechariah, the father of John the Baptist (Luke 1:68), and Paul (Acts 13:23; 17:31; 26:6-8). At the end of his life Joshua testified that God had been faithful to his promises made to Israel (Joshua 23:14).

With full assurance God's people can count on the fact that all of God's promises ultimately will be fulfilled.

FOR FURTHER READING

A. D. Verhey, "Faithfulness," in *International Standard Bible Encyclopedia*, ed. Geoffrey Bromiley. Eerdmans, 1982.

J. P. Moreland and Klaus Issler, *In Search of a Confident Faith: Overcoming Barriers to Trusting in God*. InterVarsity, 2008.

— KLAUS ISSLER

GOD, FEAR OF

EVERYDAY DEFINITION

The Bible says that the fear of God is the beginning of knowledge (Proverbs 1:7). So what does it mean to fear God? Fearing God doesn't signify a dreadful feeling about God's hidden mystery; instead, it means having a holy reverence for God's revealed majesty, love, and grace.

We can divide the fear of God into two categories: legalistic fear of God and evangelical fear of God.

1. The legalistic fear of God relates to humans having unreasonable, terrifying, and instinctive fear about God's wrath and vengeance upon their sins and transgressions. In this sense, the legalistic fear is closely connected with the shamanistic idea of horrible gods, who are prone to violently abuse their subjects and to command strict rules for their worshippers.

2. The evangelical fear of God is grounded on a solid knowledge of who God is, what he does, and what he requires of us. This is the fear of God found in the Bible. The evangelical fear of God is closely connected with his self-revelation of his holiness, love, grace, mercy, power, majesty, and righteousness. On the basis of personal experience of God's many glories, God's people begin to have holy and loving reverence toward God and they begin to trust in and rely on him for their being, happiness, and eternal life.

EVERYDAY APPLICATION

As Christians, we can apply the biblical concept of fearing God in our everyday lives. As follows:

- We should strive to know God. Unless we gain a true knowledge of God, we can't fear him in an appropriate manner. In order to know God, we should focus on what he has revealed about himself. Since God reveals himself in the Scripture, we should read, study, and meditate on the Word of God in order to know about God. Of course, this informational "head" knowledge about God needs to be accompanied by a "heart" knowledge and personal experience of God. This experience takes place through our personal worship of God and a personal life of prayer, obedience, and witness. Therefore, we should do our best to worship God in the truth and the Spirit, to pray to God earnestly, to obey God's Word, and to witness faithfully to the grace of God in Jesus Christ.

- We should make every effort to express our reverence for God in every area of our life. This is based on our personal knowledge of God's glory and occurs when we acknowledge God's lordship and priority in our everyday lives. For example, when we have true reverence for God, we can become true stewards of what God has given us, sharing our time, money, gifts, and talents with others. Therefore, our lifestyle of sharing becomes the evidence that we have a rightful reverence and fear of God of the universe.

FOR FURTHER READING
J. I. Packer, *Knowing God.* InterVarsity, 1993.

— SUNG WOOK CHUNG

GOD, GLORY OF

EVERYDAY DEFINITION
The glory of God represents the fullness and majesty of who God is. God's glory includes all of his excellences—holiness, goodness, greatness, power, wisdom, and love. Consequently, God's actions reflect his glory; God's creation reflects his glory. In essence, all that God does is praiseworthy.

People express praise and adoration in honor of God's glory. They express it through words, liturgy, music, drama, and other expressions of worship. So much of worship, in fact, focuses on the glory of God, praising God for who he is and what he does.

The Old Testament mentions glory as an attribute of God (Psalm 24:7-8; 29:3). Even God's name reveals his glory (Deuteronomy 28:58; Nehemiah 9:5; Psalm 8:1; 79:9). People experienced God's glory (Exodus 3:2; Isaiah 6:1-4); some acknowledged it (Psalm 29:2; 72:19), while others felt fear and guilt (Isaiah 2:10,19,21). Sometimes visible phenomena accompanied God's glory (Deuteronomy 5:24; 2 Samuel 22:8-16; Habakkuk 3:4). In early manifestations, God's glory appeared as a cloud (Exodus 24:15-16; 33:9-10) and then in the tabernacle and temple (1 Kings 8:10-11; 2 Chronicles 5:13-14). The Jewish term for the visible presence of God in the temple is *shekinah*, the Hebrew word for glory. Scripture speaks of the glory in all God's works, especially in the works of creation and redemption (Psalm 19:1; 111:3; Isaiah 12:5; 35:2). The whole world reveals God's glory (Numbers 14:21; Psalm 57:5,11; 108:5; Isaiah 6:3) as do God's people (Isaiah 60:19-21) and God's kingdom (1 Chronicles 29:11; Psalm 145:11-12).

In the New Testament, we learn more about the glory of God through the person and work of Jesus Christ. He is the reflection of God's glory (Hebrews 1:3), full of grace and truth (John 1:14; 13:31-32), which Jesus had before the world existed (John 17:5). Although it's thought that the fullness of God's glory cannot be fully seen (1 Timothy 6:15-16), people see it sufficiently in Jesus (John 1:18; 2 Corinthians 4:6; 2 Peter 1:17).

Theologically, the concept of God's glory suggests the transcendence—the wholly otherness—of God. It's natural for people to try to understand and describe who God is. Yet, because God is transcendent, people can't fully comprehend—much less communicate—the glory of God. People err when they think they know everything about God. Only through the self-revelation of God—for example, in Scripture—can people learn about the nature and character of God.

Early Christians used the Greek word *doxa* to describe the "glory" of God. Doxa can also mean "belief" or "opinion." However, the meaning related to God's glory is intended for a doxology, which is a short statement or hymn of praise to God. Doxologies occur throughout the Bible. Sometimes they're used in the formal worship services of Israel (1 Chronicles 29:10-13; Psalm 41:13; 72:18-19; 106:48; 150:1-6). Doxologies occur spontaneously (Romans 11:33-36) or as benedictions to prayers (Romans 16:25-27; Ephesians 3:20-21; Hebrews 13:20-21; 2 Peter 3:18; Jude 24–25). Finally, doxologies are used in heavenly worship (Revelation 4:8,11; 5:9-14; 7:12; 19:1).

In fact, the glory of God is heavily emphasized in Christian worship. So much of church experience is dedicated to praising and worshipping God in celebration of God's glory. It occurs in psalms, hymns, canticles, and spiritual songs (Ephesians 5:19) as well as other rites and rituals of churches.

EVERYDAY APPLICATION

As Christians, one of the challenges we face as we think about God is balancing the transcendence (otherness, glory) of God with the imminence (presence, approachability) of God. If we focus too much on God's glory, then we might not think of God as being approachable, understanding, and compassionate toward us and our particular needs. On the other hand, if we neglect God's glory, then our concept of God might be too small. God's glory reminds us that God is much larger than we can imagine, and we should never underestimate God's ability to understand as well as overcome the difficulties we experience in life.

As we reflect on the glory of God, one of the most prominent places we express our adoration of him will take place through praise and thanksgiving in prayer. Adoration has to do, primarily, with adoring God for who God is and not just for what he has done or might do in the lives of people. Too often, we think of prayer only as supplication or intercession on the part of others—namely, asking God for blessings. Although it's not wrong to pray for God's blessings, we miss out on the full meaning of prayer by failing to adore God in prayer. Adoration, praise, and worship of God will help our prayer life, since we will focus on God himself in addition to particular questions or concerns we might have. A helpful acronym for prayer is ACTS: adoration, confession, thanksgiving, and supplication. As we pray, we might find it helpful to spend time in all these areas of interaction with God.

Certainly our worship of God—personal and public—represents one of the most dynamic aspects of Christian life today. Churches put tremendous emphasis upon understanding, preparing, performing, and creatively expanding worship opportunities for congregants. Huge music and media industries have arisen because of the focus upon praising God and God's glory. Such developments should be welcomed for their contribution to the wealth of worship resources. However, we need to be careful about allowing the glitz of modern-day worship services to replace the heart of worship that honors God's glory. In fact, our adoration and praise doesn't need to be glitzy. It doesn't even need to be public. We all have the opportunity to honor God and to do so in many ways: personally and collectively, intellectually and emotionally, prayerfully and celebratively.

FOR FURTHER READING

Jerome H. Neyrey, *Give God the Glory: Ancient Prayer and Worship in Cultural Perspective*. Eerdmans, 2007.

J. B. Phillips, *Your God Is Too Small: A Guide for Believers and Skeptics Alike*. Touchstone, 2004.

Bruce A. Ware, *God's Greater Glory: The Exalted God of Scripture and the Christian Faith*. Crossway, 2004.

— DON THORSEN

GOD, HOLINESS OF

EVERYDAY DEFINITION

The root of the Hebrew word for holiness means "to cut" or "to separate." To be holy is to be removed from the realm of the common to the realm of the sacred.

In general, holiness signifies two qualities:

1. Being consecrated or set apart for a specific purpose.
2. Being free from the taint of evil.

Scripture ascribes to God the titles "Holy," "Holy One," "Holy One of Israel," indicating that holiness is virtually a synonym for the Almighty. Significantly, the third person of the Trinity is named the "Holy Spirit." Theologically, God's nature is eternally holy in that he is exalted in splendor and power and removed from what is unclean and defiled.

Psalm 99 verifies two aspects of God's holiness: his transcendent majesty (verses 1-3) and his absolute moral perfection (verses 4-5):

1. The transcendent majesty of God's holiness describes his essential power and splendor over the entire creation. We see this dimension following the miraculous deliverance

from Egyptian bondage, when Moses and Israel sang to the Lord: "Who among the gods is like you, O LORD? Who is like you—majestic in holiness, awesome in glory, working wonders?" (Exodus 15:11). This aspect of God's holiness is prominent in the writings of the prophets, particularly in the prophecy of Isaiah, such as when he exalted the Almighty: "great is the Holy One of Israel among you" (Isaiah 12:6; see also 29:23; 30:15).

2. The second aspect of God's holiness describes the unsullied perfection of God's character. Isaiah encountered God's transcendent and moral holiness as he entered the temple (Isaiah 6). The worshipping seraphim, the shaking foundations, the darkness and smoke, the prophet's cry of unworthiness, and the threefold ascription of holiness to God ("Holy, holy, holy is the LORD Almighty," verse 3) affirm God's majesty, power, and absolute moral perfection. In the light of God's sheer holiness godly Isaiah became acutely aware of his own uncleanness (verse 5).

The word holy and related forms of the word occur more than 150 times in the book of Leviticus, primarily in the sense of ethical purity, as the book sets forth the pattern of purity for worshipping Yahweh.

The New Testament describes God's holiness as so complete that he can't be tempted (James 1:13) and he can't lie (Hebrews 6:18). The apostle John upheld God's absolute moral purity with the declaration: "God is light; in him there is no darkness at all" (1 John 1:5). In the book of Revelation, four living creatures ceaselessly praise and glorify him who sits on the throne with the threefold ascription: "Holy, holy, holy is the Lord God Almighty, who was, and is, and is to come" (Revelation 4:8).

EVERYDAY APPLICATION

We people stand before the holy God in reverence and awe. We worship him for his infinite holiness, echoing the prophet Isaiah and the angelic hosts in Revelation: "Holy, holy, holy is the Lord God Almighty." The thrice-holy God deserves our wholehearted and exclusive worship. So the psalmist commanded, "Exalt the LORD our God and worship at his holy mountain, for the LORD our God is holy" (Psalm 99:9).

Because he is holy, God is so displeased with wickedness (Psalm 5:4) that he can't look upon evil (Habakkuk 1:13). For this reason, as God's blood-bought children, we must flee every form of evil. God commands his people, "Be holy because I, the LORD your God, am holy" (Leviticus 19:2), and then lists prohibitions against stealing, lying, deceiving, swearing falsely, defrauding the neighbor, and so on. As God is unchangeably holy in his desires, thoughts, words, and actions, we should strive to be innocent of evil in these respects.

The writer to the Hebrews penned the following provocative words: "Make every effort . . . to be holy; without holiness no one will see the Lord" (Hebrews 12:14). The inspired author didn't intend to communicate that sinless perfection is required to enter heaven. Rather, if we as God's people willfully harbor sin in our lives, we will fail to "see" God when we come to worship him, whether individually or corporately. In other words, we need to pursue purity of life to engage God in worship and prayer (see Matthew 5:8). The spiritual effectiveness of our lives for God will be proportional to the degree of our holiness.

As children of the holy God we should detest every form of evil as he does. Our indignation will be stirred against all forms of personal evil (covetousness, immorality, idolatry, etc.), as well as every form of social evil (injustice, violence, oppression, etc.). We must learn to hate with righteous ire all violations of holiness, even as the holy God himself hates them. However, while separating ourselves from moral evil, we still will remain in the world where God has planted us in order to faithfully serve as his agents of salt and light and to demonstrate his love to others.

God's ultimate purpose for his blood-bought children is to transform us into the image and likeness of his holy and righteous Son (Romans 8:29; 2 Corinthians 3:18). As we advance in holiness by God's grace and our prayerful efforts, we become more and more like Jesus. As we mature in holiness, God's purpose for us — his redeemed people — is realized.

FOR FURTHER READING

Allan Coppedge, *Portraits of God: A Biblical Theology of Holiness.* InterVarsity, 2001.

R. C. Sproul, *The Holiness of God*. Tyndale, 1985.

— BRUCE DEMAREST

GOD, KINGDOM OF

EVERYDAY DEFINITION

The kingdom of God can best be understood as God's sphere of influence in the world today. Perhaps the most common misconception about the kingdom of God is that it's a physical place—an empire with geographical borders and ruled by a monarch. A second and similar misunderstanding about the kingdom is that it's the equivalent of heaven, the place where most Christians believe they will spend eternity.

However, if we look to Jesus as the most prolific preacher of the kingdom of God (seventy-six different sayings), we discover an altogether different perspective.

Kingdom as Prophetic Announcement of Dynamic Presence. The Greek word used for kingdom (*basileia*) denotes the "reign" or activity of God, rather than a physical jurisdiction or a piece of land ruled by a king. As a result, Jesus introduces the coming of the kingdom (or reign) of God in himself. Matthew 12:28 captures Jesus' announcement as the kingdom of God directly confronts the kingdom of Satan in the form of casting out demons: "But if it is by the Spirit of God that I drive out demons, then the kingdom of God has come upon you."

Jesus' many miracles, cleansings, healings, and exorcisms all testify to the presence of God's reign in him. Jesus provides further evidence to this reign while addressing the Pharisees; Jesus challenges them to stop searching for signs of apocalyptic proportions, but to look right in front of them: "Behold, the Kingdom of God is in your presence!" (Luke 17:20-21, paraphrase). With great boldness in teaching and ministry, Jesus demonstrates the reality of the present kingdom of God.

Theology of the Kingdom of God. If Jesus ushered in the kingdom, does that mean the kingdom departed when Jesus ascended to the Father? Jesus taught the disciples that the advantage of his departure was that the "Helper" (Spirit of truth) would come to them, bearing witness and glorifying Jesus (John 16:5-15). The apostle Paul taught that "the Spirit of Him who raised Jesus from the dead dwells in you" (Romans 8:11, NASB), giving life. We find evidence of this "life" described in Acts, where the community of Jesus' followers is filled with the Holy Spirit, empowering them to not only perform miracles, but also establish a true community of believers sharing in life together.

What would our world look like if we all were under God's reign—if the kingdom of God was complete? If we look at Jesus' priorities in teaching and ministry, perhaps we can gain a glimpse of the reality of the kingdom.

In teaching, when asked "Which is the greatest commandment in the Law?" (Matthew 22:36), Jesus cited Deuteronomy 6:5: "You shall love the LORD your God with all your heart and with all your soul and with all your might" (NASB) and added Leviticus 19:18: "You shall love your neighbor as yourself" (NASB). We can glean further instruction from the Sermon on the Mount (Matthew 5-8), where Jesus lays down the ethics of the kingdom. Essentially, the reign of God involves loving God first and foremost, then loving others in such a way that we extend practical care and concern to our "neighbors." Kingdom life would mean living in a world where community concerns "trump" personal agendas; where the value of justice surpasses the value of personal gain; where the need for reconciliation overpowers pride and hurt.

The most common theme of Jesus' parables is the nature of the kingdom of God (eleven parables). The parables describe the kingdom as growing, as a valuable and wonderful discovery, and as both current and future. Given that the kingdom was ushered in by Jesus, perhaps these themes were critical, as many are unable to see evidence of God's complete reign in today's world.

Perhaps the most confusing aspect of Jesus' teaching about the kingdom is about its arrival, particularly when some Bible passages refer to the coming kingdom. For example, in Luke 22:16 Jesus told the disciples, "I shall never again eat it until it is fulfilled in the kingdom of God" (NASB). Matthew 25 outlines two parables taught by Jesus, both pointing to a future coming and judgment. The chapter concludes with Jesus teaching directly about his return as the Son of Man, coming in glory to judge the nations.

Most theologians today adopt a "realized eschatology," agreeing that Jesus initiated the kingdom presence, which will come to fruition upon his second coming. In other words, the kingdom is here today, but it won't be fully present until Jesus' second coming.

EVERYDAY APPLICATION

Although we understand Jesus' role as ushering in the kingdom of God, and the role of the Holy Spirit as continuing the work of Jesus among his believers, what's our role in the kingdom today?

First, we recognize that "the good news of the Kingdom of God permeates every part of us, not just the 'religion section' of the newspaper."[14] If the sphere of God truly invaded earth in Jesus, and continues through the ministry of the Holy Spirit, our response is simply one of submitting every aspect of ourselves to his reign.

The gift of the Holy Spirit demonstrates that God wants us to be involved in his work. But how do we actively participate in ushering in the reign of God? Perhaps ultimately by returning to the Gospels to re-examine how Jesus both taught and lived as he ushered in the kingdom of God, and then doing our best to live out his teaching.

FOR FURTHER READING

George R. Beasley-Murray, *Jesus and the Kingdom of God*. Eerdmans, 1986.

John Bright, *The Kingdom of God*. Abingdon, 1953.

Stanley J. Grenz, *Theology for the Community of God*. Eerdmans, 1994.

Glen H. Stassen and David P. Gushee, *Kingdom Ethics: Following Jesus in Contemporary Context*. InterVarsity, 2003.

Brian D. McLaren, *The Secret Message of Jesus: Uncovering the Truth That Could Change Everything*. Thomas Nelson, 2007.

N. T. Wright, *Jesus and the Victory of God*. Fortress, 1996.

—CHERYL CRAWFORD

---

14. Brian D. McLaren, *The Secret Message of Jesus: Uncovering the Truth That Could Change Everything* (Nashville, TN: Thomas Nelson, 2007), 10.

GOD, PROMISES OF

EVERYDAY DEFINITION

The promises of God are voluntary commitments God made to humanity and caused to be recorded in the Bible for all humanity. They are expressions of God's character as a loving and careful Creator.

The Bible describes the promises of God in several ways. God is faithful to keep them (Titus 1:2; Hebrews 10:23). His promises are good and precious (1 Kings 8:56; 2 Peter 1:4). They are obtained through faith (Hebrews 11:33; Galatians 3:22; Hebrews 6:12; Romans 4:13,16). In addition, not one of them will fail (Joshua 23:14; 1 Kings 8:56).

We clearly see the character of God's promises in the ones he made in the biblical story of redemption. After the fall of Adam and Eve in the Garden (Genesis 3), human history was marked by violence, hatred, and disobedience (Genesis 4–11). Humanity was alienated from God through sin. However, God moved to redeem humanity and bring reconciliation. This began with God's promise to Abraham: "I will make you into a great nation and I will bless you . . . and all peoples on earth will be blessed through you" (Genesis 12:2-3). God promised Abraham that salvation would come to the world through his family.

When Abraham's descendents lived in Egypt as slaves, it appeared that God's promise of blessing for them and all humanity had been lost. Yet God sent Moses to lead Abraham's family, called Israel, out of bondage, and into the fulfillment of the promises he had made. Through Moses, God reiterated his earlier promises to all of Israel (Exodus 19:3-6).

More than a thousand years after God's first promise to Abraham, God made another promise to David, whom God elevated to become king of the Israelites: "I will raise up your offspring to succeed you . . . and I will establish his kingdom. He is the one who will build a house for my Name, and I will establish the throne of his kingdom forever. I will be his father, and he will be my son. . . . My love will never be taken away from him" (2 Samuel 7:12-15). God spoke this promise about a very special person, a Messiah, who would be both a descendant of David and the Son of God.

After the passing of another thousand years, the promises made to Abraham and David appeared to be threatened. However, in "the fullness of time," Jesus Christ, a Jew from the house of David, was born. Through his life, death, and resurrection, the redemption of humanity was realized. God was faithful to his promise.

EVERYDAY APPLICATION
The promises of God remind us of important truths:

- We make promises to others. Sometimes we make overt promises, but often our lives imply promises to others. In ways we might not always think about, the faithfulness and care that we reflect through our lives and work affects the well-being of others around us. As Christians, we should ask ourselves how well we follow the example of God in keeping our word, even when the people we make promises to don't keep theirs.
- We need sources of hope and constancy in our lives. The brokenness of this world introduces many factors that conspire to erode our hope. As believers, we can find hope when we immerse ourselves in the Bible to discover and understand the many promises that God has given us there.
- Promises in Scripture point us to the One who promises. A promise is only as good as its giver. This is true both for what is promised and for the trustworthiness of the promise. So God's promises aren't what we should treasure most; rather, we should treasure the character and presence of God. We live our lives in the presence of the God who loves us, who is good, and who is faithful, even if we aren't always able to recognize it.

FOR FURTHER READING
Scott Hahn, *A Father Who Keeps His Promises: God's Covenant Love in Scripture.* Servant, 1998.

Jonathan Morris, *The Promise: God's Purpose and Plan for When Life Hurts.* HarperOne, 2008.

Walter C. Kaiser Jr., *The Promise-Plan of God: A Biblical Theology of the Old and New Testaments.* Zondervan, 2008.

— DAVID WRIGHT

GOD, SOVEREIGNTY OF

EVERYDAY DEFINITION

The Bible depicts the sovereignty of God as God's supreme authority and lordship over his entire creation. God has sovereignty over everything because he has created all that is. God has sovereignty over human beings because he created them for his own purpose and glory. God has absolute sovereignty over human history because he directs and rules the course of human history as he planned. This means that God's sovereignty over his creation is closely related to his ultimate ownership of all creation.

God's sovereignty is demonstrated clearly through his work of creation. God created everything by his powerful Word. God's work of creation demonstrates his wonderful creativity and almighty power. God's work of providence displays his sovereignty over the course of human and cosmic history. After creating the universe, God didn't cease involvement in the creation. Rather, he sustains the universe with his power and directs the ongoing movement of history as he purposed before the creation of the universe.

God's work of redemption dramatically demonstrates his sovereignty, as well. Through prophets and apostles, God promised to send the Messiah to save sinners from the power of sin, death, and Satan. According to God's plan and purpose, the Father sent his only Son, Jesus Christ, into the world to accomplish the redemption of sinners and the fallen creation. Jesus Christ completed the work of redemption by being born, living, suffering, dying on the cross, and being resurrected from the dead. God's sovereignty was operative throughout the course of the life and ministry of Jesus Christ our Savior.

God's sovereignty is marked by several characteristics, including the following:

- God's sovereignty is all-inclusive. Even the power of darkness and the Devil come under the rule of his sovereignty. God never endorses evil, but sometimes permits evil to exist and happen with his holy displeasure in order to fulfill his sovereign purposes. God hates and detests evil and human sin, but permits them in order to accomplish his purposes. In other words, God overrules evil in order to bring good from it.

- God's sovereignty doesn't contradict the free choice of his
  creatures, including human beings, angels, and demons.
  Rather, God's sovereignty establishes the creatures' exercise
  of their free wills. For example, the Bible affirms that Judas
  Iscariot's betrayal of Jesus was permissively planned by God
  before the creation of the universe (Acts 2:23). But the Bible
  also confirms that Judas Iscariot freely decided to betray the
  Lord. He was never coerced or forced to do so.
- God's sovereignty also establishes the moral and spiritual
  responsibility of all humans. Humans aren't puppets or robots,
  but responsible and relational beings with intellect, emotion,
  and volition (will). Humans are obligated to respond to God's
  sovereign initiatives through their own choices, decisions, and
  actions.

EVERYDAY APPLICATION
In our daily lives, we should learn how to apply the truth of God's
all-inclusive sovereignty to the business of living. We can accomplish
this in many ways, including these:

- We can learn how to acknowledge God's lordship over our
  life and destiny. We can demonstrate our acknowledgement
  of God's sovereignty by our obedience to God's will and
  commands. This doesn't necessarily mean we need to have
  profound theological knowledge about the doctrine of God's
  sovereignty; rather, we simply need to be ready to obey and
  follow God's will and command. To truly acknowledge God's
  sovereignty, we will make every effort to love God with our
  minds, hearts, wills, and souls, and to love our neighbors as
  ourselves — in spite of the cost required for such obedience.
- We can learn to be grateful to the Lord when confronted
  with all kinds of adversities and trials. The Lord commands
  us to "rejoice always, pray continually, give thanks in all
  circumstances; for this is God's will for you in Christ Jesus"
  (1 Thessalonians 5:16-18, TNIV). If we give thanks to God
  only when we enjoy favorable circumstances, we're no more
  than babies in faith. If we rejoice only in sunny seasons, our

spirituality is immature. When we truly acknowledge God's all-inclusive sovereignty, it shows that we have no doubt about God's love and favor for us even in unfavorable circumstances. We believe the truth that "we know that in all things God works for the good of those who love him, who have been called according to his purpose" (Romans 8:28).

- We can possess confidence that God's sovereignty provides us with comfort when we face difficulties and trials. Jesus said, "Whoever wants to be my disciple must deny themselves and take up their cross and follow me" (Matthew 16:24, TNIV). In addition, we're called to "enter through the narrow gate. For wide is the gate and broad is the road that leads to destruction, and many enter through it. But small is the gate and narrow the road that leads to life, and only a few find it" (7:13-14). When we do our best to obey these commands of Jesus, we'll inevitably face hardships, persecutions, and even martyrdom. Yet when we confront these difficulties, our faith in God's sovereignty provides the comfort and courage we need to overcome them. God's comfort enables and empowers us to keep pressing on toward the goal. In this sense, God's sovereignty is anything but a speculative and scholarly idea; in fact, it's a practical and relevant reality in our daily lives.

FOR FURTHER READING

James I. Packer, *Evangelism and the Sovereignty of God*. InterVarsity, 1991.

Warren W. Wiersbe, *Classic Sermons on the Sovereignty of God*. Kregel, 1994.

— SUNG WOOK CHUNG

GOD, WILL OF

EVERYDAY DEFINITION

The will of God includes all that God does, what God wants, and how God guides. God's will is necessary, it is free, and it is more mysterious than we usually admit.

- *Necessary* means that God acts consistently with his own nature. His will corresponds to his wisdom and goodness, implying that there are some things God will not do.
- *Free* means that he didn't have to create the world or perform specific actions. As free, God doesn't need to preserve the world or save it. In freedom, God acts according to his good pleasure (Ephesians 1:5,9). Humans aren't ruled by fate or blind energy, but by the will of our all-powerful heavenly Father. For this reason, we can rest in God's good and perfect will (Romans 12:2).
- *Mysterious* means that while God chooses to reveal some things to us, there is much that he hasn't made known to us. We can't plumb the depths of God's counsel (Romans 11:33-34). He reveals only those portions of his will that facilitate the maturity and fruitfulness of his people on their homeward journey.

God's will is also complex. It consists of at least four aspects, including the following:

1. *God's will of decree, sometimes called his sovereign, or secret will.* "The secret things belong to the LORD our God, but the things revealed belong to us and to our children forever" (Deuteronomy 29:29). God sovereignly ordains all that comes to pass; nothing happens outside of his control. However, God's will doesn't overrule human responsibility and choice. The tension between God's sovereignty and our free choice is beyond our human understanding.
2. *God's will of precept, sometimes called his revealed will.* People sometimes ask, "How can I find God's will for my life?" In terms of precept, God's will isn't hidden from us. We know much of God's will through his revealed Word. Reflecting on God's will as revealed in Scripture, Paul wrote, "Therefore do not be foolish, but understand what the Lord's will is" (Ephesians 5:17). We're called to obey God's perceptive will, although we can choose to disobey it.
3. *God's will of disposition.* This describes God's attitude about what is pleasing to him. Scripture teaches that God takes

"no pleasure in the death of the wicked" (Ezekiel 33:11), yet he does will the death of the wicked (3:20). Ultimately, God delights in his own glory and righteousness. In judgment, he delights in the vindication of his justice.

4. *God's individual will, meaning his specific will of guidance for each believer.* The Holy Spirit directs believers to accomplish what God purposes for them.

These four aspects represent ways to speak about or describe the will of God. Yet there is only one God who wills. Jesus perfectly conforms to each aspect of his Father's will.

EVERYDAY APPLICATION

The driving question many of us ask is, "How can I know the will of God?"

If we're referring to God's sovereign will, then we finite beings simply can't know it. We can only bow before it in submission to him. However, if we're speaking of God's revealed will, we can know it as disclosed in the Scriptures. In addition, if we're speaking of his will of disposition, we can also learn what's pleasing to him through his written Word.

What about God's individual will? Does he have a specific plan for each of our lives? Three views regarding God's will of individual guidance are prominent:

1. Some believe that God has a specific detailed plan for each person — that he speaks to us all through the day and guides us by private impressions and voices. The problem with this view, however, is that we are easily deceived. Impressions can be rooted in any number of sources: pride, fear, wishful thinking, hormonal imbalance, depression, medication, and satanic seduction. Impressions must be carefully tested because humans have a large capacity for self-deception.

2. Others believe that God doesn't have a specific plan for each individual. Rather, he wants us to use wisdom to carefully evaluate our life's circumstances. According to this view, direct revelation is extraordinary, so we must use our minds

and apply wisdom to pursue a path that pleases God. The problem with this view is that the Bible portrays God as caring for individuals and guiding them through life's maze. In the Scriptures, God communicates specific purposes and directions to our hearts (Nehemiah 2:12; Acts 8:29). Scripture tells us that God will direct our path (Proverbs 3:5-6).

3. Others think that God does guide individuals in specific ways. He has particular plans and purposes for our lives. We must prayerfully exercise discernment as we respond to God's leading. How do we exercise such discernment? By wholeheartedly trusting in the Lord, and by reading his Word and listening to the Holy Spirit speak to us through it. God's inspired Word is "a lamp to my feet and a light for my path" (Psalm 119:105). We must also pursue wisdom, because God calls us to be wise. And we must be fully open to the leading of the Holy Spirit. The Spirit guides (John 16:13), speaks (Acts 8:29), and imparts dreams and visions (Acts 2:17).

FOR FURTHER READING

Sinclair B. Ferguson, *Discerning God's Will*. Banner of Truth Trust, 1981.
M. Blaine Smith, *Knowing God's Will*. InterVarsity, 1991.
Bruce Waltke, *Finding the Will of God*. Regent, 2002.

— DONALD W. SWEETING

GOD, WRATH OF

EVERYDAY DEFINITION

God's wrath signifies his enmity to and hatred of evil combined with his righteous resolve to punish evil. In his justice, God is good to those who do right, but he's offended by and executes judgment upon those who do evil. Some have said that mercy is God's natural work, while wrath is his unnatural work. Even though wrath is contrary to God's nature, wickedness and the repulsiveness of sin compels God to righteous indignation.

The Old Testament records God's righteous anger against Israel for their persistent idolatry (Exodus 32:10-14). God's wrath against his covenant people for their perverted worship is a common theme in the book of Deuteronomy, which reiterates the law (4:25-27; 6:14-16; 29:22-28). Old Testament language concerning God's wrath is scathing; his anger burns (see Job 20:23) against all kinds of disobedience, including fabricating idols (1 Kings 16:26), consulting mediums and spiritualists (2 Kings 21:6), and disobeying his law in general (2 Kings 22:13). Scripture states that God "hate[s] all who do wrong" (Psalm 5:5). He particularly detests the sacrifices (Proverbs 15:8), thoughts (verse 26), prayers (28:9), and ways (15:9) of the wicked. In the writings of the prophets, God's anger against sin is expressed through powerful imagery of God unleashing his wrath as a farmer thrashes his field (Habakkuk 3:12), as a smelter refines metal in a crucible (Ezekiel 22:17-22), and as a powerful lion tears its pray to pieces (Hosea 5:14).

Because of God's righteous wrath against sin, the apostles summoned the wicked to decisively repent of their sins (Acts 3:19; 17:31) in the New Testament. In strong language, the apostle Paul upheld God's righteous indignation against violations of his holy law (Romans 1:18; Ephesians 5:6).

The coming day of the Lord would be a time when God's wrath would be justly executed against the unrepentant (Romans 2:5,8; 1 Thessalonians 1:10). According to the apostle John, God will mete out his wrath against all who reject his Son (John 3:36). The Apocalypse of John is striking in its symbolism describing God's wrath directed against the worldwide forces of evil. It foretells "the wine of God's fury" that must be drunk (Revelation 14:10), "bowls filled with the wrath of God" that must be poured out (15:7), and "the great winepress of God's wrath" that must be trod (14:19). The entire Apocalypse is the striking record of God's righteous wrath against end-time evil.

In the infinite grandeur of his character, God's wrath is tempered by his longsuffering, which grants opportunity for people to repent of their sins. God repeatedly promised his people that if they turned from their sin and idolatry, he would show mercy and avert his righteous wrath (Deuteronomy 13:17-18; 30:2-3).

EVERYDAY APPLICATION

Given the Bible's sober teaching that God judges sin with his righteous wrath, we shouldn't view God as some vengeful deity who delights to do people in. To grow in trustful and loving relationship with God, we need to cultivate a realistic image of what God is like.

While God is loving, merciful, and compassionate, it's also true that he is appropriately angered by evil. His goodness and love as well as his hatred of evil exist harmoniously within his perfectly integrated character. We can see this through the faithful, compassionate, and merciful qualities that Jesus demonstrated during his earthly life. However, he also experienced righteous indignation on occasions when he was confronted with unrighteousness and injustice (Luke 19:45-46). Our calling as disciples is to imitate God as revealed in Jesus, and that includes righteous indignation against sin. Paul issued the command: "Hate what is evil; cling to what is good" (Romans 12:9; see also Psalm 97:10).

Scripture teaches that God is slow to anger, patient, and longsuffering (Exodus 34:6). Yet we need to know that God's patience has limits. When God's warnings against selfishness, greed, lust, or other forms of ungodliness are spurned, he responds by detesting the evil, warning yet again about the consequences, and when his patience is exhausted, sending just punishment. God's hatred of evil must be understood against the backdrop of his absolute holiness, righteousness, and justice. The prophet Nahum declared: "The LORD is slow to anger and great in power; the LORD will not leave the guilty unpunished" (Nahum 1:3). As the book of Revelation so dramatically teaches, even the day of God's grace will run out. As Christians, we should search our hearts and examine our ways and turn from every evil.

FOR FURTHER READING

Stephen A. Bly, *God's Angry Side*. Moody, 1982.

John MacArthur, *The Wrath of God*. Moody, 1986.

A. W. Tozer, *The Knowledge of the Holy: The Attributes of God*. Alliance Publications, 1972.

— BRUCE DEMAREST

GOD'S LONGSUFFERING

EVERYDAY DEFINITION

God's longsuffering pertains to the biblical attribute of the patience of God. Specifically, it has to do with the patience or forbearance of God with people who break relationship with him due to their sin and betrayal.

The word *longsuffering* derives from the English word "suffering," and longsuffering suggests that God both suffers over the broken relationship with people and that he suffers "long" as he patiently awaits reconciliation. God's provision for reconciliation through Jesus Christ results from compassion. The word "passion" derives from the Greek word for "suffering," and the prefix "com" means that God suffers "with" people in order to bring about reconciliation.

The Old Testament often mentions God's longsuffering or patience. God was patient with individuals (1 Samuel 3:10) and nations (Jonah 3:1,10). In particular, God was patient with the Israelites (Nehemiah 9:30-31). God was patient with sinful people, especially in delaying punishment (Psalm 78:38; Isaiah 48:9). Certainly, people tried God's patience (Malachi 2:17; Isaiah 7:13; 43:24). However, God patiently bore their betrayals. Time and time again, the Old Testament describes God as being slow to anger, despite people's sin (Exodus 34:6; Psalm 86:15; Joel 2:13; Jonah 4:2).

The New Testament describes more of God's patience and reveals the extent of his patience. God is patient and imparts patience to others (Romans 15:5). The purpose of God's patience is so that people might repent (Romans 2:4). It's not God's will than anyone should perish (2 Peter 3:9); instead, God's will is that people be saved (2 Peter 3:15; see also Romans 9:22-24).

EVERYDAY APPLICATION

Too often, we feel impatient with ourselves. We haven't achieved or become who we want to be, so we're angry and unaccepting of ourselves. Such impatience can harm us from realistic self-assessment and planning for the future. Of course, we can also become impatient with others at work, school, church, or regrettably at home. Impatience at home can be especially damaging in marriage and with children. Consequently, we need to learn greater patience, which may well involve a lifetime of learning. However, the fruit of God's Holy Spirit in our lives includes patience (Galatians 5:22).

Scripture describes God's patience as long-suffering, being slow to anger, judge, and punish. So it's tragic when we lose hope, spiritually speaking, by thinking that God has lost patience with us, or that God could never love or accept us. Perhaps the best example of God's patience appears in the parable of the prodigal son (Luke 15:11-32). Jesus tells the story of a son, who asks his father to receive his inheritance early. The father consents, and the son travels to a distant country and squanders his inheritance in immoral living. After genuinely repenting of his misdeeds, the son returned to his father to serve as a servant. However, the father receives his son with joy and celebration, saying, "he was lost and is found" (verse 32). In the same way, God accepts us when we repent; we can never stray too far or be so evil that God will not welcome reconciliation with us.

In the same way, God wants us to be patient, accepting, and even forgiving of others. Jesus famously taught his disciples how to pray in the Sermon on the Mount, which included the following: "Forgive us our debts, as we also have forgiven our debtors" (Matthew 6:12). Patience includes forbearance of others to the point of forgiving them, just as God has forgiven us.

FOR FURTHER READING
Holly Whitcomb, *Seven Spiritual Gifts of Waiting.* Augsburg, 2005.

—DON THORSEN

GOOD WORKS

EVERYDAY DEFINITION
Good works are actions and deeds that bring honor to God and benefit others. The Bible is clear that good works are the expected fruit of living a committed life under the lordship of Jesus Christ. The apostle James teaches that genuine faith or saving faith isn't possible apart from actions or good works on behalf of others: "Suppose a brother or sister is without clothes and daily food. If one of you says to them, 'Go in peace;

keep warm and well fed,' but does nothing about their physical needs, what good is it? In the same way, faith by itself, if it is not accompanied by action, is dead" (James 2:15-17, TNIV).

At the same time, the apostle Paul clearly reminded us that good works do not save us or earn for us merit in heaven (Ephesians 2:8-9). Still, Paul was quick to remind us that good works are the expected outcome of our new life in Jesus Christ (Ephesians 2:10). Similarly, Paul argued that recipients of God's grace will be devoted to doing good works (Titus 3:5-8). He added that those who God has redeemed will be "eager to do what is good" (Titus 2:14).

The Protestant Reformation, a time of radical spiritual awakening and renewal in the sixteenth century, confronted the common view of the day that salvation results from the accrual of merit through a variety of good works. The Reformers strongly affirmed the Bible's teaching that salvation occurs only through the finished work of Jesus Christ on the cross. Salvation is by grace alone (God giving us something we don't deserve) and faith alone (see Romans 4–5).

EVERYDAY APPLICATION

The good works we perform, when they are the fruit of our salvations and inspired by our love for God and others, provide compelling evidence to nonbelievers that our faith is genuine. These good deeds can even result in God receiving praise. The apostle Peter urged, "Live such good lives among the pagans that, though they accuse you of doing wrong, they may see your good deeds and glorify God on the day he visits us" (1 Peter 2:12).

When we think about good works, it helps to reflect on our many circles of influence. The inner circle begins with our own family (1 Timothy 5:8). The next circle of concern is fellow Christians within the community of the church. The third circle represents all other people we might serve in their need as opportunity arises. The apostle Paul urged, "As we have opportunity, let us do good to all people, especially to those who belong to the family of believers" (Galatians 6:10).

We should keep in mind that when doing good works for the benefit of others, many times it will be inconvenient, costly, and demanding. At times, most of us will wonder if we are being taken advantage of or even being manipulated. Jesus, however, reminds us in the story of the Good Samaritan (Luke 10:25-37) that our neighbor is anyone in need who crosses our path, whatever challenges this service of good works might present to our personal comfort zone.

FOR FURTHER READING

M. E. Osterhaven, "Works" in *Evangelical Dictionary of Theology*, edited by Walter A. Elwell. Baker, 2001.

John N. Elliot, "Works" in *The Upper Room Dictionary of Christian Spiritual Formation*, edited by Keith Beasley-Topliffe. Upper Room Books, 2003.

—RANDOLPH M. MACFARLAND

GOODNESS

EVERYDAY DEFINITION

Goodness is the act of being just, loving, generous, and kind, mirroring the actions of God. Scripture states that God is good: "For the LORD is good and his love endures forever; his faithfulness continues through all generations" (Psalm 100:5; see also Exodus 34:6; Psalms 34:8; 119:68). Goodness is a characteristic of God seen in his generous and merciful actions (Matthew 7:7-12). God alone is ultimately good (Mark 10:18).

Goodness is a moral quality associated with individuals but demonstrated through actions. Goodness isn't a passive and sentimental niceness. Rather, goodness is a strong moral drive toward justice and hospitality. The notion of acting justly, loving mercy, and walking humbly before God (Micah 6:8) expresses an essential understanding of goodness.

EVERYDAY APPLICATION

As Christians, goodness is part of the content of our lives. Just as the apostle Peter described Jesus as one who went around doing good (Acts 10:38), goodness becomes a characteristic of the followers of Jesus Christ (Titus 1:8; Galatians 6:7-10; Matthew 5:16).

Barnabas, one of the companions of the apostle Paul, is described as good (Acts 11:24). Goodness is also a fruit of the Spirit (Galatians

5:22). As followers of the Lord, we're called to mirror a life characterized by goodness (Deuteronomy 12:28), doing good works in the power of the Spirit of God (Ephesians 2:10; Romans 12:2; 15:14; 2 Thessalonians 1:11; Colossians 1:10).

Goodness is focused toward others and always beneficial to others. Not selfish or self-centered, goodness seeks the well-being of others (Ephesians 5:9). Bonhoeffer said, "If we want to understand God's goodness in God's gifts, then we must think of them as a responsibility we bear for our brothers and sisters."[15]

As followers of Christ, we should reflect God's goodness toward others. Living in community is an essential part of goodness as we extend the graciousness and hospitality of God toward others. The parable of the Good Samaritan (Luke 10) shows a person who extends himself toward another. This parable shows how we are to live, and specifically how we live out "loving your neighbor as yourself." It implies not merely a selfless giving of ourselves to others, but more a sense of extending ourselves to others who might be considered marginalized.

FOR FURTHER READING
Dietrich Bonhoeffer, *The Cost of Discipleship*. Touchstone, 1995.
Dietrich Bonhoeffer, *Life Together*. HarperOne, 1978.
Philip D. Kenneson, *Life on the Vine: Cultivating the Fruit of the Spirit in Christian Community*. InterVarsity, 1999.

— KURT FREDRICKSON

GOSPEL

EVERYDAY DEFINITION
The term *gospel* (Greek *euangelion*) means "good news" or "good message." Originally, this term related to an "announcement of victory" in a military sense, but later became applied to being a "message of joy." The term is found more than seventy-five times in the New Testament and bears a distinctly Christian connotation.

This good news is first a "message of joy" that through Jesus Christ

15. Geoffrey B. Kelly and F. Burton Nelson, *The Cost of Moral Leadership* (Grand Rapids, MI: Eerdmans, 2002).

God is fulfilling his promise to Israel in sending a Messiah (Matthew 11:2-5; Luke 4:14-19).

Second the gospel comes in and from Jesus: "Jesus went into Galilee, proclaiming the good news of God. 'The time has come,' he said. 'The kingdom of God is near. Repent and believe the good news!'" (Mark 1:14-15). With this announcement, Jesus himself is continuing the promise of "the kingdom" formed and proclaimed in the Old Testament to the people of Israel, which is now opened to all through faith and discipleship to himself (Matthew 11:11-12; 28-30). The kingdom of God is the kingly reign of Jesus. In one sense, he is reigning now, yet at the same time the church awaits the full consummation of his divine reign. This is called the "already" and "not yet" reality of the kingdom of God. Still, this kingdom *is* in our midst through the gift of the Holy Spirit (John 16:5-15). As part of this invitation to life in the kingdom, Jesus offers the gift of freedom from bondage to sin, death, and victory over Satan (Colossians 1:13-14; 2).

What a great "message of joy!" The message of the gospel is proclaiming Jesus — his life, ministry, death, and resurrection. Through trust and confidence in him, we can enter the "kingdom of God" now and learn from him how to live and grow into his likeness.

This is the good news!

EVERYDAY APPLICATION

The good news of Jesus and his kingdom really is good news! This gospel is a gospel for life now, not just the afterlife. Some have proclaimed a gospel that just focuses on forgiveness of sins and receiving salvation for the afterlife. While there is truth in this gospel, it is severely reduced. This inevitably produces passive followers of Jesus.

As Christians, we need to understand that implicit in Jesus' announcement of the good news is the invitation to become his disciple, where he — through the Holy Spirit — will teach and guide us. In this relationship, we can find meaning in the ordinary and mundane activities of life. We will find joy through daily trials and tribulations (James 1:2-4). We can find comfort through the fellowship of others who are also being transformed into his likeness. And we become driven by his agenda to redeem the world.

As ministers of this reconciliation, we gladly preach and teach the

gospel, the most wonderful "message of joy the world has ever heard!"
(2 Corinthians 5:11-21).

FOR FURTHER READING
George Eldon Ladd, *The Gospel of the Kingdom.* Eerdmans, 1959.
Dallas Willard, *The Divine Conspiracy.* HarperSanFrancisco, 1998.

— KEITH MATTHEWS

GOVERNMENT

EVERYDAY DEFINITION
Government is rule exercised with authority. A government is a person,
group, or system that rules and has the right to make laws and enforce
them.

The Bible gives us some premises about government that Christians
should keep in mind:

- God is the ultimate ruler. He is the sovereign Lord who reigns
  over the world. His dominion is enduring and eternal (Daniel
  4:34). He is the ultimate Lawgiver, Judge, and King (Isaiah
  33:22). God ordains human governments and rules through
  them. In the Bible, he ruled through the Patriarchs, through
  chosen leaders like Moses and Joshua, through judges, and
  through kings. His sovereignty isn't limited to Israel alone, but
  extends to all the nations (Isaiah 45:1).
- Human government was instituted to restrain sin, preserve
  law and order, and promote justice (Genesis 9:6). Government
  wasn't intended to be a substitute for God; instead, it is meant
  to be a servant of God, functioning as a good steward over
  people. The biblical account stands in striking contrast to the
  dehumanizing character of other creation accounts, such as
  Enuma Elish (Babylonian creation account), where there is no
  affirmation of humans being created in the image of God (see
  Genesis 1:27).
- God's dominion is different from the dominion of nations.
  Nations and empires are temporary. They all rise and fall.

They are never as great as they think themselves to be. To the sovereign God, the nations "are like a drop in a bucket" (Isaiah 40:15). But his rule is absolute and eternal.

- God holds the nations accountable to himself. They derive their governing authority from God (Daniel 4:17), and they are also responsible to God. Both individuals and nations must answer to God. Individuals will answer to God on Judgment Day; nations answer to God in this life.

- Government should promote righteousness and order its life under God. This is far more important than type or structure of government. In fact, nowhere does Scripture prescribe an ideal form of human government. God's people are portrayed as living under all kinds of governments. We recognize that biblical principles have influenced a movement toward governments that respect the rights, dignity, and voice of the people.

- God evaluates government according to his moral law: "Righteousness exalts a nation, but sin condemns any people" (Proverbs 14:34, TNIV). Nations that rebel against God are foolish (Psalm 2). When empires proclaim that the state is supreme, or that salvation is found in the state, or when they dehumanize their people, they defy God. In the books of Kings and Chronicles, God calls nations to account because of idolatrous high places, pride, defiled temple worship (which promoted forms of prostitution), shedding of innocent blood, injustice, promotion of the occult and sorcery, child sacrifices, and relentless efforts to eliminate God's law.

- God holds leaders responsible because of their great influence over nations (1 Kings 9:4). The wise ruler fears the Lord and celebrates his rule (Psalm 2:11). When we as citizens of democratic nations elect leaders, we elect more than individuals; we choose a direction and a moral future and share in the responsibility for the direction of that government.

EVERYDAY APPLICATION

In the New Testament, Jesus affirms that the church and the government each have their own legitimate spheres and duties (Matthew

22:21). The state can raise taxes and holds the power of the sword for purposes of self-defense. The church, on the other hand, must proclaim God's Word, promote the gospel, nurture souls, and speak up for the weak. Even governments led by Christians are not the kingdom of God. Christians serving in government must be cautious about confusing the gospel with political agendas and be careful about attributing secular ideologies to God. At the same time, churches must be wary of getting too cozy with the government because of the risk of losing their prophetic voice.

While we might find the basis for a separation of church and state in the New Testament (in the sense that the government endorses no one denomination), we don't find any call for a separation of God and state. In fact, a vital connection exists between a society's cultural, moral, and religious life. The wise government sees that a nation's moral life is the foundation of its culture. A nation's religious life is the foundation of its moral life. Therefore, the practice of true religion, and the presence of a healthy church as salt and light, are vitally important.

As followers of Christ, we should maintain a certain realism about governments. We should realize that the political realm is never ultimate. To make it ultimate is to dethrone God and elevate humanity. Consequently, while some forms of patriotism are appropriate, other forms can edge toward idolatry.

We believers also should have a healthy appreciation for limited government. We should be wary of looking to government as the great provider, or looking at the state as children look to a parent. We will recognize that governments can't do many things. And we should be aware that while government is called to be God's servant (Romans 13), it can also be a tyrant and God's enemy (Revelation 18). Because of human sinfulness, we'll be wary of any concentration of power without appropriate checks and balances.

As citizens of a particular nation, we Christians have certain biblical duties and responsibilities. Scripture calls on us to respect the government by virtue of its God-given role (1 Peter 2:17), and we must submit to government as is appropriate (Romans 13:1,5). God wills that we support the government with taxes (Romans 13:6) and with our prayers (1 Timothy 2:1-2). Yet when a government defies God, we might be called upon to disobey it (Acts 5:29) in order to obey God.

Christians have a dual citizenship. We are citizens of two kingdoms. Yet Scripture clearly says that our ultimate citizenship is from above (Philippians 3:20). We ultimately wait for the fully realized kingdom of God when Christ returns, knowing that God alone is the "King of kings and Lord of lords" (Revelation 19:16) and that he is "desired by all nations" (Haggai 2:7, TNIV). We will be tempted to put our trust in human leaders, but as history shows, every human administration ultimately lets us down. That's why Scripture says "it is better to take refuge in the LORD than to trust in princes" (Psalm 118:9).

FOR FURTHER READING

Augustine, *City of God*. Penguin Classics, 2003.
Paul Marshall, *Thine is The Kingdom: A Biblical Perspective on the Nature of Government*. Regent, 1993.
Charles W. Colson, *God and Government*. Zondervan, 2007.

— DONALD W. SWEETING

GRACE, COMMON

EVERYDAY DEFINITION

The words in the original languages of the Bible translated as grace mean undeserved favor, kindness, and benevolence. Grace is typically bestowed by a superior toward a subordinate; in the case of the Bible's use of grace, it is bestowed by God toward finite humans.

Theologians distinguish common grace from special grace—a difference of type rather than degree or quantity. While God's special grace pertains to salvation, common grace signifies the undeserved favor he extends universally to all humans—believers and unbelievers alike—in the form of earthly and material blessings.

The following Scriptures confirm the existence of God's common grace: The psalmist claimed, "The LORD is good to all; he has compassion on all he has made" (Psalm 145:9). Jesus asserted, the "Father in heaven . . . causes his sun to rise on the evil and the good, and sends rain on the righteous and the unrighteous" (Matthew 5:45). He added, "the Most High . . . is kind to the ungrateful and wicked" (Luke 6:35). The apostle James said, "Every good and perfect gift is from above, coming down from the Father of the heavenly lights, who does not change like shifting shadows" (James 1:17).

God's common grace sustains human life (Psalm 36:6; Acts 17:28), upholds the laws and processes of nature (Job 37:13), maintains the moral order in the universe, supplies basic human needs (Psalm 65:9; 104:14; Acts 14:17), restrains evil forces (Romans 13:1-4; 2 Thessalonians 2:6-7), accounts for elements of truth in the arts, sciences, and religion (Exodus 31:2-11; 35:30-35), and delays deserved judgment (Genesis 8:21-22; Romans 2:4). The common grace God extends not only pertains to all that is true, good, and decent in fallen human culture, but also accounts for everything that enhances life. As noted by theologian John Calvin: "All the notable endowments that manifest themselves among unbelievers are gifts of God."[16]

EVERYDAY APPLICATION

Even in the absence of the special grace that saves, Christians should honor truths found in the secular arena: in the arts that enrich our lives, the sciences that expand human possibilities and achievements, medicine that enhances the quality of our lives — in short, truths in the whole of human culture. As Christians, we can and should celebrate and honor all that is true, good, and beautiful across the spectrum of human culture, because these elements come to us from God's bountiful hand. The church father Augustine's statement that all truth is God's truth receives its validity from the reality of God's common grace.

Our honor for these truths extends to respect for the institutions ordained by God in grace for the welfare of all humanity: the institution of marriage (Genesis 2:20-24) and systems of human government (Romans 13:1-2), as well as educational institutions and systems of health care. These gifts of God enrich the lives of all people. Further, because the harmoniously functioning created order is a gift of God's common grace, we must care for the planet by using resources wisely for the glory of God and the good of all. The Creator summons people everywhere to "subdue" the creation, not to spoil it; to "rule over" it, not ruin it (Genesis 1:28).

Because God in his grace deals bountifully with all humans,

---

16. John Calvin, *Institutes of the Christian Religion*, 3.14.2.

people everywhere—particularly Christian believers—should respond in kind by dealing benevolently and graciously with others. As Jesus commanded, "Be merciful, just as your Father is merciful" (Luke 6:36). The apostle Paul echoed, "Therefore, as we have opportunity, let us do good to all people, especially to those who belong to the family of believers" (Galatians 6:10).

Through his gift of common grace, God certifies that he is universally present to the world, even if the world doesn't universally acknowledge him. The omnipresent God of creation is a God of goodness and bounty. His undeserved gifts provided in common grace can help draw the hearts of unbelievers to the bountiful Giver in heartfelt repentance and faith (Romans 2:4).

FOR FURTHER READING
Richard Mouw, *He Shines in All That's Fair.* Eerdmans, 2001.

— BRUCE DEMAREST

GRACE, MEANS OF

EVERYDAY DEFINITION
The means of grace are the ways that God communicates and conveys his grace. Traditionally, the sacraments or church ordinances including baptism and the Lord's Supper have been regarded as the means through which the triune God communicates his grace to his people. For example, baptism reminds believers of the grace of regeneration, forgiveness, and spiritual union with Christ, while the Lord's Supper is a sign of the grace of Christ's suffering, atoning death, resurrection, and second coming.

God communicates his grace through nonsacramental means as well. These include preaching, prayer, Bible study, fellowship, and so on. Preaching is a means of grace because God's living Word is conveyed through it. Prayer can be a means of grace because through prayer Christians can have fellowship with the triune God and experience God's grace of provision and providence. Bible study is another means of grace; when Christians study the Bible in depth, they can absorb spiritual food for growth in God's grace. Fellowship with other believers can be a significant means of grace; through spiritual fellowship with other Christians, Christians can experience God's grace of edification and encouragement.

EVERYDAY APPLICATION

We should realize that God provides us with several means of his grace for our spiritual benefits. This provision is totally based on God's sovereign grace and love for us. As Christians, we should be passionate in employing these means of grace for both building up the corporate body of Christ, and for helping our individual spiritual growth. For example, we should understand the significance of the Lord's Supper and its role in communicating God's grace. If we truly want to obey the Lord's command to "do this in remembrance of me," we should practice it as often as possible. The Lord's Supper can be a great occasion for spiritual renewal and rededication because it reminds us of Christ's sacrificing love and care for us.

Further, we should be passionate in employing other means of grace such as preaching, prayer, Bible study, and fellowship. In particular, we should learn how to pray individually and corporately in order that both the community of faith and individual Christians may grow and become mature in Christ.

FOR FURTHER READING

Ralph L. Underwood, *Pastoral Care and the Means of Grace*. Augsburg Fortress, 1993.

Philip Yancey, *What's So Amazing About Grace?* Zondervan, 2002.

— SUNG WOOK CHUNG

GRACE, SPECIAL

EVERYDAY DEFINITION

Special grace refers to God's unmerited kindness and favor bestowed as a free gift according to his good pleasure. Through his special grace he forgives sins, regenerates, justifies, empowers, and sanctifies his people. Special grace is the grand empowerment from God that allows sinners to repent, trust Christ, receive the gift of eternal life, and grow in him.

Special grace forms the very seedbed of salvation made possible through Christ and made known through the gospel.

Grace is so central to the redemptive story of the Bible that the Hebrew words for grace (*hēn, hesed*) occur 60 and 250 times respectively in the Old Testament. The corresponding Greek word (*charis*) occurs 155 times in the New Testament—a hundred times in the letters of the apostle Paul alone.

The backdrop of special grace in the Bible is the fallen nature of humanity because of sin and our inability to extricate ourselves from this condition. Scripture tells us that the mind of the sinner is spiritually blind (2 Corinthians 4:4), that the will is dead to spiritual concerns (Ephesians 2:1,5), and that the whole person is alienated from Creator and Redeemer (Colossians 1:21). Only the grace of God can reverse the deadening effects of sin and draw people toward God. Paul wrote, "For it is by grace you have been saved, through faith—and this is not from yourselves, it is the gift of God—not by works, so that no one can boast" (Ephesians 2:8-9, TNIV). Special grace heals the wounds of depravity, illumines the sinful mind, and frees the will to embrace Christ and receive his gift of salvation. Special grace means that God initiates the first movement to salvation: "I will give them a heart to know me, that I am the LORD" (Jeremiah 24:7).

Special grace is a rich concept that possesses the following shades of meaning:

- Grace is an attitude or disposition that is part of God's character; because of this quality, he shows unmerited favor to rebellious sinners (Ephesians 1:5-6).
- Grace accounts for the whole plan of salvation (Romans 3:24).
- Grace is a power or energy from God that renews the human heart (Acts 18:27; James 4:6).
- Grace is the new state that believers enter by faith (Romans 5:2).
- Special grace is mediated exclusively through Jesus Christ and the gospel: "For the law was given through Moses; grace and truth came through Jesus Christ" (John 1:17).

EVERYDAY APPLICATION

Since grace is God's free gift, we recognize that all human efforts to achieve God's favor count for nothing. No amount of law-keeping or good works can commend sinners to God. Jesus, the personal embodiment of special grace, taught: "I am the way and the truth and the life. No one comes to the Father except through me" (John 14:6).

It's a matter of urgency that we experience the reality of special grace firsthand. As we surrender our hearts to God and his grace we find that we become morally renewed as new creatures in Christ. We become freed from the bondage of sin—from destructive and compulsive behavior patterns as well as from enslaving addictions. In addition, when we go through seasons of adversity, failure, or guilt, we are invited to come before God to find grace sufficient to meet our every need: "Let us then approach God's throne of grace with confidence, so that we may receive mercy and find grace to help us in our time of need" (Hebrews 4:16, TNIV).

As Christians, our appropriate response to God's gift of special grace and its resulting gift of salvation through Christ is to open our hearts each day to receive the abundance of God's mercy and grace. Only special grace empowers us to live obedient, fruitful, and virtuous lives. By grace through faith we become Christians, and by grace through faith we live as Christians.

Because the word grace also bears the meaning "thanks" or "gratitude," we should continually be expressing our gratitude to God for the special grace that makes all things new and beautiful. Having been touched by grace, we should thank and praise God that he has brought us to Christ and made us worthy to be his children and servants. Every blessing associated with the kingdom of God is bound up in the grace of Jesus Christ.

FOR FURTHER READING

Jonathan Edwards, *Treatise on Grace*. James Clarke & Co., 1971.
Donald Guthrie, ed., *New Testament Theology*. InterVarsity, 1981.
Philip Yancey, *What's So Amazing About Grace?* Zondervan, 1997.

— BRUCE DEMAREST

HEALING

EVERYDAY DEFINITION

Healing is an expression of God's ultimate intent for humanity. People are made by God, but marred by sin, and they need the healing touch of God as a part of their re-creation into the image of God. The Bible words associated with healing mean to cure, to make whole, or to return to health.

Because everyone dies, all healing is temporary. One exception is the sense that salvation can be seen as the comprehensive and for-all-time healing of the whole person. A key New Testament Greek term for healing is the same word (*sozo*) translated as "saved." Salvation is a process of redemption where we are saved, being saved, and will be saved.

The experience of healing is a central part of the reconciling activity of God in the world. Healing is a sign of divine mercy that moves through the world and guides it toward its final perfection. This is true whether healing takes place by sharing chicken soup, performing delicate surgery, or laying on of hands in Christian gatherings.

Healing in the Bible takes into view the whole person and the comprehensive nature of human beings, involving the body, soul, mind, spirit, emotions, social relationships, etc. Healing the sick is seen throughout the Bible. The Old Testament, for example, records the healing of Moses' leprous hand (Exodus 4:6,7,30); leprosy being cured (Numbers 12:10-15; 2 Kings 5:10-27); healing through the bronze serpent (Numbers 21:9); two sons raised from the dead (1 Kings 17:17-24; 2 Kings 4:32-37); Elisha's bones revive the dead (2 Kings 13:21), etc. While the Old Testament says it is "the LORD who heals" (Exodus 15:26), it's also clear that healing includes a divine-human partnership where humans participate in God's work of healing. For example, intercession brings healing (Numbers 12:10-15); repentance leads to healing (1 Kings 13:1-6); Jeremiah prays for healing (Jeremiah 17:14); and words bring healing (Proverbs 12:18; 13:17; 15:30; 16:24).

In the New Testament, the Gospels are full of stories of healing (for example, see Matthew 4:23-25). Clearly, Jesus placed a high priority on healing. Some Bible commentators believe that Jesus healed the sick as a sign to authenticate himself as Messiah. While healing was certainly a sign, the healing itself was crucial too. Reading the grateful responses of those healed and their families demonstrates that the healing was valued too, not just the sign.

From the first announcement of Jesus' ministry, it's clear that healing was central (Luke 4:16-21) to the New Testament revelation of God. When John the Baptist asked Jesus "if he was the one," Jesus replied, "go tell John the sick are being healed" (Matthew 11:3-5). Jesus' healings and his explanations for them (4:23; 12:28) make plain that healing is evidence of the presence of the kingdom of God among human society. In the most simple terms, the kingdom God is best understood as God's rule and reign. It's the extension of his will. When the sick, infirm, or demonized are healed, it's an expression of God's intention to restore all humanity to health and wholeness.

Jesus sent out his first followers with the command to heal the sick (Matthew 10:1; Luke 9:1-2; 10:9), and they did so (Acts 3:6; 5:15; 8:6-13; 9:32,35,38; 14:10). Following this pattern, the early church believed healing to be part of its mission. The apostle Paul mentioned healing as a gift of the Spirit (1 Corinthians 12:9). This gift isn't something a Christian owns. The gift is actually what the healed person experiences. The one praying for healing is simply a conduit for the healing.

Healing in the New Testament includes a wide variety of ailments: deafness and muteness (Mark 7:31-37); blindness (Mark 8:22-26; Matthew 20:29; Acts 22:12-13); resuscitation (Luke 7:11-18; 8:41; John 11:38-44; Matthew 9:23; Mark 5:23; Luke 8:41; Acts 9:40; 20:10); debilitating swelling (Luke 14:1-6); leprosy (Luke 5:12; 17:11-19; Matthew 8:2; Mark 1:40); healing from demonic causes (Matthew 8:28; 12:22; 15:28; Luke 4:33; 8:26; 11:14; Mark 1:23; 5:1); female disorders (Matthew 9:20); mental illness (Matthew 17:14); fever and dysentery (Acts 28:8); various skeletal and muscular issues, including paralysis (Matthew 8:6; 9:2; 12:10; Luke 13:11-17; John 5:1-9; Acts 14:10); and fever (Matthew 8:14).

The phrase "divine healing" is often wrongly used to refer to healing done by God alone, without human involvement. This too-tight definition has inadvertently led some to fail to see that God is also at work through friends, medical personnel, or in other divine-human partnerships. The great progress in the field of medicine, including complementary and alternative medicine to counteract disease and promote healing, is also a healing gift from God. Divine healing, when it involves humans, is no less *divine*, and no less *healing*.

EVERYDAY APPLICATION

Given the prominence of healing in the Bible, we can easily come to the conclusion that healing is important to God. Further, we can see that

God still heals today, and that healing is a grace from God prized by the sick and their loved ones. Yet, many people still wonder about several issues surrounding healing in today's world:

- We might question, "Why do some people who seem to deserve healing die, while others who seem to be less deserving are healed only to go right back to behaviors that caused the sickness in the first place?" There is no obvious and easy answer to this question. The best we can say is that healing is complex, and that under God sickness, and even death, in this world is not the last word.

- We also might question the cause of sickness: "Does personal or family sin cause disease?" As a practical matter, the answer is a simple "yes." For example, a child grows up around massive amounts of second-hand smoke and develops respiratory illness, or a baby born to a woman using drugs has immune system suppression. However, Jesus teaches us that we shouldn't push this too far, because as humans we don't have the ability to perfectly judge who is sick because of sin or not. On the other hand, with caution, we can use the discernment we all possess to help others who are truly sick because of sin. Maybe unbridled anger or unforgiveness is causing ulcers or headaches. Healing in this manner must be done without a judgmental attitude (Matthew 7:3-5) and with sincere love.

- We might wonder if complete healing in this life is guaranteed by the atonement offered by Jesus. Although that might sound like a theological debate, it's actually a very practical matter. If we are all healed by the beatings Jesus took (Isaiah 53), shouldn't all Christians live in total health? However, if we understand the healing we see in the Bible to be an expression of the kingdom—which is inaugurated, but not yet completed—then we can comprehend why all Christians aren't healed. Jesus didn't heal everyone he came into contact with. God deals with each of us individually. No formula guarantees that if we pray, we will be healed.

- Based on the notion that healing is assured by the atonement, some Christians have picked up the hurtful and unhelpful practice of accusing sick people of not having enough faith to be healed. Surely because of the life, death, and resurrection of Jesus, all followers of Christ will be healed in the kingdom to come. But while we live in this time between the times, Christians will continue to battle with sickness.

- Others, thinking divine healing is promised, conclude that taking medicine or undergoing medical care is inappropriate for Christians. Nothing in Scripture suggests we should take this stand. In fact, ancient forms of medicine are commended in the Bible (see 1 Timothy 5:23).

What about the role of faith in healing? The Bible is clear that faith does indeed have a role in healing (Matthew 8:10; 9:20-22; 15:28; Mark 10:52; Luke 17:17; John 4:46-53). Faith is often commended. Doubt and cynicism, even when sincere, are never commended or said to affect healing (Matthew 13:58; Mark 6:6; 14:39; 16:14). So while our faith is crucial to receive healing, our faith should never be used against God, as if we were trying to twist his arm or back him into a corner. Our faith is powerful and God loves it when we act in faith, yet our faith never challenges God's sovereign authority.

FOR FURTHER READING
Wayne Grudem, *Systematic Theology*. Zondervan, 1994.
John Wimber, *Power Healing*. HarperCollins, 1991.
Francis McNutt, *Healing*. Ave Maria Press, 1999.

— TODD HUNTER

HEAVEN

EVERYDAY DEFINITION
In Christian theology, "heaven" denotes both the abode of God and the final blessed state of those who are saved.

In the Old Testament, "heaven" or "heavens" refers to the atmosphere where the birds fly (Genesis 1:20,26; 6:7); to the cosmos containing the sun, moon, and stars (Genesis 1:14-16); or to the dwelling place of God (1 Kings 8:30). This last aspect is the most important theologically to the New Testament and to the church. Also, the abode of God isn't entirely to be conceived in terms of place because "heaven and heaven of heavens cannot contain [God]" (1 Kings 8:27, KJV). As the Creator of space and time, God is not bound by space and time.

Angels, as messengers and servants of God, travel from heaven to earth and back (Matthew 28:2; Luke 2:15). But Satan is eventually cast out of heaven (Luke 10:18; John 12:31; Revelation 12:10,12), after which there is only pure goodness in heaven.

Heaven as the final state of the righteous is a later development. The central doctrine of the afterlife in the New Testament is the resurrection to a glorious body (for the righteous) at the return of Christ (1 Corinthians 15). Still, the concept of heaven as the final state for those who are saved also has its beginnings in the New Testament. The righteous who are persecuted are promised that their reward is in heaven (Matthew 5:12). The true citizenship of Christians is in heaven (Philippians 3:20) as is their inheritance (1 Peter 1:4).

In later Christian thought, the chief joy in heaven of the saved is believed to result from a greater comprehension of and union with God. In our mortal bodies, we only have a limited capacity to understand and know God and Christ. But in heaven, we shall comprehend Christ as Christ is, for we shall be like him (1 John 3:2). As the apostle Paul said, "For now we see through a glass, darkly; but then face to face" (1 Corinthians 13:12, KJV).

A secondary joy in heaven is that of being in the company of all others who are saved. During the nineteenth century, a popular conception of heaven arose that stressed analogies to all kinds of earthly pleasures as the main reason why heaven was joyful. Theologians now largely acknowledge this to be a mistake. Rather, our chief joy is in God, but this joy is magnified by sharing it with others who have received his gift of salvation and eternal life.

EVERYDAY APPLICATION

We all desire happiness, but true and full happiness is impossible in this life. As Thomas Aquinas pointed out, our desire for happiness is an awareness in us that our purpose or end is union with the supreme good, God. We become more happy in this life the closer our union with God. And we can know that in the life to come we shall experience true and full happiness forever.

Heaven also enables us to live as we should in this life. Righteousness doesn't always seem to be worthwhile on earth. Paul acknowledged, "If in this life only we have hope in Christ, we are of all men most miserable" (1 Corinthians 15:19, KJV). The knowledge that an eternal life of happiness in union with God awaits the righteous enables us to seek a closer union with God in this life.

Finally, the knowledge that God is in heaven enables us to realize that reality is greater than what we see around us. If we are on God's side, then no matter what obstacles confront us and what enemies surround us, "those who are with us are more than those who are with them" (2 Kings 6:16). God providentially watches over us from heaven now and we shall be with him in heaven forever.

FOR FURTHER READING

Thomas Aquinas, Chapters 82–87, 92, 95–96 of *Summa Contra Gentiles*. University of Notre Dame Press, 1975.

H. Bietenard, "Heaven, Ascend, Above" in *The New International Dictionary of New Testament Theology*. Colin Brown, ed. Zondervan, 1986.

C. McDannell and B. Lang, *Heaven: A History*. Yale University Press, 1988.

— TIM FINLAY

HELL

EVERYDAY DEFINITION

According to Scripture, hell is the fiery and dark final place of torment prepared for those condemned to eternal punishment at the Last Judgment. In hell, the unrepentant suffer eternally the wrath and displeasure of God (Matthew 8:12; 13:42; 22:13; 25:41; 2 Thessalonians 1:7-9; 2 Peter 3:7; Revelation 20:11-15). As severe as this doctrine seems, most Christians have understood the existence of hell as reflecting God's just display of his holy wrath against those who refuse to repent of their sin and accept God's forgiveness and salvation through Jesus Christ.

The Old Testament explicitly teaches little about hell. The word *sheol* (translated as *hades* in the Septuagint) occurs sixty-six times in the Old Testament and refers to the final abode of all the dead, without moral distinction. The only Old Testament passage that clearly distinguishes the destinies of the righteous and the wicked is Daniel 12:1-2. The Greek word *gehenna* (hell) translates the Hebrew "Valley of Ben Hinnom," which was located south of Jerusalem (2 Kings 23:10). The valley was associated with child sacrifice (2 Chronicles 28:3; Jeremiah 7:31-32) and became Jerusalem's fiery garbage dump. The prophet Isaiah draws on this grotesque image in his eschatological depiction of the new heavens and earth: "And they will go out and look on the dead bodies of those who rebelled against me; their worm will not die, nor will their fire be quenched, and they will be loathsome to the whole human race" (Isaiah 66:24, TNIV).

New Testament authors used this graphic imagery to describe the place of future retribution. Jesus spoke more on the subject of hell than any other biblical person, graphically referring to hell as a lake of fire, a place of outer darkness, a place where there is weeping and gnashing of teeth, and where the worm never dies (Matthew 13:42,50; 22:13; 25:41; Mark 9:47-48). Various New Testament writers wrote of the penalty and the condition of hell as unending (Romans 2:5; 2 Thessalonians 1:9; 2 Peter 2:17; Jude 13).

Throughout the history of the church, debates by Christians seeking to be faithful to biblical teaching on hell have revolved around two issues: the *nature* and the *duration* of the punishment. Nature refers to the question of whether the Bible's descriptions of hell are literal or figurative, while duration refers to the question of if the punishment of hell is temporary or eternal. Whether we understand the images of a "lake of fire" (Revelation 19:20; 20:10,14-15; 21:8) and "utter darkness" (Matthew 8:12; 22:13; 25:30) literally or figuratively, the sobering picture that emerges of hell is a condition of conscious and unending torment away from the blessings of God's presence.

EVERYDAY APPLICATION
How can Christians respond appropriately to the biblical doctrine of hell?

We need to preach and teach about hell in ways that are faithful to biblical teaching. As noted, Jesus spoke more about the reality of hell than any other biblical person. Christian teaching about hell clearly and compellingly glorifies God and can motivate believers and unbelievers alike to avoid righteous punishment and seek God's mercy. These positive outcomes take place when teaching about hell illustrates and confirms the justice, holiness, and righteousness of God. If we fail to teach about hell, we leave unbelievers uncertain about their eternal destiny.

A robust doctrine of hell should spur us as believers to holy and righteous living. This means we will demonstrate our gratitude to Jesus Christ for his gracious salvation. We all deserve the just punishment of hell, and only because Jesus paid the penalty for our sins can we escape its endless horrors. Ingratitude is a sign of an unregenerate person (Romans 1:21).

The terrors of hell should lead us to renewed missionary and evangelistic zeal. Originally, God designed hell for Satan and his angels (Matthew 25:42; Revelation 20:10). However, hell is the ultimate destination of those who reject Jesus as Savior and Lord, which should serve as a lively incentive to earnest and faithful evangelistic outreach. God takes no delight in the death of the wicked (Ezekiel 18:23,32), and neither should we.

Scripture teaches the sober truth that hell exists. We need to speak soberly and with caution concerning the details of hell, while faithfully bringing the full gospel message to a needy world.

FOR FURTHER READING
William Crockett, ed., *Four Views on Hell*. Zondervan, 1996.
Christopher W. Morgan and Robert A. Peterson, eds., *Hell Under Fire*. Zondervan, 2004.

— ERIKA MOORE

HERESY

EVERYDAY DEFINITION
Heresy is the word used by the Christian church to describe beliefs that diverge in some way from fundamental Christian truth. This presupposes two ideas: (1) the Bible reveals core truths about God, creation, sin, and redemption and (2) the Christian church has been

able to recognize and articulate those truths.

Heresy is usually distinguished from error or schism. Individuals and churches might fall into erroneous beliefs, but they typically aren't considered heretical until they willfully and persistently reject or attempt to change the central truths held by the Christian church as a whole. Similarly, churches might divide over various questions of practice. This is usually called schism rather than heresy because the divided churches might both still hold to the core Christian beliefs that constitute truth.

The Greek word for heresy, *hairesis,* has the basic meaning of "choice" or "opinion." As used in the New Testament, it began as a term to identify a particular "school of thought" within a larger group, such as the Sadducees or Pharisees in Judaism (Acts 5:17; 15:5). However, as the early church grew and began to pay greater attention to what they should believe, the term heresy began to be applied to aberrant beliefs about Christ and salvation (1 Corinthians 11:19; Galatians 5:20; Titus 3:9-10; 2 Peter 2:1). This practice set the trajectory for its present understanding.

Historically, as interpretive questions about the biblical text (particularly about Christ) arose and heresies developed, Christians worked to clarify what they believed. As the church prayerfully studied the Scriptures in response, they developed a small "rule of faith" so Christians could distinguish basic Christian truth from heresy. This "rule" represents the church's core beliefs and authoritative interpretation of the Old and New Testaments, and it is summarized in the Apostles' and Nicene Creeds. While disagreements arise among Christian churches over biblical interpretation, the Creeds represent what they hold together at their core. As such, the church as a whole has judged any teaching contrary to the Creeds as heresy.

The Christian church has had an uneasy relationship with people who have been judged as heretics. The New Testament writings of John and Paul show us that, from the earliest days, the church struggled to relate to those who have held diverging points of view (Galatians 1:8-9; 1 Timothy 1:3-5,19-20; 2 John 10-11; Revelation 2:14-15). Throughout the centuries, the Christian church has tended to consider it a sacred duty to banish those who persisted in holding heretical beliefs. However, others in the church have been more tolerant. They believe heretics play a necessary role in helping the church clarify and develop their understanding of fundamental Christian truth.

EVERYDAY APPLICATION

The history of the Christian church's work to define heresy reminds us that beliefs do matter. At the heart of the Christian faith lies a conviction that some things are true and others are false. It matters that there truly is a God like the one described in the historic Christian creeds. It matters that God came into human history in the person of Jesus Christ. It matters that Jesus represents to us both the ideal for all humanity and the way that humans may be reconciled to God and become what God intended.

The Christian church's concerns about heresy also remind us of another historic conviction that lies at the heart of our faith. As Christians, we don't hold our faith in individualistic isolation. When we come to faith in Jesus Christ, we join a community that stretches across cultures, races, and ethnicities, and that stretches back across time.

Similarly, heresy reminds us as individual believers that it's good to examine our faith, to learn from and respect the history of beliefs that anchor our Christian faith in history, and to practice our faith in a living relationship with the whole community of fellow believers across the world and throughout history.

FOR FURTHER READING

Maurice Wiles, "Heresy" in *The Oxford Companion to Christian Thought*. Adrian Hastings, Alistair Mason, Hugh Pyper, eds. Oxford University Press, 2000.

Ben Quash and Michael Ward, ed., *Heresies and How to Avoid Them: Why It Matters What Christians Believe*. Hendrickson Publishers, 2008.

Alister McGrath, *"I Believe": Exploring the Apostles' Creed*. InterVarsity, 1998.

— DAVID WRIGHT

HOLY SPIRIT, NATURE OF THE

EVERYDAY DEFINITION

Defining the nature of the Holy Spirit involves taking a step that the Holy Spirit himself rarely takes in the course of the Bible. Many Christian writers through the ages have called the Holy Spirit the self-effacing member of the Trinity, because he always points to the Father and the Son. Even though the Holy Spirit inspired the Scriptures, lives within us, and even now brings new life into those who place their trust in Jesus Christ, the Holy Spirit takes the focus off himself.

During the beginning of the Charismatic and Pentecostal movements in the late nineteenth and early twentieth centuries, many Christians began to realize that they had focused too little on the third person of the Trinity, even though he is to be worshipped and glorified along with the Father and Son. Thankfully, the Holy Spirit has never become disinterested in us and our salvation.

As the earliest Christians wrestled with trying to understand the nature of the Spirit, they didn't question the Spirit's divinity (as many did with the Son's); rather, they wondered if the Holy Spirit is a person like the Father and Son, or if the Spirit is merely an impersonal "force." The Spirit's own deference to the Father and the Son, which demonstrates for us perfect submission and love, provided fodder for such arguments.

As we look at Scripture, we can see what the Holy Spirit says about himself. In the Bible, we see that not only is the Holy Spirit personal, the personal-ness of the Spirit is a significant part of the good news of the gospel. When Jesus ascended to the Father, he promised to ask the Father to send the Spirit of Truth (John 14:16). The promise is that the Spirit will be known by us, which is an extension of our knowing God through Christ. Jesus even said that it was better for him to leave because the Spirit is able be in the presence of all believers (John 16:7).

Further, if we know Jesus, we also know the Father (John 14:7) and the Spirit (14:17). This is the extension of God's mutual indwelling, because nothing of the Father or Spirit is hidden from the Son, and likewise for the other persons in the Trinity. When we meet Jesus we also "know" the Father and the Holy Spirit. Interestingly, Jesus promised that he would always be with us (Matthew 28:20). Yet how is that possible when he has ascended to the right hand of the Father? It's possible because the Holy Spirit knows the Son and brings the presence of the Son to those he dwells within. The Spirit is God's presence with his people.

One of the statements Christians have always affirmed is that God is omnipresent (everywhere in the world). While we can't limit omnipresence to the Holy Spirit, functionally he is the active presence of God in our world. Because the Spirit's nature is to share the triune God's life with us, the personal-ness of the Spirit is essential for the good news of knowing God.

Another important element of the Holy Spirit's functional nature is that he is also the convicting agent of God in the world (John 16:8-11). As the Spirit of Truth, he reveals the truth about God to both those who believe in Christ and to the world that cannot "receive" him. This also ties the Spirit into the rebirthing work of the triune God. Only when the Spirit brings about conviction can conversion take place. In conversion, through the work of the Holy Spirit, an individual becomes a new creation and the process of transformation begins (John 3:3).

The great promise of the present and coming kingdom of God is that God will be with his people (Revelation 21–22). The apostle Paul said that the Holy Spirit is the down payment of that promise. The Holy Spirit brings the presence of God right into our lives. This indwelling means that believers really are the temple of God—the place where we meet God.

EVERYDAY APPLICATION

Christians might argue over whether or not it's appropriate to pray to the Holy Spirit. However, it's clear that our recognition of the Spirit's presence in our lives is essential to our prayers, to our transformation, and to our knowing God's love in a very real and personal way. When we think just of the Father or only of the Son, we can too easily make God "out there," distant from us. When we remember that the Holy Spirit dwells within us, we realize that he brings new life daily into our old bodies of sin. We remember that God is never far away, but always present. We can know the love of the Father and the suffering of the Son because the Holy Spirit shares with us the life of the triune God in our very beings.

As children of God the Father, through the work of the Son, we can and should experience transformation and change in our lives. We must cooperate with the Spirit if we want to bear good fruit, which is the will of the Father for our lives in Christ. Therefore, the Christian life is the life of the Spirit in us.

FOR FURTHER READING

J. I. Packer, *Keep in Step with the Spirit.* Baker, 2005.
Sinclair Ferguson, *The Holy Spirit (Contours of Christian Theology).* InterVarsity, 1997.

— CHRISTOPHER MORTON

HOLY SPIRIT, WORK OF THE

EVERYDAY DEFINITION

The biblical revelation of God, as understood and taught by the church, is that God is a Trinity — one God eternally coexisting in three persons. The Holy Spirit is often called the third person of the Trinity. This doesn't mean that the Spirit is third in importance, but is called third as a matter of traditional numbering.

The Scriptures make clear the deity of the Holy Spirit. He is called God (Acts 5:3-4); he is joined with the Father and Son (Matthew 28:19; 2 Corinthians 13:14; 1 John 5:7); he is eternal (Hebrews 9:14); omnipotent (Luke 1:35); omniscient (1 Corinthians 2:10-11); omnipresent (Psalm 139:7-13); sovereign (1 Corinthians 12:6,11). The Holy Spirit makes present and real the work of God in the world. This is especially true after the death and resurrection of Jesus. The Spirit is the promised continuing presence of Jesus among the people of God.

Sadly, the Holy Spirit has too often become a controversial doctrine rather than a highly sought and prized presence, God's ongoing provision of himself to never leave believers to feel alone, orphaned, or spiritually impotent (John 14:16-26). The Father-Creator and the Son-Savior have sometimes dominated the thinking and imagination of contemporary Christians — almost to the point of ignoring the person and work of the Holy Spirit.

Perhaps this has occurred for at least two reasons: (1) Some people are afraid of falling into excess regarding the Spirit; (2) The modern, scientific, material worldview has little capacity for interacting with a non-bodily, personal power. The rational, empirical view has trouble comprehending this Person who has no body, and yet as God, is ultimate power. When this lack of comprehension occurs, the next step is often a rejection of any meaningful interaction with the Holy Spirit.

In contrast, the story of Scripture reveals that the Holy Spirit interacts personally with humanity. From creation (Genesis 1:1-2; Psalm 104:40) until the new heavens and the new earth (Revelation 22:17), the Holy Spirit equips various agents of God (Numbers 11:16-17; 16:24-30; Judges 14:1-6; Micah 3:8); is active in the birth of Jesus (Luke 1:35); is a dynamic actor in redemption (John 3:3,5; Romans 15:16; 2 Thessalonians 2:13); enables the writing of Scripture (2 Timothy 3:14-17; 2 Peter 1:19-21); teaches and leads into truth (John 16:8,13; 1 John 2:20); and gives discernment (1 Corinthians 2:10-16; 1 John 4:1-6). The Spirit fills, empowers, and animates Christian life (John 14:15-31; Acts 2:1-41; Romans 8:1-27; 14:17; 1 Corinthians 2:6-16; Galatians 5:16-26). The Spirit produces the character of Christ (Galatians 5:22-23), and gifts the church for service to others—both in the church and outside the church (Romans 12:3-8; Ephesians 4:7-13; 1 Corinthians 12:3-11). The Spirit leads and guides the work of the church (Acts 8:29; 13:2,4; 20:17-28).

Means for meaningful interactions with the Holy Spirit are found throughout the Bible. Scripture depicts the Holy Spirit with attributes of a person: speaking (Acts 28:25); teaching (John 14:26); comforting (Acts 9:31); recognizing and helping our weaknesses (Romans 8:26); being grieved (Ephesians 4:30); being resisted (Acts 7:51); and able to be lied to (Acts 5:3).

EVERYDAY APPLICATION

Various Christian traditions have understood the relationship between Christians and the Holy Spirit in different ways. Some say that receiving the Spirit occurs simultaneously with conversion. Others see initiation into an interactive life with the Holy Spirit as a second event that occurs after conversion. Among this second group are those who believe that the initial sign of receiving the Spirit is the gift of speaking in tongues.

The book of Acts contains five instances where individuals or groups are filled with the Spirit. In two of the cases they spoke in tongues (Acts 2:4; 10:46). In one case they spoke in tongues and prophesied (Acts 19:6). In one case we aren't told what happened; something occurred that was visible or audible (Acts 8:14-19). In the apostle Paul's case, he received healing and his commissioning from the Spirit (Acts 9:17). As a result, we can say that when we are filled with the Spirit, the manifestations of the Spirit will be varied. The crucial understanding—no matter what the first sign is—is knowing that God is truly with us, empowering us to live a Spirit-filled life for the sake of serving others as the cooperative friends of God.

As we desire to live a Spirit-filled life, we might ask, "How can I be filled with the Holy Spirit?" If we take the position that we receive the Spirit at conversion, then receiving the Holy Spirit is better seen as actualizing what we already possess. If we take the position that we receive the Spirit after conversion, then it is a fresh experience. In either case, the way to receive is to simply ask—in faith, sincerely desiring to live a life guided and empowered by God, the Holy Spirit.

God gives the Spirit because Spirit-power is essential to life as a Christian—for life as an ambassador of the kingdom (2 Corinthians 5:17-21). While human effort is part of life as ambassadors of the kingdom, kingdom work is never merely human. When we ignore the person and work of the Spirit, arrogance, burnout, and frustration directed at others is sure to follow. The giving of the Spirit allows Christians to be the people of God, who in their own way are what Jesus was to the world: bringing a touch of the future consummated kingdom into the present so that others are helped, healed, and saved.

The Holy Spirit is not *in* the life of the church; he does not merely create the life of the church. He *is* the life of the church. He is the animating, energizing, empowering, gift-giving, fruit-bearing power that makes the church real and alive. There is no church as we think of it without the Holy Spirit. The gift of the Spirit creates, leads, and guides the work of the church and those of us who make up the church. The Holy Spirit enables us to be the cooperative people of God in the world, empowering us to continue the work of Jesus, to spread his victory over the forces of evil in the world—announcing, embodying, and demonstrating the rule and reign of God on behalf of all fallen creation, the least, the last, and those gone astray from the purposes of God.

How do we experience the Spirit as John and Jesus promised (Matthew 3:11; Luke 24:49; Acts 1:4-5)? We do so with a heart willing to obey and with childlike determination to learn as we go. We *practice* the presence of the Spirit. We learn to pay attention, to be alert to him, trusting that he will teach us to interact with him in ways that are good for others and honoring of God.

FOR FURTHER READING

Wayne Grudem, *Systematic Theology.* Zondervan, 1994.

Gordon, D. Fee, *Paul, the Spirit and the People of God.* Hendrickson Publishers, 1996.

Gordon D. Fee, *God's Empowering Presence: The Holy Spirit in the Letters of Paul.* Hendrickson Publishers, 1994.

— TODD HUNTER

HOPE

EVERYDAY DEFINITION

Hope refers to the object that leads to a desire or a promise. The Bible lists these objects that are the hope of those who follow God:

- The bedrock object of hope for Christians is God. The psalmist claimed, "Blessed are those whose help is the God of Jacob, whose hope is in the LORD their God" (Psalm 146:5, TNIV). The apostle Paul added, "To them God has chosen to make known among the Gentiles the glorious riches of this mystery, which is Christ in you, the hope of glory" (Colossians 1:27). God the Father, God the Son, and God the Spirit are the objects of our hope as believers.

- God's Word is also a fertile object of our hope: "May those who fear you rejoice when they see me, for I have put my hope in your word" (Psalm 119:74); "I wait for the LORD, my whole being waits, and in his word I put my hope" (Psalm 130:5, TNIV).

- Although we already enter into the reality of eternal life in the present, it should be an object for our ultimate hope. Paul wrote of himself: "Paul, a servant of God and an apostle of Jesus Christ to further the faith of God's elect and their knowledge of the truth that leads to godliness — in the hope of eternal life, which God, who does not lie, promised before the beginning of time" (Titus 1:1-2, TNIV). Eternal life has already come to believers in Christ, but it will come to us fully when Jesus comes again.

- Christ's second coming should be an object of our hope. The apostle John stated: "Dear friends, now we are children of God, and what we will be has not yet been made known. But we know that when Christ appears, we shall be like him, for we shall see him as he is. All who have this hope in him purify themselves, just as he is pure" (1 John 3:2-3, TNIV). When Jesus Christ returns again to earth, our salvation will then be complete.

EVERYDAY APPLICATION

As Christians, we encounter a multitude of difficulties, troubles, and distresses in our journey through this world. The hope and promise of God carry us through the trying times in the following ways:

- When we place wholehearted hope in the living God, he enables us to endure all kinds of hardships and adversities. Paul wrote, "We remember before our God and Father your work produced by faith, your labor prompted by love, and your endurance inspired by hope in our Lord Jesus Christ" (1 Thessalonians 1:3, TNIV).
- As we embrace the hope of eternal life and the resurrection of our bodies, God fortifies us to face physical death with courage, hope, and confidence.
- When fellow Christians confront the harsh realities of life, such as a serious illness or the death of family members and close friends, we can encourage and comfort them, reminding them of our mutual hope of eternal life and the resurrection of our mortal bodies.
- When we're equipped with the hope of Jesus' second coming, we can overcome the distressing trials that assail us in this life. In this respect, hope is closely connected with the reality of our Christian faith: "Now faith is being sure of what we hope for and certain of what we do not see" (Hebrews 11:1).

We can be confident that our hope is grounded upon God's promises and his faithfulness to keep what he promises in his Word. All of us can learn how to exercise our hope on the basis of God's faithful character and promises.

FOR FURTHER READING

N. T. Wright, *Surprised by Hope: Rethinking Heaven, the Resurrection, and the Mission of the Church.* HarperOne, 2008.

Nancy Guthrie, *Holding On To Hope: A Pathway Through Suffering to the Heart of God.* Tyndale, 2006.

— SUNG WOOK CHUNG

HUMAN BODY

EVERYDAY DEFINITION

The human body describes the essential physical aspect of human beings during their earthly existence, as well as — following Christ's return and the resurrection of their bodies — in the age to come. The body is the material component of human nature distinct from — but intimately linked with — the immaterial component, commonly called the soul or spirit. Only between physical death and the return of Christ will human existence be disembodied. The soul or spirit will survive death and continue to exist while the body is sloughed off. However, this is an abnormal condition (2 Corinthians 5:1-10).

God creates embodied human beings. This was true of the first man (Genesis 2:7), the first woman (2:22), and of each and every human being since the original creation, as God is intimately involved in fashioning human life from the moment of conception (Psalm 139:13-16). Human beings are created holistically, so that in their earthly existence, their soul and body are an inseparable unity.

Human beings are either male or female (Genesis 1:26-27), which means that gender is a fundamental reality of bodily existence. Human sexuality, a wonderful gift from God, is also a reality for his embodied creatures.

As fallen and sinful, humans are called to salvation through Christ. They are not just "souls to be saved"; the human body is included in this divine work. The apostle Paul wrote, "the Lord is for the body" (1 Corinthians 6:13, NASB), meaning that his completed work of salvation will include bodily resurrection. Paul added, "the body is . . . for the Lord" (verse 13), meaning that Christians are to "glorify God in [their] body" (verse 20, NASB) by yielding it to God for his purposes (Romans 6:12-14), worshipping him (12:1-2), avoiding sexual immorality (1 Corinthians 6:18; 1 Thessalonians 4:3-8), and being holistically sanctified (1 Thessalonians 5:23). In addition, being holy in body means that Christians should engage in physical discipline (1 Timothy 4:8; 1 Corinthians 9:24-27). Even the clothes Christians wear should confirm their profession of godliness (1 Timothy 2:9-10; 1 Peter 3:3-4).

Regrettably, the church hasn't always appreciated the reality of physical embodiment, perhaps because of the negative influence of Platonic philosophy. Plato maintained that the human soul or spirit (being of divine origin) is inherently good, while the human body (being of earthly origin) is inherently bad. Salvation, therefore, would consist of the human spirit's escape from the body, facilitated by focusing on spiritual rather than bodily matters. This philosophy infiltrated the church and resulted in some Christians considering the body and its physical appetites to be a hindrance to spiritual maturity and even the root of human sinfulness. As a result, monastic movements arose that denied legitimate, physically pleasing activities such as eating and drinking certain foods, sleeping and resting comfortably, and engaging in sexual intercourse. At the same time, the church insisted on the goodness of the human body, appealing to God's creation of the physical world, the incarnation of Jesus Christ (which included the Son of God taking on a human body), and the future resurrection of the body.

EVERYDAY APPLICATION

As Christians, having a biblically informed view of life in the human body will encourage us to value the body from conception through eternity. We can live out this value in many practical ways, including:

- Ruling out abortion at the beginning of human existence and euthanasia/physician-assisted suicide at the end of life. God and God alone is the Creator of human life, and he alone decides when that life is over. His human creatures do not

possess this divine prerogative and should not take human
existence into their own hands.

- Being thankful for the gender God created us to be. This
includes avoiding any sense of superiority or inferiority
because we are male or female. Gender differences should be
celebrated, and men and women should learn to enjoy personal
and pure relationships with the other gender.

- Expressing human sexuality lovingly and with respect in the
context of a monogamous marriage relationship between
a husband and a wife. As part of this appropriate view of
sexuality, there should be no hint of sexual immorality.

- Ministering to others as holistic human beings created in the
image of God. This entails treating all people—both Christians
and non-Christians alike—with respect for their inherent
dignity. In addition, we should engage in helping the poor and
marginalized through deeds of mercy, communicating the
gospel of Jesus Christ to all, and discipling other Christians
by addressing their needs—intellectual, emotional, volitional,
physical, educational, and socio-economic.

- Worshipping the Lord with proper physical expressions.
Because we are embodied people, our worship can include
kneeling, prostration, bowing, singing and dancing, and
raising hands in praise, petition, and blessing.

- Resisting sins that are particularly associated with human
embodiment: lust (Matthew 5:27-30), gluttony and
drunkenness (Proverbs 23:20-21), and sloth (Proverbs 6:6-11;
2 Thessalonians 3:6-15).

- Following a regimen of physical discipline, including
regular exercise, proper nutrition, adequate rest and sleep,
and avoidance of body-harming substances. When spiritual
disciplines call for accompanying physical activities like
fasting, solitude, temporary celibacy, and temporarily
withholding other legitimate bodily pleasures, the goal should
always be to increase our spiritual vitality and never the
punishment of our body as an opponent or enemy.

- Standing against the destruction of human life. This includes issues
such as embryonic stem cell research that results in the destruction

of fertilized eggs, experimentation to develop human cloning that results in the destruction of human life, genetic engineering that feeds human pride and greed for the creation of perfect children, and transhumanist experimentation that fuels human autonomy in the development of superhuman beings or cyborgs (man-machine complexes).

• Focusing on our true and ultimate hope: physical resurrection for an eternal embodied existence in the new heavens and new earth.

FOR FURTHER READING
Mary Timothy Prokes, *Toward a Theology of the Body.* Eerdmans, 1996.

— GREGG ALLISON

HUMANS, NATURE OF

EVERYDAY DEFINITION
The perennial human question was posed long ago by the psalmist David: "LORD, what are human beings that you care for them, mere mortals that you think of them?" (Psalm 144:3, TNIV; see also Psalm 8:4). Humans might best be described as a complex mystery. Philosopher Blaise Pascal noted, "How novel, how monstrous, how chaotic, how paradoxical, how prodigious! Judge of all things, feeble earthworm, repository of truth, sink of doubt and error and refuse of the universe!"[17]

Scripture depicts humans as the zenith of God's creative activity, formed in God's image and likeness on the sixth day (Genesis 1:26-27). The manner of Adam's creation offers a clue to his nature: "Then the LORD God formed a man from the dust of the ground and breathed into his nostrils the breath of life, and the man became a living being" (Genesis 2:7, TNIV). God fashioned the first human from the dust of the earth and brought life into his frame by the divine inbreathing. He then formed Eve from Adam's rib (Genesis 2:22). The statement, "they shall be one flesh" (2:24, TNIV) highlights Adam and Eve's essential unity and equality within the marriage relationship.

God's act of breathing life into physical matter represents the

---

17. Blaise Pascal, *Pensées* (New York: Penguin Books, 1966), no. 131.

human person as a unitary being consisting of material and immaterial substances. Jesus gave expression to this fact: "Do not be afraid of those who kill the body but cannot kill the soul" (Mathew 10:28). "Soul" and "spirit" in Scripture are imprecise by modern standards and sometimes are used interchangeably (see Job 7:11; Luke 1:46-47). Soul and spirit differ not in essence but in function — the soul is the inner being that relates horizontally to self and others, while the spirit is the inner being that relates vertically to God.

This means that humans can be described as a holistic dualism — a unity consisting of soul/spirit and body. This fact is established in at least three ways in Scripture:

1. By the clear differentiation between inner and outer aspects of humans (Romans 7:22-23; 2 Corinthians 4:16).
2. By the doctrine of redemption, where the physical body decays but the immaterial soul/spirit is transformed (Romans 8:10; 2 Corinthians 5:1-9).
3. By the doctrine of the intermediate state, where at physical death the inner self (soul/spirit) separates from the lifeless body either to be with Christ or to be separated from him (Luke 16:19-31; Philippians 1:22-24).

The human unity of soul/spirit and body possesses several important capacities, including:

- Intellect, the human faculty of reasoning, imagination, and memory.
- Volition, the faculty of making intentions, choosing, and loving.
- Emotion, the ability to experience feelings, affections, and passions.
- Moral conscience, the ability to distinguish between good and evil with a resulting sense of innocence or guilt.
- Relationality, the capacity to connect at a personal level with self, others, and God.
- Work, the capability for performing actions and finding meaning in the tasks.

All these human capacities and functions integrate harmoniously in what Scripture describes as the metaphorical heart (Matthew 18:35; Romans 6:17). The human's choice and practice of sin has damaged all these God-created capacities.

EVERYDAY APPLICATION

Because God created us as undying souls/spirits in bodies, we must afford the highest respect and value to humans everywhere regardless of gender, ethnicity, or social status. Because people live forever either with or apart from God, they are of far more value than the worth of the materials that make up their bodies. This means that humans shouldn't be devalued when their practical utility to society diminishes due to illness or old age. As Christians, we must develop a healthy sense of self-respect and intrinsic worth as embodied soul/spirits who will live forever.

While we must not devalue the human body that might live some seventy or eighty years (Psalm 90:10), we should recognize that the undying human souls/spirit is of even greater value. Jesus taught, "What good will it be for you to gain the whole world, yet forfeit your soul? Or what can you give in exchange for your soul?" (Matthew 16:26, TNIV). This truth should challenge non-Christians to evaluate their relationship to Jesus Christ. And it should motivate us as Christians to nurture our undying souls/spirits through constructive spiritual disciplines such as prayer, biblical meditation, fasting, and service to others.

Given this nature of humans, we must respect and defend incontrovertible human rights. Humans everywhere must be treated equitably, justly, and compassionately. Rights to life, freedom of speech, fair treatment before the law, and the free practice of religion must be upheld. Tyrants who abuse or kill people must be restrained from such actions and held accountable for their callous disregard for human life.

We should also exercise hope at the fact that while the material body decays at death, the immaterial soul/spirit, or essential self, lives on forever. A. W. Tozer wrote with respect to believers, "In the time of our departure, the body that He gave us will disintegrate and drop away like a cocoon, for the spirit of man soars away to the presence of God."[18] Christians who love Christ joyfully anticipate departing this

---

18. A. W. Tozer, *I Call it Heresy* (Christian Publications, 1974), 15.

weary world to be with Christ forever. The apostle Paul wrote, "We groan, longing to be clothed with our heavenly dwelling. . . . We are confident . . . and would prefer to be away from the body and at home with the Lord" (2 Corinthians 5:2,8). Death loses its sting in the face of this blessed truth.

While living as embodied souls/spirits with various creative capacities, we should strive to achieve our fullest human potential. As Christians, especially, we should develop and enhance our God-given minds, moral consciences, relational capacities, spiritual faculties, and bodies for the glory of God, the extension of the kingdom, and our personal well being.

FOR FURTHER READING

John W. Cooper, *Body, Soul and Life Everlasting: Biblical Anthropology and the Monism-Dualism Debate.* Eerdmans, 1989.

H. D. MacDonald, *The Christian View of Man.* Crossway, 1981.

Dallas Willard, *Renovation of the Heart: Putting on the Character of Christ.* NavPress, 2002.

— BRUCE DEMAREST

IMAGE OF GOD

EVERYDAY DEFINITION

The image of God (Latin: *imago Dei*) is what distinguishes human beings from lower orders of life. On the sixth day of creation God said, " 'Let us make human beings in our image, in our likeness, so that they may rule over the fish in the sea and the birds in the sky, over the livestock and all the wild animals, and over all the creatures that move along the ground.' So God created human beings in his own image, in the image of God he created them; male and female he created them" (Genesis 1:26-27, TNIV).

A variety of interpretations exist among Christians as to the meaning of the term *imago Dei,* including the following:

- The *functional* view asserts that the *imago* consists of humanity's rule over the material world under God's authority (see Genesis 1:28).

- The *relational* view teaches that the *imago* is constituted in the context of human relationships, the most fundamental of which is the relationship between male and female (Genesis 1:27; 5:1-2).
- The *structural* or *substantive* view proposes that the *imago* consists of a set of psychological and spiritual qualities in the person. Early Christian theologians such as Justin Martyr and Irenaeus identified the *imago* with the endowment of a rational mind and free will.

The New Testament sheds light on the nature of the *imago* by highlighting the restoration, through Christ, of what was spoiled by sin. A comprehensive structural interpretation of the *imago* might lead to the following line of reasoning:

- *Metaphysically,* humans are living, active, personal, and immaterial souls/spirits in a material body. The human person is a complex unity or dualistic holism.
- *Intellectually,* humans possess rational minds with the capacity to know themselves (self-consciousness), other people (other-consciousness), their surrounding environment (world-consciousness), and God (God-consciousness).
- *Volitionally,* humans as *imago* possess the capacity to choose noble goals as well as the strategies to realize those goals.
- *Emotionally,* humans experience a broad range of feelings and affections, such as desire, compassion, fear, and anger.
- *Morally,* humans possess the ability to discern right from wrong with an accompanying sense of moral obligation. The conscience is the faculty that verifies compliance or noncompliance with the moral law of God.
- *Relationally,* humans as *imago* are capable of responding and relating to other personal subjects, whether human or divine. The human person, therefore, is created a religious being.
- *Functionally,* humans exercise dominion over the earth and lower forms of life for the glory of God and the good of humanity.

The person as *imago Dei,* then, is best understood as the sum or aggregate of these factors, with the *imago* thus residing in the total person: soul/spirit *and* body. In the words of American philosopher Alvin Plantinga, "The image will thus emerge as a rich, multi-faceted reality, compromising acts, relations, capacities, virtues, dispositions, and even emotions."[19]

EVERYDAY APPLICATION

The definition of the image of God reveals that as humans, we resemble God. Because we are created in God's image, humans are given extraordinary dignity and worth as spiritual beings who will live forever, relate to God, and answer to him. Because we're created to resemble God, humans should possess a healthy self-image, sense of identity, and sense of personal worth. We ought to accept ourselves for who we are — the valued image of God. Made "a little lower than the heavenly beings and crowned them with glory and honor" (Psalm 8:5, TNIV), human beings are elevated above every other life form. We are far more than advanced animals in God's created design, and we should be valued and treated as such (see Matthew 10:31).

The image of God extends to what seem like differences to us: Male and female, as well as people of all economic classes, all races, and all ethnicities, are created as image of God. The fact that both male and female are created image of God ensures their essential equality. Men and women must respect and honor each other as equal sharers of the divine *imago.* The intrinsic worth of all human beings, because they resemble God himself, must be fully honored and respected. The human rights of minority peoples, widows, orphans, the elderly, and the disabled should be vigorously defended by Christians and non-Christians alike. The fact of creation in the divine image should eliminate all racial prejudice and discrimination. Differences of skin pigmentation or ethnicity should never obscure our common heritage as *imago Dei.* Our creation as the image of God, not some governmental decree, constitutes the ultimate basis for inalienable human rights.

As divine image-bearers, we should nurture and develop to the best of our abilities all our God-created capacities: our minds, our wills,

---

19. Alvin Plantinga, "Images of God," *Christian Faith and Practice in the Modern World* (1988), 52.

our emotions, our moral discrimination (conscience), and our relation-ships/relational capacities. Recognizing our likeness to God, we should be eager to develop our full potential as good stewards—in particular, those qualities that God shares with his creatures: kindness, compassion, mercy, etc. As thinking, willing, feeling, and relational beings we have been created for fellowship with, and service to, God for both time and eternity. Since God has delegated to humans responsibility for ruling over and managing the earth (see Psalm 8:6-8), we should exercise this task responsibly and efficiently.

Reflecting on the dignity and worth God has assigned us, we recognize that the human person is not the perfect image of God; Jesus Christ is (2 Corinthians 4:4; Colossians 1:15). At the resurrection, however, Christians will be conformed to the image of the God-man, Jesus Christ (1 Corinthians 15:49). What a glorious prospect awaits the true children of God as we anticipate being conformed to the likeness of Christ.

FOR FURTHER READING
Philip Edgcumbe Hughes, *The True Image: The Origin and Destiny of Man in Christ*. Eerdmans, 1989.
Paul K. Jewett, *Who We Are: Our Dignity as Human*. Eerdmans, 1996.
H. D. McDonald, *The Christian View of Man*. Crossway, 1981.

—BRUCE DEMAREST

IMMANENCE

EVERYDAY DEFINITION
Immanent means that something is near or that a person is present. In theology, it is a quality that belongs to God, who is both near and far, transcendent and immanent (Jeremiah 23:23). He is over and beyond the world (transcendent) in his being, and he is actively present (immanent) in the world to accomplish his providential purposes with everyone and his redemptive purposes with his people of faith.

The immanent God actively and providentially works in history to sustain human life and activity. As the apostle Paul put it, "The God who made the world and everything in it is the Lord of heaven and earth. . . . He himself gives everyone life and breath and everything else. . . he is not far from any one of us. 'For in him we live and move and have our being'"(Acts 17:24-25,27-28, TNIV).

The immanent God also actively works in human history for our redemption. As humans, we are sinfully inclined rebels against God's moral principles. Yet in love, the heavenly Father "commands all people everywhere to repent" (Acts 17:30). He has set a day of judgment for all by Jesus Christ and "has given proof of this to everyone by raising him from the dead" (Acts 17:31, TNIV). The Holy Spirit acts redemptively to give new birth and new life to those who humbly repent and believe the gospel's truth that directs their trust to the living Christ.

Eastern and New Age pantheism (the belief that everything is part of an abstract god) misinterprets God's immanent relation to the world by mistaking God's *activity in* the world for God's *identity with* the world. By saying that God is one with finite persons as well as evil, pantheists commit the sin of worshipping and serving created things rather than their Creator (see Romans 1:25). True believers worship and serve the Creator and Redeemer whose transcendent being is unlimited by the time and space constraints of the world, which result in his immanence over providential and redemptive activity.

EVERYDAY APPLICATION

As Christians, we acknowledge and are strengthened by the fact that "the LORD is God in heaven above and on the earth below. There is no other" (Deuteronomy 4:39). Our awesome Creator God is not distant and remote. He is near at hand, faithfully providing necessities for the maintenance of life support systems on planet earth.

We humbly accept the truth that we are limited creatures in the universe, and that the immanent God orders both physical laws and many events beyond our control. Still, the God who is near has providentially chosen to accomplish many of his purposes through us. As God's children, we can appropriately pray the prayer proposed by St. Francis: "God give me the serenity to accept the things I cannot change, the courage to change the things I can and the wisdom to know the one from the other."

We gratefully receive the immanent God's once-for-all redemptive provision for the satisfaction of justice and so the forgiveness of our sins through the atoning death of Christ. As recipients of God's gift of salvation, we praise our heavenly Father for planning it, his Son for providing it, and the Holy Spirit for applying its blessings in our lives.

As we become increasingly conscious of both God's immanent providential and redemptive ministries, we can grow in our patience in adversity, faith in uncertainty, and hope for the future.

FOR FURTHER READING

Gordon Lewis and Bruce Demarest, *Integrative Theology.* Zondervan, 1996.

Gordon Lewis, "God, Attributes of" in *Evangelical Dictionary of Theology,* Walter Elwell, ed. Baker, 1984.

— GORDON R. LEWIS

IMMORTALITY OF THE SOUL

EVERYDAY DEFINITION

One of the greatest promises of the Bible is eternal life. The phrase "eternal life" appears forty-two times in the New Testament. While death is the end that every human faces since the fall of Adam, eternal life is the promise of the gospel. The soul is the part of us that is immortal, enduring beyond this life into a new life.

In Christian understanding, the soul comes into existence when it is created at birth. But it does not cease to exist at death. What happens to the soul at death is never clearly explained in the Scriptures, but the promise of resurrection — where the human soul is reunited with an imperishable and sinless human body (1 Corinthians 15; Philippians 3:21) — points to the destiny of the soul to be immortal. This is the meaning of Jesus' statement: "I am the resurrection and the life. He who believes in me will live, even though he dies; and whoever lives and believes in me will never die" (John 11:25-26).

All human souls are immortal. During the great judgment (Revelation 20:11-15) all souls will face judgment. This means that the way each person responds to the gospel message and its commands have implications beyond this life and beyond time itself.

The immortality of the soul stands in contrast to the belief that the soul ceases to exist either at the end of this life or as the outcome of some divine action. In Eastern faiths, such as Hinduism and Buddhism, the soul is believed to be reincarnated and to continue life in another form. However, the Bible makes it clear that humans have only one life, which will end in death and then judgment (Hebrews 9:27). Jesus said, "Do not be afraid of those who kill the body but cannot kill the soul. Rather, be afraid of the One who can destroy both soul and body in hell" (Matthew 10:28).

EVERYDAY APPLICATION

Our lives don't consist of just seventy or eighty years of life on earth. Rather, God created for and intended us for an eternity in the presence of the living God. The apostle Paul declared that none of our labor is in vain (1 Corinthians 15:58), meaning that in some real but not fully explainable way, the things we do to form ourselves into the image of our Redeemer and to do the works of the One who created us do matter. Christians are called to take the longview of life — to squander nothing, but to build our lives, our hearts, our loves, and our service with an eternal perspective. This long view doesn't make the pain of failure or the sufferings of this life any less real, yet Paul said that we should consider them as nothing when compared with the glory that shall be revealed (Romans 8:18).

FOR FURTHER READING

N. T. Wright, *Surprised by Hope.* HarperSanFrancisco, 2006.

Gerald F. Hawthorne, Ralph P. Martin, Daniel G. Reid, "Immortality of the Soul or Resurrection of the Dead" in *Dictionary of Paul and His Letters.* InterVarsity, 1993.

— CHRISTOPHER MORTON

IMMUTABILITY

EVERYDAY DEFINITION

Immutability means never changing and not changeable. While everything else around us changes, saying that God is immutable affirms that God — the supreme personal spirit, though living and active in the world — is unchanging in his being, character, attributes, purposes, and promises. The writer of Hebrews said directly to God, "[The heavens and earth] will perish, but you remain; they will all wear out like a garment. You will roll them up like a robe; like a garment they will be changed. But you remain the same, and your years will never end" (Hebrews 1:11-12).

Because God is immutable, we can trust that he is always holy, wise, just, and loving. God will never go back on his promises to give those who repent and believe the gift of eternal life: "God is not a human, that he should lie, not a human being, that he should change his mind. Does he speak and then not act? Does he promise and not fulfill?" (Numbers 23:19, TNIV).

Realizing that God is immutable doesn't mean that he is inactive. Dynamically, God sustains the world and providentially guides all of life. He guided Israel's history to preserve the Messiah's promised genealogical line; acted in Jesus' life, death, and resurrection; and directed the founding of Christian churches worldwide. The unchanging God is providentially active in world history, and he will work out his will at the end of the age.

Jesus exhibited how God the Father is active yet immutable in his character and purposes. In the midst of changing circumstances like ours—from rejoicing at weddings to weeping at a friend's death—the Savior always expressed his unchangeably righteous character. He also taught God's changelessly true principles and fulfilled God's never-changing moral and redemptive purposes: "Jesus Christ is the same yesterday and today and forever" (Hebrews 13:8).

Because he has this unchanging nature, God has two kinds of will or purposes:

1. God's *unconditional* will (sometimes called decretive) comes to pass even if people or nations oppose it: "Surely, as I have planned, so it will be, and as I have purposed, so it will happen" (Isaiah 14:24, TNIV).
2. God's *conditional* purposes are fulfilled depending on the affirmative response of people: "If my people, who are called by my name, will humble themselves and pray and seek my face and turn from their wicked ways, then I will hear from heaven, and I will forgive their sin and will heal their land" (2 Chronicles 7:14, TNIV).

Does God ever change his mind? It might appear that way, for example, when the people of Nineveh repented and God "relented and did not bring on them the destruction he had threatened" (Jonah 3:10, TNIV). However, the reality is that God's unconditional purposes do not change. From the Bible's language, it appears that God has changed his mind. But with further thought, we can see that it was the ungodly Ninevites who changed their minds about their sin (Jonah 3:9-10).

Does God experience changing emotions? Some argue that because the Scriptures teach that God is immutable, he must remain unmoved emotionally. While God's passions don't get beyond his control, he obviously experiences emotions, at least in our limited human understanding. For example, he loves what is right and has righteous indignation toward all forms of evil. He is angry with liars who claim to speak for God but who contradict his Word. God is emotionally moved by his people's trials and afflictions. The prophet Isaiah testified, "In all their distress he too was distressed" (Isaiah 63:9).

EVERYDAY APPLICATION

From eternity past, God chose to love the world of lost sinners, and in time he does good to all people, particularly to those who love him. As Christians, although our lives once were dominated by sin, we have accepted the God who loved us and "gave his one and only Son, that whoever believes in him shall not perish but have eternal life" (John 3:16). We can be fully confident that the love of God that sent his Son into the world to die on our behalf will never change—that is, it will never falter or fail. More than anything else, God wants us to return this unchanging love to him with all our minds and emotions.

We find encouragement and hope that God's unchangeableness extends to every promise he's made in his Word. God confirmed his promises by an unchangeable oath that "puts an end to all argument . . . so that, by two unchangeable things in which it is impossible for God to lie, we who have fled to take hold of the hope set before us may be greatly encouraged" (Hebrews 6:16,18, TNIV). In life's uncertain times, we can be greatly encouraged to know that God's promises are an unmovable anchor for our souls.

The unchangeableness of God's purposes doesn't mean that our personal involvement and activities are insignificant. In fact, we should realize their eternal significance. The immutable God includes our personal participation in his plans and strategies. Our efforts in service to God contribute to the completion of our Creator and Redeemer's grand design for the total drama of human history!

FOR FURTHER READING

John M. Frame, *No Other God: A Response to Open Theism*. P&R Publishing, 2001.

Wayne Grudem, *Systematic Theology*. Zondervan, 2000.

—GORDON R. LEWIS

JEALOUSY

EVERYDAY DEFINITION

Jealousy is an emotion that most of us can relate to. At one time or another, all of us have experienced the emotion of jealousy over someone else's car, house, or station in life. The root of the Hebrew word *qana'* translated as jealous means to "become intensely red," as a result of zeal or fervor over something important. The Greek word *zēloō* means to "be deeply concerned about" someone or something.

We find many examples of jealousy in the Scriptures. In the Old Testament, because Rachel had no children with Jacob, she was jealous of her sister Leah who had four children (see Genesis 30:1). When Joseph's younger brothers learned in a dream that Jacob favored Joseph over them and that Joseph would rule over them, they became jealous of Joseph (37:11) and even sought to kill him.

In the New Testament, the Jews—God's chosen people—witnessed God's blessing on outcast Gentiles, and they became intensely jealous. Crowds of people gathered around the apostles and as a result, "the high priest and all his associates . . . were filled with jealousy" (Acts 5:17).

As a human emotion, jealousy is a destructive trait. In God's eyes, jealousy is a grievous sin: "Love is strong as death; jealousy is as cruel the grave" (Song of Songs 8:6, KJV); "For where jealousy [*zēlos*] and selfish ambition exist, there is disorder and every evil thing" (James 3:16, NASB). As a human emotion, sinful jealousy is the strong desire for something that isn't our own—something that rightly belongs to another.

In this sense, jealousy is close to envy or covetousness. In his play *Othello,* Shakespeare described jealousy as "the green-eyed monster."

Interestingly, the Bible describes God as a jealous God. We naturally wonder, "How can jealousy be a grievous sin for us, but a treasured perfection of almighty God?" God's jealousy is different, in that this attribute in him concerns his fierce desire for and holy claim upon his people. When God's people—his treasured possession (Psalm 135:4) —profane the covenant by sinning, the righteous God responds by becoming intensely jealous. God reserves for himself the worship, devotion, and obedience of his covenant people (Exodus 19:5-6). When the redeemed forsake the covenant and lust after false gods, God's intense jealousy is aroused (Psalm 78:58; Ezekiel 16:38; 1 Corinthians 10:22). As a result, the Bible describes God—who doesn't tolerate wickedness in his people—as the "jealous God" (Exodus 34:14; Deuteronomy 6:15). Indeed, God's very name is "Jealous" (Exodus 34:14). Jealousy isn't some passing mood in God; it constitutes the very essence of his character. His jealousy, however, doesn't contain a trace of selfishness or insecurity as the emotion of jealousy typically does in us humans.

EVERYDAY APPLICATION

Jealousy is a grievous sin for us humans because it represents our strong desire to possess something that is *not* ours. On the other hand, jealousy is a noble perfection in God because it expresses his character and desire to possess what *is* his own—us his blood-bought, covenant people.

As Christians, this means we should live in a way that honors the sacred covenant relationship that God has established with us. If we— like God's people so often portrayed on the pages of Scripture—harbor sin in our lives, the divine jealousy demands that we forsake every trace of wickedness. As Jesus said in the book of Revelation, "Those whom I love I rebuke and discipline. So be earnest, and repent" (Revelation 3:19). The Lord commands us, his covenant people, to resist the sins of our culture such as crass materialism, sensuous pleasure, and sexual immorality—because all these arouse his righteous jealousy.

In addition, the jealous God demands of us total loyalty, faithfulness, and devotion. In the words of the apostle Paul, "You cannot drink the cup of the Lord and the cup of demons too. . . . Are we trying to arouse the Lord's jealousy? Are we stronger than he?" (1 Corinthians

10:21-22). Further, since God is a jealous God—a God whose very name is Jealous—we must give the Lord his full due in our lives. We must put him before and above everything else in life: our families, our possessions, our recreational lives, and our careers. We must give God our hearts, our undivided loyalty, and our wholehearted devotion. We must unreservedly give the jealous God all that he deserves, remembering that he rightfully and wholly owns us.

FOR FURTHER READING
Margarite Beecher, *The Mark of Cain: An Anatomy of Jealousy*. Harper & Row, 1971.
Paul A. Hauck, *Overcoming Jealousy and Possessiveness*. Westminster, 1886.
Richard P. Walters, *Jealousy, Envy, Lust: The Weeds of Greed*. Zondervan, 1985.

— BRUCE DEMAREST

JUSTICE

EVERYDAY DEFINITION
Justice in the Bible is the act of restoring community and healing broken relationships. "What does the LORD require of you? To act justly and to love mercy and to walk humbly with your God" (Micah 6:8).

Biblical justice doesn't compete with or contradict mercy and love. In fact, Jesus is the justice and mercy of God and demonstrates how to live so that we can seek justice exactly as God would have us do. Biblical justice (*tsedeqah, mishpat, dikaiosune*) focuses on the widow, the orphan, the poor, the outsiders, and rejected ones and calls the rich and powerful to cease their domination and be generously reconciled with those they have exploited. God calls us to justice, and the way we respond will be seen in how we live our daily lives and how we relate to others.

Justice also relates to God's desire to liberate all of humanity from sin. This entails all aspects of human existence. The terms for justice occur more than a thousand times in Scripture, and justice is never retributive or punishment focused. That would be "wrath." Instead, justice is restorative and reconciling.

Scripture also shows that God's invitation and call to justice isn't just an individual concern, but that it speaks directly to society. Deuteronomy 15 states that when the community of the faithful live justly and rightly, there will be no poor among them. God's people are to "not be hard-hearted or tightfisted toward your poor brother. Rather be openhanded and freely lend him whatever he needs" (verses 7-8). This call to economic justice echoes throughout the Old Testament and is fulfilled in the community of the believers following Pentecost. In the early Christian community, when anyone had a need, fellow believers would sell some of their possessions and share (Acts 2; 4). This echoes the promises of justice from Deuteronomy and "there were no needy persons among them" (4:34). The church—the people of God—provides an example for what the broader world is called to. In fact, we see in Scripture that God's concern for the marginalized and hurting was voiced to kings, temple elites, and politicians as well as to the common person.

Isaiah preached that social justice is the fast that God wants, not simply going without food. "Yet on the day of your fasting, you do as you please and exploit all your workers. . . . Is this the kind of fast I have chosen, only a day for a man to humble himself? Is it only for bowing one's head like a reed and for lying on sackcloth and ashes? Is that what you call a fast, a day acceptable to the LORD? Is not this the kind of fasting I have chosen: to loose the chains of injustice and untie the cords of the yoke, to set the oppressed free and break every yoke? Is it not to share your food with the hungry and to provide the poor wanderer with shelter?" (Isaiah 58:3,5-7). Here we see the consistent biblical emphasis on food, shelter, and economic concern for a living wage. God's love for humanity is seen in the invitation to do justice and stay faithful to God in all relationships—every part of our lives falls under the lordship of Christ, even our money and business practices.

The idea that justice and mercy are opposed is an unfortunate inheritance from medieval theology. Jesus' mercy to the poor is seen in the fact that he confronted the powers and authorities during his lifetime, challenging them to do justice for those who suffered injustices.

Authors Glen Stassen and David Gushee identify four areas where Jesus taught his followers to seek justice:[20]

---

20. Glen Stassen and David Gushee, *Kingdom Ethics: Following Jesus in Contemporary Context* (Downers Grove, IL: InterVarsity, 2003).

1. Jesus criticized the injustice of greed and called for justice for the poor and hungry. He told Pharisees, the wealthy religious elite, that they "justify" (*dikaiountes*) or "righteousify" their "love of money" while they devoured widows' houses (Luke 16:14-15; Mark 12:38-44). James preached powerfully for justice when he said that Christians should never treat people with money better than those without (James 2:1-7).
2. Jesus spoke against the injustice of domination and taught his followers to be servants of all instead (Matthew 23:1-6; Luke 22), calling the servants the greatest and turning the kingdom upside down.
3. Jesus taught against the injustice of violence by weeping for Jerusalem because it "kills the prophets and stones those who are sent to it!" and it does not know "the things that make for peace" (Matthew 23:37, NRSV; Luke 19:42, NRSV). The prophets were killed because they called Israel to be faithful to God and therefore just in all their actions with others. For this they died.
4. Jesus and the prophets spoke out for the justice of welcoming community and opposed the injustice of exclusion. Jesus showed that the justice of God restores relationships with lepers, prostitutes, Gentiles (ethnic/racial outsiders), immigrants, women, children, and ritually unclean people of all kinds. Jesus' teachings and practices of forgiveness, mercy, and love accomplish the vision of biblical justice because all of these restore community and heal brokenness.

EVERYDAY APPLICATION

One reason Jesus was murdered was because he spoke out against the injustice of the temple/religious system and challenged the religious elite to live differently, justly. He turned over the tables of people who were getting rich in God's name. In our communities, people are being treated just as unjustly. It may be because they're immigrants or part of an ethnic minority. Perhaps the people washing the dishes in the back of a favorite restaurant are being paid less than a living wage. Perhaps the people who make the shoes or clothes we wear are working in sweatshops. James says that the cries of the laborers who are exploited have reached the ears of God: "Look! The wages you failed to pay the workmen who mowed your fields are crying out against you. The cries of the harvesters have reached the ears of the Lord Almighty. You have lived on earth in luxury and self-indulgence. You have fattened yourselves in the day of slaughter" (James 5:4-5). Exodus 23:6 says, "Do not deny justice to your poor people in their lawsuits." Malachi 3:5 declares that God is "against those who defraud laborers of their wages, who oppress the widows and the fatherless, and deprive aliens of justice."

What can we as faithful followers of Jesus do? Some practical ways we can live out the biblical concept of justice include:

- We can try to buy sweat-free clothing that is union made or made by companies that make sure their suppliers pay a living wage, or we can buy clothes from thrift stores, such as Goodwill.
- We can also advocate for good working conditions for employees where we live (and elsewhere). For example, we can learn if aliens or immigrants are being taken advantage of in the construction industry or service industries (like at hotels) where we live. We can meet these individuals, find out their names, invite them to dinner and to church, and hear their stories. We might find that God is at work bringing more justice to creation and that we can participate in what the Spirit is doing.

FOR FURTHER READING

Stanley Hauerwas and Samuel Wells, eds., *The Blackwell Companion to Christian Ethics*. Blackwell, 2006.

Ron Sider, *Rich Christians in an Age of Hunger*. Thomas Nelson, 1997.

Glen Stassen and David Gushee, *Kingdom Ethics: Following Jesus in Contemporary Context*. InterVarsity, 2003.

—PAUL ALEXANDER

JUSTIFICATION

EVERYDAY DEFINITION

The crucial question in Christian theology (if not in life itself) is the same question asked of Job: "How then can a mortal be righteous before God? How can one born of woman be pure?" (Job 25:4, TNIV).

Christians regard the doctrine of justification by faith as central to theology. This doctrine asserts that when guilty and condemned sinners trust in the completed work of Christ on the cross (rather than their own good works), God immediately gives to them the righteousness of Christ himself.

The Hebrew and Greek verbs "to justify" bear the legal meaning to "pronounce" or "reckon as righteous." The Bible clearly states that justification involves God declaring the innocence of sinners: "No one will be declared righteous in his sight by observing the law" (Romans 3:20). Through justification, God's wrath is averted and we are restored to right standing with God; we receive forgiveness of sins, and are graced with the gift of eternal life.

Through the internal witness of the Holy Spirit, believers possess assurance that we are restored to right relationship with God and are fully pleasing to him because of Christ (Galatians 4:6-7). Early in the sixteenth century, Martin Luther reintroduced the biblical doctrine of justification by faith (not by works) to the church. Luther correctly believed that those who believe on Christ are at the same time both experientially stained with sin and positionally righteous before God.

To better understand justification by faith, we can examine several crucial elements of this doctrinal truth:

- The *problem* of justification is how God, the righteous Judge, can acquit guilty sinners without bending or violating his holy law. As Luther put it, "Here is a problem which needs God to solve it."
- The *ground* of justification is not any works of our own but the completed work of Christ on the cross. Paul wrote extensively about this element: "We have now been justified by his blood" (Romans 5:9); "God made him who had no sin to be sin for us, so that in him we might become the righteousness of God" (2 Corinthians 5:21); "Just as one trespass resulted in condemnation for all people, so also one righteous act resulted in justification and life for all. For just as through the disobedience of the one man the many were made sinners, so also through the obedience of the one man the many will be made righteous" (Romans 5:18-19, TNIV).
- The *means* of justification is faith in Christ, the Redeemer.

The seedbed of justification occurs back in the Old Testament, where "Abram believed the LORD, and [God] credited it to him as righteousness" (Genesis 15:6). For his part, Abram believed God's promise that pointed to the Messiah's sacrifice; as a result, God credited that faith to the patriarch as right standing with himself. Paul illustrated the truth of justification by faith from the life of Abraham (Romans 4:1-3,9-25) and the life of David (4:6-8). The apostle taught, "For in the gospel the righteousness of God is revealed—a righteousness that is by faith from first to last, just as it is written: 'The righteous will live by faith'" (1:17). Other passages affirming that faith in Christ is the means of justification include: Galatians 3:11; Philippians 3:9; and Hebrews 10:38.

- The *results* of justification are all-encompassing, including forgiveness of sins (Acts 13:38-39), removal of condemnation (Romans 8:1,33-34), reconciliation with God (Romans 5:10-11), peace with God (Romans 5:1), adoption into God's family (Ephesians 1:5), and the gift of eternal life (Titus 3:7).

A key New Testament text that sums up crucial elements of the doctrine of justification is Romans 3:21-26. This passage teaches that both Jews and Gentiles have sinned and fallen short of the glory of God. God demonstrated his justice by offering Christ as a sacrifice for sins. "The righteousness of God" can be received freely by faith in Christ's atoning work.

EVERYDAY APPLICATION

In order to achieve freedom from condemnation and restore right relationship with God, we can't trust in our ability to fulfill the works of the law. Because none of us can keep the law in its entirety, we can't be justified on the basis of our best and noblest works (Romans 3:20; Galatians 2:16). From long, personal experience in Judaism, the apostle Paul concluded that "All who rely on observing the law are under a curse" (Galatians 3:10). Our task is simply to accept by faith the righteousness and right standing God offers through faith in his Son's atoning work.

For Christians, the truth of the doctrine of justification offers us the following:

- *Assurance of our salvation.* John wrote, "I write these things to you who believe in the name of the Son of God so that you may know that you have eternal life" (1 John 5:13). Theologically, we know that by acceptance of Christ's atoning work we are declared righteous in God's sight. Experientially, we possess assurance of being rightly related to God in that "The Spirit himself testifies with our spirit that we are God's children" (Romans 8:16; see also Galatians 4:6).

- *Freedom from the burden of objective guilt.* When we sin in daily experience (and we all do, according to 1 John 1:8), we know both intellectually and emotionally that we have violated God's standard. Authorities such as psychologist S. B. Narramore claim that what Christians experience following a sin of omission or commission isn't guilt in the punitive sense, but constructive sorrow.[21] An example is Peter's weeping in deep sorrow after his cowardly denial of Jesus (Matthew 26:75). Christians can rest assured that God's justifying sentence declares the true believer in Jesus "Not Guilty!" before the bar of divine justice, freeing the child of God from the onerous burden of guilt. When we do sin, we should immediately confess our sin and experience the blessing of God's gracious forgiveness (1 John 1:9). In addition, because we are perfectly clothed with the righteousness of Christ, we don't need to be encumbered with the impossible agenda of perfectionism. In this life, we strive for the ideal of Christlikeness, while knowing that this goal will be achieved only when we see Jesus.

- *Opportunity to offer reconciliation.* Those of us who have been reconciled to God through the grace of justification should serve as ministers of reconciliation to others who are alienated from their Creator and Redeemer and from other human beings. The apostle Paul, who knew what it meant even as a religious leader to be alienated from God, wrote that God "reconciled us to himself through Christ and gave us the ministry of reconciliation: that God was reconciling the world to himself in Christ, not counting people's sins against them. And he has

---

21. *Baker Encyclopedia of Psychology* (1985), 488.

committed to us the message of reconciliation" (2 Corinthians 5:18-19, TNIV). As followers of Christ, we have the privilege and joy of bearing the message of reconciliation to lost and lonely souls who are estranged from the source of spiritual life. Further, we have the privilege of being used of God to mend relationships fractured through bigotry or strife. The Christian church should be a powerful force for reconciliation in a broken world.

FOR FURTHER READING

John MacArthur, *Justification by Faith*. Moody, 1984.
R. C. Sproul, *Justification by Faith Alone*. Crossway, 1999.
Peter Toon, *Justification and Sanctification*. Crossway, 1983.

— BRUCE DEMAREST

LAST JUDGMENT

EVERYDAY DEFINITION

The Last Judgment refers to the event at the second coming of Christ when all people will receive God's judgment through Christ as to whether they are righteous or wicked.

This doctrine begins with the teachings of Jesus himself. In the parable of the sheep and goats, Jesus proclaimed that at the coming of the Son of man (the second coming of Jesus), all nations would gather before him (Matthew 25:31-46). At that time, Jesus will separate everyone into the sheep and the goats. His followers, the sheep, will receive eternal life. Those who haven't followed him, the goats, will receive eternal punishment.

In the New Testament, the apostle Peter wrote that Christ was "ordained by God as Judge of the living and the dead" (Acts 10:42, NRSV). The apostle Paul warned that "we must all appear before the judgment seat of Christ, that each one may receive what is due him for the things done while in the body, whether good or bad" (2 Corinthians 5:10). The doctrine of the last and eternal judgment is also one of the six foundational doctrines mentioned in Hebrews 6:1-2.

In addition to Jesus' own teaching and that of the New Testament, both the Apostles' Creed and the Nicene Creed state that Christ will come again in glory to judge the living and the dead, thus confirming the centrality of this doctrine for the Christian church.

Several key aspects make up the doctrine of the Last Judgment.

- It will take place immediately after the general resurrection of the dead, although when this event will occur is known by God alone.
- All humans will be judged.
- The judgment will be based upon what a person has done before death.
- Everyone will be judged according to the will of God as it has been revealed to them individually.
- The judgment will be final.

EVERYDAY APPLICATION

In this world, we sometimes see people who are basically righteous suffer while evil people prosper. This observation can mislead us into thinking that it's not worth acting righteously. But the doctrine of the Last Judgment assures us that an indestructible moral order exists where God will hold all humans accountable for all of their actions, with retribution for evildoing and reward for righteousness. As the apostle Paul wrote, "Do not be deceived, God is not mocked; for whatever a man sows, this he will also reap" (Galatians 6:7, NASB).

Even the philosopher Immanuel Kant, who wrongly argued that we can't know that God exists from exercising pure reason, had to acknowledge that as a matter of practical reason we must assume both that God exists and that God providentially will reward the righteous and punish evildoers. Otherwise, people would have insufficient motivation to act ethically. The doctrine of the Last Judgment, therefore, acts both to deter us from wrongdoing and to strengthen our resolve to do right, even though we might temporarily suffer in this life for doing right.

FOR FURTHER READING

S. G. F. Brandon, *The Judgment of the Dead: An Historical and Comparative Study of the Idea of a Post-Mortem Judgment in the Major Religions.* Scribner's, 1967.

R. H. Charles, *A Critical History of a Future Life in Israel, in Judaism, and in Christianity, or Hebrew, Jewish, and Christian Eschatology.* A. and C. Black, 1913.

J. P. Martin, *The Last Judgment in Protestant Theology from Orthodoxy to Ritschl.* Eerdmans, 1963.

— TIM FINLAY

LAW

EVERYDAY DEFINITION

The Bible uses several terms to refer to the word law, including: torah, command, statute, judgment, precept, and testimony. The term torah — the most prominent of these terms — refers primarily to the system of laws given to Moses on Mount Sinai. However, torah often more broadly implies the totality of God's revelation to his people on Mount Sinai and beyond.

The "Book of the Law," found in Exodus 21–23, begins with the statement: "These are the laws you are to set before them" (21:1). Also called the "Book of the Covenant," this body of laws includes a mostly casuistic system — a set of general rules that tries to solve moral dilemmas — that addresses all aspects of personal and community life in Israel. Among the themes treated in here are laws related to slavery, murder and unintentional killing, personal injury, property damage, theft, sexual behavior, treatment of aliens, observance of the Sabbath, formal worship, and other aspects of life related to family and society. These laws came directly from God, who handed them down to the Israelites through the intermediary of his servant, Moses (Numbers 12:6-8; Deuteronomy 34:10).

The biblical concept of law is related to the idea of covenant, and it serves as a paradigm for the permanent relationship that existed between God and his people. On several occasions, during ceremonies renewing the covenant, the laws were restated before the people in order to remind the community of God's final authority over them. This also served as a reminder of their obligation to follow his decrees (Joshua 8:30-35; 2 Kings 23:1-3). After the law was read publicly, the whole community would make an oath before God, pledging to diligently follow his instructions (Nehemiah 10:29).

The Ten Commandments (recorded in Exodus 20:2-17 and Deuteronomy 5:5-21) are central to the law code of the Bible. Also called the Decalogue, these laws focused on the worship of *Yahweh*, godly behavior, and prohibition against the worship of other gods. The success of the covenant relationship between God and his people depended on the Israelites' adherence to the first commandment: "You shall have no other gods before me" (Exodus 20:3). Whenever the Israelites failed to observe this commandment and turned to other gods, they gave up the blessings of obedience and invited upon themselves the curses of disobedience (Deuteronomy 28–29).

Throughout the times of the Old Testament, Judaism adhered to a twofold system of law: written (*torah*) and oral (*halakah*). The written law was given to Moses on Mount Sinai while the oral law comes from rabbinic scribal writings that covered a period of several centuries. Generally, these two systems were of equal standing and authoritative for the Jewish community. By New Testament times, the system of Jewish law had greatly increased in complexity and comprised a legal corpus much larger than the laws included in the Old Testament. Jesus and the apostle Paul were familiar with both systems and regularly confronted members of Jewish sects (such as Pharisees, Sadducees, Zealots) with their flawed interpretations and applications of individual decrees (see Matthew 12:1-8; 15:1-6). During the centuries that followed, the corpus of rabbinic literature continued to flourish and the system of law eventually developed into an extensive body of literature, including the Mishnah, Jerusalem Talmud, and Babylonian Talmud.

EVERYDAY APPLICATION

In the Old Testament, the law served as a system of guidance and protection for all individuals. Even today, law more generally exposes wrongs and provides a paradigm for what is right and beneficial for the members of a society. The Old Testament Pentateuch includes an intricate legal system designed to guide the religious, social, familial, and individual activities of the Israelites within the framework of their covenant relationship with the Lord. This system wasn't instituted to oppress God's people; it was meant to create a peaceful society in an atmosphere of justice, harmony, and respect for human life. The law was also meant to ensure a healthy covenantal relationship between God and his children. While some think of biblical law as a restrictive system of rules, it was a divine gift of grace that facilitated a relationship of respect, order, and accountability between God and his people. Without clear boundaries, human beings have a natural tendency to become self-centered and to follow the destructive inclinations of their fallen natures.

Psalm 119, the longest psalm in the Hebrew songbook, focuses almost entirely on the purpose, blessings, value, and benefits of God's law. The ancient psalmist elevates God's statutes above all else and seeks to demonstrate the importance of establishing God's directives and principles at the center of life on earth. Among other things, the psalmist revealed that God's laws serve as a system of morality (verse 9), as a counselor (verse 24), as a teacher of knowledge and understanding (verses 34,66,98-100), and as a light that lights life's pathway (verses 105,130). In other words, God desires that all aspects of human life be ordered under his divine guidance as set forth in the law.

The following two important questions arise today:

1. "Should Gentile Christians observe Old Testament law?" While Gentile believers should be familiar with the Mosaic law—especially since it's included in our own canon of Scripture, the New Testament—the first century Jerusalem council identified only four directives that Gentile believers should follow: to abstain from food polluted by idols, to cease eating strangled animals, to avoid blood, and to refrain from immoral sexuality (Acts 15:19-20,27-29).

2. "Should Jewish Christians observe Old Testament law?" Scripture declares that through the shed blood of Jesus Christ, Jews who receive his salvation have been set free from the bondage of the law (Romans 3:19-31; Galatians 2:15-16). Yet, as recipients of a rich and deep tradition, Jewish believers are free to practice their long-standing customs as long as their motivation for doing so is based primarily on an uncompromising love for God and for neighbor rather than the law. The law served only as a shadow of better things to come (Hebrews 7:18-25; 10:1-2).

For Further Reading
Calum M. Carmichael, *The Origins of Biblical Law: The Decalogue and the Book of the Covenant.* Cornell University Press, 1992.
Samuel Greengus, "Law" in *Anchor Bible Dictionary*, ed. David Noel Freedman. Yale University Press, 1992.

— Hélène Dallaire

LOVE

Everyday Definition

Love in Christianity is a rich and full idea — so expansive that we can't adequately explore it in just a few paragraphs. But we can briefly look at two important aspects of how God views love.

God's love for us. The core message of the gospel is the sacrificial love of Jesus Christ. Jesus died for the sins of the world (1 John 2:2), not because he had to, but because he wanted to. According to the Scriptures, the cause of Jesus' death was his love. Jesus said it plainly, "I lay down My life. . . . No one has taken it away from Me, but I lay it down on My own initiative" (John 10:17-18, NASB). Indeed, it took authority for Jesus to lay down his life (John 10:18). He would not have been able to lay his life down apart from the power of love.

The Bible says, "God is love" (1 John 4:8). By nature, love is self-giving. In that God is three persons (Father, Son, and Holy Spirit), the love of God within God's self flows from each person in the Trinity. The Father loves the Son, and the Son loves the Father; the Son loves the Spirit, and the Spirit loves the Son; the Spirit loves the Father, and the Father loves the Spirit. God's love within the Trinity is social, not narcissistic. It is other-centered, not egotistical. That God himself *is* love confirms that he is triune. God himself is a community of love, even though as three, he is one (Deuteronomy 6:4).

God's love is mysterious, because the Bible declares that love is "not jealous" (1 Corinthians 13:4, NASB), yet God, who is love, is named "Jealous" (Exodus 34:14). The jealousy of God is not petty or hubristic; it is zealous and protective of the truth. Out of his love, God is jealous of the truth that he alone — and no one else — is God. Through the prophet Isaiah, God said, "I am the Lord, and there is no other; besides Me there is no God" (Isaiah 45:5, NASB). Since God can't lie (Titus 1:2), by nature God has to be jealous for the truth. Jesus said, "I am . . . the Truth" (John 14:6, MSG). When Jesus died on the cross, he upheld the highest truth that only holy God is *God*.

Our love for God and one another. In addition to the triune God's love for people, God also expects his children to return their love to him and to show love to each other. The top commandment in Scripture is to love the Lord God foremost (Matthew 22:37-38). The second command is like it, "You shall love your neighbor as yourself" (22:39, NASB). Jesus said, "On these two commandments depend the whole Law and the Prophets" (22:40, NASB). Love is the fulfillment of the Law (Romans 13:10). Love is also the greatest of all spiritual gifts (1 Corinthians 13:13). As the apostle Paul said in the famous love chapter in the Bible, "Love is patient, love is kind and is not jealous; love does not brag and is not arrogant, does not act unbecomingly; it does not seek its own, is not provoked, does not take into account a wrong suffered, does not rejoice in unrighteousness, but rejoices with the truth; bears all things, believes all things, hopes all things, endures all things. Love never fails" (1 Corinthians 13:4-8, NASB).

Jesus' command to love God foremost originated in the Old Testament (Deuteronomy 6:5) as did the Golden Rule (Leviticus 19:18). But Jesus also gave a "new commandment," saying, "A new commandment I give to you, that you love one another, even as I have loved you" (John 13:34, NASB). Jesus' love was different from any other love on earth. Jesus alone, among all human beings, could truthfully say, "Just as the Father has loved Me, I have also loved you" (15:9, NASB). Jesus' love was complete. Because his faith was unfailing, he was able to feel secure in his personal identity, and this faith-induced assurance gave him freedom to love people. "Greater love has no one than this," he explained, "that he lay down his life for his friends" (verse 13).

EVERYDAY APPLICATION

While love seems like such a simple thing, the truth is that—even as Christians—most of us find it difficult to really love God with all our heart, soul, mind, and strength. And often we find it even harder to love other people. As Bernard of Clairvaux (1090-1153) explained in his classic treatise *On the Love of God*, "Human nature is weak and therefore compelled to love itself and serve itself first." That's why it's painful for us continually to love.

Bernard described four degrees of love:

1. Love of self for self's sake. Bernard noted that this kind of love easily degenerates into lust.
2. Love of God for self's sake. This happens when a person cries out to God for help in times of trouble.
3. Love of self for God's sake. In order to love in this way, Bernard says, "We must continually go to God with our needs in prayer. In those prayers the grace of God is tasted, and by frequent tasting it is proved to us how sweet the Lord is. Thus it happens that once God's sweetness has been tasted, it draws us to the pure love of God more than our needs compel us to love him."
4. Love of God for God's sake. According to Bernard, this kind of love rarely happens. When it does, "we lose ourselves as though we did not exist."

Of course, our prayer should be that we pursue loving God for God's sake. Only then can we truly follow Jesus' command to love the Lord God and love our neighbors.

FOR FURTHER READING

Bruce Davidson, "The Four Faces of Self-Love in the Theology of Jonathan Edwards" in *Journal of Evangelical Theological Society, Volume 51, No. 1* (March 2008).

Richard Foster and James Bryan Smith, eds., "Bernard of Clairvaux: Four Degrees of Love" in *Devotional Classics: A Renovare Resource for Spiritual Renewal.* Harper, 2005.

Brennan Manning, *A Stranger to Self-Hatred.* Dimension Books, 1982.

— SARAH SUMNER

MARRIAGE

EVERYDAY DEFINITION

In current contemporary culture, marriage is usually defined by the State in secular terms as a contractual arrangement that can legally be reversed if either spouse chooses to dissolve the relationship. As viewed within a secular framework, marriage is essentially contractual.

However, within a biblical framework, marriage is covenantal and sacred. It is holy. To be holy means to be "set apart." Marriage is set apart from every other type of human bond. Unlike the family bond, which is rooted in biology and bloodlines, marriage finds its basis in a promise mutually made before God. Marriage is not meant to be broken. It's an exclusive relationship uniting a couple spiritually, sexually, and socially.

Some major differences exist between secular matrimony and holy matrimony. Secular matrimony is a private affair upheld by the feelings of two people; if their love fades, the contract can be legally broken. Secular matrimony denies and disavows that marriage was established by God. It doesn't take seriously the Genesis account where God brought a woman to the man (Genesis 2:22). Instead, secular matrimony disregards the need for a complementary relationship based on gender in marriage. Within a secular framework, heterosexuality is optional.

By contrast, holy matrimony is the union of one man and one woman. Holy matrimony is a public affair upheld by the commitment of a husband and wife; even if their love fades, the covenant still remains valid. Holy matrimony understands itself as a moral institution originated by God that serves as the basis of the family. Holy matrimony is a permanent bond precisely because it reflects the marriage of Christ and his bride, the church (Ephesians 5:32).

In Ephesians 5:23, the apostle Paul explained that the husband is the head "of the wife." Very few Christians are taught this. Most are mistaught to believe that Ephesians 5:23 says that the husband is the head "of the house." Even among conservatives who think highly of the Bible, very few quote this verse directly from Ephesians. When the biblical phrase "head of the wife" is overlooked, the picture of marriage revealed in Ephesians 5:22-33 remains hidden. As a result, the meaning of the passage far too often gets lost.

The Bible reveals that marriage is a "great mystery" (Ephesians

5:32, NLT). This mystery is a mystery of oneness. The husband and wife enter into a special kind of oneness that reflects Christ's oneness with the church. As Christ is the head of the church, so the husband is the head of the wife. As the church is the body of Christ, so the wife is the body of the husband. The language in Ephesians is metaphorical. The metaphorical picture of the head and body union of husband and wife reveals the mystery of Christ's union with the church. Metaphorically speaking, the husband (who is the head) and the wife (who is the body) become "one flesh" (Ephesians 5:31). So it makes sense when the apostle also says that "husbands ought to love their wives as their own bodies" (Ephesians 5:28).

The metaphorical use of the word head (in Greek *kephale*) found in Ephesians 5:23 is debated among contemporary scholars. While one side argues that the Greek word *kephale* means "authority," the other side argues that *kephale* means "source." In other words, one side argues that Ephesians 5:23 means that the husband is the "authority" in the family, while the other side argues that it means instead the husband is the "source" of the wife in that Adam's physical side was the source from which the Lord created Eve. A way to transcend the recent debate is to accept the word *kephale* as a metaphor that is meant to convey a mental picture of a head. A mental image of a head (the husband) connected to a body (the wife) vividly shows the mystery of the "one flesh" union of husband and wife. It also reveals the spectacular connection that the church (the body of Christ) has to Christ Jesus (the church's head).

It's important to remember that the Bible doesn't say that the husband is the "Lord" of the wife. Nor does it say he is the "Savior" of the wife. Only Christ Jesus has the power to save people from their sins. In Ephesians 5:23, the apostle says the husband is the "head of the wife," not the lord or savior of the wife. Headship has to do with the reality of oneness. Christ's lordship doesn't convey his oneness with his bride, the church. His lordship shows his leadership and power and authority. Christ's saviorhood, likewise, doesn't convey his oneness with his body. Christ's oneness with his body is exclusively revealed through his headship. As Christ unites in oneness with his bride, the church, so the husband unites in oneness with his wife.

EVERYDAY APPLICATION

As Christians, we understand sacred marriage to be a one-flesh union of a head and a body. It's not the marital union of two heads or two bodies. In practical terms, this means that marriage is the union of one male and one female. Although the husband is the wife's "head," he doesn't become her savior or lord. Jesus alone is Lord (Ephesians 4:5) and Savior (Luke 2:11). This means that the authority in marriage is Christ. Both husband and wife will look to Christ for wisdom in their marriage. In Christ "are hidden all the treasures of wisdom and knowledge" (Colossians 2:3). When couples make decisions they can look to each other for experience and learning. But they entrust themselves to Jesus Christ alone. Christ is the spiritual leader of a biblical marriage. Both husband and wife have direct access to him (Hebrews 4:14-16).

The mystery of marriage is that husband and wife, two individual people, mysteriously "become one flesh" (Ephesians 5:31). Their oneness comes about through a sacrifice-submit, love-respect dynamic in the marriage. The husband is to love his wife "as Christ loved the Church and gave himself up for her" (Ephesians 5:25), and the wife is to "submit to [her] own husband" (Ephesians 5:22) and "see to it that she respects her husband" (Ephesians 5:33, NASB). The wife submits by coming under her husband, conforming her life to his, and the husband sacrifices himself for his wife by refusing to take advantage of his physical advantage over her (1 Peter 3:7). The husband instead uses his social advantage to make sure that his wife is honored (in her giftedness and personhood) just as much as he is (John 5:23). The husband loves his wife by nourishing and cherishing her even as he does his own flesh (Ephesians 5:29), and the wife respects her husband by regarding him as highly as she does herself.

In Christian marriage, husbands and wives can cultivate oneness in many ways, especially through the sexual union. In a biblical model of marriage, both spouses have authority over each other's body. The apostle Paul said, "The wife does not have authority over her own body, but the husband does; and likewise also the husband does not have authority over his own body, but the wife does" (1 Corinthians 7:4, NASB). Husband and wife can further deepen their oneness by praying together, making decisions together, raising their children together, serving the Lord together, applying Scripture together (especially the process of conflict resolution found in Matthew 18:15-20), enjoying life together, and speaking the truth in love to one another.

Perhaps the greatest hindrance to achieving marital oneness is individual selfishness. Selfishness plays out in a myriad of sinful ways such as refusing to be honest and forthcoming, refusing to repent from practices and habits that offend God, and refusing to forgive. Conversely, the greatest help to achieving marital oneness is to worship the Lord God by loving him foremost and applying the Golden Rule within the marriage.

FOR FURTHER READING

Mike Mason, *The Mystery of Marriage*. Multnomah, 2001.
Jim and Sarah Sumner, *Just How Married Do You Want to Be?*
    Practicing Oneness in Marriage. InterVarsity, 2008.
Gary Thomas, *Sacred Marriage*. Zondervan, 2001.

— SARAH SUMNER

MATERIALISM

EVERYDAY DEFINITION

Materialism is a lifestyle dedicated to the acquisition of money, consumer goods, and services. Like any lifestyle, a materialistic lifestyle comes with its own set of priorities, habits, and practices.

In the ancient world, wealth was viewed as a sign of divine blessing, so wealthy people were regarded as particularly favored by God or the gods. In contrast, those in poverty were seen as lacking God's blessing, as evidenced by their poverty. This doctrine of "divine retribution" was almost universal in the Ancient Near East, and the book of Job was likely written to correct this idea.

By the time of Jesus, this idea was deeply entrenched in Greco-Roman as well as some Jewish thought. Of course, this added a spiritual reason for pursuing a materialistic lifestyle. However, Jesus' teachings turned this idea on its head, as he taught about God's care for the poor (see Matthew 5:3, Luke 6:20; 14:13). Further, Jesus warned the wealthy of the peril of their condition before God (Matthew 19:23-24; Luke 1:53; 6:24).

Jesus also touched on the dangers of a materialistic lifestyle in many of his parables. In one, Jesus described a wealthy farmer who, after a successful harvest, builds bigger barns to store his crops and his goods (Luke 12:16-21). The very night he designs this materialistic plan to live in comfort, he dies. God says to this man, "You fool! This very night your life will be demanded from you. Then who will get what you have prepared for yourself?" (16:20). The principle Jesus derives from this parable is: "This is how it will be with anyone who stores up things for himself but is not rich toward God" (Luke 12:21).

To combat materialism, the Bible presents a number of different approaches for handling wealth. In the Old Testament, the Law of Moses prescribes a tithe, where Israelites were to give a proportional amount of their income to support the temple and provide relief for the poor (Leviticus 27:30; Deuteronomy 12:17). The wisdom literature presents an emphasis on stewardship (Proverbs 10:17; 14:24), moderation (Proverbs 30:8-9), and generosity toward others (Proverbs 11:25). In the Gospels, Jesus frequently called people to abandon their wealth in order to follow him (Matthew 19:21; Mark 10:21). And the apostle Paul presented the idea of voluntary giving (2 Corinthians 8-9). These various approaches demonstrate that the remedy to materialism is complex and sometimes varies depending on the context.

EVERYDAY APPLICATION

Western Christians today live in the most affluent and consumer-driven culture that has ever existed in human history. Never before have so many people possessed so much. This presents a challenge as we seek to navigate the way of discipleship in a context unparalleled in Christian history. As Christians, we find ourselves bombarded with an array of different options, whether it's the purchase of shoes, educational choices, entertainment, or even varieties of food in the local grocery store.

One way we can apply the Bible's teaching about materialism and wealth is to devote ourselves to a lifestyle of giving rather than taking. This scriptural approach works no matter what our income level is. We can use a variety of different ways to develop a lifestyle of giving. The resources we can give include our time, our attention, our possessions, and our money. As we develop practices that involve relinquishing these things consistently, we combat the lure of materialism on our souls. These practices might include secretly giving to someone who has financial or material need, loaning our possessions to those in need, and consistently giving of our time and service to our local church.

FOR FURTHER READING

Craig Blomberg, *Neither Poverty nor Riches: A Biblical Theology of Material Possessions*. InterVarsity, 2001.

Richard Foster, *The Challenge of the Disciplined Life: Christian Reflections on Money, Sex and Power*. Harper, 1989.

Ron Sider, *Rich Christians in an Age of Hunger: Moving from Affluence to Generosity*. Thomas Nelson, 2005.

— TIM PECK

MERCY

EVERYDAY DEFINITION

Mercy is the emotional reaction that motivates compassionate action, extends forgiveness to the guilty, and offers assistance to the needy — whether deserved or undeserved. In addition, "mercy is condescending love, reaching out to meet a need without considering the merit of the person who receives the aid."[22] This means that mercy is both a strong emotion in a person aroused by a pressing need and the free and loving response to that need.

Mercy is categorically different from justice. As the apostle James wrote, "Mercy triumphs over judgment" (James 2:13). The difference between these two qualities comes out strikingly in a story that preachers often tell: George Washington was commander-in-chief of the colonial forces during the Revolutionary War. A mother managed somehow to reach him, begging that he spare her son who was facing severe punishment, most likely death, for sleeping while serving as a sentinel. Washington reassuringly told her, "I will see to it that he gets justice," to which the mother replied, "I am not begging for justice, but for mercy." The gospel's reassuring message is that by faith in the Savior's substitutionary sacrifice, mercy will trump justice without causing injustice.

---

22. Larry Richards, *Expository Dictionary of Bible Words*, p. 440.

In the Sermon on the Mount, Jesus uttered a beatitude focusing on mercy: "Blessed are the merciful, for they will be shown mercy" (Matthew 5:7). Mercy, as one of God's chief qualities, can be measured only by the limitless dimensions of the love he showed on the cross.

As we survey our world in this twenty-first century—war-racked and blood-soaked—mercy remains one of the greatest needs of all humanity. If instead of revenge, nations exercised compassionate forgiveness, what a transformation would take place globally! And if human relationships within marriage and family were governed by loving-kindness and tenderheartedness, suffering would be greatly minimized. Mercy grants undeserved acceptance and helpfulness even in life's unjust circumstances. In situations where punishment might rightly be expected, mercy is the exercise of peace-making pardon and forgiveness.

EVERYDAY APPLICATION

As followers of Christ, we know from personal experience that no person, however "good," has a right to God's mercy or favor. None of us deserves mercy; it's always a grace freely bestowed. As the apostle Paul said, "Because of his great love for us, God, who is rich in mercy, made us alive with Christ even when we were dead in transgressions" (Ephesians 2:4-5; see also 1 Peter 1:3). Those of us who have come to faith in Christ should thank God daily for his saving mercy so freely poured out upon us.

Because God is compassionate goodness, when we find ourselves in a season of need, we should cry out to God for mercy—as many did in Jesus' day (Mathew 15:22; 17:15). God alone is able to meet our most desperate needs. When we fail or fall into sin, we should actively seek God's mercy. As the writer to the Hebrews declared: "Let us then approach God's throne of grace with confidence, so that we may receive mercy and find grace to help us in our time of need" (Hebrews 4:16, TNIV). God delights to grant mercy to those who ask.

Finally, the merciful God exhorts his people to be merciful, witnessing to and reflecting his character. Through the prophet Micah, God announced: "He has shown all you people what is good. And what does the LORD require of you? To act justly and to love mercy" (Micah 6:8, TNIV). As recipients of God's saving mercy, he summons us to be its conduits, letting go of vengeful thoughts and instead exercising loving-kindness. In all our relationships, we should walk in the moral and spiritual footsteps of Jesus, exhibiting an attitude that is motivated by his work on the cross. In the Gospels, Jesus exhibited mercy by reaching out to relieve human want, grief, and pain. Scripture calls for us as God's people to imitate Jesus in his character and actions, including his virtue of mercy. When we reach out in these ways—as we bless the needy with mercy—we find that we ourselves are at least equally blessed.

FOR FURTHER READING
Lawrence O. Richards, *Expository Dictionary of Bible Words*. Zondervan, 1985.

—VERNON C. GROUNDS

MIND

EVERYDAY DEFINITION
Mind refers to the intellectual faculty that a moral being uses for thought, reflection, knowledge, understanding, discernment, and memory. Although the Bible has no specific word for the human brain, it does speak in various ways about the functions of the brain in its capacity to process ideas, develop conceptual understandings, and remember the past. In addition to mere understanding and knowledge, the mind in Scripture is often associated with reflection and planning that can be moral or immoral and wise or foolish. Significant overlap occurs in Scripture between mind and heart, understanding and discernment, knowledge and wisdom.

As used in the Bible, the mind processes ideas and develops understanding, but it doesn't do so in autonomous fashion independently of an individual's moral nature. The mind of an unregenerate person is both bound and blinded in how it thinks and plans: "The god of this age has blinded the minds of unbelievers, so that they cannot see the light of the gospel that displays the glory of Christ, who is the image of God" (2 Corinthians 4:4; see also Romans 8:5-8). The apostle Paul made clear that this faulty understanding is a consequence of hardness of heart toward God and his truth. He described unbelievers as those who walk "in the futility of their mind, being darkened in their understanding . . . because of the hardness of their heart" (Ephesians 4:17-18, NASB).

On the other hand, the mind of the believer has been enlightened to see God's truth as truth rather than as foolishness, to love what was formerly hated, and embrace what was formerly repelled. Paul described this enlightenment: "For God, who said, 'Let light shine out of darkness,' made his light shine in our hearts to give us the light of the knowledge of God's glory displayed in the face of Christ" (2 Corinthians 4:6, TNIV). Those who are given the ability to see God's glorious truth are called to set their hearts and minds on this truth (Colossians 3:1-2; see also Philippians 4:8). As Christians contemplate truth in this way, the renewal of the mind takes place (Romans 12:2).

EVERYDAY APPLICATION

Because the minds of unbelievers are trapped in some level of deception—seeing the truth as folly and understanding their own errant ways as right and good—we shouldn't be surprised at the ways an unbelieving world both misunderstands and mocks what we as Christians hold most precious. Jesus taught that although light has come into the world, unbelievers love the darkness rather than the light, "for their deeds were evil" (John 3:19, NASB). The antipathy unbelievers have toward God and his moral law inevitably leads to the unregenerate quest to prove that God's truth is foolish. Given this reality, we should be praying fervently for God's Spirit to work through our presentations of the truth, asking him to open blinded eyes to behold the glory of the gospel for what it is.

As believers who have been given spiritual sight, we should thank God regularly for the access we now have to the truth of his Word. We should long and study to know that truth more deeply and clearly. And we should uphold and defend this precious and glorious truth at all costs, realizing that only in knowing that truth are we and others truly set free to live for God's glory. Transformation of mind to know the truth more fully, and strengthening of convictions that uphold that truth faithfully, must be among the hallmarks of those of us whose eyes are opened and whose hearts now love the light and the truth of Christ.

FOR FURTHER READING

Harry Blamires, *The Christian Mind: How Should a Christian Think?* Regent College, 2005.

J. P. Moreland, *Kingdom Triangle: Recover the Christian Mind, Renovate the Soul, Restore the Spirit's Power.* Zondervan, 2007.

James W. Sire, *Habits of the Mind: Intellectual Life as a Christian Calling.* InterVarsity, 2000.

— BRUCE A. WARE

MIRACLES

EVERYDAY DEFINITION

Miracles are works of God within creation that can't be explained on the basis of normal scientific observation and thought. They appear in life purposefully from God. Miracles include power over nature, disease, death, and demons. However, miracles aren't just unanticipated, awe-inspiring, and astonishing; they are *good*. While miracles might seem a little scary at times, they're appreciated by those they help or heal.

While God is always at work in the world, miracles represent special ways that God works. Miracles show that because God is above creation, he's not limited to working within the created order he set up. Because they stand out from the backdrop of routine life, miracles are also a way God makes himself known to human beings. They're a way of pulling back the curtain on the normal course of events to reveal God's character, love, and provision. Miracles reveal the heart and purpose of God in ways that enlarge our capacity to see his power and glory.

Miracles are sometimes called "signs" and "wonders." They're signs because they point to something beyond themselves — something God desires to reveal in a powerful and unmistakable way (Isaiah 7:11; John 2:11). Miracles are wonders because they bring forth joy, awe, and fear of the Lord (Luke 1:11ff; Joel 2:30).

At times, God works miracles in cooperation with people. The biblical record shows Moses, Aaron, Joshua, Samson, Elijah, Elisha, Isaiah, Daniel, Jonah, Jesus, Peter, Paul, Stephen, Philip, and others working with God in this way.

In the Old Testament, we see miracles such as Creation (Genesis 1–2); the flood (Genesis 7:17-24); the burning bush (Exodus 3:3); the Exodus (Exodus 3–12; 14:21-23); the provision of manna (Exodus 16:13-36); the authentication of Aaron as leader (Numbers 17:8); healing by looking upon the bronze serpent (Numbers 21:9); the fall of Jericho (Joshua 6:6-20); the strength of Samson (Judges 14–16); a widow's son raised from the dead (1 Kings 17:17-24); an iron axe-head made to float in the Jordan River (2 Kings 6:5-7); Shadrach, Meshach, and Abednego delivered from the fiery furnace (Daniel 3:10-27); Daniel saved in the lions' den (Daniel 6:16-23); Jonah in the fish's belly (Jonah 2:1-10); and many others.

The New Testament recounts miracles such as curing of blindness (Matthew 9:27-31; Mark 8:22-26; John 9:1-7); stilling of a storm (Matthew 8:23; Mark 4:37; Luke 8:22); finding a piece of money in a fish's mouth (Matthew 17:24-27); raising from the dead (Luke 7:11-18; John 11:38-44; Matthew 9:23; Acts 9:40); water turned into wine (John 2:1-11); a miraculous catch of fish (Luke 5:4-11; John 21:1-14); feeding of thousands (Matthew 14:15; 15:32; Mark 6:30; 8:1; Luke 9:10; John 6:1-14); withering of a fig tree (Matthew 21:18; Mark 11:12); Jesus walking on the sea (Matthew 14:25; Mark 6:48; John 6:15); many miracles performed by Paul (Acts 19:11-16); miracles performed by the seventy (Luke 10:17ff); great miracles performed by Stephen (Acts 6:8); apostles released from prison or jail (Acts 5:19; 12:7-11; 16:25-26); the conception of Jesus by the Holy Spirit (Luke 1:35); the Transfiguration (Matthew 17:1-8); the Resurrection (John 21:1-14); and the Ascension (Luke 2:42-51).

Even a partial list of biblical miracles — not to mention the countless others from church history — could cause people to think that miracles are routine. God acting in and guiding his creation is routine, but miracles are special ways we see his handiwork. Yet miracles are never just for show. The biblical record never describes God doing random acts like flying on a donkey down a street in Jerusalem to prove he is God. Miracles unveil and bring about the good and loving will of God. Most of the time, while miracles do reveal the charter and power of God (John 9:2-3), they also directly benefit needy people.

EVERYDAY APPLICATION

If miracles happen, and if they're usually on behalf of needy people, does this mean we should seek them? This is tricky. On one hand, the answer is: "Sure; why shouldn't God's children seek him for divine and miraculous interventions similar to the ones noted above?" On the other hand, in asking for miraculous signs or interventions, our motive and attitude toward God make all the difference in the world. Jesus said some people seeking miraculous signs were evil (Matthew 16:4; Luke 11:29). These people weren't evil because seeking itself is wicked. They were evil because of their cynical and stubborn attitudes. They were asking for a sign after Jesus had already clearly revealed himself to them. In a sense they were actually looking for a way to reject Jesus—thinking that he couldn't do what they requested. Other times, religious leaders tried to bait Jesus into "performing" to suit their religious or political agenda.

People can interact with miracles in a way that actually prevents or slows spiritual seeking (John 6:25-30). Miracles can become another item to use in a consumer-driven culture. For example, when Jesus fed the crowd of thousands, the people around Jesus rightly valued the bread he miraculously provided but they missed the bigger picture that Jesus was the true and lasting Bread of Life.

The New Testament also describes "false miracles" (Mark 13:22; see also the acts of the Egyptian magicians in Exodus 7:11-22; 8:18-19). These miracles are false not because they aren't "real." In fact, their realness gives them the capacity to deceive. Rather, they are false because they come from the enemies of God and are designed to confuse, deceive, and lead honest seekers away from Jesus. So as we legitimately interact with God, sometimes through miraculous ways, we always need to be discerning. Thankfully, this ability has been given to all Christians (1 Kings 3:9; Philippians 1:10; Hebrews 5:14; 1 John 2:20-21), and some in the body are especially gifted in discernment (1 Corinthians 12:10).

The New Testament also provides other warnings regarding miracles. The ability to perform miracles isn't a sure sign that the one doing so is acting in concert with God. (Matthew 7:22-23). False religious leaders will perform signs and wonders designed to deceive (Matthew 24:24). This phenomena is especially attributed to the Antichrist and other powerful spiritual beings (2 Thessalonians 2:3,9; Revelation 13:13; 19:20).

With all the warnings about possible wrong interactions with miracles, we can see why some Christian leaders teach that miraculous powers are suspect and other leaders say that miracles no longer occur. However, the biblical record reveals miracles being performed by various individuals in the church through the power of the Holy Spirit. Church history continues this pattern. Further, Jesus declared that those who believe in him will do greater works than he did (John 14:12). While Christians can debate about exactly what "greater" means, Jesus surely implied that God intended to continue to work through his followers in miraculous ways.

Jesus said that the kingdom of God was "at hand" in his person and ministry. Miracles are evidence of the kingdom among us. We can expect miracles to accompany God's kingdom in the present until its consummation in the world to come.

FOR FURTHER READING
Wayne Grudem, *Systematic Theology*. Zondervan, 1994.
C. S. Lewis, *Miracles*. HarperSanFrancisco, 1947.
Graham H. Twelftree, *Jesus the Miracle Worker: A Historical and Theological Study*. InterVarsity, 1999.

— TODD HUNTER

MISSION

EVERYDAY DEFINITION
The theme of missions saturates the Bible from Genesis to Revelation. Throughout the Bible, God is on mission to display his glory among all the nations and redeem his lost world. In the Old Testament, mission was primarily a call for nations to "come and see" God's blessing and glory in Israel. In the New Testament, mission became primarily a mandate to God's people to "go and proclaim" his glory to the nations.

God's mission began when he interrupted the downward spiral of human sin and consequent judgment (Genesis 3–11) with a promise to bless Abraham and his descendents (Genesis 12:1-3). This promise held a much wider purpose: Abraham and his descendents, Israel, were blessed *in order to be* a blessing to the nations. God began to fulfill this purpose when he redeemed Israel from Egypt. He not only brought the plagues of the Exodus to free Israel, but to make himself known to Israel, Egypt, and the nations (see Exodus 6:2-8; 7:5,17; 8:10,22; 9:14,16). When the Israelites stood before Mount Sinai, God told them he had freed them from slavery so they would be a kingdom of priests, revealing him to the nations of the world (Exodus 19:6).

The rest of the Old Testament is peppered with examples of God's passion to be known among the nations. Joshua (Joshua 4:24), David (1 Samuel 17:46), and Hezekiah (2 Kings 19:19) all recognized that God's miraculous intervention on Israel's behalf was for the purpose of revealing God to the nations. God had such compassion on the people of Nineveh that, even though they were a threat to Israel, he sent a reluctant prophet, Jonah, to give them a chance to repent. The Psalms are rich with reminders that God longs to be known by all people and that he calls all nations to praise and submit to him (see 2:10-12; 47:1-3,7-9; 57:7-11; 66:1-8; 68:28-32; 87:1-7; 98:2-6; 117). Some Psalms are especially packed with missionary message. Psalm 67 reminds God's people that God blesses them in order that the nations might bless him. Psalm 96 mandates God's people to proclaim his glory to the whole world because he is worthy of the world's worship. The prophets also reflected God's desire to be known among the nations. Isaiah promised that Israel's servant would provide salvation for the nations (Isaiah 42:1-9; 49:1-7; 52:13–53:12) and foresaw a time when the nations would stream into Jerusalem to worship Israel's God (Isaiah 2:1-4; 66:18-21; Jeremiah 4:1-2; Ezekiel 36:22-23; Amos 9:11-12; Zechariah 2:7-13; 8:20-23).

In the New Testament, the message of mission continued as Jesus assured his followers that the good news about his kingdom would be proclaimed to all people groups on earth before he returned (Matthew 24:14). His mandate to his followers to proclaim this good news to all the nations is recorded five times, with each passage stressing a different aspect of his command (Matthew 28:18-20; Mark 16:15-18; Luke 24:44-49; John 20:21-23; Acts 1:8). The book of Acts traces how, through the witness of Jesus' disciples and the power of the Holy Spirit, people of many nations and ethnic groups received the salvation blessings that were promised in the Old Testament and made possible by the life, death, and resurrection of Jesus. The Epistles are also shaped with a missional purpose. Although many people think of Paul as the first great Christian theologian, he "was the first Christian theologian precisely because he was the first Christian missionary."[23] Paul's theology was written to help young churches become established in their faith and join in reaching out to others with the

---

23. David Bosch, *Transforming Mission* (Maryknoll, NY: Orbis, 1991), 124.

gospel (Romans 15:24). The climax of God's passion to see his glory proclaimed among the nations comes in Revelation 7:1-12, where people of every ethnic group on earth worship him because of who he is and his matchless salvation.

EVERYDAY APPLICATION

If mission is one of the main themes of the Bible, it should certainly be one of the main purposes in the life of every Christian and every local church. What does it mean to be involved in mission?

- As believers, we should be ready to share our own story of how Jesus gave us the assurance of eternal life and how others can also enjoy this life (Mark 16:15; 1 Peter 3:15-16).
- We should live exemplary lives that demonstrate to others the difference that Christ makes in life in order to attract them to the Savior (1 Thessalonians 1:8; 1 Peter 2:11-12).
- We should be able to help new Christians understand the teachings in the Bible so they can grow stronger in their Christian faith (note the emphasis on *make disciples* and *teaching* in Matthew 28:19-20).
- We should be involved in acts of compassion to show Jesus' love to a hurting world (Galatians 6:10; Luke 10:9,25-37).

Who do Christians engage in mission? Acts 1:8 gives us a model of the many levels where we carry out mission:

- Jerusalem and Judea: In our own towns and countries, we need to be witnesses of what Jesus has done in our lives to those who are culturally like us.
- Samaria: In areas that are geographically near us, we need to share Jesus with people who are ethnically and culturally different from us. For example, we need to be quick to share Jesus with immigrants, people of other racial and ethnic groups, and with visiting students and business people.
- The ends of the earth: We need to be involved in sharing the gospel with those who are geographically distant and culturally different from us. We get involved in "ends of the

earth" mission by engaging in prayer for the peoples of the world. We can also give generously to God's work around the world. And we should consider how God might want us to be personally involved in sharing the good news cross-culturally.

In addition, we can work to make sure that everything our own local church does occurs with the goal of sharing Jesus with a lost world. For example, children's and youth ministry should exist to bring young people to Christ, including those who don't currently attend the church. Worship should prepare believers to share Christ and point unbelievers to God. Ministries of teaching and edification should produce mature Christians, but maturity with a purpose: to reach those outside the church who don't know Christ.

God desires that every local church and all believers center their lives on making Christ known among the nations.

FOR FURTHER READING

John Piper, *Let the Nations Be Glad.* Baker, 2003.

Andreas J. Köstenberger and Peter T. O'Brien, *Salvation to the Ends of the Earth.* InterVarsity, 2001.

Christopher J. H. Wright, *The Mission of God: Unlocking the Bible's Grand Narrative.* InterVarsity, 2006.

— STEVE STRAUSS

MODERNISM

EVERYDAY DEFINITION

Although the word *modern* typically means "contemporary" or "current" when used by theologians, philosophers, and sociologists, it refers to a period of time from the middle of the nineteenth century to the late twentieth century. The eras that led up to modernism — the Enlightenment, the Industrial Revolution, and the Romantic Period — all emphasized the supremacy of human knowledge and wisdom. Modernism came about as a result of these significant changes in culture and human understanding.

In many respects, modernism was the zenith of human rationality.

Emmanuel Kant (1724-1804) was an Enlightenment philosopher who declared, "Enlightenment is man's leaving his self-caused immaturity. . . . *Have the courage to use your own intelligence!* is therefore the motto of the enlightenment." A century later, at the height of modernism, those in the Western world believed they had followed their intelligence into the "adulthood" of the human race. The advent of automobiles meant they had the ability to travel with autonomy; the invention of the airplane promised rapid, global transportation; and telecommunications (both the telegraph and telephone) changed the ways people related to one another.

Meanwhile, scholars and artists in nearly every field were purposefully leaving behind traditional and historical pieces of the past that they believed were slowing human progress. And *progress* was the buzzword of modernism. Indeed, modernists were responsible for astonishing leaps forward: Albert Einstein in physics, Edmund Husserl in philosophy, Igor Stravinsky in music, Charles Dickens and Leo Tolstoy in literature, and Pablo Picasso and Henri Matisse in painting. Even movements such as Marxism and Socialism in the United States during World War I were attempts to overcome human fighting and suffering with political systems.

Ironically, modernism's emphasis on human effort, progress, and rationality ultimately led to the end of the era. In the nineteenth century, when Friedrich Nietzsche declared, "God is dead," he meant that humans would no longer believe in a transcendent Being who determined a universal moral code. The thinking went that it would be better to trust in humanity. This kind of secular humanism led not to world peace but to the bloodiest century in human history, marked by the Holocaust, World War II, Vietnam, Apartheid, and other atrocities. It turned out that human rationality has limits, and that progress for its own sake can quickly corrupt a culture.

EVERYDAY APPLICATION

The church wasn't immune from the allures of modernism. At the turn of the twentieth century, many Christians in the Western hemisphere were consumed with the latest scholarship. Albert Schweitzer's *Quest for the Historical Jesus* was a best-seller in 1906, and the founding of the Religious Education Association in 1903 sought to bring the latest in progressive educational theory into the church. In fact, the vast majority of American church worship in the early twentieth century resembled university lectures surrounded by stately hymns. Both the fundamentalist movement of the 1890s and the birth of American Pentecostalism in 1906 were counter-reactions to these trends.

With notable exceptions, the church in twentieth century America was in harmony with American culture. Ministers were primarily educated men who often served on civic boards. Church leaders staunchly defended American-style democracy and free-market capitalism and spoke out against socialists and communists. Churches were gathered into large, bureaucratic denominations. Christian formation was modeled on the public schools and modern theories of education. Missionaries used Western ideals to shape churches around the globe.

In many ways, this structure has served the American church well. For much of the twentieth century, churches grew both in size and influence. Churches in the modern era were often cornerstones of small towns and community gathering points in large cities. Because the modernist belief in the power of the human intellect prevailed, churches became proficient at creating and passing on traditions and doctrines from one generation to the next. The modern church grew precisely because the institutional formula was easily replicated across demographic boundaries. A small church in rural Kansas could model itself on a larger church in suburban Dallas and quickly become a thriving congregation.

Still, as communication around the world has become more instant, and as Christians have learned more about the ways the gospel is lived out in cultures and communities around the world, many church leaders are realizing that modern formulas and traditions might not be sufficient for all people in all places. Over the last sixty years, a new way of thinking has arisen — one that questions the inerrancy of human thought that was the hallmark of the modern era.

Those who hold to the modern view of Christianity find support for the need for authority and absolute truth in passages such as Acts 17:16-31, where the apostle Paul encouraged the people of Athens to study God so they would know who they worshipped. He seemed to suggest that because we are created by God, humans have the capacity to know God. For modern Christians, Paul's speech seems to confirm that knowledge is the primary way to connect with God. The emphasis is on intellect, not experience.

FOR FURTHER READING
Michael Levenson, editor, *The Cambridge Companion to Modernism.* Cambridge University Press, 1999.
Alex Ross, *The Rest Is Noise: Listening to the Twentieth Century.* Picado, 2008.
Lawrence Rainey, editor, *Modernism: An Anthology.* Wiley-Black, 2005.

— TONY JONES

MYSTICISM

EVERYDAY DEFINITION

Some have quipped that mysticism begins in mist and ends in schism. Actually, the word mysticism comes from the Greek word *muō,* meaning "to hide," suggesting that mysticism concerns something that is either difficult to understand or unknown. Through history the term has been used by a wide swath of unbelievers and Christians alike.

We can better understand the diverse world of mysticism when we draw a distinction between "hard" and "soft" forms of mysticism.

- Hard mysticism affirms the radical unknowability of the Absolute Being, rather than the God who can be known through Jesus Christ. The individualistic focus of hard mysticism elevates deep mystical experience above the Word of God. Regarding salvation, it calls for a false combination of divine grace and human works. More seriously still, hard mysticism seeks union with the Absolute, a merging of the human person with the divine that causes self-consciousness to be lost. Buddhism, non-dualist Hinduism, and the Occult represent forms of hard mysticism. Only a few professing Christians (for example, Pseudo-Dionysius, Meister Eckhart) could be regarded as hard mystics.
- Soft mysticism involves the Christian's intimate communion and relational union with the God of the Bible, involving no loss of individuality. Theologian Kenneth Boa describes soft mysticism as, "An intuitive and heart-oriented approach to spiritual formation that explores the inner terrain of the

soul's journey toward God."[24] While the Bible doesn't use the term mysticism, we can find examples of soft mysticism in Scripture. One is Jacob's encounter with God by the brook Jabbok, where he stated, "I saw God face to face" (Genesis 32:30). Other biblical examples of soft mysticism include: Moses' engagement with God at the burning bush (Exodus 3:1–4:17), Elijah's encounter with the Lord on Mount Carmel (1 Kings 18:36-39), Isaiah's vision and dialogue with Yahweh in the temple (Isaiah 6), the visions and locutions received by the three disciples on the Mount of Transfiguration (Mark 9:2-9), and Saul's encounter with the living Christ on the Damascus road (Acts 9:1-9).

Jesus' teaching about believers abiding in Christ and Christ in believers (John 14:20; 15:1-17; 17:21-23), Paul's experiential language about Christ living in him (Galatians 2:20), and the frequent New Testament "in Christ" language (Romans 16:3; 2 Corinthians 5:17) all reflect soft mysticism. The apostle Peter stated that believers "participate in the divine nature" (2 Peter 1:4), indicating that such participation involves a mystical sharing in God's grace and holiness without being absorbed into his essence. Paul also spoke of this reality with the words: "the glorious riches of this mystery, which is Christ in you, the hope of glory" (Colossians 1:27).

EVERYDAY APPLICATION

Despite the unbiblical excesses brought forth by hard mystics, faithful Christians don't need to fear authentic engagements with the triune God that often transcend description in human language. We should welcome the possibility of gaining knowledge of God through personal religious experience. Similarly, we shouldn't exclude the possibility that the almighty God in freedom might reveal himself to us through inaudible speech, a startling vision, or a powerful dream. Because we believe in a supernatural God, we shouldn't exclude the possibility of genuine and edifying mystical encounters with the Almighty.

Followers of Jesus should strive to deepen personal communion

---

24. Kenneth Boa, *Conformed to His Image* (Grand Rapids, MI: Zondervan, 2001), 514.

and loving union with him through the Spirit. The great church father, Augustine, put words to his journey to a deeper relationship with Christ: "Let me enter into the secret chamber of my heart and sing to You songs of love, which are largely sighs: my attempts to express what cannot be expressed."[25] Personal engagement with the living God, as seen through the experiences of many biblical characters, is a powerful engine for transformation of life and for effectiveness in Christian service. However, we should recognize that the ultimate experience of the Christian life is not engaging other-worldly experiences, but knowing and glorifying the true God. While seeking a deeper walk with Jesus that leads to greater fruitfulness for the kingdom, we'll reject outright any notion of fusion with or absorption into the essence of God, as those who practice hard mysticism seek.

This means we should carefully test the authenticity of so-called other-worldly experiences. Do supernatural spiritual experiences exalt and glorify God? Alleged mystical encounters that elevate the individual are false and potentially heretical or even cultic. Further, do mystical encounters result in the observable transformation of the individual involved in such experiences? Jesus himself provided the ultimate test of true or false purveyors of the truth: "By their fruit you will recognize them" (Matthew 7:16). The integrity and beauty of a life transformed by Christ is the litmus test of authentic spiritual encounters.

Soft (or biblical) mysticism doesn't subvert God's Word, doesn't overthrow Christ's work on the cross, doesn't neglect spiritual and material needs, and isn't the privilege of only the spiritually elite. Rather, biblical mysticism brings together mind, affections, and intentions in the service of Christ and his kingdom.

FOR FURTHER READING

Donald G. Bloesch, *Spirituality Old & New*. IVP Academic, 2007.
Emilie Griffin, ed. *Evelyn Underhill: Essential Writings*. Orbis, 2003.
John Michael Talbot, *The Way of the Mystics*. Jossey-Bass, 2005.

— BRUCE DEMAREST

---

25. Augustine, *Confessions*, 12.16.

NEW TESTAMENT

EVERYDAY DEFINITION

The New Testament is a collection of twenty-seven books that come from the first generation of the Christian church. These books represent the teachings of Jesus' original apostles, and traditionally, each book has been viewed as written by, associated with, or endorsed by Jesus' apostles. These books chronicle the life of Jesus, the formation of the early church, and the vision for God's new creation. These books are divided into the apostle Paul's letters, the general letters, the Gospels, the Acts of the Apostles, and the book of Revelation. Although the four Gospels appear first in our New Testament, the earliest writings were the letters of Paul and some of the general letters. The earliest of these writings appeared within about twenty years of Jesus' life, death, and resurrection.

More specifically, the divisions of the books are as follows:

- Paul's letters represent his response to particular challenges in local churches, some which he began himself (1 and 2 Thessalonians, Galatians, 1 and 2 Corinthians) and some which he did not begin (Colossians, Romans). Paul's letters are written to particular church communities that were struggling to live out the gospel of Jesus Christ. This is true even of letters addressed to individuals, such as Philemon, 1 and 2 Timothy, and Titus.
- The general letters were written by various writers, such as James, Peter, and John. These letters were also written to particular church communities learning to follow Jesus within their own context.
- The four Gospels provide biographical accounts of the life of Jesus. Three of these accounts—Matthew, Mark, and Luke—tell the story from a similar perspective, so they are sometimes called synoptic (which means "see with" in Greek) gospels. The fourth gospel, John, tells the story from a different vantage point that complements the synoptic gospels. The earliest of these is probably Mark, written between thirty to fifty years after the life of Jesus. Mark likely drew together oral traditions

that were preserved within the early church and put them to paper, possibly with the help of the apostle Peter. Matthew and Luke used Mark in their own writings. In fact, Luke mentioned consulting other written accounts as he wrote his "orderly account" (Luke 1:3). The gospel of John was written later, demonstrating later theological reflection on the life of Jesus.

- The Acts of the Apostles is actually the companion to the gospel of Luke. Following a similar structure as Luke, Acts chronicles the life of the early church, from the Day of Pentecost to Paul's imprisonment in Rome. In the early chapters, Peter and the church in Jerusalem are central to the story. In the later chapters, Paul and the church in Antioch become more central.

- The book of Revelation is the account of a vision given to John while in exile on the island of Patmos. The literary style of Revelation reflects the apocalyptic (from the Greek word for revelation) writing style common in the first century. Much of the book of Revelation is designed to provide hope and courage to Christians who were undergoing persecution from the Romans. Revelation also has visions of the second coming of Christ, along with the establishment of his kingdom in the new creation.

EVERYDAY APPLICATION

Whenever we apply the teaching of the New Testament today, we need to remember that these writings were originally directed to first-century church communities. As such, we need to be sure that our application of the text is consistent with the original intention of the author as that message would have been heard by the original readers.

One way Christians have used the New Testament for their spiritual formation is a technique called *lectio continua*. This technique involves reading the New Testament books sequentially. We can use the technique of *lectio continua* to read through the entire New Testament beginning in Matthew and ending in Revelation in ninety days, by reading three chapters each day. This method works best if we don't get too focused on small details, but instead look for the overall flow of the text—the big picture. Asking the basic questions of Who?

What? When? Why? Where? and How? can help formulate an overall theme for the three chapters of reading each day, followed by a few moments asking God to help apply that theme to everyday life. Many readers keep a journal to jot notes down as they experience this spiritual practice.

FOR FURTHER READING

D. A. Carson and Douglas Moo, *An Introduction to the New Testament*. Zondervan, 2005.

Gordon Fee and Douglas Stuart, *How to Read the Bible for All Its Worth*. Zondervan, 2003.

Richard Foster, *Life with God: Reading the Bible for Spiritual Transformation*. HarperOne, 2008.

Tremper Longman and Raymond Dillard. *An Introduction to the Old Testament*. Zondervan, 2006.

J. Robert Mulholland, *Shaped by the Word: The Power of Scripture in Spiritual Transformation*. Upper Room Books, 2001.

N. T. Wright, *The Last Word: Beyond the Bible Wars to a New Understanding of the Authority of Scripture*. HarperOne, 2005.

— TIM PECK

OBEDIENCE

EVERYDAY DEFINITION

Obedience is a readiness to carry out the rules or orders of another, and then to take action and do these things in order to satisfy the will of that other person. Obedient persons listen carefully to the advice, directions, and orders of the individual they choose to obey. In human terms, we obey parents and superiors, such as employers, government officials, or military leaders. Christians also believe that obedience is due to God and Christ.

Obeying involves more than just avoiding what's prohibited (Colossians 3:8,10). It also means eagerly and carefully doing all we can to satisfy requirements instead of getting by with doing as little as possible (2 Peter 1:5,10). Obedience might call for sacrificially letting go of something that is both deserved and important. The best example is

Jesus, who obeyed God the Father as he "humbled himself and became obedient to death—even death on a cross!" (Philippians 2:8; see also verses 5-11). As humans, our diligence might include fits and starts, but it becomes a continual and habitual way of life (Galatians 6:9).

Although obedience shows itself in outward actions (good intentions to obey aren't enough), obedience does begin in the heart and it dictates our actions and words: "For out of the overflow of the heart the mouth speaks" (Matthew 12:34). Good and obedient actions can't flow from a self-focused and disobedient heart (Matthew 6:16-20). This means that obedience begins by cultivating a good and obedient heart. For example, if we cultivate an obedient heart by praying for people we find difficult, we're more likely to do outward acts of obedient love for them (Matthew 5:44).

Obedience in the Christian tradition is brought to life by love. Scripture knows nothing of teeth-gritting, bitter obedience. The Shema begins with "Hear, O Israel, and be careful to obey so that it may go well with you," and continues, "*Love* the LORD your God with all your heart and with all your soul and with all your strength. These commandments that I give you today are to be upon your hearts" (Deuteronomy 6:3,5-6, emphasis added).

In the New Testament, abiding in Christ's love initiates and empowers obedience, sustaining us when we might otherwise have second thoughts: "As the Father has loved me, so I have loved you; abide in my love. If you keep my commandments, you will abide in my love, just as I have kept my Father's commandments and abide in his love. . . . This is my commandment, that you love one another as I have loved you" (John 15:9-10,12, NRSV). The process is reciprocal: love not only creates and compels obedience, but obedient, transformed behavior deepens love for Christ (verse 10). The mutual indwelling of Christ in us and we in Christ ("abide in me as I abide in you," John 15:4, NRSV) provides us with the juices to bear fruit such as love, joy, and peace (verse 5).

Obedience also comes from a trusting faith (Romans 1:5; 16:26). Obeying, trusting, and loving God are all interconnected: "But be very careful to keep the commandment and the law that Moses the servant of the LORD gave you: to love the LORD your God, to walk in all his ways, to obey his commands, to hold fast to him and to serve him with all your heart and all your soul" (Joshua 22:5). Obedience and trust are also reciprocal: to increase our faith, we need to obey. To obey, we need to trust more deeply.

While humans are obligated to obey God, God doesn't intend for obedience to be oppressive: "This is love for God: to obey his commands. And his commands are not burdensome" (1 John 5:3). The psalmist loved God's statutes (Psalm 119:167). One reason the yoke is easy and the burden light is that an obedient life is full of advantages, particularly personal peace (Psalm 25:12-13; Acts 24:16).

Obedience to Christ results in transformation into Christlikeness. Those who carefully follow Christ by paying attention to what he said and did, and who arrange their life according to the person of Christ will sooner or later become more patient and kind, not envying or boasting. They will let go of pride, rudeness, and self-seeking ways. They won't be easily angered or keep a record of wrongs. They won't think to delight in anything evil but rejoice with the truth. They'll be the kind of persons who routinely protect, trust, hope, and persevere (1 Corinthians 13:4-7). They won't become this way by *trying* to become this way, but by abiding in Christ.

People wrongly assume that prosperity will be a result of obedience because they believe God always withholds blessing from the disobedient. However, Jesus said that God "causes his sun to rise on the evil and the good, and sends rain on the righteous and the unrighteous" (Matthew 5:45). While it's not universally true in every instance, the *normative* principle is that blessings flow from obedience because this design is built into creation — into both the human spirit and the ways of the earth. So justice and fairness *customarily* bring about wellness for a nation. Well-cultivated fields *typically* bring forth plentiful harvests (Deuteronomy 15:4-6). But these things are not *always* so.

EVERYDAY APPLICATION

Because obedience begins in the heart and is so closely tied to love for God and trust of God, the first step we need to take as obedient followers of Christ is to cultivate hearts that are full of faith and love: "Watch over your heart with all diligence, for from it flow the springs of life" (Proverbs 4:23, NASB). Of course, careful cultivation of the heart and its subsequent obedience doesn't just happen. We don't just stumble into it. It requires intentionality. We can follow Joshua's guidance to the

Israelites: "Be strong and very courageous. Be careful to obey all the law my servant Moses gave you; do not turn from it to the right or to the left, that you may be successful wherever you go" (Joshua 1:7). We choose obedience with all of our self: heart, soul, mind, and strength (Deuteronomy 30:17).

Of course, we might have trouble simply mustering up this kind of intentionality. In difficult situations when we need to obey but the heart isn't completely willing, it helps to view the opportunity as an experiment, saying, "I'm going to trust God in this and see what happens." For example, if we tell the truth in a difficult situation, we can see how it works out. What do we learn? What assurance will we have next time that was missing before? What assurance do we still need? Because obedience isn't cold and separate from a relationship with God, we can ask, "How do I need to trust God more in order to obey in this difficult area? How might my trust be built up?" Such experimentation is an opportunity to trust God to lead and empower you.

Our trust and love of God grow, as C. S. Lewis concluded, because obedience "will not be attained by any merely human efforts. You must ask for God's help. Even when you have done so, it may seem to you for a long time that no help, or less help than you need, is being given. Never mind. After each failure, ask forgiveness, pick yourself up, and [experiment] again. Very often what God first helps us toward is not the virtue itself but just this power of always [experimenting] again. . . . We learn, on the one hand, that we cannot trust ourselves even in our best moments, and, on the other that we need not despair even in our worst, for our failures are forgiven. The only fatal thing is to sit down content with anything less than perfection."[26]

FOR FURTHER READING

Andrew Murray, *The True Vine*. Diggory Press, 2007.
Dietrich Bonhoeffer, *The Cost of Discipleship*. Touchstone, 1995.

—JAN JOHNSON

---

26. C. S. Lewis, *Mere Christianity*, 93-94.

OLD TESTAMENT

EVERYDAY DEFINITION

The Old Testament is the collection of writings recounting God's saving plan from creation to the nation of Israel. Our Old Testament contains the same writings as the Jewish Bible, but the books are divided differently. The classic Jewish division of these writings is the Law (Hebrew: *Torah*), Prophets (Hebrew: *Nevi'im*), and Writings (Hebrew: *Ketuvim*), which provides the acronym *Tanakh*. The Christian Bible divides the Old Testament writings into Law, History, Poetry, and Prophecy.

More specifically, the divisions of the Old Testament books are as follows:

- The books of Law cover Genesis through Deuteronomy. Genesis 1–11 provides a foundation for God's redemptive story, narrating God's creation, the entrance of sin into humanity, and the effects of that sin. Beginning in chapter 12, God's redemptive plan begins with his selection of Abraham, Isaac, and Jacob. These forefathers are pivotal to the formation of Israel's story, as well as the story of Jesus. Jacob's twelve sons become the twelve tribes of Israel, and Genesis ends with these twelve sons and their descendants in Egypt. Exodus through Deuteronomy recount God's deliverance of Israel from their slavery in Egypt, and God's initiation of a covenant relationship with Israel. The heart of this covenant relationship is the Ten Commandments, while the rest of the laws of the Old Testament elaborate on these ten laws, as well as stipulating the consequences if Israel fails to live up to its terms in the covenant.
- The historical books begin with Joshua and end with Esther. These books contain stories of Israel's faithfulness and unfaithfulness to their covenant with God, and God's continuing advancement of his plan. Beginning with Israel's entrance into the land of Canaan, these books recount how a people once enslaved became a powerful nation. The books of Judges, Ruth, and 1 and 2 Samuel recount the eventual establishment of a monarchy, first with Saul and then later with David. The building of the first Jewish temple in Jerusalem by

Solomon and eventual collapse of this monarchy into two separate nations follows in 1 and 2 Kings. First and 2 Chronicles retell the same story from a different perspective. Both Kings and Chronicles end with the destruction of the first Jewish temple. Ezra and Nehemiah recount Israel's eventual return from exile and the beginnings of their rebuilding of the second Jewish temple. Throughout the historical books, God is presented as the primary hero of the story.

- The Old Testament books of poetry consist of both music lyrics and wisdom literature. The books of Psalms and Song of Songs contain lyrical poetry originally set to music. The 150 songs in the book of Psalms represent Israel's worship experiences. The wisdom literature of Job, Ecclesiastes, and Proverbs represent reflections about suffering, the aimlessness of life, and the ways people try to navigate life successfully.
- The prophetic books represent God's intervention at various stages in Israel's history, calling Israel back to their commitment to the covenant. These prophetic books sometimes contain predictive elements — some regarding the immediate future of the prophet, and others concerning the distant future with the coming of Christ into the world.

EVERYDAY APPLICATION

Whenever we apply the Old Testament to the spiritual formation of our lives today, we need to remember that the commands of the Old Testament were originally given to the nation of Israel. Israel was under a unique covenant that overlaps yet is distinct from the covenant we find ourselves in as followers of Christ. So while the commands of the Old Testament are God's Word *for* us, they are not God's command *to* us unless the New Testament provides clear evidence that this is the case.

Throughout the ages, Christians have found praying through the Psalms to be a spiritually transformative spiritual practice, and this is one way we can apply the teachings of Old Testament writings to our lives today. The Psalms cover the whole spectrum of emotion and life experience, from the heights of joy to the depths of despair. This might start with a thirty-day experiment of praying through the Psalms, beginning with Psalm 1 and ending with Psalm 30, dedicating fifteen minutes each day to slowly and carefully read through the psalm. Those undertaking this exercise can verbalize the words of the psalm as a prayer to God, looking for ways that the language of the psalm evokes responses from the soul and intersects with life experiences. Praying the psalms can help us develop a new language for prayer that will be embedded in our hearts for future circumstances.

FOR FURTHER READING

Gordon Fee and Douglas Stuart, *How to Read the Bible for All Its Worth*. Zondervan, 2003.

Richard Foster, *Life with God: Reading the Bible for Spiritual Transformation*. HarperOne, 2008.

Tremper Longman and Raymond Dillard, *An Introduction to the Old Testament*. Zondervan, 2006.

J. Robert Mulholland, *Shaped by the Word: The Power of Scripture in Spiritual Transformation*. Upper Room Books, 2001.

N. T. Wright, *The Last Word: Beyond the Bible Wars to a New Understanding of the Authority of Scripture*. HarperOne, 2005.

—TIM PECK

OMNIPOTENCE

EVERYDAY DEFINITION

Omnipotence means that God has the ability to do anything he wills in the way that he desires. Because God is the source of life and everything material and spiritual in the universe, he can do whatever he chooses. However, because God is love (1 John 4:16) and truth (Psalm 31:5) he never acts in a way contrary to his holy nature.

God is the essence of all that's good, and he always uses his omnipotent power in ways that bring him glory. As the sovereign King and Lord of all, he always accomplishes his perfect will. Because he is all-powerful, God created the universe out of nothing (*ex nihilo*). All that exists was called into being by his divine command and nothing exists that he did not make (Hebrews 11:3). As God Almighty, he exercises a power and control that is literally universal in scope and completely comprehensive in depth.

God's omnipotence extends beyond creation to all of human history and the free choices of individual men and women. He plans and acts so that some things happen unconditionally by his direct intervention. What God purposes to occur in history invariably comes to pass. His will can never be thwarted by events, human choices, or other spiritual forces (Isaiah 14:24; Job 42:2). God possesses unlimited power to over-rule the actions of humanity. This is most clearly seen in the crucifixion of the Messiah, who was given over to death by the wicked actions of men but transformed into eternal redemption by God's gracious power (Acts 2:23-24).

EVERYDAY APPLICATION

God's omnipotence should deepen our devotion and worship of him. The truth that God is sovereign power over every aspect of life causes us to joyfully seek him and bow before him on a daily basis. As we kneel before our omnipotent God, our lives and ministries progressively become transformed by his unlimited power (Isaiah 6:1-8).

The reality of God's omnipotence should also help us increase our trust in him. Because he is both all-powerful and perfectly good, nothing can happen outside his sovereign will. So when we find ourselves facing the difficult and painful realities of life, we can know with certainty that in his infinite power and wisdom, God will always use such trials to accomplish his noble purposes (Genesis 50:20). In addition, God will use his power to bring about the visible development of godly char-acter and spiritual maturity in our lives as we persevere in the faith (2 Corinthians 12:8-10; James 1:2-4).

God's omnipotence provides hope for us in the midst of desper-ate circumstances. Because he is the King and Lord of all, subject to no other dominion, nothing is too hard for him. Infertility can be overcome, healing from dire illness accomplished, the worst of sinners saved, and even the dead raised to life (see Genesis 18:1-14; Mark 2:1-12; 1 Timothy 1:15-16; John 12:25).

Knowing that God is all-powerful provides us comfort in the face of fear (Daniel 2:21-23). Even when faced with loss, disease, divorce, and death, the reality of God's ability to act on our behalf can ease our distressed hearts and fill us with his peace (Philippians 4:4-8). His unmatched ability to defeat any enemy, overthrow any government, cast out any demon, and even use the furious passion of sin for his glory and the greater good of the redeemed can bring spiritual and emotional reassurance to all those who believe (Acts 4:24-28; Romans 8:28-39).

Finally, a sound understanding of God's omnipotence can provide encouragement and hope in our evangelistic endeavors. Because nothing can thwart his powerful will, we pray and then share the good news of Christ with confidence, knowing that God will draw to himself those whose hearts have been touched by the gospel (Acts 18:9-11).

FOR FURTHER READING

Gordon R. Lewis, "God, Attributes of," in *Evangelical Dictionary of Theology*, Walter A. Elwell, ed. Baker Academic, 2001.

James Montgomery Boice, *The Sovereign God*. InterVarsity, 1978.

Philip Yancey, *Disappointment with God: Three Questions No One Asks Aloud*. Zondervan, 1988.

— SCOTT A. WENIG

OMNIPRESENCE

EVERYDAY DEFINITION

Omnipresence is the theological doctrine that God is everywhere and has personal access to all reality, both material and spiritual. Because he is self-existent and has no beginning, age, or ending, God is eternal. As the everlasting Creator of all things, God isn't limited by time or space. He is immense, meaning that he is fully present everywhere. God is not like a thin layer of ozone spread around the earth. On the contrary, the whole of God's being is present in every place at every time (Jeremiah 23:23-24; Acts 7:48-50).

God's eternal nature and sovereign reign mean that he providentially sustains all aspects of creation by his personal power and grace. God is perfectly aware of each moment and movement in history, including every person and what they think, say, and do. No one — regardless of age, place, or era — can ever escape or hide from him (Psalm 139:7-8).

Because God is fully everywhere at all times, he is always accessible to all people whether they recognize him or not (Acts 17:26-28). Yet to those who have accepted Christ's redemptive work, he is present in a more profound way (Isaiah 57:15; John 15:1-16). He dwells in the redeemed as his holy temple because he is their God and they are his people (1 Corinthians 3:16). Likewise, believers have been marked or sealed by the Holy Spirit, who resides in them as a guarantee of their salvation (Ephesians 1:13-14). In addition, the Lord has promised never to leave or forsake his people (Hebrews 13:5). Over time, this continual and relational oneness deepens to the point that his people know his voice and experience his presence in a deeply personal and intimate way (John 10:2-4; 2 Timothy 4:17).

EVERYDAY APPLICATION

God's omnipresence means that all people, regardless of when or where they live, are of intrinsic value to him. No tribe, nation, city, family, or individual is unimportant to the Lord of all. No matter how brief or insignificant their lives might seem, God is always aware of and in close proximity to them. As followers of Christ, this demands that all people should be of great value to us as well (Luke 15).

God's ongoing presence enables us to accomplish his will together with him. Because the Holy Spirit lives within us as believers, we have received spiritual gifts to serve him and others and build up the church (1 Corinthians 12:4-31; Ephesians 4:7-16). The Spirit empowers us to preach the gospel, serve the poor, minister to those in need, and give of our resources to advance his kingdom (Acts 2:1-38,42-47; Galatians 6:10). In addition, his indwelling presence bears rich spiritual fruit in our individual lives such as love, joy, and peace (Galatians 5:21).

God's omnipresence also means that no matter where we find ourselves or how difficult our circumstances, we can be certain we are never alone. He's always with us and around us, even as we sleep (Genesis 28:16). And even when God seems hidden or distant, we'll eventually realize that he has always been with us (Job 42:5). In the midst of life's ongoing trials and temptations, God's ever-present help always provides a sense of personal comfort and spiritual security (1 Kings 17; Psalm 46).

FOR FURTHER READING

Paul E. Little, *Know What You Believe.* Victor, 1970.

Gordon R. Lewis, "God, Attributes of," in *Evangelical Dictionary of Theology*, Walter A. Elwell, ed. Baker Academic, 2001.

John Ortberg, *God Is Closer Than You Think*. Zondervan, 2005.

— SCOTT A. WENIG

OMNISCIENCE

EVERYDAY DEFINITION

Omniscience is the term for the doctrine that means God knows all things. God's intellectual, perceptual, and experiential capacities are unlimited. He is conscious of and takes an interest in all things, from the largest cluster of galaxies to the smallest subatomic particle. Nothing in all of creation is hidden from his sight. He has determined the number of the stars and named each one (Psalm 147:4-5). He keeps watch over human behavior through all of history (Hebrews 4:13; Proverbs 15:3). Nothing in the universe is removed from his knowledge, and he always uses this knowledge fully and perfectly to accomplish his purposes (1 John 3:20).

God's infallible and exhaustive knowledge applies to all humanity, even down to the smallest personal details of each person's life. God knows the innermost thoughts, concerns, and fears of all people, as well every aspect of their physical, emotional, and spiritual world (Psalm 139:1-4,15). He is literally aware of every hair on the head of everyone and hears and sees all that they say and do (Matthew 10:29-30; Psalm 94).

God's knowledge of all things extends to the future as well as to the past and present (Isaiah 44:8,25-28). In fact, the New Testament apostles simply assumed that God perfectly knows the future (Ephesians 1:5; Romans 8:29). In the same way, he makes known the beginning from the end, whether that involves his own creative and redemptive work or the development and flow of human history (Isaiah 40:13-14; 46:10).

God's knowledge is primary, meaning that he is the ultimate source of knowledge that others can only borrow. Because God is perfectly good, his knowledge is pure; it is uncorrupted by evil, misperception, or individual subjectivity. His knowledge is also instantaneous, infallible, and comes without strain or difficulty. He has nothing to learn because he already knows all things and has always known all things. Because

God's knowledge is all-inclusive and comprehensive, it's impossible to overstate its quality, quantity, or perfection (Hebrews 4:13).

Some have argued that God can't know the future because it doesn't yet exist. At the personal level, this would mean that God doesn't know what an individual will do until that person decides and then chooses to act. Those who hold to this view are labeled Open Theists, meaning they believe the future is open and uncertain, even to God. Their doctrine is based on the belief that if God knew the future perfectly, human choice would be rendered moot and human free will compromised. However, if this belief were true, most of human existence would seem meaningless. Apart from the biblical teaching that clearly contradicts this view, open theism subtly makes God part of his own creation, restricting him to the limitations of time and space. But God is infinitely above his creation in all knowledge and understanding. Past, present, and future are temporal distinctions. By definition, God is the supernatural Creator and outside of time and space. Since he isn't subject to the nature of temporal reality, everything is immediately "present" to him.

EVERYDAY APPLICATION

The doctrine of God's omniscience offers both daily and eternal benefits to those of us who follow Christ, including the following:

- *God's omniscience reminds us of his intimate care.* Because God knows all things, including our thoughts (Psalm 139:2), we can be assured that he is fully aware of our temptations, troubles, misfortunes, and pain. We might wonder if God knows the particulars of our personal circumstance or situation, but the reality of his omniscience assures us that he does. This should provide us with comfort and hope in the midst of our trials. As God continues his redemptive work in our lives, we can know with certainty that his knowledge of our circumstances is sufficient and that he will always leverage our trials for our ultimate good (Romans 8:28-30).
- *God's omniscience functions as a call to joy.* God knows the fragile nature of our humanity and recognizes all our limitations (Psalm 103:14-16). While God knows the very

worst in us and the excesses of our humanity, he graciously has chosen to save and redeem us from our sin (Psalm 51:4-5; Ephesians 1:3-14). At the same time, he knows the very best of our thoughts, attitudes, and actions, and one day, he'll reward us for those (Matthew 25:14-23). From eternity past, God knew that he would conform us to the perfect image of his Son (Romans 8:28-29). While this is a life-long process, God's foreknowledge of his perfect end for us is cause for celebration. Even in the midst of our sins and failures, we can rejoice because, someday, we will be just like Jesus (1 John 3:2).

- *God's thorough and perfect knowledge acts as warning to all "would be" disciples.* God's intimate awareness of our thoughts and future actions should cause us to tread carefully. We might be able to fool others, but we can never deceive God. Hypocrisy is foolish and should be avoided at all costs. To do otherwise places us in a spiritually dangerous place (1 Samuel 28; John 13:21; Acts 1:25).

- *God's omniscience motivates us to walk humbly rather than boastfully.* God's knowledge of all things should prevent us from falsely asserting what we will or won't do (Micah 6:8; Matthew 26:33-35). Unlike the Lord, we don't know what the future holds, so we should live in submission to his perfect will (James 4:13-15).

- *God's omniscient means he knows the condition of our hearts.* Given that God desires our complete devotion, we need to make every effort to purify ourselves of sin and do as he commands (2 Chronicles 16:9). While God's perfect knowledge of us doesn't determine our actions, it should encourage us to nurture a deep and heartfelt love for him. In turn, this should stir us to a lifelong commitment to fulfill his calling in our lives (Colossians 3:23-24).

FOR FURTHER READING

James Montgomery Boice, *The Sovereign God.* InterVarsity, 1978.

Millard J. Erickson, *What Does God Know and When Does He Know It? The Current Controversy over Divine Foreknowledge.* Zondervan, 2003.

Gordon R. Lewis, "God, Attributes of," in *Evangelical Dictionary of Theology*, Walter A. Elwell, ed. Baker Academic, 2001.

— Scott A. Wenig

PEACE

Everyday Definition

The idea of peace as found in the Bible has a range of meanings, including well-being, abundance, the absence of war, wholeness, reconciliation, and righteousness. Above all, God desires that we are at peace with him, with others, and with ourselves.

Shalom, the Hebrew word for peace, is found more than 250 times in the Old Testament. Peace in the Old Testament often carries the idea of being well, which includes having physical needs met, being in good health, having full relationships, and being connected to community. Peace can also mean prosperity and refer to a rightly ordered life. Violence is the opposite of *shalom*.

The Old Testament prophets announced that peace will mark the fullness of God's reign. The prophet Isaiah pointed to God's messenger who will announce peace and salvation (Isaiah 2:4), and wrote of a day when weapons will be transformed into instruments of production and nations will no longer war against each other (Isaiah 52:7).

While the Old Testament frames peace as a gift from God, it also calls for people to embody peace by seeking righteousness and confronting oppression and injustice. So peace isn't just a state of existence, but also has an ethical dimension. God's peace calls on us to act and live in corresponding ways.

The New Testament Christians, living under Roman rule, would have known Rome's claim to be the provider of peace (the *Pax Romana*). But while this governmental decree allowed some to live in peace, it was built upon the oppression and suffering of others. Thus, it differed significantly from God's peace, a peace meant for everyone, not just those in privileged positions.

The primary Greek word for peace is *eirene,* which appears 100 times in the New Testament in different forms. In the New Testament, peace is always linked to the Old Testament/Jewish understandings of *shalom*.

At the same time, the New Testament understandings of peace reflect theological development that goes beyond the meanings of *shalom*.

Jesus came bearing a message of peace (Acts 10:36). Even before Jesus was born, Zechariah prophesied that Jesus would "guide our feet into the way of peace" (Luke 1:79, NASB). Jesus blesses those who make peace (Matthew 5:9). He instructed his disciples to respond to their enemies non-violently (Matthew 5:38-48). He expressed a desire for his followers to have peace, and he saw himself as the means for them to have this peace (John 16:33). He wept over Jerusalem because its people did not recognize the things that make for peace (Luke 19:42). And he prepared his disciples for his departure by giving them his peace (John 14:27). When Jesus said, "I have not come to bring peace, but a sword" (Matthew 10:34, NRSV), he didn't contradict his message of peace, but rather pointed to the divisions that his message would inevitably bring (Luke 12:51-53). Throughout his ministry, Jesus made connections between peace, the gospel, and the kingdom of God (Luke 10:1-12; Mark 9:47-50; Acts 10:36). Jesus ushers in a new era that, when fully here, will see peace extended to every corner of the earth and heavens. Even before that day is fully here, Jesus' words and his way of living call his followers to live here and now in peace and to pursue peace.

The apostle Paul also made peace a significant part of his theology. He argued that we are justified by faith and as a result of this we have peace with God (Romans 5:1). Peace is linked not just to justification, but also to salvation (Romans 5:10). Paul also made theological connections between peace and reconciliation. He stated that God, who is our peace, carries out his work of reconciliation by tearing down divisions between ethnic groups, and in this way hostility is made into peace (Ephesians 2:13-18). God's reconciling work, which affects all of creation, is brought about "by making peace through the blood of his cross" (Colossians 1:20, NRSV). Paul stated that the God of peace gives us peace (2 Thessalonians 3:16), the God of peace will be with us (Philippians 4:9), and the God of peace sanctifies us (1 Thessalonians 5:23). Paul included an ethical dimension in his understanding of peace: we are to pursue peace (2 Timothy 2:22), be at peace among ourselves (1 Thessalonians 5:13), and live peaceably with all (Romans 12:18). And Paul began all his letters by greeting his readers with God's grace and peace.

The other New Testament writers also spoke of peace. The author of Hebrews identified Jesus as the king of peace (Hebrews 7:1-3) and told his readers to pursue peace with everyone (Hebrews 12:14). James linked peace with wisdom and promised peace to the righteous (James 3:17-18). Peter urged followers of Christ to seek peace and pursue it (1 Peter 3:11).

EVERYDAY APPLICATION

Is God's peace political? Yes. Is God's peace personal? Yes. God's peace is to mark our relationships with God, with each other, with other nations, and with the whole of creation—it's comprehensive! As Christians, we must carefully hold together the ideas that peace is an internal condition of the heart, a lack of warfare between nations, and integrally related to justice, righteousness, and well-being. These spheres are all related; God's peace is a holistic peace that God wants to touch every aspect of human existence.

- God's peace is political. God is concerned with how governments, powers, and authorities treat people. Understood broadly, "political" means how we structure social relationships and institutions. In addition to caring about us as individuals, God also cares about these broad structures as we can see by the fact that God chose "to reconcile to himself all things, whether on earth or in heaven, by making peace through the blood of his cross" (Colossians 1:20, NRSV). One aspect of our participation in God's comprehensive reconciling work is to seek peace through the political processes of our country and the international community. While this involves pushing nations to resolve their differences through nonviolent means, peacemaking also means working to change cultural and economic patterns that undermine peace. This might include: working for the advancement of democracy, human rights, and religious liberty; pushing for just and sustainable economic conditions through acts of compassion; or establishing dialogue between enemies.
- God's peace is personal. God invites us into his peace and desires for our relationships to be marked by peace. One

aspect of this is the inner sense of being settled and content emotionally. God develops this peace in us by assuring us that he is always with us and reminding us not to worry about the future. The sense of peace related to contentment comes as we overcome our covetous appetites and jealousies. This personal peace is connected to our relationships with others. As we resolve our issues with others, we find more contentment and experience more fully God's peace. Forgiveness and reconciliation must be priorities for us if our relationships are to be marked by peace. Only as we learn to forgive others and seek reconciled relationships, can we move beyond hate, bitterness, resentment, and revenge and enter into God's peace.

FOR FURTHER READING

Glen Harold Stassen, ed., *Just Peacemaking: Ten Practices for Abolishing War*. Pilgrim Press, 1998.

Willard M. Swartley, *Covenant of Peace: The Missing Peace in New Testament Theology and Ethics*. Eerdmans, 2006.

— ROB MUTHIAH

PERSEVERANCE

EVERYDAY DEFINITION

The doctrine of perseverance teaches that true believers in Christ will not fall from grace, but will persist in faith to the end and be saved. True believers are kept unto final salvation through a unique combination of God's power and their spiritual diligence.

- Through his power, God faithfully preserves his followers to the end. Jesus said, "This is the will of him who sent me, that I shall lose none of all those he has given me, but raise them up at the last day" (John 6:39, TNIV). The apostle Paul affirmed: "[Jesus] will also keep you firm to the end, so that you will be blameless on the day of our Lord Jesus Christ" (1 Corinthians 1:8, TNIV); "Being confident of this, that he who began a good work in you will carry it on to completion until the day of

Christ Jesus" (Philippians 1:6). Paul expressed his confidence that "The Lord will rescue me from every evil attack and will bring me safely to his heavenly kingdom" (2 Timothy 4:18). According to the apostle Peter, believers are "shielded by God's power" (1 Peter 1:5). Jude added that Christians are "kept for Jesus Christ" (Jude 1:1, TNIV). Other Scriptures that detail God's power to help believers persevere include: God planting the seed of divine life within believers' hearts, which cannot perish (1 Peter 1:23); God giving believers new life that is by nature "eternal" (John 3:36; 6:47; Hebrews 5:9; 9:12,15, TNIV); Christ's ministry of interceding on behalf of his people (John 17:9,11,15-19,24; Romans 8:34; Hebrews 7:24-25). In sum Peter wrote that God's "divine power has given us everything we need for a godly life" (2 Peter 1:3, TNIV).

- True believers persevere through the faithful exercise of spiritual discipline. The writer of Hebrews urged, "You need to persevere so that when you have done the will of God, you will receive what he has promised" (Hebrews 10:36). Believers persevere by continuing in faith (2 Corinthians 1:24), by holding fast to Christ's teachings (John 8:31), by being faithful in prayer (1 Thessalonians 5:17), by maintaining vigilance (2 Peter 3:17), by resisting the devil (1 Peter 5:8-9), and by contending against sin (Ephesians 6:11-15). Although believers must take these actions, ultimately "The spiritual security of believers . . . depends primarily not on their hold on God but on God's hold on them."[27]

The doctrine of perseverance naturally raises some questions, particularly about the eternal security of those who claim to follow Christ. These questions include:

- *What about professing believers in the Bible who sinned grievously and lost spiritual fervor?* These include Solomon, David, and Peter. What about others, such as Demas, a coworker of Paul, who abandoned discipleship for a more comfortable

---

27. Anthony Hoekema, *Saved by Grace* (UK: Paternoster Press 1989), 4.

path? The answer is that the lapse of obedience and devotion by these followers of God was temporary rather than final and incorrigible. They didn't forfeit salvation, but in their backsliding forfeited for a season the joy of their salvation.

* *Do people who blaspheme against the Holy Spirit and thus commit "unforgivable sin" (Matthew 12:31-32; Mark 3:28-30) lose their salvation?* The answer is no. The focus of Jesus' teaching about this issue was that deliberate resistance to God's grace renders genuine repentance and faith impossible. This resistance places an individual beyond the pale of forgiveness and attainment of salvation. The passage has nothing to do with the loss of salvation or the apostasy of professing believers.

EVERYDAY APPLICATION

The doctrine of God's preservation of his followers is a profound source of confidence and hope on our earthly journeys. As true disciples of Jesus, we can find comfort in knowing that God holds us securely and he will never permit his blood-bought people to be snatched from his hands. If necessary, the Father lovingly chastens and disciplines erring believers and, in extreme cases, takes them home to himself rather than allowing them to continue in sin (see 1 Corinthians 11:30). If we choose to live carnal lives, we won't lose our salvation, but in the life to come we'll experience the loss of reward (1 Corinthians 3:14-15).

Given the divine-human nature of our eternal security, for our part we need to remain alert so we don't fall into moral laxity or lapse into a false security. The precious doctrine of perseverance in no way permits us followers of Jesus to live however we please. We must exercise continual vigilance over our spiritual lives, faithfully employing the means of grace God has given us. God faithfully preserves his children, but we must persevere by maintaining faith, relying on God's Word, enduring in prayer, resisting the Evil One, and keeping good company. We must be especially steadfast when experiencing life's inevitable trials and afflictions that easily breed distress and discouragement.

As professing believers, we should always be carefully examining the condition of our hearts. Those who fall away from the faith, in fact, were not in the family of God in the first place. The apostle John noted, "They went out from us, but they did not really belong to us. For if they had belonged to us, they would have remained with us" (1 John 2:19). This means that apostasy isn't really a falling away from a posture of faith resulting in the loss of salvation; rather, apostasy represents a defection from the Christian faith by people who make an insincere profession of faith. Only unbelievers commit apostasy, not true believers in Jesus. Scripture alerts us to the fact that there are many false teachers and prophets about (2 Peter 2) who possess a veneer of religiosity, but who deny Jesus and oppose the gospel.

FOR FURTHER READING
G. C. Berkouwer, *Faith and Perseverance*. Eerdmans, 1958.
I. Howard Marshall, *Kept by the Power of God*. Epworth Press, 1969.
Arthur W. Pink, *The Saint's Perseverance*. Tyndale Bible Society, 1977.

— BRUCE DEMAREST

PLURALISM

EVERYDAY DEFINITION
The term "religious pluralism" has two basic yet very different meanings. First, religious pluralism can simply refer to a measure of religious diversity — as opposed to religious uniformity — in a particular culture at a particular time. This is the term's *descriptive* meaning. The second understanding of religious pluralism is the term's *prescriptive* meaning. Religious pluralism in this sense is the idea that all the major religions of the world provide equal access to God.

- Regarding religious pluralism in the sense of religious diversity, a good example is that the United States today is much more religiously pluralistic than it was at the time of its founding in 1776. At that time, most Americans belonged to one Protestant group or another, with a smattering of Roman Catholics, Jews, Deists, and skeptics. Despite increasing pluralism today, more Americans still identify themselves as Christians than as members of any other religious group. And the history and culture of America has been influenced more by Christianity than by any other religion. This doesn't, however, make the United States a "Christian nation" in the sense of being God's new "chosen nation" as Israel was in the Old Testament. Sociologists and historians may debate the extent to which America is pluralistic, but the basic fact is that there are more Muslims, Buddhists, Hindus, and so on in the United States today (and they make up a higher percentage of the population) than in any other time in history. Some Americans are refusing to identify with one religious tradition or none, and are instead becoming religiously plural in their own beliefs by adopting beliefs and practices of two or more religions. For example, a woman raised a Christian may resonate with much of that tradition yet still find Buddhist meditation calming. She may attend both Christian services and Buddhist chanting sessions.

- Religious pluralism in the sense that all the major religions of the world provide equal access to God (or the Sacred) is more controversial and should be of more concern to Christians. The term the Sacred is included because some world religions — such as Buddhism — don't believe in a deity, but do affirm belief in a non-divine yet sacred reality. In this sense, religious pluralism means that no religion should claim it provides any spiritual advantage over any other religion. For example, Christians might favor Jesus as spiritual master, but religious pluralism declares that Christians shouldn't claim that Jesus is the only way to spiritual liberation. Buddha and Mohammad offer avenues of spiritual access as well. Those who think otherwise will probably end up being labeled as intolerant and bigoted in their religious judgments.

While the missionary mandate of the Bible calls Christians to take the gospel to all nations, it never endorses force or threats as a means of conversion (Matthew 28:18-20). In that sense, Scripture allows for pluralism in the descriptive sense. Not all who hear the message of the gospel will come to saving faith in Jesus Christ, although we should labor to bring the gospel to all people. The apostle Paul recognized the descriptive pluralism of his own day when he wrote to the Corinthians, "For even if there are so-called gods, whether in heaven or on earth (as indeed there are many "gods" and many "lords"), yet for us there is but one God, the Father, from whom all things came and for whom we live; and there is but one Lord, Jesus Christ, through whom all things came and through whom we live" (1 Corinthians 8:5-6).

The Bible rejects religious pluralism in the prescriptive sense. The triune God isn't one of many possible ways to gain access to transcendent reality. Rather, the living God strictly charged his people not to worship other gods and to shun all idols (Exodus 20:1-6; 1 John 5:21). False religions abound because of the distorting effects of sin in the world. Only through the life, death, and resurrection of Jesus Christ can forgiveness of sins and new life be found. As Jesus proclaimed, "I am the way and the truth and the life. No one comes to the Father except through me" (John 14:6; see also Acts 4:12).

EVERYDAY APPLICATION

Jesus said that his followers were salt and light in the world (Matthew 5:13-16). As salt and light, we should preserve goodness and present the truth of the gospel and the entire Bible to those around us. In a pluralistic culture, where many people think that Christ is just one of many ways to spiritual liberation, we must lovingly and wisely affirm that he remains the incomparable and unique source of salvation (1 Timothy 2:4). To accomplish this, we need to know deeply what we believe and why we believe it (1 Peter 5:15-16; Jude 3). Otherwise, we'll tend to blend in with the pluralism around us instead of shining the light of the gospel into the prevailing darkness (1 John 2:15-17).

In a pluralistic environment, churches can teach classes on the uniqueness of Christianity in relation to other religions. Where appropriate, pastors' sermons should mention how specific Christian doctrines differ from what is taught in other religions. Individual Christians should know the basic beliefs of other religions and how to present the gospel to those who are captive to other belief systems. Christians should take pains to communicate to unbelievers that they don't want to force their religion on anyone; and they don't want to restrict the religious freedom of those with differing religious beliefs. We should be the first to endorse and uphold the freedom of religion as enshrined in the First Amendment of the U.S. Constitution, because it gives us freedom to worship the one true God. We should take the opportunity that our pluralistic environment affords to "speak the truth in love" to our neighbors, friends, and family members who belong to other faiths. Because those outside of the gospel are enslaved to the Evil One (John 8:44; 2 Corinthians 4:4), all of our evangelistic efforts require sustained and fervent prayer as well as biblical knowledge and Christlike character (Ephesians 6:18; 1 Thessalonians 5:21)

FOR FURTHER READING

Ajith Fernando, *Presenting the Truth in Love*. Discovery House, 2001.
Harold Netland, *Encountering Religious Pluralism*. InterVarsity, 2001.

— DOUGLAS GROOTHUIS

POSTMODERNISM

EVERYDAY DEFINITION

Postmodernism generally encompasses the era from the mid-twentieth century through the present. As the name suggests, it comes after modernism — in every sense.

As the Modern period began to wane in the wake of wars and programs and corruption, various thinkers and philosophers in the culture went back to the drawing board and asked many of the same questions that vexed Socrates, Plato, and Aristotle thousands of years ago: What is Truth? What is Reality? Where does the authority to answer these questions lie? And instead of looking for some transcendent, overarching, universal answer to these questions, they looked at the details of human existence: Who we are; where we live; what we believe. In other words, they concluded, truth came out of context. Truth became subjective.

Postmodernism is marked by a general skepticism of power structures and the cultural assumptions behind them. While some postmoderns will question these structures just for the sake of questioning, others have a legitimate interest in stripping away the cultural wrapping that surrounds most institutions and ideas. The goal isn't to find some "neutral" expression of an idea — postmoderns don't believe that's possible — but rather to name and acknowledge the existence of these wrappings in an effort to better understand the way contexts influence comprehension.

This skepticism and questioning of "traditional" ideas has led to the charge that postmodernism is little more than relativism in disguise. If every idea is up for debate, critics argue, then how do we ever get to the truth? In the end, the postmodern thinkers landed on this analogy for human knowledge: We're sailing in a ship, and we don't get to take it to dry-dock and rebuild it wholesale. Instead, we have to rebuild the ship, plank-by-plank, at the same time we're sailing it. This, they said, is how human knowledge works. It's fluid, evolving, and communal. For postmodernists, truth isn't a destination, but an ongoing pursuit.

EVERYDAY APPLICATION

For some Christians, the advent of postmodernism has been all bad news. They've argued that when truth lies in the eyes and mind of an individual rather than in the closed box of tradition, then all truth ultimately fades away.

Other Christians have embraced the postmodern climate as hopeful in that it allows people of faith to unpack baggage that has been added to the Bible and Christian practice over the centuries. At some point, these Christians say, the Christian message became too closely connected to the values of Western civilization: capitalism, democracy, and individualism.

Several movements within Christianity reflect postmodern ideas. One is the emerging church, an organic movement of small churches that emphasizes authentic living, creation care, and depth of relationships. Another postmodern movement is "new monasticism," which reaches back to the fifth century for monastic practices such as simplicity, chastity, and shared resources. Many of these communities are committed to life in the inner-cities of the United States. Some critics find these movements little more than retreads of previous expressions of faith. Others see them as detrimental to the Christian faith as they question long-held traditions and beliefs.

Postmodern Christians, however, see the Bible as filled with examples of God's people questioning tradition and entrenched assumptions. They view the prophetic words of Isaiah and Jeremiah as models of God calling people to boldly challenge the establishment. They see the apostles Paul and Peter and John as masters at making culturally relevant connections to help spread the gospel. And they see Jesus as

God made flesh—the ultimate contextualization of the gospel.

How the church will find its way forward in the midst of the modern-postmodern tension remains to be seen.

FOR FURTHER READING

James K. A. Smith, *Who's Afraid of Postmodernism?* Baker Academic, 2006.

John D. Caputo, *What Would Jesus Deconstruct?* Baker Academic, 2007.

Tony Jones, *The New Christians: Dispatches from the Emergent Frontier.* Jossey-Bass, 2008.

Shane Claiborne, *The Irresistible Revolution.* Zondervan, 2006.

—TONY JONES

PRAISE

EVERYDAY DEFINITION

Praise is the active boasting in the acts of God. To understand praise better, we can examine three parts of that definition:

1. First and foremost, praise is *active.* Just as the ancient Hebrews couldn't conceive of a God who does nothing, they also couldn't merely think their praise. They had to embody it (Luke 19:40). We might think of this like the difference between reading a book on swimming and actually swimming. Praise is jumping into the water!

2. Praise is also boasting. In the ancient world, Hebrews were faced with a whole host of gods, such as the Canaanite god Baal. For them, praise was the ultimate "my dad can beat up your dad" statement: "For great is the LORD and most worthy of praise; he is to be feared above all gods. For all the gods of the nations are idols, but the LORD made the heavens" (Psalm 96:4-5).

3. Praise means acknowledging the *acts of God.* The biblical word praise is a tangible recognition of God's divine interventions. This is the inherent understanding in praise as

described in Deuteronomy 10:21: "He is your praise . . . who performed for you those great and awesome wonders you saw with your own eyes."

Christians often use the word praise interchangeably with worship, perhaps because it's difficult to distinguish God's acts from his traits. When we read the word praise in our English translations of the Bible, it's usually a translation of the Hebrew word *halal* or the Greek word *ainos*. *Halal* implies not only a command to boast, but also a sense of exclamation and abandonment. When *halal* is directed toward *Jah*, a shortened form of the name *YAWEH* (God's holy name), we arrive at the word "hallelujah," usually translated "praise the LORD!" "Hallelujah" has become so much a part of Christian vocabulary that it's often not translated at all. The word itself has become an exclamation of praise.

EVERYDAY APPLICATION

To better grasp how we live out praise, we can ask the questions of "who, why, when, where, and how."

- "*Who* should actually do this boasting about the acts of God?" Scripture is clear that praise is expected from all servants of God, "small and great" (Revelation 19:5). Eventually, all creatures will praise him (Psalm 150:6; Revelation 5:13).
- "*Why* praise?" In addition to the fact that *halal* is an imperative, Scripture suggests that praise is fitting for creatures and befitting the Creator: "Praise the LORD. How good it is to sing praises to our God, how pleasant and fitting to praise him!" (Psalm 147:1). In other words, praise fits—it fits us because we were designed for this very purpose, and it fits God because he does such amazing things.
- "*When* is praise appropriate?" This question has far-reaching implications for us as Christians. Hebrews 13:15 exhorts, "Through Jesus, therefore, let us continually offer to God a sacrifice of praise—the fruit of lips that confess his name." Praise is to be a continuous and sacrificial dialogue because of what Christ has done in his victory over sin and death. This lifestyle of praise isn't burdensome. Instead, it's a refreshing

invitation to live above the fray, as the continuous offering of praise turns us into free and joyful participants in the kingdom of God. Praise is even appropriate when we face difficulties. Scripture doesn't suggest that we praise God because bad things are happening, but rather, in spite of them. Even in prison, the apostle Paul and his mission companion Silas "were praying and singing hymns to God" (Acts 16:25) — and at midnight, no less! This type of praise is sacrificial and requires maturity to be offered sincerely. Further, we can praise God even in the face of tragedy. The apostle Peter wrote to persecuted Christians: "These [sufferings] have come so that your faith . . . may be proved genuine and may result in praise, glory and honor when Jesus Christ is revealed" (1 Peter 1:7). This is an amazing acknowledgment that God is both sovereign and good.

- *"Where* should God should be praised?"* Scripture doesn't require any specific location for praise to take place. Psalm 113:3 asserts, "From the rising of the sun to its setting the name of the Lord is to be praised" (NASB). This meshes with Jesus' teachings that, since God is Spirit, location is no longer relevant (John 4).

- *"How* should God be praised?"* The answer to this question comes from examining other less-frequent Hebrew and Greek words that are also translated or associated with "praise." In reality, these words are various types of actions. We are to *confess* his praise (*romam; yadah; exomologeo*), *sing* his praise (*tehillah; humneo*), *play* his praise (*zamar; psallo*) on all available instruments (Psalm 150), and *dance* his praise (*machol*). These actions can erupt spontaneously from a grateful heart, or be the result of studied preparation and refinement. Our praise might be articulated in a simple song of deliverance, like Moses sang, or expressed in various ways, as with Miriam when she played, danced, and sang in praise of God's deliverance (Exodus 15).

Praise is fitting for all creatures in all situations at all times. Praise should be offered everywhere and in every way. The various Hebrew and Greek words teach us that "praise" can be planned and ordered or spontaneous and clamorous. It's always a focused boast about what God has done, and it's never about us or our praise of God. What has God done in us that we could not do in ourselves? When we find concrete ways to boast about God's acts in our lives, then we will experience the meaning of praise!

FOR FURTHER READING
Ronald Allen, *Praise! A Matter of Life and Breath*. Thomas Nelson, 1980.
Andrew Hill, *Enter His Courts with Praise!* Baker, 1993.

—JIM ALTIZER

PRAYER

EVERYDAY DEFINITION
Prayer is conversing with God in words, thoughts, and gestures. It marks a life with God, where we continually pay attention to God's presence in this world and in us. Prayer builds relationship with God as we respond to his self-giving love and mercy and to his commitment to lead us into truth.

What do we pray about? Most simply put, we pray about what concerns us that also concerns God: personal well-being, well-being of others, and forward progress of the kingdom of God in this world. As we bond with God and allow his concerns to become our concerns, we learn to pray for what is good rather than just what we want. For example, we can pray for difficult people (Matthew 5:44), which helps us grow to become the kind of person who loves our enemies. In this way, prayer teaches us patience, compassion, awareness, and simplicity, leading us to an understanding of ourselves as a part of the greater community. Sometimes we need to ask God for clarity about our wants and for help in knowing what to even ask for.

People sometimes question why we should pray if God already knows our needs. We pray because we live in relationship to God, and two beings who live in a love relationship like to talk to each other. We don't pray to inform God, but to engage in a conversation that provides us with confidence, clarity, and an ability to move forward.

Jesus, as God present here on earth, prayed throughout his

ministry: before important decisions (Luke 6:12), and at his baptism and the Transfiguration (Luke 3:21-22; 9:29). He spent entire nights in prayer (Mark 6:46; Matthew 14:22-23; John 6:15). Before his death, he prayed for his persecutors (Luke 23:34), his disciples (John 17:6-19), his future followers (John 17:20-26), and for himself (Mark 15:34; Matthew 27:46).

Jesus taught others to pray in word and by example (Matthew 6:6-15; John 14:12-14; 16:24) and taught about how we can pray to be heard in faith (Mark 11:22-24). He assured the disciples that wherever they gathered to pray, he would be present (Matthew 18:19-20). The apostle Paul and other New Testament writers said that Jesus now intercedes for us in glory (1 John 2:1; Romans 8:34).

Because prayer is conversation with God, it takes many forms. The most frequent form is petition and intercession: laying our needs and the needs of others before God and asking for help (Psalm 33). The Psalms show us that prayer also involves adoration, confession, and thanksgiving. In addition, prayer involves listening to God—being still and knowing that he is God, as well as delighting in God and waiting on him (Psalm 46:10; 27:4; 62:1,2,5). Other kinds of prayer include weeping prayer, prayers of surrender, and prayers of celebration and ecstasy (Psalm 56; 131; 145–150). On a broader scale, we live in unceasing prayer (1 Thessalonians 5:17). This occurs as we practice the presence of God, moving in and out of spoken and unspoken prayer of all types with God all day long. Eventually, we discover that not doing this is like not breathing.

EVERYDAY APPLICATION

Many people find formulas for prayer helpful, but these methods often turn stale. Prayer is meant to be relational; God wants to hear from who we really are, not who we pretend to be. So instead of trying to copy the prayers of others, we can simply pray with all of our own might, being ourselves.

While "mental prayer" or speaking only in our minds, is a standard way to pray, it often degenerates into self-talk or even "holy worry." That's not prayer. Prayer involves addressing God directly and stating clearly what we need and what we think. That's why it often helps to pray aloud (even when alone) or to write our prayers. Even when writing prayer, we need to not get caught up in being concerned about grammar or penmanship. Many Christians find that writing in a private journal that will never be read by others helps them focus on content rather than mechanics. A journal doesn't need to be fancy; it fact, it might help if it looks very ordinary and if it can be torn up if too private.

When at a loss about what to pray, the Psalms provide us help. They're full of requests, thanksgiving, and adoration, as well as affirmations of having confidence in God. Phrases and ideas from the prayers of Paul (Ephesians 1:15-19; 3:16-21; Philippians 1:9-11; Colossians 1:9-12; 1 Thessalonians 3:12-13; 2 Thessalonians 1:11-12) and other Christians who have learned to put meaningful prayers into written words can also help.

Above all, we can remember that because of our personal relationship with him, God is eager to hear from us. So we can talk to him as we would any great friend.

FOR FURTHER READING
John Baillie, *A Diary of Private Prayer.* Fireside, 1996.
C. S. Lewis, *Letters to Malcolm: Chiefly on Prayer.* Harvest Books, 2002.
C. S. Lewis, *Reflections on the Psalms.* Harvest Books, 1964.
Richard Foster, *Prayer: Finding The Heart's True Home.*
    HarperSanFrancisco, 1992.
Jean Nicholas Grou, *How to Pray.* Lutterworth Press, 2008.

— JAN JOHNSON

PREDESTINATION

EVERYDAY DEFINITION
Predestination represents God's sovereign determination about who will be saved to inherit heaven and who will be lost to suffer punishment in hell. The doctrine of predestination is one of the most misunderstood and debated of doctrines.

Most Christians believe that, according to God's wisdom and pleasure, he in eternity past sovereignly chose from among all of fallen humanity yet to be created the ones he willed to be saved by grace. The rest he left to suffer the just punishment of their sins. John Bunyon, author of *Grace Abounding* and *Pilgrim's Progress*, wrote, "This act of God in electing is a choosing or fore-appointing of some infallibly unto eternal life."[28]

The saved are the objects of God's decretive or unconditional will, while the lost are the objects of his permissive or conditional will. A minority of Christians uphold double predestination, which asserts that from eternity past God sovereignly chose both those who would be saved and those who would be condemned. According to this position, both the saved and the lost are objects of God's unconditional will. Advocates of this position say that if God predestined some to be saved, he necessarily must have predestined the rest to be lost.

The Old Testament contains numerous examples of God's sovereign choice of some to be saved and to serve him. God chose Abram for covenant relationship not on any basis of foreseen faith (Genesis 12:1-3; 17:1-8). Also, contrary to cultural custom, God chose Abraham's younger son, Isaac, rather than Ishmael to be the offspring of promise (Genesis 17:19-21). In addition, God made a sovereign choice of the younger son, Jacob, over the elder son, Esau (Genesis 25:23; Romans 9:10-13), even though Jacob stole the cultural birthright. The psalmist wrote: "Blessed are those you choose and bring near to live in your courts!" (Psalm 65:4).

Many New Testament Scriptures support the doctrine of predestination. Jesus taught, "For just as the Father raises the dead and gives them life, even so the Son gives life to whom he is pleased to give it" (John 5:21). Jesus calls the people whom the Father gave to the Son his "sheep" (John 10:27). Jesus the Shepherd "knows" his sheep and "calls" them by name (10:3,14,27). The sheep recognize the voice of the shepherd and follow him (10:4,27). Jesus said of those not his sheep, "you do not believe because you are not my sheep" (10:26). Believing is the outcome of being chosen (or elected) as one of the sheep.

When the apostle Paul and his mission companion Barnabas ministered in Pisidian Antioch, Luke stated, "All [the Gentiles] who were appointed for eternal life believed" (Acts 13:48). Paul provided a comprehensive treatment of predestination (Ephesians 1:3-12), heaping together several powerful terms asserting God's selection in salvation: "chose" (verse 4), "predestined" (verse 5), "his pleasure and will"

---

28. John Bunyon, *Works*, 3 vols. (1862), vol. 2, 337.

(verse 5), "mystery of his will" (verse 9), "his good pleasure" (verse 9), "purposed in Christ" (verse 9), "chosen" (verse 11), "predestined" (verse 11), and "purpose of his will" (verse 11). To the church in Thessalonica Paul added, "We ought always to thank God . . . because God chose you as fruitfruits to be saved through the sanctifying work of the Spirit and through belief in the truth" (2 Thessalonians 2:13, TNIV). The apostle Peter addressed his first letter, "To God's elect . . . who have been chosen according to the foreknowledge of God the Father, through the sanctifying work of the Spirit . . ." (1 Peter 1:1-2). In his second letter, Peter urged scattered believers to "make every effort to confirm your calling and election" (2 Peter 1:10, TNIV).

EVERYDAY APPLICATION

The doctrine of predestination isn't a matter for idle speculation, such as asking, "I wonder if that person has been chosen by God to be saved?" Any person who comes to faith in Jesus Christ is certain to be among the predestined. That God loves us and has chosen us to be his children and heirs of eternal life is a teaching of inestimable blessing and comfort. Our fitting response is to bow before the Lord in humble gratitude and give thanks and praise to him for his saving mercy. While we might not fully understand the mystery of God's redemptive purpose, we can and should offer him our heartfelt gratitude.

The doctrine of predestination doesn't render preaching, evangelism, and prayer unnecessary. On the contrary, as servants of the Lord we witness and pray confident that God's purposes through our ministry will come to complete fruition. When confronted with severe opposition during his second missionary journey in Corinth, Paul was encouraged by a word from God. The apostle must continue preaching the gospel in Corinth, in God's words, "because I have many people in this city" (Acts 18:10). God had chosen a people for himself in that cosmopolitan city, and Paul's courageous preaching would bring in the appointed harvest that God had planned. The doctrine of predestination confirms that ministry that bears fruit ultimately is due to the power of the Holy Spirit in accord with God's purpose, rather than to any skill or prowess of our own.

The doctrine of divine predestination also in no way undercuts the legitimate offer of the gospel. As Christians, we can proclaim with complete confidence, "Whosoever will may come!" (see John 3:15-16;

11:25-26; Acts 2:21). "Whosoever will" constitutes the very means that God through the Spirit draws sinners to Christ. God's purpose or end—meaning salvation—always involves the use of chosen means: preaching, prayer, and the gospel invitation. The reality is that the person who would receive the blessings of salvation must *will* to come to Christ.

The doctrine of predestination, far from being a roadblock to holiness of life, is instead a positive incentive and motivation. Rather than undermining the pursuit of holiness, the doctrine of predestination serves as encouragement to live a holy life. Scripture is clear that God elects individuals not only to heaven, but also to personal holiness in this life. The apostle Paul wrote that the Father "chose us in him [Christ] before the creation of the world to be holy and blameless in his sight" (Ephesians 1:4; see also Romans 8:29). When we experience God's goodness and favor toward us, we desire from the depths of our hearts to honor him with lives that are well-pleasing in thought, word, and deed. Overwhelmed with his saving grace freely poured out upon us, we dedicate ourselves to living lives of holiness and truth that please and honor him.

FOR FURTHER READING
Samuel Fisk, *Election and Predestination*. Wipf and Stock, 2002.
Norman H. Geisler, *Chosen But Free*. Bethany, 2001.
John Gerstner, *A Predestination Primer*. Baker, 1960.
Fred H. Klooster, *Calvin's Doctrine of Predestination*. Baker, 1977.
R. C. Sproul, *Chosen by God*. Tyndale, 1986.

— BRUCE DEMAREST

PROPHECY

EVERYDAY DEFINITION
Prophecy is a message from God to people who need to hear it. Most of the time in Scripture, prophecy is a message that deals directly with the way people are living their lives or how the political leaders are ruling, as well as how God wants them to live more faithfully and less sinfully.

The substance and content of biblical prophecy varies, but it's consistently a call toward holiness and faithfulness to God. In the Old Testament, Hebrew prophets pointed out social and personal sins within Israel, Judah, and other countries. This usually caused the prophets to be unpopular and sometimes even cost them their lives. The prophet Amos said that the people of Israel sell the needy for a pair of sandals, trample the heads of the poor, deny justice to the oppressed, "hoard plunder and loot" (Amos 3:10), and "oppress the poor and crush the needy" (Amos 4:1). The prophet Habakkuk rhetorically asked God, "Why do you make me look at injustice? Why do you tolerate wrong?" (Habakkuk 1:3). He then claimed that the violence that Israel did to Lebanon would come back and "overwhelm" them (Habakkuk 2:17). The prophet Obadiah also claimed that the oppressive unfaithfulness of the people of God would boomerang back on them, "as you have done, it will be done to you; your deeds will return upon your own head" (Obadiah 15).

In the Gospels, Jesus repeated this idea when he prophetically taught that judgment, condemnation, and forgiveness often work according to this principle: "A good measure, pressed down, shaken together and running over, will be poured into your lap. For with the measure you use, it will be measured to you" (Luke 6:38).

Who can speak a word of prophecy? On the Day of Pentecost, Peter quoted the prophet Joel and preached that "your sons and daughters will prophesy" (Acts 2:17). Both men and women, young and old, insiders and outsiders can share messages from God that can shape and form the community of believers. Often, prophecy comes from the least expected individuals, who hear most clearly from God and who live prophetically: a mother from Ephraim (Deborah), a shepherd from Tekoa (Amos), or a carpenter from Galilee (Jesus).

The Bible also warns of false prophets. These individuals speak well of powerful religious and political leaders who oppress others and who justify the greed, materialism, idolatry, and sin of the people. Because of their popular messages, false prophets were often accepted while true prophets were opposed by the kings and queens. The prophet Elijah had to run for his life from Ahab and Jezebel. In a sense, Jesus was murdered for challenging the status quo with his prophetic statements.

Prophecy is often misunderstood to be a prediction of future events. But predictions are infrequent in the messages of biblical prophets, and references to future events are usually consequences of present actions. In other words, the prophet's message might include a description of how an outcome might change if the people of God (and others) live differently. Therefore, the prophets not only warned of impending trouble because of current unfaithfulness, they also charted paths of faithfulness that would glorify God and bring greater healing to the world.

EVERYDAY APPLICATION

Perhaps the most significant way that Christians can be prophetic in our current culture is by challenging the status quo with the good news of Jesus. Jesus, as our Prophet, Priest, and King, taught us not to pile up treasures on earth or worry about what we'll wear: "for the pagans run after these things" (Matthew 6:24-33). So perhaps we live prophetically by challenging ourselves and other Christians to live more simply, to be content, and to refocus our energy on making sure that those who truly suffer have enough food, clothing, shelter, education, and health care. Further, we can prophetically remind ourselves and fellow Christians of God's call to forgive our enemies, and even to talk with them when it's difficult. Jesus taught that "if you do not forgive others their sins, your Father will not forgive your sins" (Matthew 6:15).

In these and other ways, we can apply the meaning of prophecy to our lives and to our churches by hearing and accepting the priorities of the biblical prophets on issues that continue to challenge us as the people of God to be more faithful to the God we love and serve.

FOR FURTHER READING

Walter Brueggemann, *The Prophetic Imagination*. Fortress, 2001.
Alan Kreider, *Social Holiness: A Way of Living for God's Nation*. Wipf & Stock, 2008.

— PAUL ALEXANDER

PROVIDENCE

EVERYDAY DEFINITION

The term providence doesn't appear in the English Bible, but its truth is deeply imbedded in the fabric of Scripture and Christian theology. The word entered Christian thought from the Latin of Genesis 22:7-8, where Isaac asked, "Where is the lamb for the burnt offering" Abraham, Isaac's father, replied, "God himself will provide [*providebit*] the lamb for the burnt offering, my son." The doctrine of providence implies that the universe and human affairs are sustained, guided, and governed not by evolutionary forces, chance, or fate but by the will of a wise, loving, and holy God.

Providence has two principal aspects: God's preservation in existence of the universe he created and his governance of the world's affairs, actively ruling and directing them to their intended end:

1. God's sustaining providence of the earth is taught in Nehemiah 9:6 (NLT): "You alone are the LORD. . . . You made the earth and the seas and everything in them. You preserve them all, and the angels of heaven worship you." Hebrews expands the scope of divine preservation: "The Son is the radiance of God's glory and the exact representation of his being, sustaining all things by his powerful word" (Hebrews 1:3; see also Colossians 1:17). God holds the universe together by his supernatural power, but he generally exercises this preserving providence through the functioning of secondary causes, typically by the laws of nature that God established. Nature psalms (Psalm 65; 104) illustrate God's sustaining and caring providence for earth, vegetation, and animal life.

2. God's providential governance of the world and its affairs at times operates immediately and supernaturally (such as the parting of the Red Sea), but usually is executed indirectly according to natural principles (such as famines and droughts). The omnipotent God could accomplish all his providential purposes through the direct application of supernatural power (the intervention of God), but he most commonly works through human intermediaries (the interaction of God).

C. S. Lewis observed that God seems to do nothing by himself that he can delegate to his creatures. God commands us to do slowly and blunderingly what he could do in the twinkling of an eye. Because God is an incarnational God, his customary way of working is through humanity.

God exercises several types of providence in human affairs, including:

- His provision and care for all living creatures (Matthew 6:25-30).
- His directive providence in guiding the course and destiny of the nations (Daniel 2:21).
- Permissive providence such as when he allowed Satan to assault Job's family and possessions (Job 1:8-19). This demonstrates that while God permits sin in the world, he's not the cause of sin.
- Safeguarding providence in protecting his people, such as in the case of Shadrach, Meshach, and Abednego in the fiery furnace (Daniel 3:8-27).
- Restraining providence by preventing sin and harm from happening, such as preventing Abimelek from taking Abraham's wife, Sarah, as his concubine (Genesis 20:1-6; see also Psalm 19:13).
- Limiting providence, such as forbidding Satan from destroying Job's person (Job 1:12; 2:6).
- Redirecting providence, such as when he turned the treachery of Joseph's brothers into provision that saved many people's lives (Genesis 50:20). Of course, the primary example of this last mode of providence was God's work of redirecting the death of Jesus on the cross into salvation for the world (Acts 2:23).

EVERYDAY APPLICATION

For Christians, knowing that God is actively involved in the affairs of human life and history gives meaning and purpose to life, and even more importantly, certain hope for the future.

Providence assures us that human history isn't meaningless or out of control. We don't need to fear, as some do, that planet earth will randomly be struck by some errant meteorite or accidentally consumed by some human-caused catastrophe. We can trust in God's wise governance of the universe and live in the reality of his direction and provision. The doctrine of God's loving providence eliminates pessimism and despair. Even though our lives are sprinkled with good times as well as difficult times, God providentially allows both, knowing that we need both to grow strong spiritually. We mature in Christ through providentially permitted seasons of hardship and suffering.

Because God usually exercises his providential direction in partnership with humans, especially those who follow him, we must be alert to the faithful exercise of the responsibilities he gives us. At times, we might be aware that God is using us to carry out his purposes. At other times, we might not be so directly aware. In either case, however, we must be prepared for God to use us for the fulfillment of his wise, providential purposes. As we cooperate with God, the labors of our hands are invested with eternal significance.

Many people wonder about the role of prayer in relationship to God's providence. If all things come to pass in accord with God's sovereign and providential rule, why should we pray? Of course, we pray because God in the Bible commands us to pray and to do so consistently (1 Thessalonians 5:17). But at a deeper level, we pray because God has ordained prayer as one of the crucial means he has chosen to accomplish his purposes. In other words, God in eternity past factored prayer — as well as preaching, witness, missionary effort, etc. — into his sovereign providential plan.

We also need to recognize that God sometimes uses unbelievers as instruments of his providence. In 539 BC, the pagan king of Persia, Cyrus, issued a decree that freed Israel from captivity and allowed them to return to their native land. Scripture records that God summoned Cyrus to this particular task (Isaiah 45:13), even calling the pagan king my "anointed" (Isaiah 45:1) and "my shepherd" (Isaiah 44:28). Similarly, God used the decree issued by Caesar Augustus (Luke 2:1) to fulfill biblical prophecy that Jesus, the Messiah, would be born in the town of Bethlehem.

FOR FURTHER READING

G. C. Berkouwer, *The Providence of God*. Eerdmans, 1952.

Paul Helm, *The Providence of God*. InterVarsity, 1994.

Lloyd John Ogilvie, *If God Cares, Why do I Still Have Problems*. Word, 1985.

J. I. Packer, *Evangelism and the Sovereignty of God*. InterVarsity, 1961.

— BRUCE DEMAREST

RACISM

EVERYDAY DEFINITION

Race is a way that people categorize each other based primarily on physical attributes, such as skin color and facial features. Racism is the intentional or unconscious use of power and domination by one race to withhold equal privileges and to discriminate against individuals and communities of another race. Racism can exist on a personal level between individuals, and it is also embedded in broader social structures such as education and the workplace. Racism is often connected to economic issues. Those in the racial majority usually have economic advantages over those in the minority. Seeking to keep such advantages in place as well as benefiting from such advantages are both forms of racism. All forms of racism are wrong.

EVERYDAY APPLICATION

Love, justice, repentance, and reconciliation are four core biblical themes that form a Christian response to racism.

1. When Jesus spoke about the nature of *love,* he told the story of the Good Samaritan, a story with racial overtones. The hero of the story is a Samaritan who crosses ethnic lines to love a Jew who had been robbed and beaten up (Luke 10:25-37). We should engage in this same type of boundary-crossing, a move that invariably challenges racism. The type of love we are to embody is a love that initiates across lines of animosity and resentment, a type of love that includes loving those who don't love us (Matthew 5:46). Regardless of where we find ourselves,

we each bear the responsibility of making the first move to love others. We can't wait for others to come to us before we exhibit the love of Christ.

2. God's *justice* also demands that we confront the oppressive and destructive spirit of racism in both its personal and structural forms (Matthew 25:31-46; Ephesians 6:12). When the divide between rich and poor in any economic system falls along racial lines, we must see that as unjust and challenge it. Educational and medical systems that better serve people of one race over people of another race must be judged as inadequate. If a court system treats people differently based on their race, that system stands under God's judgment as unjust. The biblical witness shows God's passion for justice. Because racism defies God's justice, Christians must work to see it overcome.

3. When we fail to live out God's love and justice, the necessary action is *repentance.* We are to turn away from our sinful ways (Ezekiel 18:30; Matthew 3:2). We are to repent so that our sins may be forgiven (Acts 2:38). The sin of racism also requires repentance. This turning from sin is the prologue to God's work of reconciliation.

4. Because racism results in a bitter divide between people, Christians are to seek *reconciliation* between people on both sides of this divide. The wall erected between Jews and Gentiles prior to Christ was torn down by the work of Christ, and the one newly created body is reconciled to God (Ephesians 2:11-22). This serves as a paradigm for addressing divisions between all ethnic and racial divisions. As Christians, we are reconciled to God through Christ, and as a result, we're called to the ministry of reconciliation (2 Corinthians 5:18-19). In order to confront issues of racism we must continue this reconciling work.

People on either side of any racial divide can have attitudes marked by bigotry and hatred. We are *all* called to work for reconciliation. As Christians, we must take these themes seriously, and to do so requires us to address racism in responsible and biblical ways. How can Christians accomplish this? Consider these practical ways:

- Acknowledge that the problem of racism exists.
- Learn about how others have experienced racism. Ask people of other races to share their stories. Read articles and books written from the perspectives of those in racial minorities.
- Choose to be around people of other races. Many of us have little contact with people of other races. While friendships across racial lines are the deepest expression of reconciliation, simply finding ways to be around people of other races — whether by choosing where you shop, where you go for recreation, or where your children go to school — is a starting point. At the same time, people can prayerfully look for ways to develop friendships across racial lines that go beyond preliminary niceties.
- Work for the common good. The common good can be served by starting a tutoring program for underprivileged children or by choosing to set up a business in a disadvantaged neighborhood. The common good is served by calling and writing your members of Congress to pass laws that intentionally take into account what's best for people of all races. It can be promoted by working to change things such as company policies, city ordinances, and medical practices so that people of all races benefit equally.

FOR FURTHER READING

Michael O. Emerson and Christian Smith, *Divided by Faith: Evangelical Religion and the Problem of Race in America*. Oxford University Press, 2000.

Spencer Perkins and Chris Rice, *More Than Equals: Racial Healing for the Sake of the Gospel*. InterVarsity, 2000.

— ROBERT MUTHIAH

RECONCILIATION

EVERYDAY DEFINITION

Reconciliation is the healing and reuniting in relationship of those who previously harbored hostility toward one another. Scripture describes reconciliation as taking place both between human beings (horizontal reconciliation) and between sinful human beings and God (vertical reconciliation).

Reconciliation involves three aspects.

1. Reconciliation occurs in an existing relationship marked by animosity, hostility, disregard, or enmity between two parties. One or both parties hold something against the other, and as a result, a breach of relationship exists between them.
2. Intervention to address the cause of the enmity is introduced, providing the means to remove the hostility and breach of relationship.
3. The removal of enmity isn't just a form of amnesty, truce, or lack of conflict; reconciliation is a positive renewal of relationship marked by peace and acceptance. Both parties now experience true delight and fellowship with one another.

Several New Testament passages highlight the reconciliation that sinners can have with God through faith in Christ and his atoning death on their behalf. The apostle Paul provided one of the most beautiful expressions of reconciliation imaginable (2 Corinthians 5:16-21). The important assertion that anyone who is in Christ is a "new creature" (5:17, NASB) is immediately followed by the declaration that this came to us from the God "who reconciled us to himself through Christ and gave us the ministry of reconciliation" (5:18). So we not only become new creatures through faith in Christ, but this transformation is marked by our being reunited with God through what Christ has done. As we proclaim salvation in Christ, then, we make an appeal for sinners to "be reconciled to God" (5:20). Of course, a lingering question is how we, as sinners, can be reconciled to this holy God.

Christ himself is the intervention that takes place to remove the enmity that previously existed between us sinners and God. Astonishingly, Paul wrote that God the Father made Christ, who knew no sin, "to be sin on our behalf, so that we might become the righteousness of God in Him" (5:21, NASB). This is often called the "great exchange." Our sin was charged to Christ, and in exchange, his righteousness was credited to us. Only because our sin is dealt with in the death of Christ is reconciliation with God possible. We are made new creatures "in Christ" (5:17) and our reconciliation comes to us "through Christ" (5:18). This restores our right standing with God and gives us joyous peace and acceptance.

In his letter to the church in Ephesus (Ephesians 2:11-18), Paul further described the truth of our reconciliation to God through Christ. But to this vertical reconciliation, Paul told of the horizontal reconciliation (sinners with other sinners) that accompanies true saving reconciliation. Paul described in these verses the enmity that has existed between Jews and Gentiles. In many ways, both despised the other, and clearly the Jews thought of Gentiles as apart from God's favor because they weren't given the covenants with God and didn't abide by God's law (2:11-12). But now in Christ, both Jews and Gentiles are reconciled to God. This is remarkable in itself, because no Jew would have imagined that Gentiles who remain uncircumcised could be reconciled with God. Even more amazing is the fact that the reconciliation of Jews and of Gentiles with God only happens as Jews and Gentiles are themselves brought together in one body through the cross of Christ, and reconciled together, in one body and by one Spirit, to God the Father (2:14-18).

Paul also wrote that reconciliation took place with God "while we were enemies" of God (Romans 5:10, NASB). He made this point to remind us that we aren't responsible for bringing about our reconciliation. Rather, God has done this for us—despite the fact that he did so even while we despised him and his ways. In his love for us, and through Christ's death on our behalf, we receive the gift of reconciliation with God through faith.

EVERYDAY APPLICATION

The key biblical passages dealing with reconciliation suggest the following important aspects that we as Christians should consider:

- We should pause to revel in the unfathomable greatness of what our reconciliation in Christ means. The truth that sinners—who deserve God's righteous judgment and eternal wrath—can instead be reunited in loving relationship with the God of all joy and eternal gladness, is astonishing. Because the "bad news" of our separation from God is so bad, the good news of reconciliation indeed is glorious and wonderful.

- Because reconciliation only occurs through faith in Christ and his substitutionary death for sinners, the good news of the gospel must be proclaimed for others to be reconciled with God (2 Corinthians 5). God has made his own people his ambassadors. We are granted the gracious gift of reconciliation, and we are granted the gracious responsibility of spreading the good news of this reconciliation through faith in Christ with others.

- Only as believers experience and demonstrate reconciliation with one another in Christ, despite whatever former hostility existed, will the gospel truly be lived out so others can clearly see the power of the Cross. There is simply no place among Christians for attitudes of superiority or prejudice, on any grounds, when all true believers are united into one common body in Christ. When we practice horizontal reconciliation among us sinners saved by grace, we demonstrate the reality of the vertical reconciliation we have, as one, with our God through Christ.

- As with every aspect of our salvation, God should receive all the glory. The work of reconciliation is his alone, so the praise and thanksgiving belong to him alone. It should humble us to recognize that although we are responsible for the sin and rebellion that made us God's enemies, we had nothing to do with the reconciled standing that we now enjoy in Christ. God has done this great work, and our endless praise should be given to God alone.

FOR FURTHER READING

Ralph P. Martin. *Reconciliation: A Study of Paul's Theology*. Wipf & Stock, 1997.

Daniel P. Thimell and Trevor Hart, eds. *Christ in our Place: The Humanity of God in Christ for the Reconciliation of the World*. Paternoster, 1994.

—BRUCE A. WARE

REDEMPTION

EVERYDAY DEFINITION

Broadly, redemption means "to rescue." Specifically, it means to buy something back or rescue something with the payment of a price. The Bible refers to redemption in three ways: to property and people, to the nation Israel, and to a world trapped in sin.

1. Redemption is used as a commercial term with property and people. They can be redeemed by a payment. Once paid, a transfer of ownership occurs (Leviticus 25). In this way, land or slaves could be redeemed. The book of Ruth speaks of land being redeemed, but Boaz also became Ruth's kinsman-redeemer (Ruth 4:1-12).

2. Redemption is used with reference to Israel, especially as its people languished as slaves in Egypt. Through the series of plagues, God redeemed his people from bondage (Exodus 6:6; 15:1-21). The price paid was the destruction of Egypt (Isaiah 43:3). God himself became Israel's redeemer (Jeremiah 50:34). He later redeemed his people from exile in Babylon, and the language of redemption again was used of their release (Jeremiah 31:11).

3. The most expansive way the Bible speaks of redemption is in the spiritual realm. This idea appears in the Old Testament (Psalm 130; Isaiah 40:2; 59:20). However, the New Testament speaks more explicitly and extensively about the profound slavery that binds sinners. Jesus said, "Everyone who sins is a slave to sin" (John 8:34). This idea is repeated in the Epistles (Romans 6:16-18; 2 Peter 2:19). We are helplessly trapped by sin and can't extricate ourselves. Self-redemption is impossible (Psalm 49:7-8). Jesus the Messiah is the Redeemer who alone can free us (John 8:36). Christ accomplished his redemption through the cross, where he gave his life as a ransom for many (Mark 10:45). Specifically, the ransom paid was his life laid down in death (Ephesians 1:7). We were redeemed "with the precious blood of Christ" (1 Peter 1:19).

A host of Bible terms refer to Christ's redeeming work on the cross. It is spoken of as a sacrifice for sins (Hebrews 9:28). Christ's sacrifice redeemed by acting as a payment for our sin. It redeemed because it reconciled us to God. It reconciled us to God because it turned away his just wrath (propitiation). It propitiates (renders God favorable to us) by being substitutionary and enduring God's just judgment in our place. Because of this, when we trust in Christ as our Redeemer, our sins are forgiven and we are justified (Romans 3:24). In addition, we are freed from sin's domination (Romans 6:7,22), from an empty way of life (1 Peter 1:18), and from the curse itself (Galatians 3:13). All this is involved in Christ's redeeming work on the cross.

God the Father planned the work of human redemption before the beginning of time (Ephesians 1:3-10). It was announced following the Fall (Genesis 3:15). Because redemption involves the death of God's Son, it is of infinite worth. In its saving effect, it is sufficient for all (the human race) and efficient for some (those who believe).

The apostle John stated, "with your blood you purchased for God members of every tribe and language and people and nation" (Revelation 5:9, TNIV). Christ's redeeming death is presented as the primary means of breaking down all the racial and ethnic barriers that divide us today. Scripture also says that the day is coming when the redemption won by Christ will be extended to our bodies, and finally to all of creation (Romans 8:23).

EVERYDAY APPLICATION
One way to apply the full reality of redemption is in our Bible reading. We are edified as we view the entire Bible as a story of redemption. Too often, we look at the Bible's small parts and lose its grand storyline. God's great redemptive plan unites the whole of Scripture. Our rescue from sin and its destructive effects comes from the promised Redeemer and his sacrifice. Some have called redemption "the scarlet thread" that runs through the entire Bible.

After the Fall, with its world-fracturing effect, God announced the coming of a Savior (Genesis 3:15). He then provided a covering for Adam and Eve by the killing of an animal. He allowed sacrifices to be used as a temporary covering for sin. He promised Abraham that he would provide a lamb. The blood of the Passover lamb provided a covering of protection. The sacrificial system of the temple continued that provision. Then came the day when John the Baptist cried out, "Look, the Lamb of God, who takes away the sin of the world!" (John 1:29). The final book of the Bible contains a vision of blood-washed souls. The redeemed multitude is washed in the blood of the Lamb, who overcomes all the world's evil (Revelation 17:14).

We also apply redemption to our lives when we place our trust in Jesus Christ as our own personal sin bearer and Savior. Christ's sacrifice of atonement must be individually received by faith (Romans 3:24). Redemption isn't automatic; it comes by God's grace through our faith. As Paul expressed: "Believe in the Lord Jesus, and you will be saved [redeemed]" (Acts 16:31).

In addition, redemption involves a "from" and a "for." Just as Israel was redeemed *from* slavery in Egypt, we are redeemed *from* the bondage of sin and our former empty way of life (1 Peter 1:18). But then Israel was redeemed *for* God, and called to be a holy nation. In the same way, we are redeemed to live *for* God. In our freedom, we are to glorify God with our lives. We are now children, not slaves!

Just as Israel celebrated its redemption in the Passover, we Christians celebrate Christ's redemptive work on the cross. God told Israel to be careful to remember and not to forget his awesome redeeming work on their behalf (Deuteronomy 15:15). Similarly, as Christians we remember our redemption through Christ each time we gather with God's people for Communion, in annual Holy Week celebrations, or through a Christian Seder meal. In fact, it can happen every time we contemplate the cross.

The more we believers grasp this great redemption, the more it changes our outlook and perspective on everything. We begin to think differently about the world and the things we see and hear. Our worldview gets reshaped. The biblical and Christian worldview is like a grid that affects how we perceive things. Redemption is a crucial element in this worldview, which consists of five parts:

1. Creation. We were created in God's image and likeness.
2. Fall. We all were ruined by sin.
3. Redemption. Christ's death on the cross was the payment price for our deliverance.

4. Regeneration. We can be reborn by the Spirit through faith in Christ's sacrifice.

5. Consummation. Christ will come a second time and create a new heaven and a new earth.

Another way we can apply redemption is by observing the theme of redemption echoing in the arts. We find redemption embedded in literature, music, and film. It echoes everywhere because the deepest longing of the human heart is for redemption, and this longing can't be suppressed.

Finally, when we consider Christ's work of redeeming us, we can't ignore the tragic consequences of the Fall. And while we acknowledge that the world is fallen, lostness is not the whole story. Rather than overlooking this reality or giving in to despair, as Christians we should live with confident hope—even the hope of redemption both here and hereafter. We who understand redemption must devote ourselves to exalting Christ the great Redeemer celebrated throughout the Scriptures and by great believers throughout history. As the redeemed, we seek to magnify our Redeemer in everything we do.

FOR FURTHER READING
Leon Morris, *The Apostolic Preaching of the Cross*. Eerdmans, 1965.
John Murray, *Redemption: Accomplished and Applied*. Eerdmans, 1955.
Willem Van Gemeren, *The Progress of Redemption: The Story of Salvation from Creation to the New Jerusalem*. Baker, 1996.

— DONALD W. SWEETING

REGENERATION

EVERYDAY DEFINITION
Regeneration is the theological term describing the instantaneous creation by the Holy Spirit of a new spiritual nature in a sinful person who trusts Jesus Christ as Savior. The person who has been regenerated is said to have been born again. This phrase comes from the account of Jesus talking with a Pharisee named Nicodemus: "Jesus declared, 'I tell you the truth, no one can see the kingdom of God unless he is born again'" (John 3:3).

When humans are born, they possess *bios*, or biological life. But believers in Jesus who are born of the Holy Spirit possess *zōē*, or new spiritual life. This explains why, in the same conversation with Nicodemus, Jesus said, "Flesh gives birth to flesh, but the Spirit gives birth to spirit" (John 3:6).

Unlike conversion, humans don't have a part in regeneration; it's a supernatural work of God alone. The apostle Paul spoke of regeneration this way: "Therefore, if anyone is in Christ, the new creation has come: The old has gone, the new is here!" (2 Corinthians 5:17, TNIV). James described this new birth in these terms: "He chose to give us birth through the word of truth, that we might be a kind of firstfruits of all he created" (James 1:18). And the apostle Peter added the following perspective: "In his great mercy [the Father] has given us new birth into a living hope through the resurrection of Jesus Christ from the dead, and into an inheritance that can never perish, spoil or fade" (1 Peter 1:3-4).

Regeneration brings about radically new outcomes for those who believe. The new birth cleanses holistic depravity (Matthew 7:17-18), imparts to the soul a new spiritual nature (Ephesians 4:24; 2 Peter 1:4), and unites the life to Jesus Christ (Galatians 2:20; Hebrews 3:14). By imparting a new nature, Holy Spirit regeneration infuses into the soul renewed intellectual, volitional, moral, emotional, and relational powers that initiate the renewal of *imago Dei*—being made in the image of God—in the Christian through the process of lifelong sanctification.

EVERYDAY APPLICATION

Anyone who seeks to obey God can't trust upbringing in a Christian home, the rite of baptism, or church membership to supply the new birth. As helpful as these means of grace are, they don't impart supernatural, spiritual life to the soul. Mere affiliation with a church or simply performing religious rites doesn't automatically purify ingrained sin or produce the new spiritual creation Jesus and his apostles proclaimed. Rather, the Word of God teaches that "if anyone is *in Christ*, the new creation has come" (2 Corinthians 5:17, TNIV, emphasis added). We can only rely on inward regeneration by the Holy Spirit to make us new creatures in Christ and, as a result, pleasing to God.

Regeneration is vital when it comes to attempts to change any political, social, or economic institutions. No matter how well-intentioned, all attempts to build a more compassionate community or a more just society apart from the new birth in Christ are like building a house on shifting sand (see Matthew 7:24-27). As often has been said, "The heart of the human problem is the problem of the human heart." Agendas of political, social, and economic transformation alone without widespread spiritual conversion and regeneration are doomed to come up short. Any positive institutional changes we hope for must be preceded by substantial moral and spiritual change. Throughout history, noteworthy instances of improvement in society typically have been preceded by periods of spiritual revival, such as the Wesleyan revival in the eighteenth century and the Welsh revivals early in the nineteenth century. Philosopher and apologist Francis Schaeffer offered his opinion that no society achieves a state of decency, justice, and compassion unless at least ten percent of its populace has personally experienced the new birth.

FOR FURTHER READING
Helmut Burkhardt, *The Biblical Doctrine of Regeneration*. InterVarsity/ Paternoster Press, 1978.

A. W. Pink, *Regeneration: or the New Birth*. Reiner Publications, 1960.

Peter Toon, *Born Again: A Biblical and Theological Study of Regeneration*. Baker, 1978.

— BRUCE DEMAREST

RELATIVISM

EVERYDAY DEFINITION
Relativism is the term used to describe an unbiblical, false, irrational, and socially dangerous philosophy that commands the beliefs of many Americans, including some Christians. In general, relativism holds that no objective, absolute, and universal truth exists, either in morality or religion. However, this claim—more accurately called *moral relativism*—denies the core of biblical revelation and the confession of Christians for two thousand years.

Moral relativism can be divided into two general types: cultural relativism and private subjectivism.

Cultural relativism claims that moral truth is determined by cultural consensus. Morality depends on culture and is as diverse as the plurality of cultures in the world. Simply put, what is right in one culture may be wrong in another culture. However, while moral values sometimes differ to some extent between cultures, this doesn't warrant cultural relativism. As C. S. Lewis argued in *The Abolition of Man*, few major moral differences exist between cultures throughout history. Lewis demonstrated this by categorizing moral beliefs across time and cultures to include: the law of general beneficence, the law of beneficence for family members, the law of justice, the law of good faith, the law of mercy, and the law of magnanimity.

Further, simply because cultures have a diversity of viewpoints on some issues (for example, monogamy versus polygamy), this doesn't support the conclusion that both cultures are correct morally. Just as cultures can make mistakes about science (thinking the sun revolves around the earth), they might err on morality as well (thinking that some people are "untouchables," as in India).

Cultural relativism claims that moral disagreement can't occur between cultures. So an American shouldn't reach the conclusion that slavery in the Sudan is morally wrong, since Sudanese culture (or at least those in power) have determined it correct. Of course, this logic is absurd, so cultural relativism must be wrong.

Cultural relativism leaves no category for moral reformers—such as Martin Luther King or Gandhi—who speak out against the cultural consensus in the name of a higher law. If they oppose the social norms of their day, they must be considered deviants. Again, this is absurd and makes relativism false.

Finally, cultural relativism makes genuine moral progress impossible. If no moral standard exists outside of cultures, then cultures can't be evaluated morally regarding how close or how far they are from the standard. However, this is unacceptable because we have evidence that moral progress occurs. For example, when the United States outlawed slavery, it moved closer to the moral ideal of treating human beings justly and honoring their "unalienable rights" (in the words of the Declaration of Independence). When the country gave African Americans additional rights during the civil rights era, it moved closer to the standards of equality.

Private subjectivism says that right and wrong is determined by individuals, not cultures. Private subjectivism teaches that morality is not dependent on culture at large, but on the individual's moral judgments. This is also called individual relativism. This belief is defeated because we know intuitively and directly that some things are morally wrong, no matter what any individual might claim. For example, rape, murder, torture, and racism are wrong, because they violate essential human rights. The mass murderer and rapist Ted Bundy, who was put to death in 1992, believed that the universe was morally neutral and that social laws were arbitrary and had no authority over him. He even deemed himself superior to the cowardly crowd that went along with social custom. If private subjectivism is true, then Ted Bundy was right. But, again, this conclusion is ridiculous and profoundly counterintuitive; therefore, private subjectivism is false.

EVERYDAY APPLICATION

As Christians, we can resist relativism by developing a strong sense of objective, absolute, and universal moral truth. We believe in and serve a moral and personal God, who is the source of objective moral law for all people at all times. God is the source, standard, and stipulator of what is good, right, just, and virtuous. Scripture affirms the existence of moral absolutes, which are summarized in the Ten Commandments (Exodus 20:1-18). Jesus summarized the commandments by saying that we should love God with all our being and love our neighbors as ourselves (Matthew 22:37-40). Nowhere in Scripture can we find exceptions to this radical call to love. Because we all fall far short of the divine goal (Romans 3:23), we need to be made right with God through Christ's work on our behalf (Romans 5:5-8), and we must submit to the work of the Holy Spirit in becoming more Christlike in thought and deed.

Since relativism prevails today, Christians need to affirm and live out the realities of moral truth. We can do this in several ways, including:

Stressing both the form and freedom of the Christian life. While there are moral truths that depend on God's eternal character and we must live within the circle of God's standards, there is still great freedom in how Christians find their calling and live out their faith on a daily basis. This isn't moral relativism. God allows for many ways to serve him and our fellow creatures according to our gifts and opportunities

(1 Corinthians 12). So while no one is allowed to steal (Exodus 20:15), some might choose to receive a lower income in order to work with the poor. While all should worship God in ways that honor his character (Exodus 20:1-6), various forms of worship are allowed, given cultural differences. The same form and freedom tension holds true for cuisine, dress, and art. Popular opinion to the contrary, God's law provides a meaningful structure that human beings can flourish within.

Evaluating the morality of our culture according to biblical standards. Given the power of popular culture — as seen in television, radio, films, video games, the Internet, and so on — it's easy for Christians to become worldly and submit to values based on the world, the flesh, and Satan instead of on Christ. Thus Paul warned believers, "Therefore, I urge you, brothers and sisters, in view of God's mercy, to offer your bodies as a living sacrifice, holy and pleasing to God — this is true worship. Do not conform to the pattern of this world, but be transformed by the renewing of your mind. Then you will be able to test and approve what God's will is — his good, pleasing and perfect will" (Romans 12:1-2, TNIV). A prime example of an area where we need to resist relativism is in the area of materialism. The culture communicates that how people spend their money is relative. There is no objective standard. If an individual can afford four cars and wants them, then buy them! However, as Christians, we look to God's Word to find his objective standard. While Scripture sanctions private property and doesn't condemn profit in general, it has plenty to say against greed and insensitivity to needy people. The Old Testament prophets often railed against those who exploited the poor and refused to help them (Amos). Jesus' parable of the sheep and goats affirms that the redeemed serve and bless "the least of these," Christ's brethren (Matthew 25:40; see also verses 31-46). No matter what our culture communicates, there's no place for materialism in the Christian life.

FOR FURTHER READING
C. S. Lewis, *The Abolition of Man.* Simon & Schuster, 1996.
Greg Koukl and Francis Beckwith, *Relativism: Feet Firmly Planted in Mid Air.* Baker, 1998.

— DOUG GROOTHUIS

REPENTANCE

EVERYDAY DEFINITION

Repentance carries two central ideas from the Old and New Testaments: (1) turning back to God, and (2) doing so as a willful decision.

In the Old Testament, repentance involves "changing one's mind" or "being sorry and turning back." We see this language of repentance pertaining to God's people Israel (Exodus 13:7; Job 42:6; Jeremiah 8:6; 31:9) and others who "turned" and wandered away from God over and over again. We also find the term describing God himself, who has a "heart" of repentance (see Genesis 6:6; 1 Samuel 15:11; 35; Jeremiah 18:10). Cleary, the Old Testament dynamic between God and his people portrays the beauty and folly of humanity and God in covenant relationship. God is committed to his people through thick and thin. This call to repentance on the part of humanity is a call to return to this covenant relationship, modeled through dependence on God. Even negative consequences for non-repentance are meant to return God's people back to their rightful state in relationship with him.

In the New Testament, the Gospels are full of the language of repentance. John the Baptist began his preaching by instituting a "baptism of repentance," preparing the way for Jesus the Messiah to come on the scene (Matthew 3:2,11; Mark 1:4; Luke 3:3,8; Acts 13:24; 19:4). When Jesus began his ministry, he made it clear that the doorway into his kingdom comes through repentance: "The time has come . . . The kingdom of God is near. Repent and believe the good news!" (Mark 1:15). For Jesus, repentance doesn't represent a "sad" state of mind. Instead, repentance is a "willful decision"—a thoughtful action based on desire to go through the doorway into a life with Christ!

EVERYDAY APPLICATION

Repentance is perhaps the most misunderstood and maligned word in the Bible. It might bring to mind "fire and brimstone" sermons that warn of hell to those who don't repent, or a feeling of sadness or sorrow over sin, something we must do to avoid hell. However, what appears to be a word that evokes negative feelings is really the word that brings us the most freedom. Eugene Peterson beautifully captures the meaning of this wonderful word when he writes:

Repentance is not an emotion. It is not feeling sorry for your sins. It is a decision. It is deciding that you have been wrong in supposing that you could manage your own life and be your own god; it is deciding that you were wrong in thinking you had, or could get, the strength, education and training to make it on your own; it is deciding that you have been told a pack of lies about yourself and your neighbors and your world. And it is deciding that God in Jesus Christ is telling you the truth. Repentance is a realization that what God wants from you and what you want from God are not going to be achieved by doing the same old things, thinking the same old thoughts. Repentance is a decision to follow Jesus Christ and become his pilgrim in the path of peace. Repentance is the most practical of all words and the most practical of all acts. It is a feet-on-the-ground kind of word.[29]

In addition, repentance isn't a one-time action. Instead, it's an ongoing disposition of our will to always rely on God, to believe that what he says is true and trustworthy, and to live in his freedom (Galatians 5:1). Repentance is the doorway to life in God, and it's something we must do. While God offers forgiveness to us when we repent, he will not ask repentance for us. It's our requirement for entering and living in his kingdom.

FOR FURTHER READING
Eugene Peterson, *A Long Obedience in the Same Direction: Discipleship in an Instant Society.* InterVarsity, 2000.
Richard Owen Roberts, *Repentance: The First Word of the Gospel.* Crossway, 2002.

— KEITH MATTHEWS

REST/LEISURE

EVERYDAY DEFINITION
Rest and leisure are words used to describe a break from normal routine. This change of pace is essential to human life.

---

29. Eugene Peterson, *A Long Obedience in the Same Direction* (Downers Grove, IL: InterVarsity, 2000), 25-26.

Life is made up of a fundamental rhythm that is part of the way we reflect the image of God: we work and we also rest. As we see in Genesis 1, God is a worker. He sets about to the work of creation, but at the end of his creative activity, he rests. The seventh day is set aside for a different type of living.

God commands us to follow this divine example: "Six days you shall labor and do all your work, but the seventh day is a Sabbath to the LORD your God. On it you shall not do any work, neither you, nor your son or daughter, nor your male or female servant, nor your animals, nor any foreigner residing in your towns. For in six days the LORD made the heavens and the earth, the sea, and all that is in them, but he rested on the seventh day. Therefore the LORD blessed the Sabbath day and made it holy" (Exodus 20:9-11, TNIV).

With our fast-paced lives, rest and leisure are far from a common experience. Many people work long and hard hours. Even our vacations are hectic. Recreation becomes extreme, rather than restorative.

The seasonal rhythms of the "Agricultural Age" gave way to the conformity and precision of the "Industrial Age," which has given way to the hectic 24/7 pace of the "Information Age." Before clocks, the sunset determined work schedules. Daylight hours were times for working, while the evening, after sundown, was for rest and fellowship. Clocks were invented in the Middle Ages so that monks could better attend to their prayers. Clocks today don't have that sacred function; rather, they've become our master, driving the ways we function in our world. Time-saving technologies and the immediacy of communication has compressed time and space so that commerce and communication occur at any time of the day or night. It makes the world accessible, and it makes us frantic. In *The Tyranny of the Urgent,* Charles Hummel wrote about our tendencies to see some things that are extremely demanding as so necessary that we end up ignoring some of the truly important things. Because we so easily lose focus, we need a break from the expectations, demands, and pressures of everyday life.

Jesus regularly spent time apart from his active work: "Very early in the morning, while it was still dark, Jesus got up, left the house and went off to a solitary place, where he prayed" (Mark 1:35, TNIV). In this alone time, Jesus was restored, found fellowship with God, and was given clarity in order to make crucial decisions (see Luke 6:12ff). We can learn from Jesus' example.

EVERYDAY APPLICATION

We all need times away that are restorative, give focus, and provide grounding. If we feel guilty about making time for rest and leisure, we need to remind ourselves that God commanded it. These ideas can help us make rest and leisure practical:

- We cease from our normal activities and routines. Rest isn't rest unless we change our practices.
- The pace of life changes. These are times for leisure, recreation, and sleep.
- We slow down enough to appreciate life and others.
- We experience joy and celebration and eating in the midst of community.

Further, rest needs to be a part of our regular lifestyle. We should create space each day for a change of pace. We should create space weekly for a rest experience like the Sabbath. We should find time monthly or quarterly to remove ourselves from normal paces of life. And annually, we should find vacation time that restores us so that we can return to work and service with renewed vigor.

At the same time, rest shouldn't be dreary or rule laden. Instead, the notion of rest and leisure should be a regular practice that leads us to a spiritually centered, restorative, and whole lifestyle.

FOR FURTHER READING

Richard J. Foster, *Celebration of Discipline*. HarperSanFrancisco. 1978.

Robert Johnston and J. Walker Smith, *Life Is Not Work, Work Is Not Life: Simple Reminders for Finding Balance in a 24/7 World*. Wildcat Canyon Press, 2001.

Charles Hummel, *Freedom from Tyranny of the Urgent*. InterVarsity, 1997.

— KURT FREDRICKSON

RESURRECTION

EVERYDAY DEFINITION

Resurrection is the act of rising from the dead. The first person in the Bible to resurrect was Jesus Christ. He suffered and died on the cross, and three days later he rose from the tomb. Jesus was not merely resuscitated to live as before, with his body unchanged. Instead, Jesus was made new and would not die again. The Resurrection included his body as well as spiritual, mental, emotional, and others dimensions of his life.

Because of Jesus' life, death, and resurrection, people can be saved and live eternally with God in heaven. The Resurrection, in fact, confirmed the truthfulness of what Jesus said about God, people, sin, and the way of salvation. Scripture says that all people will someday resurrect and be judged. Because of God's provision for salvation, believers will resurrect to eternal life. They don't need to fear condemnation. Instead they will live eternally in a tangible and physical way, and not just in an intangible, spiritual way. The resurrection emphasizes the holistic dimensions of people's salvation.

The Old Testament implies that there is life after death. Sometimes people were even revived from death (1 Kings 17:22; 2 Kings 4:35; 13:21). However, their bodies remained unchanged in the sense that they would die again. The resurrection of the dead is predicted (Daniel 12:2), and some interpreters think that Jesus' resurrection is foreshadowed in the Old Testament (Genesis 22:5; Isaiah 53:11; Hosea 6:2).

In the New Testament, resurrection becomes central to biblical revelation. For example, Jesus predicted his own resurrection (Matthew 16:21; Mark 8:31; Luke 9:22). His suffering and death were real, and voluntarily undertaken for the salvation of others. During his life, Jesus challenged the Sadducees, who doubted the prospect of resurrection (Matthew 22:23-32; Mark 12:18-27; Luke 20:27-38). Jesus firmly believed in and proclaimed the reality of resurrection. After the Crucifixion, Jesus indeed resurrected (Matthew 28:1-2; Mark 16:2-4; Luke 24:1-3; John 20:1-2). His resurrection was announced by angels, and afterward Jesus appeared to many people: Mary Magdalene (Mark 16:9; John 20:11-18), two men on the Emmaus road (Luke 24:13-15), and eventually to the disciples and more than 500 people (1 Corinthians 15:6). Jesus also appeared at a later time to the apostles Paul and James.

Paul was aware that belief in the resurrection of Jesus and of others was a religious stumbling block to Jews, who were unsure of the resurrection. Further, resurrection was intellectual foolishness to the Gentiles (Acts 17:32; 1 Corinthians 1:23). Paul argued on behalf of Jesus' resurrection and the resurrection of everyone. His classic defense of the historical truth of the Resurrection appears in 1 Corinthians 15:

> But if it is preached that Christ has been raised from the dead, how can some of you say that there is no resurrection of the dead? If there is no resurrection of the dead, then not even Christ has been raised. And if Christ has not been raised, our preaching is useless and so is your faith. (1 Corinthians 15:12-14)

From Paul's perspective, the entire gospel message of Jesus hinged on the truth of the Resurrection. He believed in the Resurrection and attested to the evidence, witnessed by the disciples and hundreds of others.

The disciples were reluctant to believe in Jesus' resurrection (Mark 16:13-14; Luke 24:25-26; John 20:24-25). However, Jesus appeared to them in his resurrected body, talked and ate with them, and eventually convinced all the disciples. Jesus later ascended to heaven, further convincing the disciples of all that he said and did (Acts 1:6-11; Romans 8:34); he was indeed the Son of God (John 20:30-31). As a final point, the Resurrection confirmed the power of God and God's Holy Spirit in the life of Jesus (Ephesians 1:18-20; Romans 1:4; 1 Timothy 3:16; 1 Peter 3:18).

The Resurrection was central to early preaching and teaching by the disciples. It served as the basis of their faith (1 Corinthians 15:14-15), and of their justification (Romans 4:25; 8:34). Thus, the Resurrection became the basis of people's hope in resurrection, justification, and eternal life (Acts 24:15; 1 Corinthians 15:19-23). In fact, being made alive in Jesus is linked to the concept of resurrection (Ephesians 2:1,4-6). Through him, people cross from death to life (John 5:24-26), and they live by the ongoing power of the risen Christ (Philippians 4:13).

Someday all people will be resurrected, and then they will face judgment (John 5:28-29). However, Christians can rejoice in the coming judgment because that's when Jesus will fully manifest their salvation and reconciliation with God. Both the righteous and unrighteous will be resurrected, and they will receive their respective salvation or damnation (Matthew 25:31-32; Acts 24:15). Those who believe in Jesus for salvation will inherit eternal life.

As an event that took place historically, the resurrection of Jesus can't be examined scientifically, so some people raise doubts about what actually occurred after his death. Historical investigation, in some respects, resembles the kind of argumentation that occurs in courts of law. Evidence is presented, analyzed, assessed, and then a decision must be made. This invariably requires an element of faith or belief, sufficient to dispel reasonable uncertainties. Christians argue that Scripture provides factual data, and that numerous other extra-biblical accounts are reliable, including accounts both from those who were and were not disciples of Jesus. Such argumentation is considered persuasive, given ordinary criteria for historical investigation. However, Christians also argue that the conclusion individuals come to about Jesus' resurrection is not like decisions about other historical events. Their verdict about Jesus' resurrection has eternal significance. Thus, as author Josh McDowell wrote, evidence for the resurrection "demands a verdict" by those who investigate it.

Of course, people aren't saved by historical arguments; they're saved by God's grace through faith. Still, Christians think that their faith is reasonable, and that alternative explanations of Jesus' resurrection are inadequate.

EVERYDAY APPLICATION

Resurrection is the blessed hope of Christians, even though so much of what Scripture says about salvation pertains to our life here and now. While the Resurrection reminds us of the reality of an afterlife, it also reminds us of the tangible importance of Christian life in the present. After all, the Resurrection involves the body as well as the spiritual aspects of our lives. So our present, physical lives are part of God's good creation as well as God's eternal life for believers. This means that we can face the prospect of afterlife with great confidence. Still, we should also wrestle with how our confidence in eternal life should affect life in the present. What freedoms can we live out, knowing that our future is secure?

What about the nature of resurrection that God has in store for all believers? Jesus' resurrected body gives us some clues. Jesus' resurrection wasn't merely spiritual; it included his entire body. When the resurrected Jesus appeared to the disciples and other followers, he was visible, tangible, and ate with them. What's more, his resurrected body wasn't just physical, as we understand physicality. Jesus appeared, disappeared, and eventually ascended to heaven. When the disciples first met the resurrected Jesus, they didn't recognize him. Yet there was enough similarity that they recognized him eventually. His resurrection made Jesus, so to speak, new and improved. Further, he didn't just resurrect to die again. His resurrection was forever. As Christians, we also have the hope of being resurrected in a way that is new and improved, freeing us from the present limitations of death and dying.

As followers of Christ, we're not immune from struggling with whether or not Jesus' resurrection really occurred. Some doubters describe Jesus' resurrection as a hoax, or a fabrication by the disciples. The question of the truth of Jesus' resurrection still troubles people, despite the centrality of it to the biblical account of Jesus and the disciples. In order to understand the reasonableness of what Scripture says about the Resurrection, we need to keep in mind that historical studies can only determine what occurred, beyond reasonable doubt. In the case of Jesus' resurrection, the historical evidence is impressive; whole books are dedicated to in-depth studies of it. In fact, a good spiritual discipline would be to read one or more books on the topic. This allows believers to consider the relevant data for themselves.

Finally, each of us must determine if we will accept the truth of Jesus' resurrection. However, this isn't like other decisions to accept or reject certain historical events. Acceptance of Jesus' resurrection has eternal significance! Just as Jesus resurrected, we too may resurrect and enjoy eternal life with God in heaven.

FOR FURTHER READING

Josh McDowell, *Evidence that Demands a Verdict*. Authentic Lifestyle, 2004.

Richard Swinburne, *The Resurrection of God Incarnate*. Oxford University Press, 2003.

N. T. Wright, *The Resurrection of the Son of God*. Augsburg, 2003.

— DON THORSEN

REVELATION, GENERAL

EVERYDAY DEFINITION

What, if anything, do non-Christians know about God? The apostle Paul's statement that "pagans . . . do not know God" (1 Thessalonians 4:5, TNIV) might suggest that the unsaved know little or nothing. The doctrine of general revelation sheds light on this important question. We can make a distinction between general revelation and special revelation. General revelation refers to the knowledge God discloses outside Christ and the Bible to all people everywhere. The created universe, God's providential kindness in history, and the moral law implanted in the human heart constitute the means of general or universal revelation. General revelation provides awareness of God's existence, creative work, aspects of his character or attributes, as well as his moral demands. God's essence can't be seen by mortals (John 1:18), but the works of his hands testify to him.

Scripture gives us many examples of God's general revelation. Psalm 19:1-6 teaches that nature's display brightly mirrors the greatness of Elohim, the God of creation: "The heavens declare the glory of God; the skies proclaim the work of his hands" (verse 1). The apostle Paul proclaimed to the people of Lystra that God "has not left himself without testimony" (Acts 14:17), specifically in terms of his gracious provision of human needs. Before preaching Christ and the Resurrection to Athenian pagans (Acts 17), Paul cited truths that both he and his hearers held in common — that as Creator of heaven and earth (verse 24) God is: self-sufficient (verse 25), an intelligent being (verse 26), active in the world (verse 27), and the source of human life and all that is of value (verses 25,28).

Paul's letter to the Christians in Rome contains the fullest teaching on general revelation (Romans 1:18-32): "since the creation of the world God's invisible qualities — his eternal power and divine nature — have been clearly seen, being understood from what has been made, so that people are without excuse" (verse 20, TNIV). Five times this passage affirms that pagan people know God (verses 19-21,28,32). This doesn't mean they know him redemptively, but that they know God in the sense of being conscious of his existence, character, and moral demands. Tragically, however, the sinful human heart suppresses this rudimentary knowledge (verses 21-23). Paul then taught, as a form of general revelation, that God has written on the human heart his eternal moral law (Romans 2:14-15). Human conscience testifies to each person's compliance or non-compliance with this universal law.

The knowledge afforded all by general revelation communicates the essentials of theism: that a personal God exists who created the universe and who is actively involved in its affairs. The philosopher and theologian Augustine wrote, "Noble philosophers looked and knew the Maker from his handiwork."[30] Throughout history, people have professed atheism, pantheism, and polytheism; this represents the consequence of rejecting the light of general revelation. Sinful people distort this elemental but true knowledge of God into false views. As a result of rejecting this light, humanity is guilty before the bar of divine justice (Romans 1:20).

EVERYDAY APPLICATION

If general revelation doesn't bring salvation, what purposes does it serve? Here are several purposes:

- God's disclosure to all people through general revelation communicates his kindness and care for those he has created. All of us, therefore, should respect, value, and care for ourselves, even as God does. To devalue or despise ourselves, when God loves us and reveals himself to us, constitutes human arrogance.
- Because God through general revelation and common grace shows kindness to all humans made in his image, Christians will do all within their power to enhance human life. Believers blessed with material resources will provide for the needs of others, even as God does. Universal revelation that tells of God's providential goodness provides a more viable basis for alleviating human needs than does the altruism promoted by nontheists.
- General revelation demonstrates that the loving God seeks out lost sinners. God's revelation to all as Creator and Sustainer invites pre-Christians to respond positively to, and receive, additional light. As Paul declared, God revealed himself "so

---

30. Augustine, *Sermons on the New Testament*, 91.2.

that they would seek him and perhaps reach out for him and find him" (Acts 17:27, TNIV). And because general revelation imparts awareness of a higher power that life depends on and a sense of moral accountability, it provides the basis for God's complete, saving revelation disclosed through Christ and the Scriptures, which theologians designate special revelation.

- General revelation bears important relevance for discipleship and evangelism. Even though suppressed, pre-Christians instinctively know that God exists. Even more important, the unsaved sense that they are accountable for their actions to the Judge of the universe. Apprentices of Christ, like Paul at Athens, seek points of contact, or areas of common ground, with unbelievers. They remind pre-Christians of their need for acceptance with God. And like the apostle Paul, they challenge unbelievers to repent of their selfish independence from God, trust Christ, and be saved.

- General revelation applies to social and political issues. Since general revelation communicates universal moral law (such as the difference between right and wrong, truth and falsehood), Christians hold the secular culture accountable to maintain truth, pursue honesty, and act justly. Jesus' disciples rightly challenge dishonesty, immorality, and injustice wherever found in the social arena. Moral values are established not by societal consensus but by the will of God revealed in general revelation. On the basis of general revelation, Christians can cooperate without compromise with other theists for just social and political ends.

FOR FURTHER READING
G. C. Berkouwer, *General Revelation*. Eerdmans, 1955.
Bruce Demarest, *General Revelation*. Zondervan, 1982.

— BRUCE DEMAREST

REVELATION, SPECIAL

EVERYDAY DEFINITION
Christian teaching distinguishes between general revelation and special revelation — between God's general disclosure to all people at all times,

and God's redemptive disclosure to particular individuals at specific times. While general revelation communicates with some clarity God's existence, character, and moral demands, it fails to impart certain knowledge of the plan of salvation. Special revelation is necessary for sinners to be saved. According to the Latin church father Augustine, "We were too weak by unaided reason to find out the truth, and for this cause needed the authority of holy writings."[31]

Hebrews 1:1 tells us that God gave special revelation "at many times and in various ways." The principal ways God gave special revelation are as follows:

- *Direct speech from God.* At the burning bush, God described himself to Moses as "I AM WHO I AM" (Exodus 3:14, NASB). Later, God spoke in an audible voice to Moses on Mount Sinai (Exodus 19:3-6), as well as to Isaiah in the temple (Isaiah 6:8). The angel of the Lord communicated to Mary that she would conceive by the Holy Spirit and give birth to the Son of God (Luke 1:26-37).
- *Dreams and visions that unfolded God's redemptive purposes.* Joseph had a dream at Bethel that he saw angels ascending and descending a stairway between earth and heaven (Genesis 28:10-17). God gave Daniel a dream of four beasts that outlined the course of world history (Daniel 7) and Ezekiel a vision of a valley littered with dry bones that predicted Israel's restoration from captivity (Ezekiel 37:1-14). Saul, the rabbi, had a vision of the glorified Christ that told him of God's purpose to commission him an apostle to the Gentiles (1 Corinthians 9:1).
- *Theophanies, or visible manifestations of God.* In the form of an angel, God engaged Moses in a fiery bush at Horeb and disclosed his plans for Israel's deliverance from Egyptian bondage (Exodus 3:1-22). The cloud and fire that guided Israel through the desert represented another theophany (Exodus 13:21-22).
- *Mighty acts of God in history.* Examples of this form of special revelation include Israel's miraculous deliverance from

---

31. Augustine, *Confessions*, VI.5.8.

Egyptian bondage (Exodus 14:13-31), Elijah's victory over 850 false prophets on Mount Carmel (1 Kings 18:16-39), and the outpouring of the Holy Spirit at Pentecost when thousands were added to the church (Acts 2:1-4). Add to these Jesus' glorious resurrection from the dead (see Romans 1:4).

- *God's messages of redemption spoken to Old Testament prophets and New Testament apostles.* Prophets stated that the very word of the Lord was given to them (Jeremiah 18:1; Ezekiel 12:1; Joel 1:1; Jonah 1:1) as a spiritual burden to be delivered. Paul testified that he received the gospel by special revelation from Christ himself (Galatians 1:12) — likely as he waited upon God in the desert.

- *God's messages spoken through Old Testament prophets and New Testament apostles and disciples.* These revelations included interpretations of saving events in history (Romans 5:12,15,17), predictions of the coming Messiah (Isaiah 7:14), foretelling future events that would come to pass (Isaiah 42:9), and words of comfort (Isaiah 40). Prophets typically began their messages with the phrase, "This is what the LORD says" (see Amos 1:3,6,9; Nahum 1:12; Micah 3:5). The preaching of Peter, John, Barnabas, and Paul was declared to be "the word of the Lord" (Acts 8:25; 15:35) and "the word of God" (Acts 13:46; 2 Corinthians 2:17).

- *Jesus' appearance on earth.* In his earthly life and ministry, Jesus served as the ultimate saving revelation. Hebrews identifies the incarnate Son as the final revelation of the Father (Hebrews 1:1-2). As the apostle John put it, "No one has ever seen God, but the one and only [Son], who is himself God and is in closest relationship with the Father, has made him known" (John 1:18, TNIV). When Philip petitioned Jesus, "Lord, show us the Father," Jesus responded, "Anyone who has seen me has seen the Father" (John 14:9).

- *Jesus' teachings.* Christ's teachings originated not with himself but with his Father in heaven (John 7:16). Speaking of his disciples Jesus said, "I gave them the words you gave me" (John 17:8). Examples of Jesus' revelatory teaching include the Sermon on the Mount, his many parables, and his instruction about the end times in the "little apocalypse" (Matthew 24; Mark 13).

- *Jesus' mighty works.* Jesus performed many miracles — signs and wonders — that demonstrated his deity and messianic authority and that also sought to elicit faith in himself as Savior (see John 2:11). Jesus calmed the violent storm on the Sea of Galilee (Mark 4:37-41) and brought Lazarus back from the dead (John 11:1-44). The record of what was revealed to prophets and apostles (through dreams, visions, prophetic and apostolic teachings, and Jesus Christ) is itself special revelation. Special revelation is progressive — New Testament revelation clarifies and supplements Old Testament revelation.

EVERYDAY APPLICATION

Because God is unbounded love, it is reasonable that he would communicate to humans he created. A father drafted into the Army in World War II called his eight-year-old son aside and gave him a list of things he needed to know and do in order to care for his mother, younger sister, and household affairs. Special revelation is like that. Jesus lived among us for a while before returning to heaven. Until he returns at the end of the age, the Father has given us, his children, detailed instructions on how to live and how to attend to kingdom business. We must take seriously and live out faithfully what God has communicated in his instructions to us. We must obey the teachings spoken by authorized prophets, by Jesus himself, and by his chosen apostles. As Jesus said, "Anyone who loves me will obey my teaching" (John 14:23, TNIV).

We need special revelation to show us who God is as Father, Son, and Holy Spirit. Special revelation informs us that Jesus Christ isn't merely a human teacher, but the only Son of God and Savior of the world. We need special revelation to know how to worship God properly, with heart, soul, mind, and strength. We need special revelation to understand the fundamental problem of humanity, which is the quest for personal autonomy and resulting alienation from God (Genesis 3). We need special revelation to show us how to live wisely and to conduct ourselves in a godly manner (the book of Proverbs; exhortations in the New Testament letters). Special revelation informs us of the imperative of love, as in 1 Corinthians chapter 13.

Without special revelation, we wouldn't know how to be formed into the image of Jesus Christ. As Jesus petitioned his Father, "Sanctify them by the truth; your word is truth" (John 17:17). Without special revelation we wouldn't know how to serve God acceptably. We'd be ignorant about God's command to execute mercy and justice (see Amos 5). Without special revelation we'd be ignorant of God's marvelous plan of salvation from sin and Satan. We'd be unaware of the Great Commission to take the gospel to the entire world (Matthew 28:18-20). Without special revelation we'd be ignorant of the return of Christ to consummate the present age as taught in the book of Revelation.

Special revelation shouts from the rooftops that God has spoken and acted on our behalf! What a comfort to know that God hasn't remained silent and that he hasn't left us to our own devices.

Special revelation, defined as truth content pertaining to salvation, doesn't continue today. Through Christ and the Scriptures, the Father has spoken his complete and final revelation (Hebrews 1:1-2). In the Bible, God has given us all we need to be saved and to live godly lives. To add anything to inspired Scripture would be to call it inadequate and incomplete, which would also dishonor its Author. We reject the claims of sects and cults that claim additional revelations beyond those contained in the Bible. Indeed, Scripture predicts that many false teachers and prophets would appear (2 Peter 2:1), purveying false revelations. The conviction that special revelation has ended with the close of the biblical canon, however, doesn't deny that God on occasion speaks to people today, that he gives people dreams and visions, or that he works miracles.

FOR FURTHER READING

Leon Morris, *I Believe in Revelation*. Eerdmans, 1976.
A. W. Pink, *The Doctrine of Revelation*. Baker, 1976.
Bernard Ramm, *Special Revelation and the Word of God*. Eerdmans, 1961.

— BRUCE DEMAREST

REVERENCE

EVERYDAY DEFINITION

Reverence is a sense of giving respect and bestowing value upon something or someone. A biblical understanding of reverence begins with a sense of worship, love, and honor toward God.

Wisdom literature in the Bible reveals the starting point regarding reverence: "The fear of the LORD is the beginning of knowledge" (Proverbs 1:7). In similar fashion, when asked, what is the greatest commandment, Jesus replied, "'Love the Lord your God with all your heart and with all your soul and with all your mind.' This is the first and greatest commandment. And the second is like it: 'Love your neighbor as yourself'" (Matthew 22:37-39). A sense of reverence emerges from this priority of love toward God and then toward others. In Jesus' answer, we hear the echo of the prophet Micah: We are to be people who act justly, love mercy, and walk humbly with God (Micah 6:8). This sense of holistic worship affects all areas of our daily living. The apostle Paul wrote that followers of God are to live lives of worship that reorient the way they live (Romans 12:1-2).

The two commands Jesus offered as the "greatest" are a summary of the Ten Commandments found in Exodus 20. These commands become the basis for how we can live out reverence. The Ten Commandments begin with a proper ordering. We are to love the Lord our God. We honor him and worship him by giving him priority, not misusing his name, creating no idols that replace him, and giving space in our lives for him. Living out this life of worship orients our lives properly. Out of these ways of honoring God, we are also to live lives of respect and reverence toward others.

EVERYDAY APPLICATION

As Christians, out of reverence for God, we are to be people who respect authority. We honor our parents. We pray for those in government. While we are aliens in this world with ultimate allegiance to the ways of God, we seek to live lives of respect and honor.

Out of reverence for God, we respect human life as a gift given by God. This means that we must critically and compassionately engage in issues that deal with reverence for life such as abortion, euthanasia, waging war, issues of justice, and care for the poor and marginalized. These aren't easy issues, but living out our reverence demands that we give these issues attention.

Out of reverence for God, we also have respect for covenant. We don't commit adultery, the breaking of a marriage covenant between two persons. We must also uphold other covenants: when we make promises, we keep them. Out of reverence for God we also value truthfulness, so we don't lie.

Out of reverence for God, we have a respect for property. We respect and cherish and serve as good stewards for whatever God provides. We don't covet what belongs to others. We don't steal what belongs to others.

This is the way of the people of God—a practical way of living a life of reverence. Out of reverence for God, we love God and love our neighbor. This reverence provides the foundation for us as the body of Christ to have an ever-increasing imprint of God on the society around us.

For Further Reading

Lewis Smedes, *Mere Morality: What God Expects from Ordinary People.* Eerdmans, 1983.

Glen Stassen, *Living the Sermon on the Mount: A Practical Hope for Grace and Deliverance.* Jossey-Bass, 2006.

Scott McKnight, *The Jesus Creed.* Paraclete Press, 2004.

— Kurt Fredrickson

RIGHTEOUSNESS

Everyday Definition

Righteousness is the state of being right or morally justified in thoughts, words, and actions. In the Bible, righteousness primarily refers to God. As God incarnate, Jesus Christ is also referred to as righteous. People are referred to as righteous, but it is mostly because of God's gracious work of salvation in their lives. Righteousness has an ethical dimension, pertaining to faithful conduct in response to God's laws and covenantal relationship with people. Righteousness also involves having a right relationship with God, principally involving faith as trust.

Righteousness represents one of the attributes of God's nature. God embodies righteousness and acts righteously in saving people from sin and death. According to Scripture, God's nature is righteous (Deuteronomy 32:4; Psalm 119:137; John 17:25), and it demonstrates God's sovereignty and eternity (Psalm 71:19; 111:3). God's righteousness is worthy of praise (Psalm 7:17; 35:28; 71:15,24; 145:7; Isaiah 24:15-16). Likewise, God's actions are righteous, as revealed through God's rule, laws, justice, judgment, and salvation of people (Psalm 7:11; 9:8; 19:8-9; 65:5; Jeremiah 11:20). The Bible contrasts God's righteousness with human unrighteousness (Romans 3:5; 10:3).

Righteousness is best revealed in Jesus (Acts 3:14; 1 Corinthians 1:30; 1 John 2:1). Through him, God enables people to become righteous by his atoning work on the cross (Romans 4:22-24; 2 Corinthians 5:21). Despite people's unrighteousness, God makes it possible for them to become righteous. The Holy Spirit also reveals God's righteousness and graciously enables people to be justified or saved (Romans 14:7; Galatians 5:5).

Once individuals receive salvation, God's righteousness provides a pattern for Christian living, especially as found in the example of Jesus (Ephesians 4:24; 1 John 3:7). Jesus challenged people to "be perfect" (Matthew 5:48) as God is perfect, striving above all for the kingdom of God and God's righteousness (Matthew 6:33; 1 Thessalonians 5:23).

Throughout church history, the topic of righteousness arose numerous times in Christian theological reflection. For example, righteousness was seen as important in regard to understanding the nature of Jesus' atoning work on behalf of people. Because humans have transgressed God's righteousness, they are guilty of sin and judgment. However, because of Jesus' life, death, and resurrection, he atoned for their sin. Jesus' righteousness replaced people's unrighteousness and provided salvation.

Roman Catholic and Orthodox Churches thought of salvation as the righteousness of God made available to people by means of God's grace. They had faith in God for their salvation, which they believed was mediated to them through the sacraments of the church. They also emphasized the importance of living righteous lives, emulating Jesus, and other teachings of Scripture. For example, they emphasized living virtuous lives, emulating the theological virtues of faith, hope, and love. They also emphasized the cardinal virtues of prudence, temperance, justice, and courage. Justice especially reflected the righteousness of God, and Christians should endeavor to be just and to confront injustice.

Protestants understood righteousness and the order of salvation more individualistically, not believing that people needed the church as a mediator between themselves and God. Instead, people by themselves are saved by God's grace through faith. Thus, the righteousness of God was available to people by "grace alone" (*sola gratia*) and "faith alone" (*sola fide*); these differences became key principles of the Reformation.

After the Reformation, Protestants increasingly explored the importance of living righteous, Christlike lives. Some denominations stressed holy living and the power of God's Holy Spirit to enable people to live increasingly like Christ. Other groups emphasized justice and the transformational power of God to liberate people from that which binds them physically, socially, politically, and economically as well as spiritually.

EVERYDAY APPLICATION

For Christians, the most important aspect of righteousness involves the free gift of salvation provided by God to us through the atoning work of Jesus. Jesus provided for our salvation, since his righteousness substitutes on behalf of our unrighteousness. We cannot earn salvation for ourselves; it's a free gift from God. We receive it by grace through faith. Our salvation depends upon the righteousness of God and Jesus, rather than through any righteousness we have ourselves. The gift of salvation is an unimaginable grace from God to us; we neither can nor need to earn our salvation. God freely offers it so that we can be free from the guilt of sin and death. Perhaps the question that remains is how we should live, knowing that we don't need to earn or merit God's gracious gift of eternal life.

Although salvation is a free gift, God wants to work further in our lives through the presence and power of the Holy Spirit. Because God is righteous, he wants to make us more and more righteous—more like Christ. Scripture describes this process of growth in many ways. Sometimes God works it miraculously. Other times, God states ways or means for us to cooperate with God's grace in becoming more Christlike. Historically, these means of grace have been referred to as spiritual disciplines. They include vigorous measures such as prayer, scriptural study, worship, celebration, fellowship, confession, and service. Spiritual disciplines also include abstinent measures such as solitude, silence, meditation, contemplation, fasting, frugality, simplicity, and sacrifice. Of course, other prudent means have been employed by Christians in order to grow spiritually, such as small-group accountability, mentoring, and so on. So we have many ways that God promises grace to enable us to become more like Christ. We don't lack with regard to finding ways that help us grow and become more reflective of God's righteousness.

Some Christians believe in the special work of the Holy Spirit in aiding people to become more righteous—more like Christ. This might involve a second experience, subsequent to conversion, when people realize that Jesus wants to become more than their Savior; Jesus wants to become Lord of their lives. As they consecrate their lives to God, the Holy Spirit helps them to grow and sanctifies them entirely. Other Christians believe in a special work of the Holy Spirit, subsequent to conversion, known as Holy Spirit baptism. When believers are baptized by the Holy Spirit, they are empowered by God to receive spiritual gifts as well as holiness. God's righteousness is promoted as believers use their spiritual gifts.

Concern for God's righteousness is increasingly expressed by Christians through their concern for issues of justice, such as caring for the poor as well as for those who have been neglected, marginalized, oppressed, persecuted, and killed. Indeed, Jesus cared for both the spiritual and physical needs of people. So as we live out God's righteousness through our lives, we need to become more inclusive in our love for others and demonstrate the kind of holistic care for others that reflects Jesus' life and ministry. This includes being concerned for the various ways people are physically impoverished as well as spiritually impoverished.

FOR FURTHER READING

Donald L. Alexander, ed., *Christian Spirituality: Five Views of Sanctification*. IVP Academic, 1988.

Mark A. Seifrid, *Christ, Our Righteousness: Paul's Theology of Justification*. InterVarsity, 2001.

N. T. Wright. *Paul: In Fresh Perspective*. Fortress, 2006.

— DON THORSEN

SABBATH

EVERYDAY DEFINITION

Sabbath is time set apart for rest and worship.

During creation, God rested on the seventh day—blessing it,

hallowing it, and setting it aside as special. So he set the pattern of ceasing work as part of the divine rhythm. God rested not out of weariness or fatigue, but because rest is a good part of the created order just as air and plants and animals are. This divine rhythm isn't to be neglected or overlooked because it's part of how we were created and how we are to be. God mandates that both hard work and good rest are essential — that humans must have both. Such "time-outs" keep us from becoming addicted to work and from believing, "I am what I do."

In observing Sabbath, we make space for God. Lynne Baab describes Sabbath as "a day to stop [doing] the things that occupy our workdays and participate in activities that nurture peace, worship, relationships, celebration, and thankfulness. The purpose of Sabbath is to clear away the distractions of our lives so we can rest in God and experience God's grace in a new way."[32] This experience is essential for all who want to hear God in life because it teaches us to develop the capacity to stop the rush of thoughts and activity and simply be with God. For six days a week, we observe *chronos* time (1:00, 2:00, and so on) but on a Sabbath interval, we observe *kairos* time (living only in this moment with an awareness of God).

Practicing Sabbath requires trust that God is able to act in the world apart from human effort or achievement. It requires self-examination, asking, "Do I believe that God can manage the world *without me?*"

Although the Sabbath day predates the law, it is emphasized in the Ten Commandments as a day of rest for every person and creature in the household. Sabbath wasn't observed just because God rested in creation, but also as a time for Israel to remember how God rescued them (Exodus 20:9-11; Deuteronomy 5:12-15). Jesus' ministry further clarified that the Sabbath can't be contained by universal legalisms (as the Pharisees insisted) because God might act on the Sabbath to heal and restore life (Mark 3:4; Luke 14:3). Sabbath, then, is a day of mercy not only for one's self, but also for others.

Sabbath also refers to a rhythm of weeks and years. For example, Israel needed a sabbatical year (one in seven) when the land rested and debts were forgiven, as well as a Jubilee year (the fiftieth year after seven cycles of seven years) when all slaves were freed and land returned

---

32. Lynne Baab, *Sabbath Keeping* (Downers Grove, IL: InterVarsity, 2005), 11.

(Deuteronomy 15:1; Exodus 23; Leviticus 25). Regarding economics and culture, Sabbath observance teaches us that nonstop buying and selling aren't good for us, and that workers and debtors need a time to be "off the hook." Such rhythms keep us from an addiction to buying and selling (shopping), and helps us avoid believing "I am what I consume."

EVERYDAY APPLICATION

For Christians, making space for God in Sabbath might involve prayer or play, self-denial or celebration. As with every spiritual discipline, Sabbath works best if we start where we are. Some people begin with a Sabbath morning—a slow time where nothing is scheduled. Sabbath might look different at different seasons of life.

Each individual and family unit needs to seek God's wisdom in how to practice Sabbath. But as a general guideline, if something seems like work, we shouldn't do it. For some people, planting flowers is work, so they shouldn't do it; for others, the same activity is paradise, so they should do it. A family with children might practice a Sabbath day by spending time together in leisure, while a busy careerist might need a day with nothing to do and nowhere to go. Some people find that Sabbath involves taking naps; for others it involves taking hikes—not to *get anywhere,* but to *be.* For many Christians, Sunday morning worship services are full of work and do not serve as a Sabbath, so another time needs to be arranged. Personal retreats and sabbatical seasons are necessary for longer reflection and to be reminded, "I am God's person not a human machine."

FOR FURTHER READING

Lynne Baab, *Sabbath Keeping.* InterVarsity, 2005.
Dorothy Bass, *Receiving the Day: Christian Practices for Opening the Gift of Time.* Jossey-Bass, 2000.
Tilden Edwards, *Sabbath Time.* Upper Room Books, 2003.

—JAN JOHNSON

SACRIFICES

EVERYDAY DEFINITION

The Old Testament system of sacrifices is described in detail in Leviticus 1–7. The instructions were given to Moses soon after he had received the law on Mount Sinai and the instructions to build the tabernacle in the wilderness.

Centuries earlier, sacrifices had been offered to God by Cain and Abel (Genesis 4:3), Noah (Genesis 8:20), Abraham (Genesis 22), and Jacob (Genesis 31:54). Sacrifices were first offered on man-made altars (Genesis 8:20), and later they were presented before the priests in the tabernacle (Leviticus 17:5-9) and in the temple in Jerusalem (1 Kings 8:62-63).

The five main sacrifices described in Leviticus 1–7 include:

1. The whole burnt offering (Leviticus 1).
2. The cereal offering (Leviticus 2).
3. The peace offering (Leviticus 3).
4. The sin or purification offering (Leviticus 4–5:13).
5. The guilt offering (Leviticus 5:14–6:7).

The first three sacrifices could be offered spontaneously as expressions of repentance or thanksgiving, while the last two sacrifices were required for expiation of intentional sins (sins of commission) and nonintentional sins (sins of omission).

The burnt offering was to be entirely consumed by fire, leaving no edible parts behind. The grain or cereal offering was to be baked or cooked and given to the priests to eat. The peace or fellowship offering represented communion with God, and a portion of the offering could be returned to and consumed by the donor. The sin or purification offering was intended to atone for sin and restore the broken relationship that existed between God and the offerer. The guilt offering served to repay debt.

The shedding and sprinkling of animal blood — usually an unblemished domesticated animal — was required for the whole burnt offering, for the peace offering, and for the sin offering (Leviticus 22:18-25; Numbers 19:2). Whenever an animal was offered before the priest, the donor was required to lay hands on its head as a symbol of the transference of sin (Leviticus 1:4; 3:2,8; 4:4; etc.). On the Day of Atonement, two animals were presented to the priests. The high priest would lay his hands on one animal and transfer the sins of the worshipper. That animal was sent away into the wilderness, while the second animal was offered on the altar as a burnt offering (Leviticus 16:20-22).

In ancient times, an individual would never come into God's presence in the tabernacle or in the temple in Jerusalem empty-handed. Worshippers always brought from their substance and presented their gifts as offerings, indicating either a need for purification or an expression of thanksgiving for divine blessings received. The sacrificial system of the Old Testament was ordained by God to ensure that his people remained in right relationship with him, free from the consequences of sin, and distinct from the foreign nations that surrounded them. Several passages identify the sacrifices offered to God as a "pleasing aroma," indicating divine acceptance of the offering by God, and divine forgiveness for the sinner (Exodus 29:41; see also Leviticus 1:9,13,17).

Sacrifices were never intended to replace true repentance or the pursuit of holiness. Scripture clearly tells us that God wasn't pleased when his people came before him with empty and meaningless sacrifices and failed to pursue justice for the poor, the oppressed, and the afflicted (Jeremiah 6:20; Matthew 9:13). Old Testament prophets proclaimed repeatedly that God abhorred their detestable and shameful sacrifices (Isaiah 1:11-13) because their hearts were turned away from him, often toward other gods. God yearned to see his people engage in acts of kindness, justice, and righteousness on the behalf of the needy who lived in their midst (Micah 6:6-8). These were the sacrifices that pleased him.

EVERYDAY APPLICATION

In the Old Testament, sacrifices were closely related to the notion that the tabernacle or temple was the physical structure where God dwelt (Exodus 25:8; 29:44-46), where his name was established (1 Kings 5:5; 8:29), and where his people met with him in worship (Joshua 22:27-29). Although the temple no longer exists today, the presentation of offerings and sacrifices to God still holds an important place in the worship of God's people. The New Testament tells us that now our bodies are the temple of the living God (1 Corinthians 6:19), and that because worship is meant to take place in God's temple, true worship comes from within the individual and proceeds out of that person's own heart. In his letter to the Romans, the apostle Paul instructed us to honor God by presenting our bodies as "a living sacrifice, holy and pleasing to God" (Romans 12:1, TNIV).

We should understand that sacrifices were never intended to fulfill a purely mechanical role in Jewish liturgy. Rather, they were intended to be an expression of love given from the heart to God in true sincerity and purity. David's prayer of repentance (Psalm 51) tells us that the sacrifices of God are a "broken spirit" and a "broken and contrite heart" (Psalm 51:17). The prophet Micah echoed the words of David when he said, "With what shall I come before the LORD and bow down before the exalted God? Shall I come before him with burnt offerings, with calves a year old? Will the LORD be pleased with thousands of rams, with ten thousand rivers of oil? Shall I offer my firstborn for my transgression, the fruit of my body for the sin of my soul? He has shown all you people what is good. And what does the LORD require of you? To act justly and to love mercy and to walk humbly with your God" (Micah 6:6-8, TNIV).

By shedding his own blood and dying on the cross for us, Jesus became the ultimate sacrifice—the unblemished and perfect Lamb of God who took away the sins of the world. This signified the greatest possible expression of God's love for us. Through Christ's atoning sacrifice, we now have confidence that when we sin we have an advocate with the Father—even Jesus who is just and faithful to forgive us our sins and cleanse us from all unrighteousness (1 John 1:9; 2:1). This side of Calvary, no sacrificed animal can atone for our sins. The blood of the Lamb has been shed, and the price for our eternal redemption has been paid by Jesus Christ once and for all (Hebrews 9:26).

FOR FURTHER READING

Richard S. Hess, *Israelite Religions: An Archaeological and Biblical Survey*. Baker, 2007.

Patrick D. Miller, *The Religion of Ancient Israel*. Westminster John Knox Press, 2000.

—HÉLÈNE DALLAIRE

SAINTS

EVERYDAY DEFINITION

A saint (from the Latin *sancti)* refers to a person who is holy or set apart for God's service.

In the Old Testament, the psalmist says of saints that they are the glorious ones in whom God delights (Psalm 16:3), and the faithful whose walk is blameless (Psalm 101:6).

In the New Testament, the term saint (Greek: *hagios*) refers to the members of the body of Christ, the church. Christ's holiness is the source of the saint's holiness, which was imparted to them through the gift of the Holy Spirit.

For the first three centuries of the church, all members were considered saints; because all followers of Christ received their holiness from God, no individual was consider above any other Christian. As Christianity expanded into the Mediterranean world, it encountered sometimes severe persecution. Some Christians faced the persecution courageously and suffered torture and even death without denying their deeply held beliefs. Others caved under pressure and quickly blended back in with their pagan counterparts until the persecution subsided. These faithful witnesses (*martyrs*) became highly regarded in the church's memory and emerged as the first "saints." Stories of their faithfulness under duress circulated widely. Their burial sites became important sites to gather for prayer and services of worship. Over time, this special status was extended to bishops and monastics, whose lives were characterized by courageous holiness and a single-minded devotion to God. As saint-hood became associated with heroes of faith and was later coupled with Roman notions of patronage, a perception emerged that saints were intercessors who had the authority to benefit the faithful. Fanciful stories spread detailing the healing power of objects (*relics*) associated with the saint or special favor accrued by pilgrimages to the graves of the saints. It's important not to allow these later distortions to distract from the importance saints or heroes of the faith played in the life of the faithful.

EVERYDAY APPLICATION

The courageous trust and faithfulness of saints to God provide an inspiring example that encourages us "ordinary saints" to leave behind our worldliness and follow Jesus with "ruthless trust." Saints remind us that at the heart of our gospel is the promise of transformation. Saints aren't born; they're made by the power of God and daring obedience. We can learn from spiritual ambitiousness of saints, who embrace the demands of obedience and difficult circumstances because they want to be more than what can be achieved by human power. They desire to be holy.

FOR FURTHER READING

Gerald Sittser, *Water from a Deep Well.* InterVarsity, 2007.
Matthew Woodley, *Holy Fools: Following Jesus with Reckless Abandon.* SaltRiver, 2008.

— MIKE GLERUP

SALVATION

EVERYDAY DEFINITION

Simply put, "salvation" constitutes the work of God on behalf of his people. Although the term "salvation" is popularly understood to primarily concern eternal destiny, the biblical model doesn't limit the saving work of God to only the afterlife. On the contrary, the saving purposes of God are at work in this life as well as the next. In fact, "salvation" is translated from Hebrew and Greek words that are conspicuously nonreligious.

In the Old Testament, salvation is most often used to describe God as the agent of deliverance from physical danger and distress. For example, the miraculous crossing of the Red Sea is understood as a saving act of God, as he liberated his people from slavery in Egypt: "Thus the LORD saved Israel that day from the Egyptians; and Israel saw the Egyptians dead on the seashore. Israel saw the great work that the LORD did against the Egyptians. So the people feared the LORD and believed in the LORD and in his servant Moses (Exodus 14:30-31, NRSV). Salvation is also used to describe the final, national restoration of Israel: "I will save my flock, and they shall no longer be ravaged; and I will judge between sheep and sheep" (Ezekiel 34:22, NRSV). In the prophetic words of Ezekiel, like a valley of dry bones, the people of God will rise again, their land will be restored, and the promise given to Abraham in Genesis 12:1-3 will be renewed (Ezekiel 37:1-14).

In the New Testament, salvation is decisively shaped by spiritual, other-worldly concerns, although the physical sense of deliverance from distress isn't lost entirely. For example, after encountering the blind beggar Bartimaeus, Jesus proclaimed, "Go; your faith has made you well" (Mark 10:52, NRSV). Or in the story of the stilling of the storm on the Sea of Galilee, the disciples cry out to the sleeping Jesus, "Lord, save us! We are perishing!" (Matthew 8:25, NRSV).

Still, in the New Testament, the ultimate salvation of the believer through the work of Jesus Christ assumes a central place in God's provision for his creation. For example, in the healing of the paralytic man, physical restoration is linked with the forgiveness of sins: " 'For which is easier, to say, "Your sins are forgiven," or to say, "Stand up and walk"? But so that you may know that the Son of Man has authority on earth to forgive sins' — he then said to the paralytic— 'Stand up, take your bed and go to your home'" (Matthew 9:5-6, NRSV). In other words, physical salvation and spiritual salvation are interconnected.

Further, salvation isn't imagined as a singular moment, but a process being worked out over time until Christ returns. In his letter to the church at Corinth, the apostle Paul describes the unfolding nature of salvation in the opening chapter: "For the message about the cross is foolishness to those who are perishing, but to us who are being saved it is the power of God" (1 Corinthians 1:18, NRSV).

EVERYDAY APPLICATION

The provision of God for his people is beautifully captured in the person of Jesus. In fact, the origins of the name Jesus proclaim a divine purpose: "God is salvation." Through the Incarnation, the salvation of God has arrived. Yes, Jesus was crucified, but he is not dead; death could not hold him. Jesus rose from the dead and dwells among us still, actively engaging the world. Likewise, the saving purposes of God can't be bound or contained; salvation has not only come, but is in the process of coming to all of creation, great and small, now and forever.

FOR FURTHER READING

Paul K. Jewett, *Election and Predestination*. Eerdmans, 1985.
Clark Pinnock, ed., *The Grace of God, the Freedom of the Will*. Bethany, 1989.

John Piper, *The Justification of God*. Baker, 1993.

— MATT HAUGE

SALVATION, ASSURANCE OF

EVERYDAY DEFINITION

In the Bible, assurance of salvation refers to our confidence that God has accepted us through the work of Christ and our certainty in God's promise to complete our salvation.

The author of Hebrews describes Christians as those who "draw near to God with a sincere heart in full assurance of faith" (10:22). The word for assurance here (Greek: *plerophoria*) refers to "being completely sure of the truth of something."[33] The apostle Paul described this assurance in terms of our certainty of being God's children that comes from God's Spirit (Romans 8:16). In fact, the very presence of the Holy Spirit represents God's seal of ownership on us and his pledge to finish what he has started (1 Corinthians 1:22; Ephesians 1:13). The apostle John described Christians as those who possess sure knowledge that they possess eternal life (1 John 5:11-13).

This assurance of salvation has at least four distinct dimensions, as found in the Bible and in spiritual formation literature throughout the history of the church.

One dimension is the inner certitude that comes from the presence and work of the Holy Spirit in our lives. Paul captured this inner dimension when he wrote, "The Spirit himself testifies with our spirit that we are God's children" (Romans 8:16). This testimony (Greek: *summartoreo*) refers to "confirming evidence by means of a testimony."[34] The inner testimony of the Spirit provides this evidence in a way that goes beyond rational thinking or feeling. This inner assurance goes deeper than a mere rational proposition; it is a deeply relational reality, much like the way children are assured of their acceptance by their parents.

A second dimension is assurance based on the promises of God's Word. Throughout the Bible, God's Word refers first and foremost to communication that proceeds from God. It also refers to the written

---

33. J. P. Louw and E. Nida, *Greek-English Lexicon Based on Semantic Domains*.
34. *Greek-English Lexicon Based on Semantic Domains*.

record of God's communication as found in the Bible. We find an example of this dimension of assurance in John's statement that he was writing his letter to Christians so that they might "know" that they possess eternal life (1 John 5:13). Confidence based on a written record assumes that this written record is trustworthy and possesses God's own authority. As Christians, we confess that the Bible indeed is trustworthy and possesses God's own authority. So, in contrast to the inner assurance described above, this dimension of assurance is a more rational reality. By acknowledging God's trustworthiness and the trustworthiness of the Bible, we deduce our assurance by faith.

A third dimension of assurance relates to the communal nature of our faith. In the Bible, no one believes in Jesus in isolation from others. From the decision of faith and repentance, believers are joined to the communion of saints. This community creates a social environment where believers both give and receive affirmation that their faith is authentic. In some traditions, this comes by means of a confirmation or baptismal event. In other traditions, it comes by reciting testimonies of faith. These actions continually reinforce each individual's confidence regarding their pardon through Christ and hopeful expectation for the completion of their salvation. The Bible connects this dimension to the action of "confessing" one's faith (Romans 10:10-11).

The fourth dimension of assurance of salvation is the sacramental dimension. Jesus gave us the sacraments of baptism and the Lord's Supper to nourish our faith. As believers regularly participate in the sacraments, they nourish their assurance of faith so it can thrive (John 6:51-58). When believers abandon consistent participation in the sacraments, their assurance is stifled and wanes.

EVERYDAY APPLICATION

We must remember that God grants us assurance of our salvation as a gift to be received, not as a right to be flaunted. Our assurance of God's acceptance and the completion of our salvation isn't an indication that we're more righteous than others. We should remember God's assurance to Israel: "The LORD did not set his affection on you and choose you because you were more numerous than other peoples, for you were the fewest of all peoples. But it was because the LORD loved you and kept the oath he swore to your forefathers that he brought you out with a mighty hand and redeemed you from the land of slavery, from the power of Pharaoh king of Egypt" (Deuteronomy 7:7-8). Nor does God choose us because of our fame, numbers, intellect, moral superiority, or anything within us. Our application of assurance of salvation requires that we live in this reality humbly, without self-righteousness and self-congratulation.

God invites us to find him in all four dimensions noted above.

1. We grow in our inner assurance as we cultivate sensitivity to the Holy Spirit by consistent participation in spiritual disciplines. These disciplines fine tune our inner hearing so we can discern the Spirit's testimony about our identity as God's children.
2. We grow in the biblical dimension by soaking our minds in the Bible, allowing the narrative world of the Bible to become the narrative world of our lives. Consistent involvement in *lectio divina* and *lectio continua* contribute to this process, as well as regular hearing of the Bible read and preached.
3. We grow in the communal dimension of assurance by surrounding ourselves with like-minded disciples of Jesus who will reinforce our decisions of faith and remind us of the promises of God.
4. We grow in the sacramental dimension by regularly participating in the celebration of Christ's sacraments in community with other followers of Jesus.

FOR FURTHER READING
Bill Hull, *The Complete Book of Discipleship*. NavPress, 2006.
John G. Stackhouse, *What Does It Mean to Be Saved?* Baker Academic, 2002.

— TIM PECK

SANCTIFICATION

EVERYDAY DEFINITION
The root of the word sanctification (Latin: *Sanctus*) denotes a separation unto God or the act or process of being holy or cleansed. However,

it has taken on a broader theological meaning, especially in terms of Christian formation. Practically, sanctification refers to a consciously chosen and sustained relationship to God in Christ, where an individual is able to do—and routinely does—what is right before God. This condition of the human heart comes about through grace, the work of the Holy Spirit, and by personal and corporate formation, where an individual progressively takes on the inner character and outward actions of Jesus Christ through discipleship to him.

Sanctification is sometimes used to describe an event as well as a process. For many Christians, sanctification means becoming "sanctified" through the infilling of the Holy Spirit. This "event" is sought, and it's seen as a significant spiritual marker in the Christian's life.

However, being sanctified is *not* primarily an experience, a status, or an outward form. Rather, sanctification shows through a Christian's character, and it creates a track record of action. A truly sanctified person embodies in thought and action the life described by the apostle Paul in Galatians 5:22-23, when he describes the "fruit of the Spirit." Throughout a sanctified individual's life, this process might be furthered through unique and special experiences or events brought about by the Holy Spirit. Yet none of these events equate to a finality of growth in Christlikeness. Instead, they make an ongoing contribution to the formation of Christlike character and action in the disciple of Jesus.

Over the course of life, a follower of Christ should expect to experience many different kinds of sanctifying experiences, but at the same time, mostly finding Christ's pattern of formation in the ordinary and mundane of daily life.

EVERYDAY APPLICATION

As Christians, the sanctifying work of the Holy Spirit within our lives is a synergistic process. We see this process clearly in the words of Paul, who admonished, "Continue to work out your salvation with fear and trembling, for it is God who works in you to will and to act in order to fulfill his good purpose" (Philippians 2:12-13, TNIV) and added, "To this end I labor, struggling with all his energy, which so powerfully works in me" (Colossians 1:29). These verses describe the dual role of human effort and the supernatural energy of God simultaneously at work within us, forming us into Christ's image.

Our role in the sanctification process includes daily submission and surrender to God's rule in our life and the awareness of God's gracious provision in all things. Then, we commit to the taking on of specific "spiritual disciplines" that place us before God, allowing us to learn from him and be changed. When we act, we find that God is there, giving us the energy to act all along! Our sanctification is sustained and fueled by grace, through our active discipleship to Jesus Christ.

We should see this sanctification process most clearly in the ordinary activities of life, such as work, play, friendships, family commitments, and church, not just the unique or spectacular moments. Many Christians of the past demonstrated this truth; that even in doing the dishes we can be formed into the image of Christ.

FOR FURTHER READING

Brother Lawrence, *The Practice of the Presence of God.* Shambhala, 2005.
Dallas Willard, *Renovation of the Heart: Putting on the Character of Christ.* NavPress, 2002.

— KEITH MATTHEWS

SATAN

EVERYDAY DEFINITION

Relatively little is said in the Bible about Satan, the leader of the opposition to God. Yet what Scripture does say is very important to understanding the differences between God and Satan, the devil's activity, and the ultimate end to this enemy of God and his people.

The Bible uses a number of terms to describe the personal force who opposes God and his good purposes. The most common terms are the devil, Beelzebul (or Beelzebub in some translations), and "the Evil One." In fact, each of these terms reveals something about Satan's character, way of operating, and intentions:

- The word Satan literally means adversary. Satan, the adversary of God, seeks through his limited power to oppose God, the all-powerful King of the universe.
- The term devil means slanderer or accuser, which is one of

Satan's chief modes of attack against God's people and those whom God's Spirit is drawing to himself.

- Beelzebul comes from the name of the god of the Philistines. The religion of this god called for child sacrifices and other practices the Torah described as an abomination.
- The Evil One, used by many New Testament writers, identifies Satan's character as wicked and his person the source of all malicious actions.

Satan first appears in the Bible in Genesis 3, where he tempted Eve by distorting God's word in order to bring about disobedience to God. The Bible reports little about Satan's biography, describing rather his actions and his ultimate downfall. Job 1 portrays Satan in the role of accuser of the righteous — in this case God's servant, Job. From the book of Job, we learn that Satan's power is limited in the sense that he's able to do only what God permits, according to the Lord's perfect will.

The Gospels depict Satan again in God's presence, this time in the presence of the incarnate Son of God during his temptations in the desert. As Satan did with Eve, he seeks to twist the Word of God for his purposes, but the devil is overcome by Jesus. Jesus said, "I saw Satan fall like lightning from heaven" (Luke 10:18). Satan is cast down from his place of power through Jesus' work and in the work of the kingdom. Satan, the author of disease and death, is defeated, although he refuses to accept his defeat.

The New Testament teaches that Satan stubbornly attempts to reassert his malevolent power. He parades as an "angel of light" (2 Corinthians 11:14), seeking to lead God's people astray. He also prowls about like a lion looking for someone to devour (1 Peter 5:8). Satan does this, in part, by the use of demons, who seek to further his influence. Satan must use demons because, unlike God, he is neither omnipresent (everywhere) nor omnipotent (all powerful).

The book of Revelation portrays Satan as a dragon who rages because he knows that his time is short (12:10). The Apocalypse depicts Satan's ultimate defeat by the power of the Lamb, the Lion of Judah, who is Jesus Christ. Satan is bound for a thousand years and thrown into the abyss. After that, he is freed by God. But Satan returns to his practice of deceiving, only to be permanently cast into the lake of fire, forever overthrown and rendered powerless.

EVERYDAY APPLICATION

Because Jesus took Satan very seriously, we are wise to do the same. Jesus understood Satan to be a real, personal, and intentional being who strives to oppose the will of God. At the same time, Jesus didn't inordinately focus on Satan, and we shouldn't either. While respecting the power of Satan and being aware of his ability to deceive us and lead us astray, we shouldn't give him the attention that only God deserves. To be aware of his wicked work, we can glance at Satan while we gaze at God. God alone deserves our focus. As the source of truth and goodness, he alone enables us to discern the devices of Satan as he works his deceptions. Viewing Satan as imaginary or powerless is a great danger, especially for the modern scientific mind that seeks natural explanations for all things. Satan exerts his power when people assume him to be mythical and therefore ignore him.

As Christians, we have three great enemies: the flesh (the temptation that comes to us because we are fallen), the world (the structures and patterns of culture that are programmed to draw attention away from God), and Satan. The difference between Satan and these other two enemies is that Satan's personal focus—assailing the weakest areas of our lives—makes his attacks very dangerous. Additionally, his deep desire to retain all human beings in the power of rebellion and death means that he will stop at nothing to hold in his sway those who don't know Christ and to attack those who follow the Savior.

As followers of Christ, we possess the strength to overcome Satan. This isn't natural power, but power that results from the ongoing work of the Son of God and the indwelling presence of the Holy Spirit. All hostile forces must submit to Christ (Philippians 2:10), and that includes Satan. When humans seek to oppose Satan in their own strength, they will fall victim to his great charms and power. Victory over Satan and the evil he personifies is found in the victory of Jesus and through faith identification with him in his death and resurrection.

FOR FURTHER READING

Michael Harper, *Spiritual Warfare*. Servant, 1984.

Timothy M. Warner, *Spiritual Warfare: Victory over the Powers of Darkness*. Crossway, 1991.

Michael Youssef, *Know Your Real Enemy*. Thomas Nelson, 1997.

— CHRISTOPHER MORTON

SECOND COMING

EVERYDAY DEFINITION

In Christianity, the Second Coming refers to the anticipated return of Jesus from heaven to earth. This event fulfills prophecy about Jesus as the Messiah, such as the resurrection of the dead, the Last Judgment, and the establishment of the kingdom of God on earth.

Through his first coming, Jesus fulfilled the Old Testament promises and prophecies about redemption of sinners. Jesus died an atoning death for sinners and was resurrected to give eternal life to those who put personal trust in him as personal Savior. Before his ascension, Jesus himself promised to come again in the last days, commonly referred to as the Second Coming, in order to judge the living and the dead and to take his people to the millennial kingdom and the new heavens and the new earth.

The second coming of Jesus has several important theological meanings:

- The Second Coming stands as the ultimate hope of all believers that have lived, are living, and will live on this earth. Because of this hope, Christians eagerly look forward to the second coming of their Lord.
- The second coming of Jesus is connected to the ultimate victory of God over the power of evil and Satan. God will vindicate himself by judging the evil one and his followers and condemning them into the lake of fire for eternity.
- The Second Coming will demonstrate that God is faithful in fulfilling his promises and prophecies. God's words and promises can't be broken and God can't deny himself. Through

the Second Coming, God will prove himself to be faithful in his words and promises.

Although the Bible doesn't specify when Jesus Christ will come again, it does give several important signs concerning the second coming of Jesus:

- The nation of Israel will be restored.
- Many false prophets will rise.
- The gospel of God's kingdom will be preached all over the world and to the ends of the earth.
- The church will become increasingly apostate—meaning that some Christians will turn away from God.
- The Antichrist will rise as the ruler of the entire globe.

EVERYDAY APPLICATION

If the second coming of Jesus is a future event, how can we apply it to our everyday lives now? Here are some meaningful approaches:

- As Christians, we don't know when Christ will come again. The exact date and time is not known. So we should meditate upon Jesus Christ's promise to come again and learn how to eagerly expect his second coming. We should believe wholeheartedly that Jesus can come even today. This means that we should be equipped with eschatological faith. Today can be the last day of global and personal history.
- We should be watchful about the signs of the Lord's second coming. The nation of Israel has already been restored. The gospel of the kingdom has been spreading all over the globe, although some nations and peoples don't yet know the gospel. Many false prophets have arisen, and some churches are in the state of apostasy and spiritual degradation. According to the signs given in Scripture, the second coming of Jesus is very near.
- We need to prepare ourselves for the great Tribulation that will come soon. Although some Christians believe that they will escape from the Tribulation through a rapture, the Bible

seems to teach that even Christians will go through the great Tribulation when the Antichrist will severely persecute believers. We should be ready for the coming Tribulation.

FOR FURTHER READING

Craig Blomberg and Sung Wook Chung, eds., *A Case for Historic Premillennialism: An Alternative to the "Left Behind" Eschatology.* Baker, 2009.

George E. Ladd, *The Presence of the Future.* Eerdmans, 1974.

— SUNG WOOK CHUNG

SECULARISM

EVERYDAY DEFINITION

Secularism is a perspective that sees the world through the lens of a nonreligious commitment, especially in the areas of social and intellectual life. This worldview is derived from the term that means worldly, and it focuses on the natural order of the universe to be the only reality.

Secularism is a philosophy associated with the eighteenth-century Enlightenment that partitioned spiritual matters from nonspiritual matters. Most often, the term is used to describe the belief that political practices should be free from religious ideas. This is the idea behind the separation of church and state found in democracies.

The Bible doesn't directly address the topic of secularism. In the Old Testament, Israel's government is clearly a theocracy, where God is the King of Israel and where God's laws are applied by the government. In the New Testament, the people of God are so marginalized from the Roman government that the idea of influencing government policy doesn't frequently occur to New Testament writers. However, Scripture does teach that all areas of life are under the domain of God, such as when the psalmist wrote, "The earth is the LORD's . . . and all who live in it" (Psalm 24:1).

EVERYDAY APPLICATION

In today's society, secularism is fast becoming a cultural option for many, especially for people who have become frustrated with the mixing of religion into public and political life. Often, secularism is viewed as an attitude, scoffing at anything attributed to the supernatural. Many individuals who embrace a secular mindset look surprisingly similar to mainstream culture—seeking the good life and devoting themselves to family and careers, service, and political activism. However, they reject a religious perspective or interpretive grid for life and ultimate issues. Ultimately, many secularists end up embracing atheism or agnosticism.

As Christ followers, we have a view of the present and ultimately the future grounded in the fact that God has revealed himself to humanity in Jesus Christ and that history is securely in his redemptive planning (Colossians 1:15-23). We believe that the shaping of our future depends on Christ and the carrying out of his agenda by his people for the redemption of the world. Within this distinctively Christian world-view, we need to be especially wary of allowing our lives to be partitioned into spiritual and nonspiritual categories, because no dimension of life is off limits for discipleship. In fact, Jesus calls us to place all of our lives under his lordship.

FOR FURTHER READING

Jurgen Moltmann and Margaret Kohl, *God for a Secular Society*. Augsburg Fortress, 1999.

James Turner, *Without God, Without Creed: The Origins of Unbelief in America*. Johns Hopkins University Press, 1986.

— TIM PECK

SELF-CONTROL

EVERYDAY DEFINITION

The principal New Testament word for self-control means "to have power over oneself." This quality of character was deeply valued in ancient Greek philosophy and ethics and is considered to be a fulfillment of the Greek ethical system. Self-control is the ability of humans to monitor and control their responses in word and behavior in specific circumstances in order to respond appropriately to other people. People without self-control are powerless in their reactions and can speak and act in ways that inflict harm upon themselves and others. The Bible speaks to the vulnerability and danger for those who lack self-control: "Like a city whose walls are broken through is a person who lacks self-control" (Proverbs 25:28, TNIV).

Self-control is a fruit of the Spirit (see Galatians 5:23). Jesus Christ clearly exhibited this character quality throughout his life, most notably in the events leading up to the cross and during the crucifixion itself: "Do you think I cannot call on my Father, and he will at once put at my disposal more than twelve legions of angels? But how then would the Scriptures be fulfilled that say it must happen in this way?" (Matthew 26:53-54).

Jesus experienced rejection by the religious leaders of his day (Sadducees and Pharisees), betrayal by those closest to him (Judas, one of the twelve disciples), denial and desertion at his darkest hour (Peter and the rest of the disciples). Yet even in the most difficult of circumstances, Jesus demonstrated a life of self-control before both friends and enemies.

EVERYDAY APPLICATION

Life in the Spirit (see Galatians 5) enables Christians to display self-control, this character quality of Christ, as we face temptations or difficult people and circumstances. If service for Christ is to be faithful and effective, self-control is a character quality that we must cultivate. Paul reminded us (Titus 1:8) that self-control is a necessary characteristic for those selected for leadership in the church.

Author Eugene Peterson paraphrases "self-control" to mean "train hard" (1 Corinthians 9:25, MSG). Just as a runner who expects to win a race seeks mastery over his body and chooses behaviors or disciplines suited to that end, Christians will adopt behaviors and disciplines that honor God. This includes prayerfully resisting desires that dishonor God because of the unfruitful attitudes and behaviors they yield (see Galatians 5:19-21). At the heart of practicing and exhibiting self-control is the practice and behavior of abiding in Christ (see John 15:4-8).

As we encounter difficult people and challenging circumstances, we can ask the Holy Spirit to grant us self-control. If tempted to seek revenge when we are mistreated, we can completely entrust the problem situation to Christ (see Romans 12:17-19). Self-control helps us to return good for evil (Romans 12:20-21) and to respond to people and events in ways that display the character of Christ and that please him.

FOR FURTHER READING

P. W. Clement, "Self-Control" in *Baker Encyclopedia of Psychology & Counseling,* edited by David G. Brenner and Peter C. Hill. Baker, 1984.

David S. Dockery, "Fruit of the Spirit" in *Dictionary of Paul and His Letters,* edited by Gerald F. Hawthorne, Ralph P. Martin, and Daniel G. Reid. InterVarsity, 1993.

— RANDOLPH M. MACFARLAND

SERVICE

EVERYDAY DEFINITION

In the Bible, service has both vertical and horizontal dimensions. Vertically, service is an expression of love and obedience to God. Horizontally, service is an expression of helpfulness and giving toward other people. So as Christians, we define service as unselfish and tangible acts of helpful giving toward others offered out of devotion to Jesus Christ.

The background to the idea of service is the hierarchical nature of ancient society. In the ancient world, hierarchy defined all relationships. People in positions of subservience were viewed in a servant role, with the epitome of this being slaves (see Exodus 21:2-11). Most often, people on the margins of society found themselves in these subservient roles: women, foreigners, the poor, etc.

The Bible takes the ancient concept of service and places it at the very center of what it means to love God through Jesus Christ, in both the Old Testament (Deuteronomy 6:13) and the New Testament (Romans 6:16-22). Consistently, those who obey God for the sake of others are referred to as God's servants, whether it be Moses (Deuteronomy 34:5), Joshua (Joshua 24:29), or Paul (Romans 1:1). Ultimately, Jesus is the perfect incarnation of a servant of God (Isaiah 53:1-12; Acts 8:28-35; Philippians 2:7). In the Christian life, acts of worship are viewed as service (Romans 12:1-2), as are acts of ministry toward other people.

The horizontal and vertical dimensions of service must be carefully balanced. For example, the apostle Paul was adamant that although he was a servant of Christ (Titus 1:1) and strived to serve others with the gospel (1 Corinthians 9:19), he ultimately was a slave to no human

(Galatians 1:10). His ultimate allegiance was to serve Christ, and he served people because that service was faithful to his allegiance to Christ. Church leaders are specially called to model lives of service, as seen in Jesus' words, "Whoever wants to be first must be your slave" (Matthew 20:27).

EVERYDAY APPLICATION

When we understand that service was typically reserved for those on the margins of society, applying service to our spiritual life means being willing to engage in actions that are countercultural and embrace authentic humility. Often, these actions are foreign to our natural sense of entitlement and social conditioning. Jesus himself exemplified this role when he washed the feet of his followers (John 13). This action not only required humility on the part of Jesus, but also required a reversal of social norms by the disciples.

When we apply service to our own journey of spiritual transformation, we must also adopt a kingdom-oriented mindset regarding social norms. This can take place in what might seem like insignificant ways, such as a church leader who cleans the restrooms, a small group facilitator who does the dishes after a group meeting, or a church officer who changes diapers in the church nursery. Our willingness to engage in actions that could be delegated to others and that we might view as beneath us are true actions of service. A steady pattern of these actions cultivates the virtue of humility within us and helps us see ourselves rightly in light of God and his purposes.

FOR FURTHER READING

I. A. H. Combes, *The Metaphor of Slavery in the Writings of the Early Church*. Sheffield Academic Press, 1998.

Robert Greenleaf, *Servant Leadership*. Paulist Press, 2002.

William J. Webb, *Slaves, Women and Homosexuals: Exploring the Hermeneutics of Cultural Analysis*. InterVarsity, 2001.

— TIM PECK

SEXUAL SIN

EVERYDAY DEFINITION

Sin is any lack of conformity to God's will regarding how we should live our lives. It can occur in thought or action and is particularly apparent in our relationships. Sexual sins are those thoughts, impulses, or behaviors that diverge from God's instructions given in Scripture regarding how our God-given sexual natures are to be expressed.

God declared sexuality itself as good because we were created as sexual and relational beings and God stated that his creation was good (Genesis 1:31). Sex is described in Scripture as the way a married couple becomes united with each other. This marital oneness of a woman and a man can only fully be realized when they are committed to a lifelong relationship of mutual support and intimacy. The union of the couple in sexual intercourse symbolizes the complete oneness that should occur between the two of them, and reflects the oneness that God wants to have with us as his creation. However, due to the Fall (Genesis 3), all people have been infected by sin, and while we want to do what is good we keep sinning anyway (see Genesis 4:7; Romans 6:6). Our sexuality is influenced by sin, so what was created as good often becomes a struggle to live out faithfully as God intended.

The emphasis of biblical teaching on sexual sins is that sin occurs when we behave in specific ways that contradict God's intention for us (for example, breaking his commandments; Exodus 20:1-17), when we *think and dwell on* specific things that contradict God's desire for us (for example, committing adultery in our hearts; Matthew 5:28), and when we *damage our relationships* with others and harm ourselves and them (1 Corinthians 6:18-19).

Some Christians have different opinions about which specific sexual behaviors, thoughts, and types of relational disrespect result in sin. However, Scripture clearly indicates that the following are sexual sins: violent sexual acts (rape), selling or buying sexuality (prostitution and pornography), coercive sexual relationships (sexual abuse and harassment), unfaithfulness (infidelity in marriage and committed relationships), same-sex sexual relationships (homosexual behavior), premarital sexual behavior (sexual intercourse and cohabitation prior to marriage), dwelling on and pursuing what does not belong to you (fantasy and lust), and sexually demeaning others (teasing and joking).

We sin sexually when we express our sexuality in ways that hurt others, take advantage of others, dominate others, let others use us for their sexual gratification, or even hurt ourselves. We sin sexually, are sinned against sexually by others, and live within societies where we are exposed repeatedly to sexual sins in both explicit and subtle ways. God's creational intent is for us to live with each other in mutual respect and love, honoring the dignity and value of each person as God's creation.

In the area of sexuality we all fall short of God's desire for us. As a result, we desperately need God's forgiveness in order to be reconciled with him and with each other. When we have sinned, one of the ways we unconsciously seek forgiveness and reconciliation is by the shame and remorse that so often is a consequence of sexual sin. In healthy, God-ordained sexuality within marriage, being naked and unashamed is a wonderful gift of God that is to be celebrated (Genesis 2:25). When we commit sexual sin, we might feel temporarily satisfied, but in the end it results in emptiness, shame, or even self-loathing and condemnation.

EVERYDAY APPLICATION

The fall of humanity resulted in many behavioral dysfunctions of healthy sexuality, a multitude of distortions in our thoughts, and many powerfully destructive emotions such as shame and guilt. For many of us, one of the greatest challenges of growing in the Christian life — of following Jesus as his disciples — is in overcoming the sexual sins that plague us. Sexuality has an addictive element that locks us into patterns of behaving, thinking, and relating that are contrary to God's desire for us. However, rather than giving us simply a list of sexual dos and don'ts and showing us how we have failed, Scripture continually points our attention to the depth and transparency of our relationship with God and the wholesomeness of our relationships with each other.

In practical ways, this is done by reflecting on the roots of our sinfulness. For some people, current sexual sin is related to having been sinned against earlier in their lives. Working through this issue with a trusted friend or counselor can bring healing and freedom. Emotional struggles with disappointment, loneliness, rejection, abandonment, anger, or even anxiety about other things in life can twist normal and understandable emotions into compulsive sexual behaviors and obsessive thoughts.

Discussing and understanding these feelings can bring us considerable relief from sinful sexual desires and behaviors. Fleeing temptation is another helpful strategy, demonstrated in the story of Joseph (Genesis 39). Confession to trusted fellow Christians and prayer for each other are also important steps (James 5:16). Accountability with friends and spouses is an essential component of how God helps us by providing fellow travelers on our journey of faith.

Galatians 5 is one of the Bible passages that lists a variety of sins, including a number of sexual sins. But immediately following the list of sins, the apostle Paul described the fruit of the Spirit. We're encouraged to join the Spirit in his work in our lives. Many of these fruits apply to our efforts to combat sexual sin. For example, our society promotes immediate relief and instant gratification. Patience is one fruit of living in the Spirit, and we need to be patient with ourselves as we struggle to develop greater Christlikeness. Self-control is listed last, perhaps a recognition that while we can often see other fruit in our lives — such as love, joy, and peace — one of the most difficult things is to control ourselves, particularly in the area of sexuality. For those of us who with the Spirit's help achieve some measure of success in the important area of self-control, the passage goes on to warn us that we must not become conceited because it is the Holy Spirit who does his work in us as we cooperate with him.

Following the Galatians passage concerning the fruit of the Spirit is a clear instruction to the church (6:1-2). While the text describes how sin in general is to be handled by the church, it applies equally to sexual sin. The passage suggests that if we live by the Spirit of God, we are to restore each other gently and do so with humility because any of us can be tempted into sin. We need to understand that sexual sin is no worse than other sins that threaten to separate us from God and each other. And we need to understand that God offers his forgiveness and restoration for sexual sin just as he does for any other sin.

Over time, as we grow older physically and as we are increasingly transformed into Christ's image, we realize that sexual sins don't have the power over us they once had. As we focus on healthy relationships within the body of Christ, deepen intimacy within our marriage relationships, and grow closer to God and understand more fully his ways of working in the world and in us, sexual sins can begin to fade in intensity. As we mature spiritually, we become more convinced of the precious nature of this wonderful gift that God has given us.

FOR FURTHER READING

Stephen Arterburn and Fred Stoeker, *Every Man's Battle Workbook: The Path to Sexual Integrity Starts Here.* WaterBrook, 2002.

Shannon Ethridge and Stephen Arterburn, *Every Woman's Battle: Discovering God's Plan for Sexual and Emotional Fulfillment.* WaterBrook, 2003.

— FRED GINGRICH

SEXUALITY

EVERYDAY DEFINITION

Sexuality is a core component of humanity given by God to males and females for reproductive and relational purposes. The Genesis account of creation teaches us that our maleness and femaleness is foundational to what it means to be a human (1:27) and that our sexuality received the blessing of God (1:28). Sexuality enables humans to fulfill one of the mandates given to Adam and Eve, to "Be fruitful and increase in number; fill the earth and subdue it" (1:28). Sexuality is related to what it means to be created in the image of God (1:27), although Scripture nowhere teaches that God engages in sexual behavior. After the creation of the human race endowed with sexuality, "God saw all that he had made, and it was very good" (1:31).

From Genesis 2, we learn that Adam was lonely (2:20). So God created Eve in response to the incompleteness of Adam when he existed alone. She was created from the side of Adam (2:22-23), meaning that they were one flesh before her creation, and their sexual interaction was designed to restore that oneness (2:24). In the Garden of Eden, human sexuality existed without either Adam or Eve experiencing any shame.

Three important facts about sexuality stand out in Genesis 1 and 2:

1. Sexuality comes directly from God as a good and blessed gift to humans.

2. Satan wasn't involved in the design of sexuality or in the bestowal of sexuality upon humans.

3. Sexuality existed in human experience before sin entered the Garden.

These features of human sexuality help protect us from entertaining some common but false ideas about sex: that it is a burden, that it is evil in nature, or that it is sinful to engage in sexual behavior as God designed it.

Sin, however, negatively impacted human sexuality. After their disobedience, Adam and Eve realized they were naked and covered themselves with fig leaves (Genesis 3:7). As a result, shame became a part of sexuality. This post-fall shame also serves to provide some of the sexual privacy needed as the human race began to grow in number. God added other boundaries around the gift of sexuality that were eventually codified in the law given to Moses. God's standard calls for the restriction of sexual intercourse to marriage between a man and a woman (Exodus 20:14). Scripture prohibits sexual activity with close relatives, children, or animals (Leviticus 18:1-23). Maintaining sexual purity was an important standard for the people of Israel and became an important standard for followers of Jesus (Acts 15:20). Sexual impurity is incompatible with the kingdom of God (1 Corinthians 6:9-10).

The New Testament teaches us that maintaining sexual purity is related to our sanctification and that God calls us to live a sexually pure life (1 Thessalonians 4:4,7). God will punish those who indulge in passionate lust (1 Thessalonians 4:6). These standards aren't man-made efforts to impose hardship and misery on people; rather, they are standards that come directly from God (1 Thessalonians 4:8). The washing, sanctifying, and justifying aspects of our salvation can restore sexual purity for those who have previously ignored God's teaching about sexuality (1 Corinthians 6:11).

The New Testament also teaches us that our sexuality is intimately connected to our body. Violating God's standards regarding sexuality has human implications greater than those for other sins (1 Corinthians 6:18). "The body is not meant for sexual immorality, but for the Lord, and the Lord for the body (1 Corinthians 6:13). The body will be resurrected, the body of the believer is linked to Christ himself, and our bodies are temples of the Holy Spirit (1 Corinthians 6:14-15,19). These theological truths give us all the more reason to flee from sexual immorality and to pursue sexual purity (1 Corinthians 6:18).

EVERYDAY APPLICATION

As believers, we are responsible for managing our personal sexuality. When members of the body of Christ reach out for help in dealing with sexual issues, church leaders and mature Christians need to respond to those requests with relevant help from Scripture. This can help people deal with the past sexual sins and the future with its promise of sexual faithfulness.

We can place a great deal of confidence in the Word of God to address matters of sexuality. Both Old and New Testaments of Scripture were written in centuries when the surrounding cultures were sexually disordered. The paganism surrounding ancient Israel featured the worship of gods who were viewed as sexually active beings. Pagans used sexual intercourse as part of the worship of these gods. Numerous types of sexual license characterized the Greek and Roman world of the New Testament era. The Bible's call for sexual purity is relevant and timely for our age, which is likewise sexually disordered in many ways.

The Bible offers an abundance of practical advice for living a sexually pure life (see major portions of the book of Proverbs). We are commanded to flee immorality (1 Corinthians 6:18; 2 Timothy 2:22). We have hope for sexual restoration because the Bible indicates that we can learn to control our bodies (1 Thessalonians 4:3-5).

Sexuality is both strong and fragile at the same time. Sexuality is a strong drive as reflected in the vast expansion of the human family throughout the planet. It is also fragile in that the drive can be expressed in many deviant forms. As Christians, we must regard our sexuality as a blessed gift from God and as a fragile component of life to be protected by following the Bible's standards for purity.

Many people have found it difficult to maintain a sensible balance regarding sexuality without falling into either license or asceticism. Both imbalances were found in the Corinthian congregation. Some parties in the Corinthian church argued that "Everything is permissible for me" (1 Corinthians 6:12), while other people advocated restraint from sexual activity even within marriage (1 Corinthians 7:1-5). A balanced view of sexuality for Christians should involve a careful combination of celebration for the gift and profound respect for the boundaries given by God to protect and enrich that gift.

FOR FURTHER READING

Daniel R. Heimbach, *True Sexual Morality*. Crossway, 2004.
Dwight H. Small, *Christian: Celebrate Your Sexuality*. Revell, 1974.

—JAMES BECK

SHAME

EVERYDAY DEFINITION

Shame, as used in the Bible, refers to disgrace, dishonor, or ridicule, especially the humiliation of the cross in order to emphasize the greatness of God's love in Christ: "Jesus . . . for the joy set before him endured the cross, scorning its shame, and sat down at the right hand of the throne of God" (Hebrews 12:2). A few times, the apostle Paul used the word shame to cause regret and shake up his readers' thinking: "I say this to shame you. Is it possible that there is nobody among you wise enough to judge a dispute between believers?" (1 Corinthians 6:5; see also 15:34).

In recent decades, shame has lost the part of its meaning related to appropriate guilt, and has instead come to mean a strong sense of being uniquely and hopelessly "less" than other human beings. Appropriate guilt is at the core of the conscience, resulting from behaving contrary to our internalized standards. Appropriate guilt offers the possibility to learn, repair, and grow.

Christians welcome healthy guilt with godly sorrow and repentance (2 Corinthians 7:9-11). However, with shame, there is no hope for repair because shame is tied into identity. Guilt says, "I *made* a mistake." But shame says, "I *am* a mistake." People feel guilty for what they do but they feel shame for what they are. In their shame, they believe they are bad people or losers. The end result is not conviction, but despair, believing, "There's no hope for me."

With this contemporary definition, the consequences of shame are that it tarnishes, smears, and even violates the true identity that individuals are made in the image of God (*Imago Dei*), and therefore have inherent value independent of their utility or function. Shame's activities come in the form of self-scolding (imitating the enemy of our soul, the Accuser; Revelation 12:10). People in shame repeat to themselves self-recriminations, which become a part of their identity. They think, *Others might know God, but I've done something so bad—indeed, I am someone so bad—that God is disappointed and no longer extends grace to empower me to become one with him.*

Shame aborts transformation into Christlikeness as it leads to destructive tendencies such as verbally attacking others, blaming others to lift up self, trying to prevent future shame by controlling others, seeking power and perfection, or being overly nice or self-sacrificing in a people-pleasing manner to prove worth. Still others become immobilized, withdrawing from the world to numb painful feelings of shame. Shame can also fuel addictive behaviors (not only alcoholism and drug addiction, but also mood-altering experiences such as overeating and shopping). In despair, people believe they must depend on something outside themselves to feel better. As a result, recovery from addiction requires more than to "just say no," but to work through the shame.

Recovering from shame requires help on two fronts: uncovering the roots of the shame and dealing with life habits that have grown out of shame. As followers of Jesus, we need to immerse ourselves in the truth of our identity as individuals whom God loves and dearly treasures apart from our actions. God's love is so great that performance—or lack of performance—can't increase or decrease his love. Therefore, God's great love and power can heal us.

EVERYDAY APPLICATION
Healing from shame involves examination of the past, especially incidents that fostered shame, in order to reeducate ourselves about God's intentions that embody grace and truth. This examination might entail grieving over lost time or destructive behaviors.

Healing also requires examination of the present, especially our thought life. Because the automatic inner voices in our minds (such as the relentless inner critic) can reinforce shame-based behaviors, they need to be recognized, confronted, and replaced. This leads to examination of the behaviors that feelings of shame foster. We come to understand that we're not helpless and powerless because of our past experiences.

This healing needs to occur relationally, not in isolation. Such discoveries, grief, and awareness occur while interacting with godly people who show empathy and love. They also help us think carefully about motives behind shame-based thoughts and behaviors. Relational healing is needed to replace critical voices and facial expressions of the past with accepting and nurturing ones.

Recovery and healing from shame is aided by tools such as support groups, therapy, healing prayer, and Scripture meditation. Interaction with others about the troublesome events in daily life can help us see how shame plays itself out in compulsive behaviors and makes us aware of triggers for shame-based behavior. With continued healing, we can let go of these behaviors.

Of course, healing from shame is work, requiring us to constantly examine our thoughts. For example, when we think, "Why am I such a failure?" we need to recognize that as a sign of shame that doesn't lead to considering the next steps of taking responsibility and healing. Instead, we might ask God, "Why did I fail in this instance?" Then we can explore our motives and pray about what steps to take next.

FOR FURTHER READING
Sandra D. Wilson, *Released from Shame.* InterVarsity, 2002.
Henry Cloud and John Townsend, *12 "Christian" Beliefs That Can Drive You Crazy.* Zondervan, 1995.
John Bradshaw, *Healing the Shame that Binds You.* Health Communications/HCI, 2005.

—JAN JOHNSON

SIN

EVERYDAY DEFINITION
The biblical description of the term sin (*harmartia*) is derived from the idea of "missing the mark." Scripture makes clear that sin is a condition of humanity, as well as all of creation, which longs for deliverance (Romans 8:19-23).

The reality of our sinful condition is without question. Truly, "all have sinned and fall short of the glory of God" (Romans 3:23). This missing of the mark is beyond mere mistakes; at its core it is a rebelliousness or breach of relationship between God and humanity, which shows up in all degrees of selfishness, evil, pain, and suffering. Because sin has permeated the universe, it affects more than our personal relationships. It also is embedded in the systems and structures of society, from corporate offices to governmental operations. So sin is personal and corporate.

On a personal level, the most characteristic feature of sin is that it's directed toward God himself. Essentially, humanity has committed self-idolatry, refusing to live under God's loving redemption through Jesus Christ (Romans 5:6-8). We might say that sin on a personal level is "a radical addiction to our own self-sufficiency." This violation of relationship with a loving God has severe consequences of separation and pain. Apart from redemption, sin results in helpless cycles of manifold evils between humanity and God.

However, while we are helpless when it comes to sin, we are not without hope! This condition of sin sent Jesus Christ in pursuit of humanity, to set us free from the bondage of sin and death and restore us to freedom (Colossians 2:13-14; Galatians 5:1; 2 Corinthians 5:17-21).

EVERYDAY APPLICATION

We only need to read the daily newspapers or watch the evening news to catch a glimpse of the reality of sin in our world. Truly there is "nothing new under the sun" (Ecclesiastes 1:9). All levels of evil abound right under our noses. As Christians, we even contribute! Most of us will admit that we sin, but don't want to admit that we are sinners. Yet even the best of us find a way to protect ourselves at all costs. This clearly reveals that all of us suffer from that "radical addiction to our own self sufficiency."

Thankfully, we have a rescuer in Jesus, who has broken our bondage to sin and death. The grace that frees us from sin now becomes the grace that teaches us how to live in freedom (Titus 2:11-14). Yes, we can live free of sin's bondage! "It is for freedom that Christ has set us free" (Galatians 5:1). Does that mean we won't sin? No, we'll always have battles, but through trust and confidence in Jesus, progress is assured!

Further, Jesus involves us in his redemptive plan, making us ambassadors of his reconciliation and freedom from sin. Through Jesus, we can become a people who look like our Savior in character and action.

As his followers and representatives, we can actually affect the people, systems, and structures still in bondage to sin.

FOR FURTHER READING

Jerry Bridges, *Respectable Sins: Confronting the Sins We Tolerate.* NavPress, 2007.

Cornelius Plantinga, *Not the Way It's Supposed to Be: A Breviary of Sin.* Eerdmans, 1995.

— KEITH MATTHEWS

SIN, ORIGINAL

EVERYDAY DEFINITION

Original sin refers to the state of guilt and corruption that all human beings are born into as the result of Adam and Eve, the originators of the human race, falling into sin. Original sin involves two aspects: all people are guilty before God, and all people are characterized by a sinful human nature.

God originally made human beings in a state of integrity. Created in the divine image (Genesis 1:26-27), Adam and Eve were good and upright, enjoyed a face-to-face relationship with their Creator, and were oriented toward doing God's holy will. However, when Eve was deceived by Satan and Adam openly disobeyed God by the taking of the prohibited fruit (Genesis 3:1-7), they fell into sin. Specifically, Adam's sin wreaked havoc on the entire human race after him. However, original sin doesn't refer to the first sin of Adam. To distinguish his sin from original sin, Adam's act can be referred to as the originating sin. From this originating sin of Adam flows the reality of original sin, the state of guilt and corruption that is part of all human beings from their birth.

The corruption that is part of original sin consists of total depravity, which refers to the extensiveness of sin on human nature. The corrupting influence of sin is so expansive that it extends to a person's entire being. Total depravity doesn't mean that human beings are as sinful as they could possibly be, nor that they are incapable of doing any good. Rather, depravity is all-pervasive, affecting every part of a human nature, including the body, mind, emotions, will, motivations, purposing, and the like. The corruption of original sin also consists of total inability, which refers to the intensiveness of sin on human nature. The corrupting influence of sin is so intense that none of us, in our own strength and according to our own ability, can do anything that essentially pleases God or changes our nature from self-centeredness to love for God. Total inability doesn't mean that human beings don't possess a will to decide and act, or that they are incapable of doing good in the natural (civil, social, artistic, scientific) realm. Rather, total inability means that there is no spiritual soundness in people that would enable them to do good in order to merit God's favor, nor do they possess any inclination on their own to take a step toward God for salvation.

Biblical support for original sin is specifically found in the apostle Paul's discussion of the parallel between Adam's disobedience and Christ's obedience (Romans 5:12-19). Through the "one trespass" of "the one man," Adam, all human beings experience the penalty for sin, which is death (verses 12,15,17). They are judged (verse 16) and condemned (verses 16,18), and they are sinners (verse 19). Specifically, original sin is due to human solidarity with the sin of Adam, who acted as the representative of the human race in covenant relationship with God. As Adam, the head of the race, went—through disobedience to destruction—so went all humanity represented by him. Elsewhere, Paul described human beings as spiritually "dead in your transgressions and sins" so as to be "by nature objects of wrath" (Ephesians 2:1,3). This dreadful state is true of people from the very beginning, as the psalmist David lamented, "Surely I was sinful at birth, sinful from the time my mother conceived me" (Psalm 51:5).

EVERYDAY APPLICATION
Original sin prompts serious reflection on the plight of humans and our corresponding need for salvation:

- We must never think of people as being "safe" before God or even in a neutral position before the holy Judge. Original sin means that all people are guilty before God and are sinful in nature. All are prone to divine judgment, death, and condemnation.

- We should never imagine that sin affects people only partially or exerts just a minor influence on them. Original sin means that every aspect of human nature is depraved and that the debilitating influence of corruption renders them incapable of doing anything to rescue themselves from this dreadful situation. The hopelessness of the human condition is utterly complete. Original sin is the tragic and all-consuming problem of the entire human race.

- Awareness of human depravity and inability should propel us to be missional—committed to communicating the divine solution in Jesus Christ (Matthew 28:18-20; 2 Corinthians 5:17-21). Sharing the gospel is the only hope to save sinful, condemned human beings (Romans 10:9-15). Several mighty works of God are set in motion at salvation to deal with the problem of original sin. Justification (the declaration that people are not guilty before God but are made righteous through the righteousness of Jesus Christ) counteracts the aspect of original guilt. Regeneration (the new birth) and sanctification (the Holy Spirit's work to bring about growth in Christlikeness) answer the aspect of original corruption. Indeed, every aspect of human nature is renewed through salvation (1 Thessalonians 5:23): the mind (Romans 12:1-2), the heart (1 Timothy 1:5), the conscience (Hebrews 9:14), the will (Philippians 2:13), the "inner being" (Ephesians 3:16; Colossians 3:10), and the body (1 Corinthians 6:12-20).

- As followers of Christ—those rescued from original sin—we should express our thankfulness by no longer living for ourselves but for him who saved us (2 Corinthians 5:14-15). Our identity as justified and new creatures in Christ qualifies us to be genuine worshippers of God (John 3:1-8) and prompts us to live for the praise of the glory of his grace (Ephesians 1:3-14). The original dignity that we'd fallen from as human beings created in the image of God is progressively being restored (Romans 8:29; 2 Corinthians 3:18).

FOR FURTHER READING
Henri Blocher, *Original Sin: Illuminating the Riddle*. Eerdmans, 1997.
John Murray, *The Imputation of Adam's Sin*. Presbyterian and Reformed, 1959.

— GREGG ALLISON

SOUL/SPIRIT

EVERYDAY DEFINITION
Understanding what the Bible has to say about the soul or spirit — for that matter any components of the human person — can be confusing. Three main problems confront the attempt to define the terms.

1. The words *soul* and *spirit* often are used as parallel expressions and in many ways can be viewed as synonymous.
2. Close examination of the distinctions between soul and spirit in Scripture reveals that spirit also can refer to both heart and will.[35]
3. Hebrew and Greek conceptions of the soul's relationship to the body were very different. While Greek thought often presented a view of the soul as an entity separate from the body, Hebrew anthropology was more holistic.

Modern theology has gravitated toward the Hebrew view. Theologians no longer debate whether human beings are composed of two parts (soul and body) or three parts (soul, spirit, body). Most scholars today don't consider the soul/spirit to be "part" of the human makeup, but instead it characterizes the person in its totality.

In contemporary usage, the term soul/spirit refers to the nonmaterial aspect of a human that imparts individuality. In Christian theology, soul/spirit carries the further connotation of being the part of the person that has the potential to relate to God and that survives the death of the physical body.

In his book *Renovation of the Heart,* professor and author Dallas

---

35. Dallas Willard, *Renovation of the Heart* (Colorado Springs, CO: NavPress, 2002), 33-35.

Willard proposes that six basic aspects of a human being together and in interplay make up "human nature."[36] They are:

1. *Thought* (images, concepts, judgments, inferences).
2. *Feeling* (sensations, emotion).
3. *Body* (action, interaction with the physical world).
4. *Social Context* (personal and structural relations with others).
5. *Spirit* (choice, will, heart, decision, character, the CEO of the person).
6. *Soul* (the factor that integrates all the above into one life).

This model not only outlines the components of the person, but also the only five things a human can do. Humans can think, feel, behave, interact with others, and choose. Spirit/will/heart is the center or core of a person's life and might be called the "ego." "Choice" is perhaps the best one word encapsulation for the activity of this spirit/will/heart dimension. It underscores the most fundamental decision faced by humanity. Christians awaken each day to the choice of living in an intimate, conversational, and communal relationship with God, or to initiate and maintain a separate existence. The spirit/CEO's critical decision is between willingness and surrender versus willfulness and autonomy.

The soul, as distinguished from the spirit/CEO, can be viewed as the invisible computer that keeps everything running and integrated into one person. The soul is the aspect that integrates all of the components of the person to form one life. The soul is not the "person." The person includes all aspects of the self—including the soul. The soul, according to Willard, "is that aspect of one's whole being that correlates, integrates, and enlivens everything going on in the various dimensions of the self. It is the life center of the human being."[37]

EVERYDAY APPLICATION

If God created the spirit/heart/will/CEO as the key influence in our lives as his followers, then how the heart becomes transformed from distant and darkened (Deuteronomy 29:18-19; Matthew 15:8; Romans 1:21) to noble, good, and open to God (Luke 8:15; Romans 10:9)

---

36. Dallas Willard, *Renovation of the Heart* (Colorado Springs, CO: NavPress, 2002), 30.
37. Willard, *Renovation of the Heart*, 199.

becomes the most important question that can be asked in theology, philosophy, and psychology.

To get a better grasp of the person in the context of transformation, we can explore the imagery of a large company. At an executive meeting of this large company, the CEO (spirit/heart/will), who makes the key choices, sits at the head of the table in a conference room. She is surrounded by five division heads representing research and development (thought), human resources (feeling), labor (body), corporate relations (social context), and information services (soul). In an ideal situation for the company, all essential parts are effectively organized around its mission statement—its purpose and reason for existence—that was put in place by the board of directors (the Trinity). The CEO (spirit/heart/will) seeks the higher good of the organization and its mission. In the best of worlds, the five division heads cooperate and comply with the administrative will of the CEO, which is one with the will of the board of directors.

The problem, however, is that most "companies" (or human beings) aren't headed by a CEO who operates in perfect alignment with the "board." The key question is how transformation can occur that will realign the vision of the CEO (spirit/heart/will) to comply with the mission statement of loving God with one's whole heart and one's neighbor as oneself?

The biblical answer is clear. The spirit/heart/CEO is changed through a relationship with the Trinity—specifically Jesus Christ. When Jesus says to his disciples, "Now this is eternal life: that they know you, the only true God, and Jesus Christ, whom you have sent" (John 17:3, TNIV), he is directing the CEO of the human person to an intimate and interactive friendship with God. The CEO in relationship with the board produces singleness of purpose, willing surrender, and the ultimate organization of all the division heads around one purpose. Spiritual formation in Christ is the process leading to that ideal end where all essential parts of the human self are effectively organized around God. The ideal result is love of God with all the heart, soul, mind, and strength, and of the neighbor as oneself (Deuteronomy 6:4-5; Mark 12:29-31).

Christian spiritual transformation involves "knowing" God at such a deep, relational level that one's spirit is progressively aligned to God's will while the soul is humming in the background like a well-functioning computer, integrating all the components of the person into one fully-functioning organism.

FOR FURTHER READING

Colin Brown, "Soul," in *The New International Dictionary of New Testament Theology*. Zondervan, 1978.

Dallas Willard, *Renovation of the Heart: Putting on the Character of Christ*. NavPress, 2002.

— GARY W. MOON

SPIRITUAL DISCIPLINE

EVERYDAY DEFINITION

Spiritual discipline, while not a biblical term, is born out of Christian tradition. The term is directly related to the biblical idea of "training" like an athlete (1 Corinthians 9:24-27).

The practice of spiritual discipline began with the model of Jesus himself, such as when he withdrew to a solitary place (Luke 4:42). The wise and fatherly mentor Paul instructed Timothy, "Train yourself to be godly. For physical training is of some value, but godliness has value for all things, holding promise for both the present life and the life to come" (1 Timothy 4:7-8).

So, what is this training in godliness? Is there such a thing as a "spiritual gym"? To answer those questions, it helps to more clearly understand what spiritual disciplines are and why they're important. Author and philosophy professor Dallas Willard writes, "A spiritual discipline is an activity in our power that enables us to accomplish what we cannot do by direct effort."[38] When practiced, these disciplines move our attention to the spiritual realm of our own heart as well as our outward behavior. They help us withdraw from our natural dependence on ourselves and rely on God and his kingdom.

While no "official" list of spiritual disciplines exists, many wise teachers in spiritual formation have given us a helpful model. Willard designates two types of these disciplines:[39]

---

38. Dallas Willard, *The Great Omission* (San Francisco: Harper San Francisco, 2006).
39. Willard, *The Great Omission*.

1. *Disciplines of Abstinence:* Activities where we *abstain from* something and place ourselves before Jesus, in order to find our significance, nourishment, and wholeness in him. These spiritual disciplines include: solitude, silence, fasting, frugality, secrecy, chastity, and sacrifice.

2. *Disciplines of Engagement:* Activities where we *engage in* and place ourselves before Jesus, in order to find our significance, nourishment, and wholeness in him. These disciplines include: study, prayer, worship, fellowship, submission, service, and sacrifice.

Practicing these disciplines — going to the spiritual gym — involves arranging our lives to incorporate these activities into our daily routines. Practicing these disciplines is all about wise living and not earning righteousness with God. In other words, we don't earn "points" with God by undertaking these disciplines. Rather, we should think of them as opportunities to bring ourselves before God to be changed.

EVERYDAY APPLICATION

For many of us, the word "discipline" isn't pleasant. It reminds us of punishment, hard work, and no fun. However, most of what we produce in our lives that carries any value requires us to exercise some form of discipline. For example, to play a musical instrument, we arrange our life routines to practice. We take on activities, such as playing scales, working on techniques, and studying musical scores, in order to master the instrument and music.

Our spiritual lives work much the same way. Spiritual disciplines form one leg of a three-legged stool in regard to our transformation into Christlikeness. One leg is our formation through daily trials and tribulations, the second is the action and work of the Holy Spirit, and the last leg — the only one under our unique control — is practicing spiritual disciplines.

Spiritual disciplines form us into the people God created us to be. Through these exercises, we learn to do the right things, in the right way, with the right attitude, and the right timing. We aren't after perfection — just daily living out of God's resources.

FOR FURTHER READING

John Ortberg, *The Life You've Always Wanted: Spiritual Disciplines for Ordinary People*. Zondervan, 1997.

Dallas Willard, *The Great Omission*. HarperSanFrancisco, 2006.

Adele Ahlberg Calhoun, *Spiritual Disciplines Handbook*. InterVarsity, 2005.

—KEITH MATTHEWS

SPIRITUAL GIFTS

EVERYDAY DEFINITION

Spiritual gifts are qualities given by the Holy Spirit to Christian believers.

The prophet Isaiah foretold the coming of a king, who through the Spirit would possess "wisdom," "understanding," "counsel," "might," "knowledge," and "fear of the LORD" (Isaiah 11:1-2, NLT). The apostle Paul wrote to the Corinthians about "the gifts of the Spirit" (1 Corinthians 12:1, TNIV), to the Romans about their "different gifts" (Romans 12:6; see also 1 Peter 4:10), and to the Ephesians about "Christ's gift" (Ephesians 4:7, NRSV).

Four key passages discuss spiritual gifts: 1 Corinthians 12:1-31; Romans 12:3-8; Ephesians 4:7-16; and 1 Peter 4:10-11. Each passage uses the metaphor of gift with a distinct image and purpose in mind.

- In 1 Corinthians 12, Paul emphasized the range of God's expression of grace and its common source in the triune God (1 Corinthians 12:4-6,11). These gifts aren't manifestations of personal importance, but reveal the unique parts of a united body (verses 12-28). Paul's metaphor identifies the gifts with abilities or roles exhibited in the body: wisdom, knowledge, faith, healing, apostles, prophets, teachers.
- In Romans 12, Paul summarized his theological views and offered practical advice. He urged his readers to renew their minds and humble their thoughts (Romans 12:1-3). The inspiration for this humility lies in the diversity of the church as one body composed of different members. Here,

as in 1 Peter, the gifts are identified with different functions: prophesying, serving, teaching, and so on (Romans 12:4-8; 1 Peter 4:10-11). These passages encourage the reader to render faithful service to the local community through faithful use of their God-given abilities.

- In Ephesians, Paul pictured God's gifts as people: apostles, prophets, evangelists, pastors, and teachers (Ephesians 4:11), given by God for the edification of the church.

None of these lists of gifts is meant to be comprehensive. Rather, they suggest the kinds of abilities and roles that the Holy Spirit gives to generally work among God's people. Some of the gifts involve speaking (teaching, evangelism, encouraging, kinds of tongues) and some involve action (administration, leadership, service). Some appear more spectacular or miraculous (faith, healing, prophecy, miraculous powers), while others appear more ordinary (serving, contributing to the needs of others, showing mercy, helping others).

EVERYDAY APPLICATION

As Christians, important outcomes rely on our understanding of the nature of spiritual gifts, including the following:

- Our life as a local community and our ministry to one another as individuals flows from God, who gives to each one "just as he determines" (1 Corinthians 12:11). God's grace (*charis*) is expressed in God's gifts (*charismata*). We can't boast in our gifts; we simply receive them from the Spirit and pass on their graces to others. In addition, these gifts have their end in God and in one another "for the common good" (1 Corinthians 12:7) and for "attaining to the whole measure of the fullness of Christ" (Ephesians 4:13). The spiritual gifts operate from God, through one another, to one another, and for God. The movement of the Spirit directs our attention not in prideful ways to ourselves but humbly to God and to others.
- By learning the way God distributes the gifts of the Spirit, we recognize our need for each other. God has poured out the Holy Spirit on the church in a way that we experience

and demonstrate Christ fully only through a diversity-in-unity: "Are all apostles? Are all prophets? Are all teachers?" (1 Corinthians 12:29). No. The prophet needs those with the gift of administration. The teacher needs those with the gift of service. Apostle, evangelist, pastor, and teacher are all necessary to "prepare God's people for works of service, so that the body of Christ may be built up" (Ephesians 4:12). There is no such thing as a lone-ranger believer.

- Knowing about God's work of gifting the body leads us to seek, develop, and use those gifts that God chooses to grant us. Within the context of the local church we both seek and discern our gifts and discover the work of God through us toward others. In conversation with the local community, we develop our gifts, practicing skills and learning a sense of the anointing that flows through us on behalf of others. And in relationship with the local community, we use our gifts, doing our best with what we have been given according to the faith we have received.

- All is to be done in a spirit of love. Immediately following one listing of spiritual gifts (1 Corinthians 12:27-30), Paul proceeded to write, "I will show you the most excellent way" (verse 31). Similarly, Paul followed his discussion of gifts in Romans with the words, "Love must be sincere" (Romans 12:9). The passage in Ephesians concludes with reference to the whole body of Christ which "builds itself up in love, as each part does its work" (Ephesians 4:16). The gifts bestowed by God and used in God's way have as their end the display of love and the attribution of glory to God.

FOR FURTHER READING

C. Peter Wagner, *Your Spiritual Gifts Can Help Your Church Grow.* Regal, 1979.

Max Turner, *The Holy Spirit and Spiritual Gifts: In the New Testament and Today.* Hendrickson Publishers, 1998.

—EVAN B. HOWARD

SPIRITUALITY

EVERYDAY DEFINITION

The word spirituality in noun form isn't found in the Bible, but it's closely related to the Christian use of the word spiritual (Greek: *pneumatikos*). Christian belief has always maintained that humanity images God in the fact that we are "embodied spirits." In effect, all of humanity fits into the category of "unceasing spiritual beings" and this spiritual condition is what makes humanity uniquely special to God.

Scripture makes clear that, prior to regeneration, we are all "dead in trespasses and sins" (Ephesians 2:1, KJV) in relation to God. However, this doesn't mean that our spirits aren't in operation. Rather, our spirituality is continually being formed. As humans, we find ourselves in the position of being helpless to enliven ourselves to God. But we're not hopeless, because God in Jesus Christ constantly reaches out to restore us and make us alive to God.

In common use today, spirituality offers people two primary things:

1. A sense of identity (gives me a sense of who I am as a person).
2. A sense of empowerment (a reason for action or living).

Finding spiritual identity in Christ is just one of a vast number of spiritualities available to our human condition. While other false spiritualities promise people identity and power, as Christians, we understand that the only true spirituality is a "Christian spirituality," which creates an identity and power that reflects the love and life of Jesus Christ.

EVERYDAY APPLICATION

Spirituality is certainly a topic deeply embedded in the minds of most people, Christians and non-Christians alike. Most of us have heard the statement, "I'm not into religion, but I am very spiritual." Often this translates into the disdain for institutional religion and dogma and a simple belief that people can design their own unique experiences to fulfill their inner life needs and wants.

Christian spirituality is quite different. It is a spirituality that is grounded in obedience to Jesus Christ—not Ghandi, or Buddha, or even my own experience. As followers of Christ, we realize that Jesus has the most important and relevant information and understanding of the human spirit, because he created us. If we apprentice ourselves to him, he will teach us how to become like himself (Matthew 11:28-30). This is his promise to his followers (Romans 8:29; 1 John 3:1-3).

As Christ followers, we also have the gift and responsibility to present a "Christian spirituality" to others that offers the true identity and power they inherently seek. As Christians, we can pray for our own deep dependence and obedience to Christ, so that our own spirituality clearly reflects his love and grace.

FOR FURTHER READING
R. Paul Stevens, *Down to Earth Spirituality*. InterVarsity, 2003.
Jim Thomas, *Streetwise Spirituality*. Harvest House, 2001.

— KEITH MATTHEWS

STEWARDSHIP

EVERYDAY DEFINITION
The word stewardship is often used as shorthand for financial stewardship. But its scope is much broader than that. Stewardship involves how followers of Jesus handle the gifts that God has given them.

In its most basic sense, a steward manages another's estate or house. For example, Joseph was a slave, appointed to administer Potiphar's house (Genesis 39:4-6). But even before this, humanity was entrusted with a massive stewardship assignment. After God created humans, he said to them, "be fruitful and increase in number; fill the earth and subdue it." Then he told them to rule over it (Genesis 1:28). This is sometimes called "the creation mandate," or "the great cultural commission." Humanity is appointed as God's vice-regent over the earth. Our creation calling is a stewardship calling. We are to manage God's house.

This idea is carried over into the New Testament, illustrated in the parable traditionally called the parable of the talents told by Jesus (Matthew 25:14-30). In this story, a man went on a journey and entrusted his property to his servants while he was away. They were to manage his estate. From this parable, four basic stewardship principles follow:

1. God owns everything. He made the world and is the owner of it. All that we are and have come from him. The master who went on the journey is a picture of God himself.
2. God entrusted these possessions into his servants' hands. The very concept of stewardship is connected to the idea of grace. All that comes to us from God is a gift. We are stewards of God's possessions. He loans it to us for a little while.
3. We are called to invest whatever we are given. We must manage it and put it to work for our master. In this sense, Christian stewardship is the use of God-given resources for the accomplishment of God-given purposes.
4. God calls his servants to account for what they've done. In the parable, two of the servants invested their talents, but one hid his talent in the ground. Two received the master's "well done, good and faithful servant!" (Matthew 25:21). The other received the master's rebuke.

What are these "talents"? In the parable, a talent represented an amount of gold. While money is the focus of this parable, we do know that the scope of stewardship is far broader than money. It includes our time, talent, and treasures, our bodies, the people under our care, and creation itself. These are the gifts we are called to manage for our master.

EVERYDAY APPLICATION
Our response to God's gifts should involve the following:

- We should recognize his ownership, because nothing that we hold is really ours; it is on loan.
- We should be grateful for his gifts.
- We should acknowledge our dependence not on the gifts themselves but upon God. Scripture says, "it is he who gives you the ability to produce wealth" (Deuteronomy 8:18).
- We must take care of what he has given to us and invest it. He calls us to faithfulness.

How does this work out in practice? The following ideas can help us be good stewards of what God gives us:

- Regarding the gift of time, we should "make the most of every opportunity" (Colossians 4:5). Some older Bible translations use the phrase, "redeem the time."
- Regarding actual talents, we shouldn't bury them but exercise them fruitfully.
- With treasures, we should store them up in heaven and put them to work for the master's estate (Matthew 6:19).
- With our bodies, we should care for them because they are the "temple of the Holy Spirit" (1 Corinthians 6:19).
- When it comes to people, we must wisely oversee their abilities and gifts. Paul compared the work of an elder in a church to a father in a home. If an elder cannot manage his own family, how will he care for the household of God? (1 Timothy 3:5). Business owners face the same challenge. They are to be stewards over the resources of employees. The same job faces the trustee of a university or charitable institution.
- With creation, we must care for the earth God gave us. Adam and Eve were to "work it and take care of it" (Genesis 2:15). It comes as a surprise to some people that the first statement of stewardship in the Bible involves care of the earth.

With regard to financial stewardship, we are to give to the Lord's work, but we are also to manage our households well. This involves getting out of debt, saving, paying taxes, providing for loved ones, and guarding ourselves against materialism and greed. Giving to the Lord's work may involve a tithe, but will go beyond that when possible. In the New Testament giving is to be planned and regular (1 Corinthians 16:1-2). It should be sacrificial (Mark 12:41-44). It should be done voluntarily and cheerfully (2 Corinthians 9:7). Such giving will result in blessing (Malachi 3:10). The point is that we can't out-give God. He brings blessings both in this life and in the life to come to those who exercise good stewardship in the full sense of the term (see Matthew 19:29).

Meanwhile, we should live our lives in a way that when our master calls us to give account, we too will hear the words, "well done, good and faithful servant!" (Matthew 25:21).

FOR FURTHER READING

Randy Alcorn, *Money, Possessions and Eternity*. Tyndale, 2004.

Ben Gill, *Stewardship: The Biblical Basis for Living*. Summit, 1996.

Fred Van Dyke, David C. Mahan, Joseph K. Sheldon, and
    Raymond H. Brand, *Redeeming Creation: The Biblical Basis for Environmental Stewardship*. InterVarsity, 1996.

— DONALD W. SWEETING

SUBMISSION

EVERYDAY DEFINITION

Submission is a relational term (Greek: *hupotasso*) that literally means to "come under." In Ephesians 5:21, the apostle Paul told believers in Ephesus to "submit to one another out of reverence for Christ." Like all the "one another" passages ("love one another," "forgive one another," "encourage one another"), the New Testament commandment to submit to one another is given for the sake of building genuine community among believers. Apart from submission, there can be no authentic church unity.

Tragically, many Christians reject the biblical notion of mutual submission. They claim that only those who are under authority should submit. However, this is a *misunderstanding* of biblical submission. Ephesians 5:21 doesn't state, "Submit to those in authority." It says, "Submit to one another." The proper understanding of submission is that followers of Christ will relate to one another by "coming under" in order to honor one another and to regard others as more important than ourselves (Philippians 2:3).

EVERYDAY APPLICATION

We can understand biblical submission by looking at the step-by-step process Jesus gives for confronting a fellow Christian who has sinned (Matthew 18). Submission is important in this process, because unless the offender trusts that God wants each of us "to submit to one another," that individual might refuse to cooperate when confronted.

Jesus says the first step of biblical confrontation is for the offended party to "go and show him his fault in private" (Matthew 18:15,

NASB). If the offender refuses to submit to the person in private by refusing to engage at all or listen humbly, then the offended party is to go back again with "one or two more" (Matthew 18:16, NASB) and explain the offense again. If the offender still refuses to submit, then the offended party is to share the persistent problem with the wider church community, so that everyone can try to speak the truth in love to the offender.

The whole purpose of this process is restoration. Because everyone sins, all Christians at times need to be restored with the help of other believers. In other words, we all need to submit because we all need to be confronted sometimes. We need to be willing to submit, not just to authorities in general, but specifically to anyone we've offended. Although devised by Jesus himself, the Matthew 18 process simply doesn't work without mutual submission among believers. The goal of submission is building oneness. The body of Christ is supposed to experience oneness with Jesus Christ, the church's Head.

Many Christians struggle with the apostle Paul's call for wives to submit to their husbands (Ephesians 5). However, when a wife submits to her husband, she doesn't give up her will. On the contrary, she *exercises* her will to be one with her husband. She doesn't become a subordinate who obeys him; she conforms her will to his precisely for the sake of uniting herself to him. Something similar happens when a husband obeys God by taking the initiative to sacrifice himself for his wife as Christ "gave himself up" for the church (Ephesians 5:25). The husband doesn't become henpecked; instead, he consciously chooses to sacrifice his will to his wife's.

Submission to authorities such as employers and officials in the government can be likened to the submission of a wife in the sense that biblical submission is always to be done "unto the Lord" (Ephesians 5:22, KJV). Submission is an act of obedience to God, and it never runs counter to God's Word.

FOR FURTHER READING
Richard Foster, *Celebration of Discipline*. Harper, 1988.
Watchman Nee, *Authority and Submission*. Living Stream Ministry, 1993.

Jim and Sarah Sumner, *Just How Married Do You Want to Be? Practicing Oneness in Marriage.* InterVarsity, 2008.

—SARAH SUMNER

SUFFERING

EVERYDAY DEFINITION

Suffering is the experience of severe loss, damage, pain, distress, or even death by an individual or a group of people. Suffering has been a part of the human story since Adam and Eve lost one of their sons to a violent death (Genesis 4:8), and it will be a part of human history until the end of time (Revelation 7:15-17).

The Bible records the accounts of many individuals whose suffering was great: Job, Zedekiah (2 Kings 25:7), Herod (Acts 12:23), as well as groups of people who suffered terribly: the clan of Jacob from famine (Genesis 41:56–42:2), the people of Jerusalem under the siege by the Babylonians (2 Chronicles 36:17), the early Christians in Jerusalem (Acts 11:28; 24:17), and first-century believers living in hostile settings (Acts 8:1; 1 Peter 1:6).

Suffering is a topic of interest to believers for many reasons, but the aspect of suffering that promotes the most discussion and is at the same time the most difficult is the question, "Why does suffering occur?" The presence of suffering in the world is a major hurdle for skeptics to overcome if they are to come to faith and belief in God. "Theodicy" is a specialized field within theology that seeks to defend the goodness of God in light of the presence of suffering in the world. The Bible presents its major teachings regarding suffering in three areas: the book of Job, accounts of the Passion of Jesus, and the epistles sent to suffering Christians. We can understand suffering by examining each of these accounts:

- The book of Job records the nearly unimaginable and unprecedented suffering of a righteous man named Job. The story is recorded by an unknown author on two different levels. First, the author reveals to readers information that was unknown to both Job and his friends. God allowed

Satan to afflict Job with various types of suffering in order to demonstrate to Satan that Job's faith wasn't merely due to Job's prosperity (1:8-12). On the second level, we read about Job's profound losses, his puzzlement over why these events had occurred to him, and the utter ineffectiveness of Job's friends either to understand the losses or to offer consolation to Job. From the story of Job we learn that sufferers might never know the true reason behind their suffering. Even the wisest of our friends might not know the true reason. Suffering isn't always an expression of punishment for wickedness. Ultimately, the greatest source of comfort for sufferers is the knowledge that we serve and worship a powerful God whose presence is always with us even as we suffer (Job 38-41; 1 Peter 4:19).

- Jesus suffered greatly during his earthly life. The suffering of Jesus is at the heart of the gospel (Hebrews 2:10). Nearly half of the Gospel accounts of the life of Jesus recount the events of the last week of his life—a week that included great suffering (Matthew 26:37-39; 27:27-31,45-50). Jesus, though sinless, suffered by bearing our sins in his body on the cross (1 Peter 2:21-25). The Passion of Christ teaches us again that suffering isn't automatically related to the committed sins of the sufferer, but that suffering is related to the presence of sin in the world, and that suffering can have great outcomes for others (1 Peter 1:10-11).

- First-century Christians were increasingly subjected to suffering in the form of persecution. Peter wrote to his readers that suffering might be part of the believer's calling (1 Peter 2:20). The believer's suffering mysteriously participates in the suffering of Christ (1 Peter 4:13), a theme also mentioned in Paul's letters (Colossians 1:24).

EVERYDAY APPLICATION

In addition to these general principles about suffering, the Bible also gives us some additional insight into possible causes behind human suffering that can help us understand our own suffering and enable us to provide help for fellow sufferers.

Some of these reasons for suffering are causative (looking backward) and others are purposive (looking forward). Suffering may be a judgment for sin (Daniel 4:28-33), a form of discipline (Hebrews 12:4-11), or an incentive to promote maturity (2 Corinthians 12:7; 1 Peter 1:6-7; James 1:2-4; Romans 5:3-5). Suffering might also be a prelude to greater things, just as birth pangs anticipate the joy of a baby's birth (Romans 8:18-27). Suffering might simply be the price of being associated with Christ (John 15:20).

What other attitudes should the believer cultivate toward human suffering? We should follow the example of the Savior. At the beginning of his public ministry he boldly declared that he had come from glory to bring to suffering people sight, freedom, deliverance, and the Lord's favor (Luke 4:18-19). Jesus actively pushed back against myriad forms of human suffering (Mark 1:32-34), giving us an example of what our attitude and actions should be in the face of preventable suffering. Great suffering results from natural disasters, events we might be helpless to avoid or prevent. But we should still reach out to display the mercy and love of God to those affected by these disasters. Followers of Jesus, using the example we find in Luke 4, have even greater responsibility toward preventable suffering. Man-made disasters such as human trafficking, war, or genocide inflict great levels of suffering to people of all ages, situations toward which we are to act justly, to love mercy, and to walk humbly with our God (Micah 6:8).

The Bible gives no indication that believers should seek out suffering. Suffering is an inevitable part of life and a part of our finitude and mortality. God speaks and works through suffering. We can sometimes discern the hand of God in suffering if we approach the matter with humility and sensitivity. But the Bible doesn't guarantee that we'll always be able to understand fully the mysteries of human suffering during this lifetime.

FOR FURTHER READING

Chris Tiegreen, *Why a Suffering World Makes Sense*. Baker, 2006.
Henry Cloud and John Townsend, *God Will Make a Way*. Integrity, 2002.

—JAMES R. BECK

SUICIDE

EVERYDAY DEFINITION

The word suicide comes from two Latin terms meaning "to kill" (*caedere*) "oneself" (*sui*). Suicide describes the self-termination of life when death is intended rather than accidental or a result of risky activities.

While life ends for people who commit suicide, their reasons vary significantly. We usually associate suicide with psychological factors such as depression, despair over financial trouble, and difficulty in or the dissolution of relationships. However, suicide also has a broad array of other motivations, such as a ritual intended to preserve honor (such as Samurai suicides as a ritual admission of defeat), a form of protest (such as self-starvation to protest war or oppression), a means of escaping punishment, or as a form of escaping pain because of terminal illness.

Generally, religions of all types have maintained a dim view of suicide. A few exceptions exist where causing one's death is seen as an acceptable expression of religious duty, such as suicide by self-immolation (*sati*) by Hindu widows to accompany their husbands in death, or self-starvation by Jain or Buddhist monks to protest war. The mass suicide of Jews as Masada to deny the Roman army the opportunity to exterminate them offers a similar case.

Scripture itself records six suicides. Perhaps the most well know of these is Judas' self-hanging after he betrayed Jesus (Matthew 27:3-5). Samson's suicide occured when he pulled down the pillars of the Philistine temple, an act that he knew would cause his death as well as the deaths of others in the building (Judges 16:23-31). Some argue that Samson's death should not be viewed as suicide because his primary intent wasn't to bring about his own death; instead, he was seeking revenge against the Philistines, who had tortured and blinded him. Saul committed suicide to avoid capture by the Philistine army (1 Samuel 31:2-5). Three other incidents are the suicides of Ahithophel (2 Samuel 17:23), Zimri (1 Kings 16:15-20), and Abimelech (Judges 9:50-54). None of these self-caused deaths are accompanied by a moral evaluation that either commends or condemns them.

While Scripture doesn't directly comment on the moral status of suicide, Christians have historically viewed it as contrary to God's will. Augustine, a Latin church father, is usually credited with the first complete exploration of suicide in the Christian tradition. In his view, causing one's own death intentionally was self-murder, and thus a violation of the fifth commandment (Deuteronomy 5:17). In medieval Christianity, priest and philosopher Thomas Aquinas grounded his prohibition of suicide on three foundations:

1. God designed human beings so that they naturally seek self-preservation and life, and suicide violates this God-given impulse.
2. Because we are created to contribute to the good of others, ending one's life is sinful because it makes it impossible to fulfill our social and spiritual obligations to others.
3. Life is a gift from God and it's not within our right to determine the time of life's conclusion. Suicide represents an act of ingratitude toward the God who gives life and determines when it should end.

EVERYDAY APPLICATION

Suicidal thoughts and attempts are not the result of a life that an individual sees as full and hopeful. Instead, these are indicators of despair, hopelessness, pain, and desperation. At the center of the gospel is the message that God comes to us in Jesus, who brings hope by sharing our suffering and pain. Christianity acknowledges the deep sense of despair and suffering that can come in life's circumstances. Yet in place of emptiness, it offers hope, newness, and abundance to our lives. On a basic level, then, Christianity's message itself is a response to the conditions that lead people to consider or attempt suicide.

Because God brings hope by entering into the sufferings of the world, this establishes a mandate for Christians. Our task is to recognize the signs of suffering around us and respond with a message of hope. Suicide attempts are often preceded by activities that are harmful, but nonlethal, such as cutting or binge drinking. Quite often, just when their support is most critical, people are tempted to withdraw from those who engage in these activities. However, as Christians, we should be walking closely with those who go through dark periods, intervening in appropriate ways.

While much of society has reflected Christian attitudes toward suicide, as the culture has become more pluralistic and secularized, suicide is often viewed as a psychological or medical issue rather than a theological matter. While Christians must reject tendencies to reduce suicide to a medical or psychological matter, it's also a mistake to fail to recognize that these disciplines often provide useful tools for dealing with those at risk of suicide. Chemical imbalances or deep psychological wounds can make people incapable of escaping despair and hopelessness. Thus, while medicine and psychology don't offer the message of hope that Christianity does, proper use of medical and psychological resources can help people get to the place where they can hear that message.

Scripture seems to clearly indicate that suicide is contradictory to God's will. Taking one's own life fails to acknowledge the value that God places on life, and it creates tremendous burdens and guilt for those left behind. At the same time, nothing in Scripture indicates that suicide is an unforgivable sin. Further, we all die with unconfessed sins. So as Christians, if we need to deal with the suicide of a loved one or minister to those in such a situation, the gospel reminds us that God is in the business of redeeming pain, suffering, and death. Our job is to join with Christ by suffering with those in pain and reflect the new life and hope he promises.

FOR FURTHER READING

Timothy J. Demy and Gary P. Stewart, eds., *Suicide: A Christian Response: Crucial Considerations for Choosing Life*. Kregel Academic & Professional, 1998.

— STEVE WILKENS

TEACHING

EVERYDAY DEFINITION

Christian teaching is an intentional interaction, directed by the Holy Spirit (Romans 8:12; 1 Peter 1:2) who indwells (John 14:16) and empowers (Ephesians 3:16) Christian teachers and students to facilitate learning and transformation into Christlikeness (Romans 8:29; Ephesians 4:13-16).

God is infinitely omniscient, needing no instruction (Isaiah 40:13-14). But humanity was created in his image as finite beings that change and must learn to come to maturity. This transformation isn't possible without God's supernatural and mysterious work in sanctification. Yet God has ordained that human teachers have a legitimate role to play. In his Great Commission, Jesus commanded the church to "make disciples of all nations . . . teaching them to obey everything I have commanded you" (Matthew 28:19-20; see also Colossians 3:16). Consequently, all Christians are called to be teachers.

However, some teachers have greater accountability in light of roles related to two primary instructional contexts: parents in the home (Deuteronomy 6:4-9; Ephesians 6:4) and teachers in the local church (2 Timothy 2:2). Those in the local church teach in two capacities: the spiritual gift of teaching (1 Corinthians 12:28-29; Romans 12:7) and the office of teacher (Ephesians 4:11; 1 Timothy 5:17).

Another important context in each believer's life is when God initiates or permits learning opportunities to "share in his holiness" (Hebrews 12:10). For example, God taught Jonah about his unforgiving attitude toward Nineveh (Jonah 4:1-10) and taught Peter that Gentiles too can receive salvation (Acts 10:1-48).

Jesus' calling on this earth also included a teaching mission. The most common title given to him was "Teacher" ("rabbi," "Master" (KJV); John 13:14).

EVERYDAY APPLICATION

As Christians, we should prayerfully examine our hearts to determine whether we have the gift of teaching, so that gifted teachers — guided by the Holy Spirit — can take the lead role in the educational ministry of the church. However, because all of us, whether gifted as teachers or not, are called to teach, we can all learn from gifted teachers to improve our instructional skills in various ministries and context, such as parenting, small groups, children's and youth ministries, mentoring, and preaching.

Careful study of Jesus' teaching ministry in the Gospels offers a rich resource to improve our teaching skills.[40] Gifted and experienced

---

40. For additional information, see Roy Zuck, *Teaching as Jesus Taught* (Wipf & Stock, 1995).

teachers can mentor disciples aspiring to teach, observing us in the teaching process and offering feedback and guidance. We can also study teaching-learning principles that have gained wide acceptance among good teachers past and present. In addition, we are also learners, so we play an important role by giving concerted effort to be attentive and to review and to apply new insights. When teachers and students genuinely walk by the Spirit of God, the teaching-learning process can yield results beyond what is humanly possible (Galatians 5:16-25; James 3:13-18).

FOR FURTHER READING

D. K. McKim, "Instruct," in *International Standard Bible Encyclopedia*, Geoffrey Bromiley, ed. Eerdmans, 1982.

C. N. Jefford, "Teach," in *International Standard Bible Encyclopedia*, Geoffrey Bromiley, ed. Eerdmans, 1982.

Klaus Issler and Ronald Habermas, *How We Learn: A Christian Teachers' Guide to Educational Psychology*. Wipf & Stock, 2002.

William R. Yount, *Called to Teach: An Introduction to the Ministry of Teaching*. Broadman & Holman, 1999.

— KLAUS ISSLER

TEN COMMANDMENTS

EVERYDAY DEFINITION

The Ten Commandments appear in two passages in the Old Testament: Exodus 20:2-17 and Deuteronomy 5:7-21. According to the Bible, the Ten Commandments were given by God to Moses on Mount Sinai (Exodus 20:1-17; Deuteronomy 5:2-22), amid dramatic sights and sounds, approximately three months after deliverance from Egypt.

In both passages, the Ten Commandments are introduced by a divine statement of self-identification ("I am the LORD your God"; Exodus 20:2; Deuteronomy 5:6), confirming the source of the decrees and providing the theological foundation for the directives that follow. This introductory statement precedes a historical note ("who brought you out of Egypt"; Exodus 20:2; Deuteronomy 5:6), pointing back to God's recent deliverance of Israel from four hundred years of Egyptian bondage.

The Ten Commandments were written on two sets of stone tablets. The first set, inscribed by the finger of God (Exodus 31:18; Deuteronomy 9:10-11), was broken by Moses who threw them on the ground when he discovered the Israelites worshipping a golden calf, a representation of the Canaanite god Baal (Exodus 32:19; Deuteronomy 9:16-17). The second set of tablets was given to Moses to replace the broken set. This set was placed in the ark (Deuteronomy 10:1-5; 2 Chronicles 5:10), carried along during the wilderness wanderings (Numbers 10:33-36), kept in the tent-like tabernacle (Exodus 40:18-21), and eventually placed in the Holy of Holies after the completion of Solomon's temple in Jerusalem (1 Kings 8:3-9; 2 Chronicles 5:4-10).

Two of the Ten Commandments offer positive instructions, while eight provide universal prohibitions. The two positive commands include:

1. Sanctifying the seventh day (the Sabbath; Exodus 20:8-11; Deuteronomy 5:12-15). This God-centered concept was unique to Israel and absent from the religious practices of foreign nations. Observance of this commandment was intended to provide an opportunity for God's people to withdraw from life's activities and to reflect on his mighty deeds. The Exodus passage focuses on Creation as a theme for Sabbath reflection (Exodus 20:8-11), while the Deuteronomy passage points to the Israelites' recent deliverance from Egyptian bondage as a reason for celebrating this special day (Deuteronomy 5:12-15).

2. Honoring father and mother (Exodus 20:12; Deuteronomy 5:16). This human-centered command serves as a link between the divinely focused directives and the human-focused social decrees.

The other eight commands prohibit certain behaviors. These include:

- Prohibiting the worship of any other god and forbidding the making of divine images (Exodus 20:3-7; Deuteronomy 5:7-9). Unfortunately, the Israelites disobeyed and repeatedly participated in these secular practices. Consequently, they were denied some of the blessings that accompanied their exclusive relationship with God (1 Kings 14:8-9; 2 Kings 17:9-14). Without a command against the making of idols, the Israelites would no doubt have officially sanctioned the crafting of statuettes, and would have embarked in the making of man-made icons for human profit.

- Prohibiting universally accepted unethical or immoral principles. These include commandments related to murder (Exodus 20:13; Deuteronomy 5:17), adultery (Exodus 20:14; Deuteronomy 5:18), theft (Exodus 20:15; Deuteronomy 5:19), false testimony (Exodus 20:16; Deuteronomy 5:20), and covetousness (Exodus 20:17; Deuteronomy 5:21). These commands were present in other Ancient Near Eastern law codes (such as Ur-nammu, Hammurapi).

Based on the Hebrew word used for "murder" (*r.f.µ*), it's worth noting that the sixth commandment ("You shall not murder"; Exodus 20:13; Deuteronomy 5:17) does not signify an absolute ban on killing; neither does it forbid capital punishment or killing during military conflicts. And because Scripture makes provision for special legislations regarding accidental killings (Deuteronomy 19:1-13), the sixth commandment also excludes unintentional homicide. According to the text, intentional homicide or the premeditated taking of a human life is prohibited by the sixth commandment.

Partial lists of the Ten Commandments appear in several Old Testament passages. A short version is found in Hosea where the prophet accused the community of cursing, lying, murdering, stealing, and committing adultery (Hosea 4:1-3). A second partial list appears more than a century later when the prophet Jeremiah confronted the community in Judah with their evil practices and accused them of stealing, murdering, committing adultery, lying, and bowing down before foreign gods (Jeremiah 7:9-11).

Although the New Testament doesn't include the entire list of the Ten Commandments as they appear in Exodus 20 and Deuteronomy 5, individual decrees are often found in the Gospels and the Epistles (for example, Matthew 5:21; 19:18-19; Romans 13:9; Ephesians 6:2; James

2:11). In the Sermon on the Mount, Jesus expounded on the sixth and seventh commandments against murder and adultery (Matthew 5:21-22,27-32). In his encounter with the rich young ruler (Matthew 19:16-25), Jesus instructed the young man to obey the commandments, specifying the fifth to the ninth (honoring parents, against murder, adultery, stealing, and false testimony), adding an important passage from the Holiness Code (Leviticus 17–26) related to loving one's neighbor as oneself (Leviticus 19:18).

EVERYDAY APPLICATION

In a postmodern world where morality and ethics have become largely subjective, we can boldly declare that the Ten Commandments still represent the ultimate paradigm for a well-ordered society. As intended when they were given to Moses, they still provide for us the only universal principles for righteous and godly living. Throughout history, the Ten Commandments have stood at the center of Judeo-Christian thought and have inspired the decisions of leading religious and political leaders.

Unfortunately, our generation has witnessed a wave of strong sentiments that has resulted in the removal of the Ten Commandments from public places around the country. This contentious effort has not only attacked the divinely inspired message of the Ten Commandments, but it has attempted to undermine the moral and ethical value system that provides the foundation for much of civilization. Such harmful and ungodly efforts on the part of politicians, business leaders, and ordinary citizens serve only to impoverish a nation and damage its foundation.

The Ten Commandments were given to the children of Israel a short time after they were rescued from the bondage of Egypt. God then gave them specific instructions for wise living and set them on a course that was intended to honor him and bless them. Without the divinely ordained framework of the Ten Commandments, the Israelites would not have survived as a people. They would have forgotten the great deliverance they had experienced and would have perished in the wilderness.

Our story today is similar. Through Christ's work we have been set free from the bondage of sin, and we have been set on a path designed by God himself. Without his instructions and presence with us, we will not survive the journey to our heavenly home. We would perish in the wilderness of our secular world and wander along dangerous paths. But as God remained with his children in the wilderness, he hasn't left us to our own means. Motivated by his abounding love for us, God has provided his Word, his Spirit, and his eternal decrees to guide us until we meet him face to face.

The Ten Commandments were never intended to restrict the freedom of God's people. On the contrary, they were meant to provide guidelines to assist us in our behavior toward God and toward one another. The Ten Commandments touch on all aspects of human life, including faith in God, respect of neighbors, protection of parent-children relationships, appreciation for God's creation, the value of human life, faithfulness and honesty, integrity and truthfulness. Unfortunately, in all societies we find the harsh realities of fallen humanity where hatred, violence, adultery, pornography, divorce, injustice, poverty, broken homes, murder, jealousy, cheating, and other ungodly acts prevail. When the message of the Ten Commandments is dismissed or forgotten by members of a society, everyone suffers. Yet, it's never too late to return to the instructions of these commands and to declare them openly to all who would dare to listen and obey.

FOR FURTHER READING

Carl E. Braaten and Christopher R. Seitz, eds. *I Am the Lord Your God: Christian Reflections on the Ten Commandments.* Eerdmans, 2005.

Walter J. Harrelson. *The Ten Commandments and Human Rights.* Mercer University Press, 1997.

Paul Grimley Kuntz. *The Ten Commandments in History: Mosaic Paradigms for a Well-Ordered Society.* Eerdmans, 2004.

Roberts Kimball-Shinkoskey, "Deep Roots in Thinning Soil: The Ten Commandments in American Law and Family Life" in *The Family in America* 9.4, 1995.

— HÉLÈNE DALLAIRE

THEISM

EVERYDAY DEFINITION

Theism affirms that an ultimate Being creates and governs all things and that this ultimate Being is both one and personal.

Three established religions fall under the umbrella of theism:

1. Islam is a theistic religion because Muslims believe that there is an ultimate Being of the universe who creates and governs all things.
2. Judaism is another theistic religion.
3. Christians, however, believe that Christian theism is the only true theism that can provide authentic knowledge of the living God. According to Christian theism, the ultimate Being of the universe is the triune God, and this triune God is a personal being who creates and governs all things.

Several important truths frame the core of Christian theism, including the following:

- The triune God—Father, Son, and Holy Spirit—is the ultimate Being of the universe. When Jesus Christ gave his disciples the Great Commission, he commanded them to "go and make disciples of all nations, baptizing them in the name of the Father and of the Son and of the Holy Spirit, and teaching them to obey everything I have commanded you. And surely I am with you always, to the very end of the age" (Matthew 28:19-20). When Jesus used the name of the Father, the Son, and the Holy Spirit, he was identifying the name of the ultimate Being of the universe that we should worship, serve, and obey.
- The triune God is a personal being that has intellect, emotion, volition, communicative power, and relational capacity. Some world religions deny that the ultimate Being of the universe has personality. Hinduism, for example, believes that the Brahman—ultimate in the universe—is not a person but an impersonal principle. Buddhism also is an atheistic religion in that it denies that the ultimate Being of the universe has personality.
- The triune God created the whole universe including human beings with his own plan and purpose and continues to govern the whole world through his providence. As stated in Genesis 1:1, "In the beginning God created the heavens and the earth."

Christian theism unhesitatingly affirms that the triune God is the Creator of the entire universe and that he is the sovereign ruler of it. The writer of the letter to the Hebrews agrees: "The Son is the radiance of God's glory and the exact representation of his being, sustaining all things by his powerful word" (Hebrews 1:3). In this sense, Christian theism is totally different from philosophical Deism, which teaches that God created the universe and left it to run on its own course without any divine intervention and involvement with the creation.

- Human beings were created in the likeness and image of God, but they rebelled against God by committing the sin of prideful disobedience. In creating human beings, the three Persons of the Godhead had holy discussion: "Let us make human beings in our image, in our likeness, so that they may rule over the fish in the sea and the birds in the sky, over the livestock and all the wild animals, and over all the creatures that move along the ground" (Genesis 1:26, TNIV).

- When sin entered into the universe, all kinds of curses came together, including death and eternal judgment. Further, in order to redeem fallen humanity and creation, God the Father sent his only begotten Son, Jesus Christ, into the world. Jesus Christ accomplished redemption by his life, death on the cross, and resurrection from the dead.

EVERYDAY APPLICATION

All believers are called to have confidence in the truthfulness of Christian theism. The validity of Christian theism is also closely connected with its coherence and consistency. As followers of Christ, we can be certain that Christian theism is the only truth system that is believable and practicable. This implies that Christian theism possesses great apologetic significance. As Christians we are called to "Always be prepared to give an answer to everyone who asks you to give the reason for the hope that you have. But do this with gentleness and respect" (1 Peter 3:15). As a result, we need to understand the structure, system, attractiveness, coherence, and practicality of Christian theism and be prepared to answer questions and objections that nonbelievers may raise regarding Christian theism.

For example, we currently live in a context of widespread religious pluralism. Religious pluralism holds that every religion teaches essentially the same thing and that every religion has equal access to ultimate truth and salvation. When some Buddhists and Muslims equipped with a religiously pluralistic perspective raise questions about the absolute uniqueness of Christian theism, we need to answer those questions with gentleness and respect. In order to do so, we must learn how to analyze basic beliefs of non-Christian religions and how to identify their inconsistencies and falsehoods. In addition, we need to learn how to share the gospel with them and persuade them to believe in Jesus Christ. When we are equipped with Christian theism, we will be able to perform this apologetic and evangelistic task well.

Christian theism can be applied in an ethical context as well. Since Christian theism teaches that the triune God is the ultimate Being of the universe, we as Christians should trust, serve, and worship him alone. If we embrace other gods before him, we then commit the sin of idolatry. Idolatry involves not only making idols with stone or wood and worshipping them, but also giving priority to anything other than the triune God in our thoughts, words, decisions, attitudes, and behaviors. Falsely, we might give priority to personal honor, money, popularity, and pleasures rather than to the triune God. These kinds of loyalties contradict the life that God requires of his covenant people. As Christians, we should learn how to give priority to God in all areas of our life, including our finances, education, sports, politics, or culture.

FOR FURTHER READING
James Sire, *The Universe Next Door: A Basic Worldview Catalog.*
InterVarsity, 2004.
Brian J. Walsh, *Transforming Vision: Shaping a Christian World View.*
InterVarsity, 1984.

—SUNG WOOK CHUNG

THEOLOGY

EVERYDAY DEFINITION
The word theology is derived from two Greek words, *theos* and *logos*, meaning reflection or discourse about God. Christian theology is

essentially a compilation of our most fundamental beliefs. Christian theology primarily is derived from God's special revelation in authoritative Scripture, with an eye to the cultural settings of the biblical writers. Theology also builds on truths from God's general revelation and to a lesser extent on the results of the human disciplines that are agreeable with biblical norms (such as history, archaeology, geology, anthropology, and others). We understand that all truth wherever found is God's truth. Theology involves reflection on fundamental beliefs about God, creation, the human person, the person and work of Christ, salvation, the church and its mission, and the end times. Far from being a dry and dusty enterprise, theology deals with the most important issues of life.

Theology can be divided into several disciplines, including the following:

- Systematic theology seeks to organize teachings of the whole Bible logically and topically into a comprehensive world-and-life view with applications for Christian living.
- The related discipline of biblical theology studies doctrinal themes within specific sections of the Bible (for example, Old Testament prophecy or the Pauline epistles). Biblical theology highlights the progress of revelation through the centuries of biblical history.
- The discipline of historical theology traces the development of doctrinal themes through the periods of church history, with emphasis on the perspectives of leading theological authorities such as Augustine, Luther, Wesley, and Edwards.

The discipline of theology has taken place throughout the history of the church.

In the early centuries of the church, theology was intimately bound up with spiritual life, pastoral practice, and evangelistic outreach.

In the Middle Ages, doctrinal writers such as Thomas Aquinas and Bonaventure were, in the words of Hans Urs von Balthasar, "complete theologians" — that is theologians who also were saints.[41]

In the sixteenth century, the Protestant Reformers wrote treatises on

---

41. See also Philip Sheldrake, *Spirituality and Theology* (Maryknoll, NY: Orbis, 1999), 40.

theology that united doctrine, spirituality, and ministry into a seamless whole in ways that could be used by individuals and churches for spiritual formation and advance of the gospel. An excellent example of this unity is John Calvin's *Institutes of the Christian Religion* (1559), which fundamentally is a manual on doctrine, devotion, and kingdom building.

Puritan preachers and theologians likewise integrated in their theological writings propositional knowledge, Spirit-directed religious experience, and pastoral ministry. The Puritans knew the truth with their minds, felt the truth in their hearts, and proclaimed the truth with their lives.

In the seventeenth and eighteenth centuries, academic theology and spirituality separated. Theologians wrote lengthy treatises of dogma, often with the purpose of refuting ecclesiastical opponents, while others wrote stirring essays that nurtured the spiritual life.

Much of mainline theology today (so-called "scientific theology") focuses on the intellectual dimension of theology while leaving issues of spirituality to other writers. Reggie McNeal notes that evangelicals emphasize committing our lives to Jesus. "Then, as soon as the deal is done, we switch the language and go to head stuff. We pull out the notebooks. We go over what we believe, information about the church, and so on. We aim at the head. We don't deal in relationships. And we wonder why there is no passion for Jesus and his mission?"[42]

Christian theology, while drawing primarily on biblical revelation, is informed by twenty centuries of Christian wisdom. Since the Holy Spirit has been active (with varying degrees of human responses) in the church throughout its history, theology engages rich insights expounded by godly church fathers, devout medieval writers, the Eastern Christian tradition, Post-Reformation Christian authors, and contemporary writers. Evangelical church historian Richard Lovelace, writes, "We need to listen to other kinds of Christians. Mainline Protestants, Roman Catholics, and Orthodox believers have preserved biblical values that we lack. And they often have clear insights about our faults that could help us toward repentance."[43] Disciples of Jesus are informed and edified as we engage truths from our two thousand year

---

42. Reggie McNeal, *The Present Future* (New York: Jossey-Bass, 2003), 70-71.
43. Richard Lovelace, "Evangelical Spirituality: A Church Historian's Perspective," *JETS* 31/1 (March 1988), 35.

Christian tradition that nurture spiritual life and foster gospel ministry. Our formulations of Christian theology are open to new evidence (always faithful and true) as that comes to light. Theology, then, brings together logically and topically truths from God in a unified whole. Theology forms an integrated worldview for the nurture of spiritual life and advance of the kingdom.

EVERYDAY APPLICATION

As believers, we must recapture the importance of theology, because the Christian faith rests entirely on this solid foundation. Because theology sets forth essential truths about the nature of God, his purposes in history, and instructions for living, it's not an optional undertaking. We must honor theology that is true to God's Word. First-century apostles recognized that some professing Christians had turned aside from sound theology (1 Timothy 6:21). They also predicted that in the end times many will depart from revealed truth (2 Timothy 4:3-4) and will put forth destructive heresies (2 Peter 2:1). The apostle Paul urged Timothy to "command certain persons not to teach false doctrines" or to give themselves to "controversial speculations" (1 Timothy 1:3-4, TNIV). As followers of Christ we must follow the Bible's warnings against theological error. The apostle John wrote, "Dear children, do not let anyone lead you astray" (1 John 3:7). Also, in keeping with Paul's instruction, we must positively "teach what is appropriate to sound doctrine" (Titus 2:1, TNIV).

We must allow theology not only to inform our minds but also to nourish our hearts. Christian theology is more than a set of truths to be believed, for even the demons believe (James 2:19). Expressed otherwise, theology isn't just learning about Christ, because simply "knowing about" is insufficient. Rather, authentic theology is a matter of our learning Christ, as the Greek of Ephesians 4:20 establishes, "that isn't what you learned about Christ" (NLT). God-honoring theology involves holistic knowing, centered not in the intellect only but in the heart. Heart (*leb, kardia*) is the place of our orientation to God—the place where God touches us and kindles our passion for Christ and his kingdom.

Upholding Christian theology means that led by the Spirit, we will integrate doctrine with godly living. We must incorporate theology into our lives and communities in ways that result in wonder, worship, and deeper devotion to Christ. A major goal of theology—as reflection on God and his purposes—is the spiritual transformation of believers, churches, denominations, and people groups. Faithfully embraced, Christian theology will also inform our message and catalyze our ministry among the poor, the wounded, and the lost. Christian theology presents God's people with motivation and directives for fruitful evangelism, church planting, and kingdom building, as well as for dealing with a wide range of practical problems as they arise.

We should also recognize that because our knowledge of God and his purposes is partial (1 Corinthians 13:9), complete agreement among committed Christians on secondary matters of theology isn't likely this side of glory. As Paul wrote, "For now we see only a reflection as in a mirror; then we shall see face to face. Now I know in part; then I shall know fully" (1 Corinthians 13:12, TNIV). As followers of Jesus, we need thorough conviction regarding essential issues of the Christian faith, but humility regarding matters judged nonessential to the gospel and to life in the kingdom.

FOR FURTHER READING

Millard J. Erickson, *Introducing Christian Doctrine*. Baker Academic, 2001.

Wayne Grudem, *Bible Doctrine: Essential Teachings of the Christian Faith*. Zondervan, 1999.

Gordon R. Lewis and Bruce A. Demarest, *Integrative Theology*. Zondervan, 1996.

— BRUCE DEMAREST

TRADITION

EVERYDAY DEFINITION

Tradition (from Latin *tradure*, meaning "to hand over") is the handing down of beliefs, customs, and information from generation to generation.

According to the gospel of Mark, Jesus criticized the teachers of the law for holding fast to tradition (*paradosis*): "You nullify the word of God by your tradition that you have handed down" (Mark 7:13). The apostle Paul, on the other hand, employed tradition positively, writing to the church in Corinth, "For I received from the Lord what I also passed on to you" (1 Corinthians 11:23). Curiously, Paul reported that he received this teaching from the Lord, yet he wasn't present when Jesus delivered this teaching. So how did Paul receive it from the Lord? Early commentators suggest that Paul was taught this tradition—the received memory of the apostles—by others. Since the Holy Spirit (2 Corinthians 3:17) was involved in the process of recollection and accurate transmission, Paul could say with confidence that he received this teaching from the Lord. Tradition, as the process of transmission enabled by the Spirit of God, involves not just the act of transmission, but also includes the content of the transmission.

In 1 Corinthians 15:3-6, Paul indicated that he passed on what he had received—the core teaching of the gospel in narrative form: "That Christ died for our sins according to the Scriptures, that he was buried, that he was raised on the third day according to the Scriptures, and that he appeared to Peter, and then to the Twelve. After that, he appeared to more than five hundred of the brothers at the same time." When Paul wrote "according to the Scriptures," he was emphasizing that tradition must be based on a faithful interpretation and correct recollection of God's action in history as recorded in Scripture. For the early church, creeds served as accurate summaries of the teachings of Scripture.

EVERYDAY APPLICATION

Our age has been characterized as an *ahistorical* age, meaning a time when rather than learning from the past, we must overcome our past. Yet our Christian faith does have a tradition—a tradition of conversion. Accounts of the conversions of John Wesley, John Bunyan, and Charles Colson shape our imagination. Unfortunately these stories of radical departure from previous ways of living, read through our cultural lens of individualism, reinforce the belief that the past can't help us to follow Christ in the present or in the future. Yet generations and generations of faithful Christians, which the writer of Hebrews calls a cloud of witnesses (Hebrews 11), suggest that faithful remembering of the past—tradition—protects us from disaster.

Imagine traveling over a mountain pass on an icy and snow-covered road. Travel on such a treacherous road would be significantly more dangerous if the guardrail didn't protect cars from slipping off the side of the road and tumbling down the steep embankment. We can think of tradition as the guardrail for the faithful. Like the guardrail, learning from the past (tradition) keeps us from the tragedy of slipping off the road of right belief (orthodoxy) and right living (orthopraxy).

FOR FURTHER READING

D. H. Williams, *Evangelicals and Tradition: The Formative Influence of the Early Church*. Baker Academic, 2005.

Matthew Woodley, *Holy Fools: Following Jesus with Reckless Abandon*. SaltRiver, 2008.

— MIKE GLERUP

TRANSCENDENCE

EVERYDAY DEFINITION

Transcendence means over and beyond, above and independent. It's the quality by which God's being is above and beyond the being of the world. God, a living and active personal spirit (John 4:24), is independent of and unlimited by matter-energy, space, and time. God is also uniquely holy, above all that is evil and dedicated to uprightness: "'To whom will you compare me? Or who is my equal?' says the Holy One" (Isaiah 40:25).

The transcendence of God has been misunderstood by those who believe that God's way of thinking is "totally" different from ours. They often justify worship of an unknown and impersonal higher power by quoting out of context: "'For my thoughts are not your thoughts, neither are your ways my ways,' declares the LORD. 'As the heavens are higher than the earth, so are my ways higher than your ways and my thoughts than your thoughts'" (Isaiah 55:8-9). Although God's mind is beyond sin-blinded minds, and believers can never fully comprehend all that the transcendent God knows (see 1 Corinthians 13:12), by God's self-revelation his image bearers can grow in knowing revealed truth.

Even though sin has defaced the Creator's image in us, Christians "have put on the new self [or nature], which is being renewed in knowledge in the image of its Creator" (Colossians 3:10). Jesus received words from the Father and gave them to his disciples in their language (John 17:6,8,14,17). This means that the infinite and transcendent God has chosen to speak directly to us through his Son (see Hebrews 1:2). "The secret things belong to the LORD our God, but the things revealed belong to us and to our children forever" (Deuteronomy 29:29).

EVERYDAY APPLICATION

The good news is that to love God we don't have to try to ascend beyond time, space, and thought. The transcendent Lord of all has actively come to us! He has made his existence and moral principles known to all persons in creation (Romans 1:19-20) and the dictates of conscience (2:14-15). God has supremely exhibited his grace and truth in the life and words of Jesus (John 1:1,14,18). The truths revealed to the prophets and apostles have been preserved for us in the inspired Scriptures (2 Peter 1:16-21). The Bible makes known the way to eternal fellowship with the transcendent God and equips his people for every good work (2 Timothy 3:16-17).

In response to revealed truth, we must fulfill the great commandment reiterated by Jesus: "Love the Lord your God with all your heart and with all your soul and with all your mind" (Matthew 22:37). The transcendent God's words don't return to him empty, but achieve what he purposed in sending them (see Isaiah 55:10-11). Revealed truths effectively direct our passionate commitment away from idols and to God, who wants to enjoy daily fellowship with us (1 John 1:1-4). "For this is what the high and exalted One says—he who lives forever, whose name is holy: 'I live in a high and holy place, but also with those who are contrite and lowly in spirit'" (Isaiah 57:15).

FOR FURTHER READING

J. I. Packer, *Knowing God.* InterVarsity, 1993.
Gordon R. Lewis, "God, Attributes of," in *Evangelical Dictionary of Theology,* ed. Walter A. Elwell. Baker, 1984.

— GORDON R. LEWIS

TRANSFORMATION

EVERYDAY DEFINITION

In a culture that has television series, diet plans, exercise clubs, and stores all dedicated to makeovers, transformation isn't an entirely foreign concept. Our culture is littered with different ways to improve ourselves. In the Christian faith, however, transformation is not about us improving our current selves. The primary word used in the New Testament for transformation, *metamorphoo,* is the same word that we translate metamorphosis, with image of the caterpillar going into its cocoon and coming out a butterfly. In that image, we know of the relationship between the caterpillar and the butterfly, yet something is radically different in the end result. The work of God in transformation is similar, in that it's about making us into something new, something that retains some relationship to the old, yet something that is also so totally different that it's a new creature.

The work of transforming the human being, and with all of creation, is the work of God. However, while transformation is God's work, people have always tried to transform themselves. The story of Adam and Eve is the first example of humans trying to bring about transformation in their own power and with an end result that they design. Of course, Adam and Eve were transformed—from innocent, shameless, sinless, and in the freedom of the Garden to guilty, shamed sinners, and barred from the Garden. They indeed created their own transformation, but they didn't transform into a new and better creation. Throughout the history of Israel right up to the Pharisees of Jesus' own time, men and women attempted through human power to do the right things to make themselves better people. Yet even with the best efforts and the best tool—the Law—humans cannot transform themselves. Throughout the early church, throughout church history, and right up until the present, people continue to look to their own power rather than to God to "metamorphasize" themselves into something new.

Human beings can never make themselves into a new creation. Only when we ask Christ to be our Savior and the Lord of our lives can we begin the process of transformation—where the old dies and the new comes into existence. The process begins when Jesus gives the great image that we must be born again if we want to see the kingdom of God. When we are born again by receiving Christ, he becomes the center of our being, and we are born again of the Spirit. The apostle Paul underscored this truth with his great statement: "If anyone is in Christ, he is a new creation; the old has gone, the new has come!" (2 Corinthians 5:17). When we are born again of the Spirit, we begin a life of radical newness.

Sometimes we think of transformation as an event that is totally future, which will occur to us when we die or Jesus returns. Certainly, much of our transformation does await a future day of new creation, of God's kingdom when the rest of the universe will experience full transformation into the new heaven and new earth (Isaiah 65:17; 2 Peter 3:13; Revelation 21:1). Paul even told us that then, "Jesus Christ, who, by the power that enables him to bring everything under his control, will transform our lowly bodies so that they will be like his glorious body" (Philippians 3:20-21). Yet, as Paul also reminded us, the process of transformation begins now and remains a present-tense process (2 Corinthians 5:17; Galatians 6:15).

So how are we transformed? Paul told us that we are called to be "living sacrifices, holy and pleasing to God" (Romans 12:1), which will lead to transformation by the renewing of our minds (Romans 12:2). Paul didn't mean that we just fill our heads with knowledge. He also meant that we begin to see the world and understand it from God's perspective, instead of the merely human or evil perspective that Adam and Eve fell victim to in the Garden (Genesis 3). As part of the process of transformation, the apostle John pointed to our need to become filled with the love of God (1 John 3:11,16,18), and Paul further urged us to train our bodies for the race, which is a life that glorifies God (1 Corinthians 9:24-27).

However, these aspects of transformation all sound like actions we take as humans. Yet we've already seen that people can't transform themselves. Thus, this is where we enter into the dynamic of God's work in us and our work with God. Paul said, "continue to work out your salvation with fear and trembling, for it is God who works in you to will and to act according to his good purpose" (Philippians 2:12-13). So yes, we work with God by participating in our transformation, yet our transformation isn't a human self-improvement plan but a "God who works in you" plan. This Spirit-led, Spirit-inspired, and Spirit-empowered process transforms us in the direction of God's great destiny for those who are in Christ.

EVERYDAY APPLICATION

Nothing is wrong with diets, home-improvement projects, and the like. But none of these efforts can bring us new life. The Christian life is the transforming life. Transformation needs all the parts of our lives to be tuned to God. We need to be immersed in Scripture. We need to participate in the life of God's people. We need to practice spiritual disciplines that God has given us, such as fasting, solitude, prayer, and worship, so that the Holy Spirit can work to help us taste the promises of being new creations even now. Further, our transformed life will show up in a life of good spiritual fruit (Acts 5:22), in a life that demonstrates love for God and neighbor (Matthew 22:37-39), and in a life that serves as a testimony to the world of the ongoing truth of Jesus' victory on the cross and his resurrection.

The Bible makes many promises to those who are in Christ. As we participate along with the Spirit in the process of transformation, we also increase our faith and trust in God's promises. The process begins with our work with God, as well as deciding to trust the work of God in us.

FOR FURTHER READING

Kenneth Boa, *Conformed to His Image*. Zondervan, 2006.
Dallas Willard, *The Divine Conspiracy*. HarperSanFrancisco, 1998.

— CHRISTOPHER MORTON

TRIBULATION

EVERYDAY DEFINITION

Tribulation is spoken of in the Bible in two ways. It refers to the general trials, difficulties, and suffering that people experience in a fallen world, and to the specific righteous judgment of God on those who have turned away from God and, in their rebellion, now receive his just wrath. While all who live in this fallen world experience trials and tribulations, the Bible associates the concept of tribulation in two ways and with two groups:

1. With *believers* who experience *wrongful tribulation*, persecution, and affliction for their faithful devotion to Christ.
2. With *unbelievers* who receive *rightful tribulation* as the just judgment of God for their sin and rebellion against him.

Scripture often admonishes believers to bear up under tribulation, knowing that this is part of what discipleship to Christ entails. Jesus warned his disciples, "Then they will deliver you to tribulation, and will kill you, and you will be hated by all nations because of My name" (Matthew 24:9, NASB). If a sinful world hated and persecuted Christ himself, surely his followers also should expect the same. As the apostle Paul reminded fellow believers after he was stoned and thrown out of town, "Through many tribulations we must enter the kingdom of God" (Acts 14:22, NASB). But this realization should never lead a believer to despair. Again, Jesus said, "These things I have spoken to you, so that in Me you may have peace. In the world you have tribulation, but take courage; I have overcome the world" (John 16:33, NASB). What comfort and strength this promise grants those who follow Christ, the persecuted but victorious Lord. Indeed, believers are called to exalt (Romans 5:3) and persevere (Romans 12:12) in tribulations precisely because such perseverance in tribulation leads to their final hope. In this light, Paul asked the question, "Who will separate us from the love of Christ? Will tribulation, or distress, or persecution, or famine, or nakedness, or peril, or sword?" (Romans 8:35, NASB). The answer is that since we have been united to God through the victory of Christ, nothing can ever separate us from this love of God in Christ Jesus.

The second emphasis Scripture gives to the theme of tribulation involves God's righteous punishment brought upon sinners who stand before him in their unrepentant wickedness and rebellion. Jesus spoke of a coming day of "great tribulation, such as has not occurred since the beginning of the world until now, nor ever will" (Matthew 24:21, NASB), after which "the sun will be darkened, and the moon will not give its light, and the stars will fall from the sky, and the powers of the heavens will be shaken" (Matthew 24:29, NASB). Interpretations of the Tribulation vary. Some see it describing the immanent judgment to befall the city of Jerusalem; others see it as the judgment of God on sin throughout the church age; still others understand Jesus' words to refer to a final eschatological and climactic judgment at the time of the second coming of Christ.

What is clear is that God will be victor over all sin and evil, and he shall vanquish every foe and bring every wicked person to justice in that day. Jesus' teaching is confirmed by Paul's reference to a coming day of "tribulation and distress for every soul of man who does evil, of the Jew first and also of the Greek" (Romans 2:9, NASB). Indeed, a day of final judgment awaits all, but the judgment of unbelievers will surely be an experience of unparalleled and everlasting tribulation (Revelation 20:11-15).

EVERYDAY APPLICATION

The tribulation believers will face for their devotion and faithfulness to Christ presents them with a clear choice. As Jesus warned, "Do not fear those who kill the body but are unable to kill the soul; but rather fear Him who is able to destroy both soul and body in hell" (Matthew 10:28, NASB). In the face of persecution for faith in Christ, the temptation may be strong to "fear men" rather than to "fear God." As believers, it should strengthen our faith and hope to know that just as Christ endured great tribulation and was rewarded by his Father for his obedience to the end, those of us who follow him can persevere through the tribulations of our lives. We can easily be misled by voices today promising the certainty of health, wealth, prosperity, and happiness throughout life for the followers of Christ. While everlasting joy certainly awaits all of Christ's faithful ones, the pathway to this life of joy might well take us through deep valleys and dark affliction.

For those who haven't trusted Christ, the Bible's teaching on the coming Tribulation should elicit deep concern and lead them to seek rescue from this horrible day. For just as the future judgment of all unbelievers is certain, so too is the salvation from this punishment for all those who trust in Christ alone for the forgiveness of their sins and the hope of eternal life. The preaching by the apostles in the book of Acts often includes warning of the coming day of judgment. But along with this warning is the promise of deliverance from the Tribulation through faith in Christ. Peter, for example, proclaimed that Christ had been "appointed by God as Judge of the living and the dead." But he immediately followed this warning with the promise that "of Him

[Christ] all the prophets bear witness that through His name everyone who believes in Him receives forgiveness of sins" (Acts 10:42-43, NASB). The coming Tribulation will be a day of unspeakable suffering and pain. All who stand outside of Christ are in peril. Yet rescue is possible, and we can have the confidence that God has provided a Savior.

FOR FURTHER READING

Jim Andrews. *Polishing God's Monuments: Pillars of Hope for Punishing Times*. Shepherd Press, 2007.

Steven J. Keillor. *God's Judgments: Interpreting History and the Christian Faith*. InterVarsity, 2007.

John Piper and Justin Taylor, eds. *Suffering and the Sovereignty of God*. Crossway, 2006.

— BRUCE A. WARE

TRINITY

EVERYDAY DEFINITION

The Christian doctrine of the Trinity affirms that the one true God exists eternally in three coequal persons who bear the names Father, Son, and Holy Spirit. God reveals himself as one unified and infinite spirit being consisting of three divine persons. The Trinity lies at the heart of Christian faith and life.

The word trinity doesn't appear in the Bible; it first occurred in the writings of the leading theologian and apologist, Tertullian (ca. 155-220). The Council of Nicea (325) put forth the doctrine of the Trinity, paving the way for further development of this doctrine by the church through the centuries.

The Old Testament stressed the oneness or unity of God as a corrective to the many gods of Israel's pagan neighbors and the chosen people's tendency toward polytheism. This includes the great *Shema* of Israel, "Hear, O Israel: The LORD our God, the LORD is one" (Deuteronomy 6:4). Still, the Old Testament includes hints of multiplicity in the Godhead, as when God said, "Let us make man in our image" (Genesis 1:26; see also 3:22; 11:7; Isaiah 6:8). Also, we find mention in the Old Testament of one called "Branch" (Isaiah 11:1),

"Immanuel" (Isaiah 7:14), "king" (Isaiah 32:1), "Lord" (Psalm 110:1), "prophet" (Deuteronomy 18:15), "servant" (Isaiah 42:1), "Son" (Psalm 2:7), "son of man" (Daniel 7:13), and "wisdom" (Proverbs 8:1). A third person with divine qualities appears, designated "the Spirit of God" (Genesis 1:2), "the Spirit of the LORD" (Judges 3:10; Isaiah 11:2), and "Holy Spirit" (Psalm 51:11). When the Israelites tempted the Lord in the desert (Exodus 17:2,7) they were enticing the Holy Spirit (Hebrews 3:7-9). Prophets predicted that God would pour out his Spirit in the coming age (see Ezekiel 36:25-27; Joel 2:28-32).

When Jesus came forth, he acknowledged himself as God (John 8:58; 10:30). Following Jesus' death and resurrection, inspired apostles confessed him as Son of God and Messiah (Romans 9:5; Philippians 2:6; Titus 2:13; 1 John 5:20). At Pentecost, the Holy Spirit was poured out with power as a personal divine being (Acts 2). The Spirit's deity was further confirmed by many supra-human activities throughout the book of Acts (see 4:31; 8:29,39; 11:28). Jesus acknowledged the Holy Spirit to be invested with divine powers (John 3:6-8; 14:26; 16:13). Peter testified that the Holy Spirit was essentially God (Acts 5:3-4), as did the apostle Paul (2 Corinthians 3:17-18).

Key New Testament figures reiterated the unity of God. Jesus repeated Israel's *Shema* (Mark 12:29) as did the apostles Paul (1 Corinthians 8:4) and James (2:19). The New Testament contains many convincing Trinitarian texts: for example, Jesus' baptism in the Jordan (Matthew 3:16-17), the Great Commission (Matthew 28:18-20), Paul's Trinitarian benediction (2 Corinthians 13:14), and other passages such as Ephesians 4:4-6; Titus 3:4-6; 1 Peter 1:2; Jude 20-21; and 1 John 4:13-15.

Various illustrations of the Trinity have been proposed. Everyday experience confirms that many things are both one and many. Examples include space (length, breadth, and height), a family, a nation, or the church as the body of Christ (Romans 12:5). The fact that ultimate Reality—God—consists of unity with diversity shouldn't seem odd or illogical. Reflecting on God as love (1 John 4:16), Augustine observed that love requires a lover, a beloved, and the love that flows among them. The great theologian concluded that the Father is Lover, the Son the Beloved, and the Spirit the personal love that flows between them.

Both Scripture and Christian theology teach that the three persons are equal in their intrinsic being. But functionally, or in modes of operation, an ordering relation exists between them. Thus the Father sends the Son (John 5:37; 17:3) as well as the Spirit (1 Corinthians 2:12; Galatians 4:6), and the Son sends the Spirit (John 15:26). With respect to this functional sense that Jesus said, "the Father is greater than I" (John 14:28). At the end of the age the Son will yield his authority to the Father (1 Corinthians 15:24,28).

Scripture attributes principal works to each of the three divine persons in the realms of creation and redemption. John Calvin commented, "To the Father is attributed the beginning of activity, and the fountain and wellspring of all things; to the Son, wisdom, counsel, and the ordered disposition of all things; but to the Spirit is assigned the power and efficacy of that activity."[44] In the area of salvation, the Father planned redemption (1 Corinthians 8:6), the Son accomplished that redemption (Ephesians 1:7), and the Spirit applies redemption to all who believe (2 Thessalonians 2:13).

EVERYDAY APPLICATION

A. W. Tozer commented that "A right conception of God is basic not only to systematic theology, but to practical Christian living as well."[45] He added, "The heaviest obligation lying upon the Christian church today is to purify and elevate her concept of God until it is once more worthy of Him—and of her."[46] If we harbor faulty conceptions of God, Christian faith and living flounders on a foundation of sand. If we yield our loyalty to a god less truthful than the Trinity, we commit idolatry. How critical, therefore, that we believe in the one true God who subsists as three divine persons: Father, Son, and Holy Spirit. How important is it also to teach the true Trinity to our children.

In addition, we need to relate to each of the three persons of the Trinity personally, lovingly, and intimately. We need to return to the Father his unmerited love and favor; we ought to entrust ourselves completely to Jesus who died in our place; and we ought to invite the Spirit to infuse his life and power into our mortal frames. We should offer prayer not to the Father only, but also to his Son (Acts 22:16) and to the comforting Spirit (Jude 20). Through contemplation and

---

44. John Calvin, *Institutes*, I.13.18.
45. A. W. Tozer, *The Knowledge of the Holy* (New York: Harper and Row, 1961), 10.
46. Tozer, *The Knowledge of the Holy*, 12.

attentive listening, we should practice the presence of each of the three divine persons. We might engage the sacred Presence during a quiet stroll in nature, while reading the Scriptures, or as we come to the Lord's Table.

More profoundly still is the reality, often overlooked, that by virtue of Christ's saving work we believers are caught up into the life of the Three-in-One God. The Trinity is a dynamic community where the loving energy of each person flows between the others (see John 10:38; 14:10-11; 17:5,21,23). John wrote, "If anyone acknowledges that Jesus is the Son of God, God lives in them and they in God" (1 John 4:15, TNIV; see also verses 13,16; Ephesians 2:6-7). Living in this supernatural realm, we should relate to one another with trust, love, and mutual submission, even as the three persons of the Trinity so relate. As John put it, "As we live in God, our love grows more perfect" (1 John 4:17, NLT).

The Trinity is also crucial to a sound missional theology. The Father conceived the good news and planned the worldwide mission. The Father then sent his Son on the magnificent mission of redeeming the lost world (John 3:17). The Savior in turn commissioned his followers as missioners to the dying race, with the words, "As the Father has sent me, I am sending you" (John 20:21; see also Mathew 28:28-30). Our evangelistic message centers on free access to Christ's kingdom through faith in the Savior's cross and resurrection. In addition, the Spirit directs and empowers us to bring in the harvest of sheep the Father has given to the Son (John 10:1-16). The Trinitarian God is a missional God, and out of loving obedience to him we should be missional people. The church today must recover a theology and practice of mission that is solidly Trinitarian.

Reflecting on the Trinity as a community of three divine persons in one infinite spirit being, we ponder the words of Charles Spurgeon: "My firm conviction is that in proportion as we have more regard for . . . the wondrous Trinity in unity, shall we see a greater display of God's power and a more glorious manifestation of his might in our churches."[47]

FOR FURTHER READING

Michael Downey, *Altogether Gift: A Trinitarian Spirituality*. Orbis Books, 2000.

---

47. Charles Spurgeon, *Metropolitan Tabernacle Pulpit* (1855), vol. 1, 379.

Millard J. Erickson, *Making Sense of the Trinity.* Baker, 2000.

Darrell W. Johnson, *Experiencing the Trinity.* Regent College
Publishing, 2002.

James R. White, *The Forgotten Trinity.* Bethany House, 1998.

— BRUCE DEMAREST

TRUTH

EVERYDAY DEFINITION

The word truth would seem to have the straightforward sense of a statement that corresponds to a factual state of affairs. So, it would be a
truth to say that the shape of planet Earth is more round than it is flat.
Scripture certainly uses "truth" in this manner (Deuteronomy 17:4;
Proverbs 22:21; John 4:18). However, the Bible more frequently uses
truth in a broader and richer sense.

In the Old Testament, the word generally translated as "truth" carries
moral connotations of fidelity, stability, and integrity. In fact, depending on the context, the same term is sometimes translated as "faith" or
"faithfulness" in the Greek translation of the Old Testament. This use is
found in the sense of God's faithfulness or trustworthiness to us: "But
you, O LORD, are a compassionate and gracious God, slow to anger,
abounding in love and faithfulness" (Psalm 86:15), and it's also used to
describe human trustworthiness toward others or in carrying out duties
(Exodus 18:21). Intensifying the moral and personal nature of truth in
the Old Testament is a common linkage with the term *hesed,* frequently
translated as love, steadfast love, or kindness. These instances remind
us that God's truthfulness or fidelity toward his people are connected
with his enduring love: "All the ways of the LORD are loving and faithful toward those who keep the demands of his covenant" (Psalm 25:10,
TNIV; see also Genesis 24:29; Exodus 34:6; 1 Kings 3:6).

In the New Testament, the use of "truth" or "true" retains the close
link between word, action, and being by communicating the sense of
being reliable or genuine. When the apostle Paul referred to Titus as his
"true son" (Titus 1:4), it carries the meaning of authentic, trustworthy,
and real (see Luke 16:11; John 8:17; 2 Peter 2:22; Hebrews 10:22). The
relationship between truth and character is seen in phrases such as "live by

the truth" (John 3:21, TNIV) or "live out the truth" (1 John 1:6, TNIV).

As might be expected, truth often appears in contrast with falsehood in the New Testament. However, in virtually every case, the falsehood isn't simply something untrue in the sense of being inaccurate or erroneous; rather, the contrasting element is deceptive and capable of bringing ruin to life (Mark 12:14; Romans 1:25). For example, Jesus described Satan as "a murderer from the beginning, not holding to the truth, for there is no truth in him. When he lies, he speaks his native language, for he is a liar and the father of lies. Yet because I tell the truth, you do not believe me" (John 8:44-45). In a positive sense, truth brings salvation (John 17:17). In several places in the New Testament, truth is a shorthand way of referring to the message of the gospel (1 Timothy 2:4; 2 Timothy 3:7; 1 Peter 1:22; James 5:19).

Finally, "truth" is sometimes used in reference to God himself. The clearest expression of this is found when Jesus speaks of himself as "the way and the truth and the life" (John 14:6). John's gospel also refers to the "Spirit of truth" (John 14:17; 15:26; 16:13), describing the ways the Holy Spirit echoes and continues the work begun by Jesus. These passages speak of a truth that is not abstract or cut off from history. Rather, this truth is God, who is revealed in history.

EVERYDAY APPLICATION

The meanings and connotations of words change over time. For example, the word "vulgar" used to mean "of the common people" or "unrefined." Now it means something quite different. With this in mind, we need to remember that words like true and truth can have different connotations in our everyday usage than they did in the biblical world. When we see the word "truth" in Scripture, we often unwittingly default to the definition of truth as the quality of being accurate. However, this definition doesn't capture the full effect of the way Scripture uses words like true and truth.

While truth as used in Scripture does often include the idea of accuracy and fact, we limit our understanding of truth if we stop there. Rather, Scripture most frequently speaks of truth in terms of a person's actions, motives, and character. In the biblical sense, an individual's (or God's) words are truthful because the person (or God) is truthful. Truthful words are the result of a truthful or faithful character.

Further, Scripture doesn't let us detach the idea of *saying* the truth from *doing* and *being* the truth. Truth requires an integrity and authenticity where all aspects of our life correspond with each other.

In addition, biblical truth requires an integrity that corresponds to an even higher standard. When Jesus identifies his message and person as truth, it reminds us that Scripture's use of truth is grounded in the divine, personal reality of God.

FOR FURTHER READING
J. Richard Middleton and Brian J. Walsh, *Truth Is Stranger Than It Used to Be.* InterVarsity, 1995.

— STEVE WILKENS

UNIVERSALISM

EVERYDAY DEFINITION
Universalism is the idea that Christ's atoning death accomplishes the ultimate reconciliation of all humanity to God. Universalism goes beyond the traditional Christian view that Christ's death makes *possible* the salvation of all people, to claim that salvation is *guaranteed* for all people, regardless of their decisions and attitude toward God's grace in this life.

The apostle Paul's discussion of the contrast between Jesus and Adam has been understood by some as affirming universalism: "But the gift is not like the trespass. For if the many died by the trespass of the one man, how much more did God's grace and the gift that came by the grace of the one man, Jesus Christ, overflow to the many! Again, the gift of God is not like the result of the one man's sin: The judgment followed one sin and brought condemnation, but the gift followed many trespasses and brought justification. For if, by the trespass of the one man, death reigned through that one man, how much more will those who receive God's abundant provision of grace and of the gift of righteousness reign in life through the one man, Jesus Christ" (Romans 5:15-17). The argument for universalism here is that because Adam's sin had universal consequences, resulting in the death and condemnation of all humanity, Christ's act of sacrifice must also have the same effect.

In a similar way, Paul wrote to the Corinthian Christians: "For since death came through a man, the resurrection of the dead comes also through a man. For as in Adam all die, so in Christ all will be made alive" (1 Corinthians 15:21-22). And in Colossians, Paul described Christ as ultimately accomplishing the reconciliation of all things in creation (Colossians 1:19-20).

The majority of Christian theologians reject the idea of universalism, largely because of the many other passages in Scripture which state that some will reject God's grace and ultimately be lost. Among these occurrences are: Jesus' warning about the narrow gate (Matthew 7:13); Paul's affirmation that some will ultimately be shut out from God's presence in the end (2 Thessalonians 1:9); and the book of Revelation's affirmation of endless torment (Revelation 14:9-11).

EVERYDAY APPLICATION

While the Bible doesn't affirm universalism, it does affirm God's love and concern for all humans, regardless of their attitude toward him. The Bible consistently speaks of God's love for all. God longs for all to come to repentance (2 Peter 3:9). Christ's sacrifice is sufficient for all who respond to God's grace in faith. This should motivate us as followers of Jesus to enlarge our own circle of love to include those who are difficult to love. In addition, the tension between the sufficiency and efficiency of Christ's atonement presents an important lesson about reconciliation and forgiveness for followers of Jesus. Through Christ, God expresses his love by providing a way of reconciliation for all. However, God doesn't force people to reconciliation. He invites them to reconciliation without coercing them. For those who refuse that path, God respects their decision by providing a means of existence apart from a relationship with him.

In a similar respect, Paul advised followers of Jesus, "If it is possible, as far as it depends on you, live at peace with everyone" (Romans 12:18). This means that as Christians, we are also called to open paths of reconciliation for those we are estranged from. We invite others to join us on the path to reconciliation, yet we respect people's decision when they choose not to walk that path.

FOR FURTHER READING

Larry Dixon, *The Other Side of the Good News*. Christian Focus, 2003.
C. S. Lewis, *The Great Divorce*. Harper, 2001.
Miroslav Volf, *Exclusion and Embrace*. Abingdon, 1996.

— TIM PECK

VICE

EVERYDAY DEFINITION

We usually think of vice as the opposite of virtue. However, vice is more accurately defined as the corruption of virtue.

Augustine, an early philosopher and theologian, described evil not as a substance or "thing," but as a privation, absence, lack or corruption of goodness. In other words, just as cold is the absence of heat and darkness is the lack of light, vice is a lack or corruption of virtue.

The seven virtues are commonly described as wisdom (prudence), courage, temperance, justice, faith, hope, and love. These are contrasted with seven vices: folly, cowardice, lust, venality, blasphemy, despair, and hatred.

Virtue is a good trait of character, manifested in habitual action. Virtues might best be understood as a means between two extremes, between excess and deficiency. Picture an Olympic gymnast on a balance beam. The gymnast is to perform her routine on the narrow beam. Her intention is to stay in the middle of the beam, not veering to the left or right, which would result in a fall from the beam. If virtue is likened to the beam, then a fall on either side of the virtue leads to a vice.

For example, the excess and deficiency of courage is cowardice and foolhardiness — both are vices. If courage is the virtue describing the proper attitude toward danger and fear, then the cowardly person shrinks from any challenge and hides from danger, while the foolhardy person displays a deficient amount of fear, rushing forward blindly in the face of danger. To have courage is to find the mean or balance between these two vices.

EVERYDAY APPLICATION

While the Bible doesn't strictly use the term vice, we can certainly find the concept within the notion of sin. Historically, the church (most notably, Thomas Aquinas in the thirteenth century) has identified a lack of holiness, righteousness, and virtue under the seven deadly sins. While not found in a single passage of Scripture, the seven deadly sins encapsulate the misery of vice. These sins—pride, greed, envy, wrath, sloth, lust, and gluttony—are all warned against in Scripture from the beginning of Psalm 1, through Proverbs, and ultimately throughout the Bible. If we see vice as a lack of wholeness or virtue, then God's supernatural program is to restore wholeness, goodness, and virtue to humanity.

Pride, sometimes seen as the deepest vice from which the other vices develop, is self-absorption, self-assertion, and selfishness; it can't be simply removed or "zapped" from our soul and body. God must "restore" goodness, wholeness, and virtue in order to release a vice's grip on us. The apostle Paul expressed this process, exhorting, "Train yourself to be godly. For physical training is of some value, but godliness has value for all things, holding promise for both the present life and the life to come. This is a trustworthy saying that deserves full acceptance. That is why we labor and strive, because we have put our hope in the living God, who is the Savior of all people, and especially of those who believe" (1 Timothy 4:7-10, TNIV). We are to train in the power and presence of the Holy Spirit, imitating Jesus our example, bringing glory to the Father as we escape the gravity of vice in our lives and extinguish its presence as God brings goodness and wholeness through virtue in our lives. This process results in the fruit of the Spirit (the virtues of Christ, contrasted with vices of sin) as Paul described in Galatians, "So I say, walk by the Spirit, and you will not gratify the desires of the sinful nature. For the sinful nature desires what is contrary to the Spirit, and the Spirit what is contrary to the sinful nature. They are in conflict with each other, so that you are not to do whatever you want. But if you are led by the Spirit, you are not under the law. The acts of the sinful nature are obvious: sexual immorality, impurity and debauchery; idolatry and witchcraft; hatred, discord, jealousy, fits of rage, selfish ambition, dissensions, factions and envy; drunkenness, orgies, and the like. I warn you, as I did before, that those who live like this will not inherit the kingdom of God. But the fruit of the Spirit is love, joy, peace, patience, kindness, goodness, faithfulness, gentleness and self-control. Against such things there is no law. Those who belong to Christ Jesus have crucified the sinful nature with its passions and desires. Since we live by the Spirit, let us keep in step with the Spirit. Let us not become conceited, provoking and envying each other" (Galatians 5:16-26, TNIV).

FOR FURTHER READING

Peter Kreeft, *Back to Virtue*. Ignatius Press, 1986.

Gilbert Meilander, *The Theory and Practice of Virtue*. University of Notre Dame Press, 1985.

Dallas Willard, *Renovation of the Heart: Putting On the Character of Christ*. NavPress, 2002.

Jonathan R. Wilson, *Gospel Virtues: Practicing Faith, Hope & Love in Uncertain Times*. InterVarsity, 1998.

—GEORGE HARAKSAN

VIRGIN MARY

EVERYDAY DEFINITION

The Virgin Mary is the traditional title used by most Christians to describe Mary, the mother of Jesus. The Bible affirms that Mary was a virgin.

Matthew's gospel explains that Mary was engaged to Joseph, but before they had sexual intercourse, she became pregnant with Jesus through the Holy Spirit (Matthew 1:18). Matthew further notes that Joseph and Mary didn't engage in sexual intercourse until after she gave birth to Jesus (Matthew 1:25), meaning that Mary remained a virgin throughout her pregnancy.

Luke's gospel similarly emphasizes that Mary was a virgin (Luke 1:27). Luke even presents Mary's consternation at the angel's announcement that she was pregnant: "How can this be, since I am a virgin?" (Luke 1:34, NASB). The angel's reply explains the *how* of the virginal conception: "The Holy Spirit will come upon you, and the power of the Most High will overshadow you" (Luke 1:35). This means that Mary's genetic material biologically provided twenty-three of the forty-six chromosomes for Jesus' humanity, while the Holy Spirit supernaturally supplied the twenty-three. In the Incarnation, the eternally existing Son of God took on human nature and became a real and fully human being.

EVERYDAY APPLICATION

Mary's virginity is significant because it means that Jesus had no human father. Rather, God was the Father of the Son, both eternally and at the Incarnation. This Father-Son relationship explains Jesus' unique consciousness of being on the mission of the Father (John 20:19-23), in order to always carry out the Father's will (John 15:10; 8:29). Mary's virginity further means that Jesus didn't have a sinful human nature like other human beings (Luke 1:35). Because the power of the Holy Spirit was operative in the conception of Jesus, he didn't inherit original sin.

From Mary's story, we can learn a lesson about pleasing God. When Mary learned she was pregnant, even though she hadn't engaged in sexual intercourse with Joseph or any other man, she reacted with perplexed concern. As a woman engaged to be married, she would be vulnerable to the charge of immorality and would certainly be put to shame (Matthew 1:19). Yet her ultimate response was marked by faithful obedience to God: "I am the Lord's servant. . . . May it be to me as you have said" (Luke 1:38). In Mary, we see a strong example of God-honoring responsiveness.

FOR FURTHER READING

J. Gresham Machen, *The Virgin Birth of Christ*. James Clarke, 1987.
Robert Gromacki, *The Virgin Birth: A Biblical Study of the Deity of Jesus Christ*. Kregel Academic, 2002.

— GREGG ALLISON

VIRTUE

EVERYDAY DEFINITION

Virtue is moral excellence, right living, or goodness. It can also refer to a specific type of moral excellence. More specifically, virtue can be considered a good quality or feature, purity, chastity, or effectiveness in living. The English word virtue comes from the Latin word *virtus*, which meant manliness or virility.

Observers of modern morality have been concerned that the systems of morality in place currently aren't sufficient to produce good people, families, communities, and nations. Much of the current discussion about ethical systems and applied ethics have revolved around challenges to morality (such as relativism), actions and their consequences (labeled utilitarianism or deontology), or how to answer ethical dilemmas. While some question whether these considerations are either insufficient for the moral life or not necessary, virtue theorists suggest we should be focusing on how to live and how to live well. This entails asking questions, such as: What is a good person? What is the good of human life? What traits of character will lead to a good life? How do we acquire and cultivate these traits? What would a virtuous person do in a particular situation? How will these varying actions impact an individual's character?

Current moral discussion has tended to stress what we want or what we ought to do. Virtue ethics concerns itself with what sort of person we should try to become and what we should want and/or care about. In addition, it asks what sort of habits and activities cultivate qualities that lead to a flourishing, good life. What are these qualities? The so-called Cardinal virtues articulated by the likes of Plato and Aristotle were wisdom (or prudence), courage, temperance, and justice. They described cultivated conduct rather than innate qualities. The ancients stressed that these qualities are achieved through proper training and discipline.

These Cardinal virtues are sometimes referred to as "natural virtues" as they are contrasted with the three Christian theological virtues faith, hope, and love (1 Corinthians 13:13). Historically, Christians combined the natural virtues with the three theological virtues to make the seven great virtues.

Virtue ethics is character-oriented rather than action-oriented. Action-based ethics focus on the results or consequences, conduct, duty of the act. Character-based ethics focus on the "actor" and how that person displays virtue or character in life. It focuses on character development, on the nature and formation of a good person, and the sort of dispositions and character traits that constitute a good person resulting in good families, good communities, etc. Virtues promote moral goodness, which leads to good actions. Moral goodness is the quality of an action, attribute, or person that measures whether it agrees with the virtues.

Jesus, the New Testament, and the Christian church employ notions of virtue in teaching and the understanding of moral and spiritual formation. Jesus and the writers of the New Testament reflect the deep and different concerns of virtue theory and the good life. Being a disciple of Jesus, journeying and following him in everyday life, imitating and practicing the activities of his life, lead to a flourishing life in God's kingdom. Jesus is deeply concerned with the character and inner disposition of people as they relate to God, other people, and creation. This agrees with what the Hebrew prophets spoke as they exhorted the people of God toward holy internal motivations and beliefs. In the Beatitudes, Jesus stressed attitudes and internal states of the heart that are "blessed," meaning objectively good, promoting human flourishing, and in harmony with God's ways. Jesus' account of virtue is both theological and teleological. That is, virtues are viewed and cultivated against the broader canvas of God's creation, supernatural kingdom, and redemption (both individual and communal) of humankind and the resulting people it produces (both now and everlasting). For Jesus and his followers, God is essential to the nature, cultivation, and formational experience of virtue. Virtue is not developed and cultivated on one's own power, but in a grace-infused partnership with Jesus Christ, to the glory of the Father, and in the power of the Holy Spirit.

EVERYDAY APPLICATION

Virtue in the life of the follower of Jesus flows from the new life received from God, which comes from the life and work of Jesus in the power of the Spirit. The apostle Peter declared, "To those who through the righteousness of our God and Savior Jesus Christ have received a faith as precious as ours: Grace and peace be yours in abundance through the knowledge of God and of Jesus our Lord" (2 Peter 1:1-2). God's divine power provides us "everything" we need to live a godly life through the knowledge of him by his own glory and excellence. As followers of Christ, we should "make every effort" to add to our faith certain "qualities" that if increased in measure result in an effective and productive (flourishing) life in the "knowledge of our Lord Jesus Christ" (2 Peter 1:8). These qualities supply us with "moral excellence" or virtue. We should add to this moral excellence "knowledge; and to knowledge, self-control; and to self-control, perseverance; and to perseverance, godliness; and to godliness, mutual affection; and to mutual affection, love" (2 Peter 1:5-7, TNIV). The same Greek word (*arête*) used for God's excellence is used by Peter to describe our moral excellence, goodness, or virtue. Virtue in our lives leads to a set of qualities and character traits that, when infused and fueled by God's ongoing grace, leads to a life of flourishing and benefit to others who receive the positive impact of our character and actions.

This leads to the question, "What is character?" Simply, character is the sum total of our habits. A habit is a tendency to act, think, or feel without willing to do so. Thus, a virtue is a habit of excellence, a beneficial tendency, a skilled disposition that enables us to realize the crucial potentialities that constitute proper human flourishing in light of God's redeeming activity in our lives.

Further, we can understand virtue as a mean between two extremes — between excess and deficiency. For example, take humility. Christians see humility as vital to operating in the kingdom and power of God. Intrinsic to the "blessed" way of living that Jesus advocates is the virtue of humility (such as "The first shall be last"; Mark 9:33-35). Humility is the proper recognition of our position in God's creation; and in more human terms, humility is a mean between the vices of arrogance and low self-esteem or no love for self. The grand theological virtue of love is closely related to humility because these virtues lead to forgiveness. Jesus didn't advise forgiving others merely for the sake of our mental, emotional, or physical health — however beneficial this might in fact be — but taught and displayed forgiveness as an ethical duty expressing a virtue. Jesus modeled this power of virtue while dying on the cross when he prayed, "Father, forgive them, for they do not know what they are doing" (Luke 23:34).

A virtue, then, is a good trait of character that shows in habitual action. For Christians, the cultivation of virtue occurs in an ongoing, moment-by-moment partnership with God, a relationship that builds a godly character with powerful and profound results. Jesus announced to his followers that "All authority in heaven and on earth has been given to me. Therefore go and make disciples of all nations, baptizing them in the name of the Father and of the Son and of the Holy Spirit, and teaching them to obey everything I have commanded you. And surely I am with you always, to the very end of the age" (Matthew 28:18-20). Jesus, in the power and presence of the Holy Spirit, promises to be in our midst, teaching and training us to lead a life of virtue—a flourishing, morally excellent life that glorifies God and blesses others.

FOR FURTHER READING
Douglas Groothuis, *On Jesus*. Wadsworth Philosophers Series, 2003.
Peter Kreeft, *Back to Virtue*. Ignatius Press, 1986.
Gilbert Meilander, *The Theory and Practice of Virtue*. University of Notre Dame Press, 1985.
Jonathan R. Wilson, *Gospel Virtues: Practicing Faith, Hope & Love in Uncertain Times*. InterVarsity, 1998.

—GEORGE HARAKSAN

WISDOM

EVERYDAY DEFINITION
Biblical wisdom (Hebrew *μ-k-m*, Greek *sophía*) appears in the Old Testament primarily in Proverbs, Job, and Ecclesiastes—books identified as "wisdom writings." Wisdom also is widely unfolded in the New Testament throughout the Gospels and Epistles.

The Old Testament personifies wisdom as a woman who was present at the moment of creation, who actively participated in the crafting of God's handiwork, and who delighted in the presence of human beings (Proverbs 8:22-31). Lady Wisdom, who appears in Job, Proverbs, and in certain Apocryphal writings (such as Baruch, Sirach, Wisdom of Solomon) is contrasted with loud, undisciplined, unsophisticated, and immoral Lady Folly (Proverbs 9:13-18). In the book of Proverbs, Lady Wisdom is portrayed as an exceptional orator whose piercing and prophetic voice is heard in the market places, and whose message invites her hearers to follow her voice in order to find security and peace (Proverbs 1:20-33).

Several Old Testament passages refer to "wise men," members of a guild of official counselors who appear before rulers (together with magicians, sorcerers, and astrologers) in order to provide counsel or interpret dreams (Genesis 41:8; Exodus 7:11; Daniel 2). Likewise, skilled artisans whose talents were used to build the tabernacle are represented as persons of wisdom (Exodus 35:31-35). Of all the wise men of the Bible, none equaled King Solomon. According to Scripture, Solomon's wisdom surpassed the wisdom of any other human in his day and before him (1 Kings 4:29-34).

Old Testament wisdom writings typically exclude references to famous biblical figures of the patriarchal accounts and historical books and avoid discussions dealing with history and theoretical issues. Rather, they focus on universal and timeless maxims and highlight practical and behavioral themes such as: human suffering (Job 2:8-13; 30:16-27), the result of immorality (Proverbs 2:12-16; 7:4-23), challenges of human relationships (Proverbs 31:10-31), the power of human speech for good and evil (Proverbs 10:19-20; 15:2), truth and integrity (Job 2:9-10; Proverbs 10:9), wisdom versus foolishness (Proverbs 10:23; 14:26), diligence versus laziness (Proverbs 10:4; Ecclesiastes 10:18), and pride versus humility (Proverbs 11:2; 16:18).

The New Testament contrasts the meaningless outcome of worldly wisdom with the remarkable benefits of godly wisdom (1 Corinthians 2:5; 3:19). Godly wisdom is identified as a divine gift available to all believers (Ephesians 1:8; James 3:17). The secular wise men cited in the New Testament frequently are confounded by the wisdom of God revealed through the words and deeds of Jesus (Matthew 11:19; Luke 2:40,52), Stephen (Acts 6:10), and the apostle Paul (1 Corinthians 1:17).

EVERYDAY APPLICATION
A secular definition of wisdom includes the right application of knowledge and the ability to make sound judgments. For us as Christians, however, divine wisdom is more than behavioral choices made from a bank of information. Motivated by the fear of God (Psalm 111:10) and the hatred of evil (Proverbs 8:13), the Christian who attains wisdom is equipped to face a multitude of challenges and to overcome many of life's obstacles. As wise followers of Christ, we will not only benefit personally from the blessings that accompany wisdom, but also will be equipped to lead others in the paths of wisdom.

As we pursue wisdom, we discover how practical it is in nature and application. Wisdom reveals the glory and majesty of God, confounds the self-designated sages of this world, and establishes God's purposes on the earth. If we forsake godly wisdom we, in fact, forsake God. But as we embrace wisdom we choose fullness of life as God intended it.

The term "wisdom" frequently is accompanied by words such as "understanding," "judgment," "knowledge," "learning," and "skill." Scripture urges us to seek after these qualities diligently, to listen to them attentively, and to embrace them in order to be enriched by them in our daily lives. Not only will these graces help us discern right from wrong, but they will accompany us on our daily journey and counsel us along the way. Every aspect of our Christian lives can be influenced and changed by God's wisdom. Scripture provides sound wisdom for financial dealings, family relations, moral and ethical issues, political and vocational endeavors, social interactions, and religious decisions.

According to King Solomon, we live wisely when we acknowledge God and his created order in the world (Proverbs 2:1-6; 19:23; Ecclesiastes 8:5). Scripture tells us that God created the universe with a deep sense of order and stability, with justice and integrity, and with wisdom and harmony. When our Christian experience is based on godly wisdom, we'll respect and preserve this God-ordained order, and we'll seek to live morally and ethically in all areas of our lives.

In Scripture, wisdom is connected to the human heart, the center of all moral and ethical deliberations (Psalm 90:12; Proverbs 2:10). Without fully embracing wisdom, our hearts are easily deceived and tend to succumb to foolish behaviors, stubborn dealings, selfish ambitions, and evil practices (James 3:14-16). The apostle James invites us to seek godly wisdom that comes from above and to live peaceful and holy lives before God (James 3:13,17-18). Inspired by the Spirit, he reminds us that true wisdom comes from God alone, and that its fruit is humility, purity, love, peace, mercy, impartiality, and sincerity (James 3:13-18).

Scripture acknowledges that the experience of living over many years imparts great wisdom (Job 12:12; 32:7). Those of us who are mature in age should be expected to live wise and godly lives. Believers younger in years do well to attend to and follow a wise mother's instructions and to heed a wise father's discipline—in short, to respect an elder's guidance in order to live prudent and productive lives (Proverbs 1:1-9). We discover that wisdom doesn't come easily or without a price. We must intentionally pursue wisdom to find it. But we're encouraged by the truth that whoever finds wisdom finds life (Proverbs 8:34-36).

FOR FURTHER READING

Robert Hicks, *In Search of Wisdom*. NavPress, 1995.

H. Wayne House and Kenneth M. Durhan. *Living Wisely in a Foolish World: A Contemporary Look at the Wisdom of Proverbs*. Thomas Nelson, 1992.

— HÉLÈNE DALLAIRE

WORK

EVERYDAY DEFINITION

Work is physical or mental activity directed toward the completion of a task.

One of the first truths in the Bible is that God works (Genesis 1:1; 2:2-3). The Scriptures teach that the universe came into existence, is actively sustained, and is being guided to its ultimate purpose by the work of God (Psalm 8:3; Isaiah 45:11; Matthew 10:29; Acts 27:28; Colossians 1:15-19).

When the Old Testament speaks about God creating humanity in the divine image, it's not surprising that work is closely connected: "Then God said, 'Let us make human beings in our image, in our likeness, so that they may rule over the fish in the sea and the birds in the sky, over the livestock and all the wild animals, and over all the creatures that move along the ground'" (Genesis 1:26, TNIV). God placed Adam and Eve in the Garden of Eden for the expressed purpose "to work it and take care of it" (Genesis 2:15).

Within the pattern of human life, God ordained a Sabbath rest from work, a time for worship and rejuvenation (Exodus 20:8-11). The importance of rest in the divine plan is seen in the fact that humanity's first full day of existence is spent in rest and not labor. Humanity was created by God on the sixth day; the seventh day humanity rested with God (Genesis 2:2).

While work is intrinsic to being made in God's image and is good, the Old Testament makes clear that human work has been corrupted by sin. As a result of the fall of Adam and Eve, humanity and the world are broken by sin. Work isn't spared from sin's consequences. As a result, work is now "painful toil" and necessary for survival (Genesis 3:17-19). Work is no longer as God originally created it.

Still, work is an expression of the divine image. The New Testament teaches that as Christians we are being renewed in the likeness of God (2 Corinthians 3:18; Colossians 3:9-10) and our work should reflect this transformation. More specifically, the New Testament focuses on two types of work: the work done for daily living to provide for the necessities of life, such as food, shelter, etc. (1 Thessalonians 4:11-12; Ephesians 4:28), and the work given to believers as a part of the body of Christ and God's kingdom (1 Corinthians 7:17). Regardless of its type, all work should be done faithfully for the glory of God, as service unto the Lord, and defined by love of God and humanity (1 Corinthians 10:31; Colossians 3:23-24).

In the age to come, work will not cease, but it will be fully redeemed. The curse placed upon work as a result of human sin will be lifted and God's ultimate intentions for it will be realized in our lives (Revelation 22:3).

EVERYDAY APPLICATION

As Christians, having a sound theology of work can help us address unhealthy misconceptions that society sometimes has about work. First, some of us are tempted to see work as a "curse" that we should avoid as much as possible. We can overindulge in leisure and dream of a day when we are freed from all labor. But in this kind of self focus, we can forget the goodness of work and our call to work as a way to serve God and other people.

Further, when we don't take time to relax and worship, work can consume our lives. This can make work an idol. When we don't rest, we risk burning out and compromising our physical health. When we don't worship the true God, work can become a god to us. We'll erroneously look for work to provide all our needs, to become our "refuge and strength," to gives us self-worth, and to command our heart's allegiance.

Finally, our society places value on work based on how much it's worth, the praise it receives, or the fame it garners. However, as followers of Christ, we should evaluate our work by other criteria: whether it's done well, is performed for the glory of God, and is an expression of love and service to God and others.

FOR FURTHER READING

Uwe Siemon-Netto, "Work Is Our Mission: Why the Godly Baker's Most Significant Task Is Baking Good Bread," in *Christianity Today,* November 1, 2007.

Miroslav Volf, *Work in the Spirit: Toward a Theology of Work.* Wipf & Stock Publishers, 2001.

Karl Barth, "The Holy Day," "The Active Life," and "Vocation" in *Church Dogmatics* III.V. T and T Clark, 1961.

— DAVID WRIGHT

WORSHIP

EVERYDAY DEFINITION

Worship means reflecting God's self-revealed worth back to him. The word "worship" comes to us from the Middle English word *worthschipe* and refers to something that shows or possesses a state of worth.

When we worship, a communication cycle takes place. Theologians call it "dialogical process." Simply put, this cycle consists of God revealing himself to humans and humans responding accordingly. God shows and tells what he is like, and humans respond with thoughts and feelings of amazement and wonder. When we talk about worship, we're speaking merely of our end of this cycle. We can think of ourselves as being like the moon; it has no light of its own, but simply reflects the light of the sun.

When the word "worship" is used in our English Bibles, it's translated from one of two groups of Hebrew and Greek words, which refer to either acts of homage or acts of service:

1. The first group of words relates to acts of bowing down. The Hebrew word *shachah* means to prostrate, bow down, or

stoop, and the Greek word *proskuneo* means to do reverence, to prostrate, or to kiss toward.

2. The second group consists of words that primarily relate to labor or service. The Hebrew word *Abad* means to serve or stand, and was generally used to refer to the work of the priests and Levites in their roles relating to worship. The Greek word *Leitourgia* refers to the service, work, or ministry of worship.

Unlike praise, worship is a response to the being and nature of God rather than to his works. In everyday terms, "praise" would be like boasting about the great things your spouse has accomplished, while "worship" would be like appreciating your spouse for being loyal, compassionate, honest, and encouraging. Worship, then, centers on character traits rather than deeds. Both worship and praise are necessary and both are biblical. They represent different components of the same relationship. Christians worship God for who he is and praise him for what he has done.

EVERYDAY APPLICATION

It's essential that Christians remember to worship God for who he says he is rather than for who we want him to be. This means that our worship must be:

- Trinitarian—one God, revealed as Father, Son, and Holy Spirit. It's common to hear that all religions worship the same concept of god, but this isn't true. The Christian God is the One True God, who has revealed himself as simultaneously singular and plural: Father, Son, and Holy Spirit, yet one God. This concept of God is unlike any other.
- Christocentric—centered on the person and work of Jesus. Jesus has both shown us the Father (John 14:9) and made us acceptable to be in his presence (Hebrews 10:19-20).

Jesus also taught that worship must be offered "in spirit and truth" (John 4:24). This verse is interpreted in various ways, but in all circumstances it functions as a continuum that helps us maintain balance in worship, so that we don't fall into either license or legalism.

Further, Christians should practice three general types of worship:

1. *Personal worship.* Christians are the temple of God, and God's very Spirit dwells in them (1 Corinthians 3:16). Various terms are used for this worshipful devotion: the "secret place" (Psalm 27:5, NASB), the "inmost place" (Psalm 51:6), and the "inner being" (Ephesians 3:16). Here, at the intersection of time and eternity, we are privileged to commune with God. The apostle Paul noted the wonderful by-product of practicing personal worship: "That you, being rooted and established in love, may have power, together with all the saints, to grasp how wide and long and high and deep is the love of Christ, and to know this love that surpasses knowledge — that you may be filled to the measure of all the fullness of God" (Ephesians 3:17-19). The thought that we can have both knowledge and experience with the Living God is unfathomable, but true!

2. *Corporate worship.* The apostle Peter addressed Christ-followers in cooperative terms like "people," "priesthood," and "nation." Peter used these terms to describe that the body of Christ can "declare the praises of him who called you out of darkness into his wonderful light" (1 Peter 2:9). Sometimes we question the need for the corporate gathering, in lieu of the practice of personal worship. Again, both are important; both are biblical. Jesus said, "For where two or three come together in my name, there am I with them" (Matthew 18:20). In corporate worship, Christians reflect the very nature of the triune God; when we gather to worship, we are simultaneously singular and plural, and we experience God corporately through both the presence of the Holy Spirit and through one another. This dual audience is reflected in Paul's words to the Ephesians: "Speak to one another with psalms, hymns and spiritual songs. Sing and make music in your heart to the Lord, always giving thanks to God the Father for everything, in the name of our Lord Jesus Christ" (Ephesians 5:19-20).

3. *A lifestyle of worship.* When Adam and Eve breathed their initial breaths and brushed the dirt from their newly created

skin, they must have looked up and seen God wiping the primordial clay from his hands. They instantly knew Who created them and Who they should live for. They knew they were created worshipping! When they sinned, they simply traded gods, but kept on worshipping. A lifestyle of worship means that we show our love—and as a result, our worship—through our obedience to God. Jesus said, "Whoever has my commands and obeys them, he is the one who loves me" (John 14:21). When tempted by Satan to trade gods, Jesus replied, "Worship the Lord your God, and serve him only" (Matthew 4:10). The apostle Paul urged Christians to consider the mercies they had received and to worship by offering themselves as a living sacrifice (Romans 12:1). Scripture doesn't demand perfection. However, the daily life of a worshipper will be fueled by God's mercies to live a life pleasing to God.

To understand worship, we can simply answer the question: "What does the God of the Bible say that he is like?" As Christians, we should mirror God's attributes back to him with reverence, adoration, fascination, and admiration. When we do this, we obey the greatest commandment: "Love the LORD your God with all your heart and with all your soul and with all your strength" (Deuteronomy 6:5).

FOR FURTHER READING
A. W. Tozer, *The Knowledge of the Holy.* HarperOne, 1992.
Ronald Allen, *The Wonder of Worship.* Thomas Nelson, 2001.

—JIM ALTIZER

ABOUT THE GENERAL EDITORS

DR. BRUCE DEMAREST was educated at Wheaton College and Trinity Evangelical Divinity School. He earned his doctorate in biblical and historical theology at the University of Manchester. A professor at Denver Seminary, he has written numerous books in theology and spirituality including *Integrative Theology*, *The Cross and Salvation*, *Satisfy Your Soul*, and *Seasons of the Soul*. Dr. Demarest lives in Littleton, Colorado.

DR. KEITH J. MATTHEWS is an ordained pastor and professor currently teaching in the Graduate School of Theology at Azusa Pacific University. He is a "Senior Teaching Fellow" with the Renovare Institute and has written articles in *Sojourners* magazine and *Leadership Journal*, as well as designed and coauthored *Dallas Willard's Study Guide for the Divine Conspiracy*. Keith resides in Southern California with his wife, Christa, and kids, Cori, Kyle, and Kate.

CONTRIBUTORS

Paul Alexander, PhD
Professor, Theology and Ethics; Director of the Doctor of Ministry
Graduate School of Theology
Azusa Pacific University

Gregg R. Allison, PhD
Professor of Christian Theology
The Southern Baptist Theological Seminary

Jim Altizer, D.WS
Adjunct Instructor in Worship Leadership
Graduate School of Theology
Azusa Pacific University

James Beck, PhD
Senior Professor of Counseling
Denver Seminary

Christopher T. Bounds, PhD
Associate Professor of Theology
Indiana Wesleyan University

Sung Wook Chung, D.Phil.
Associate Professor of Theology
Denver Seminary

Cheryl A. Crawford, PhD
Assistant Professor of Practical Theology
Azusa Pacific University

Hélène Dallaire, PhD
Associate Professor of Old Testament
Denver Seminary

Bruce Demarest, PhD
Professor of Christian Formation
Denver Seminary

Matt Elofson, PhD
Assistant Professor of Practical Theology
Azusa Pacific University

Tim Finlay, PhD
Associate Professor of Biblical Studies
Graduate School of Theology
Azusa Pacific University

S. Donald Fortson, III, D.Min., PhD
Associate Professor of Church History and Practical Theology
Reformed Theological Seminary

Kurt Fredrickson, D.Min.
Director, Doctor of Ministry Program
Assistant Professor of Pastoral Ministry
Fuller Theological Seminary

Fred Gingrich, D.Min.
Associate Professor of Counseling and Counseling Division Chair
Denver Seminary

Michael Glerup, PhD
Projects Director
Center for Early African Christianity
Drew University

Douglas Groothuis, PhD
Professor of Philosophy
Denver Seminary

Vernon Grounds, PhD
President Emeritus and Chancellor
Denver Seminary

George Haraksin, Doctoral Candidate
Adjunct Instructor in Philosophy
Azusa Pacific University

Matthew R. Hauge, Doctoral Candidate
Instructor of Religion
Department of Biblical Studies
Division of Religion & Philosophy
Azusa Pacific University

Evan Howard, PhD
Lecturer, Author, Spiritual director
Montrose, Colorado

Todd D. Hunter, D.Min.
Adjunct Professor of Evangelism, Spiritual Formation, Leadership,
    and Contemporary Culture
George Fox Evangelism Seminary, Wheaton Graduate School, Fuller
    Seminary

Klaus Issler, PhD
Professor of Christian Education and Theology
Talbot School of Theology
Biola University

Jan Johnson, D.Min.
Writer, Speaker, and Spiritual Director
Assistant Adjunct Professor
Hope International University

Tony Jones, PhD (ABD)
Theologian in Residence at Solomon's Porch Church
Writer/Speaker

Gordon Lewis, PhD
Senior Professor of Christian Philosophy and Theology
Denver Seminary

Randy MacFarland, D.Min.
Provost and Academic Dean
Denver Seminary

Keith J. Matthews, D.Min.
Professor of Spiritual Formation & Contemporary Culture, and Chair
    of the Ministry Department
Graduate School of Theology
Azusa Pacific University

Gary W. Moon, PhD
Vice President and Chair of Integration: Richmont Graduate
    University
Executive Director: Renovaré Institute for Christian Spiritual
    Formation

Erika Moore, PhD
Associate Professor of Old Testament
Trinity School for Ministry

Christopher Morton, PhD
Chief Theological and Cultural Researcher
The Navigators

Robert A. Muthiah, PhD
Associate Professor of Practical Theology
Graduate School of Theology
Azusa Pacific University

Tim Peck, D.Min.
Director of Chapel Programs and Adjunct Instructor
Graduate School of Theology
Azusa Pacific University

Steve Strauss, PhD
Professor of World Missions and Intercultural Studies
Dallas Theological Seminary

Sarah Sumner, PhD
Professor of Theology and Ministry; Special Assistant to the Dean for
    Strategic Development
Graduate School of Theology
Azusa Pacific University

Donald Sweeting, PhD
Senior Pastor, Cherry Creek Presbyterian Church
Centennial, Colorado

Don Thorsen, PhD
Professor of Theology, and Chair of Advanced Studies
Graduate School of Theology
Azusa Pacific University

Bruce A. Ware, PhD
Professor of Christian Theology
The Southern Baptist Theological Seminary

Scott A. Wenig, PhD
Professor of Applied Theology and Chair of the Division of Christian
    Ministry
Denver Seminary

Steve Wilkens, PhD
Professor of Philosophy and Ethics
Azusa Pacific University

David Wright, PhD
Provost
Indiana Wesleyan University

Discover more about the Bible with The Navigators Reference Library.

The Complete Book of Discipleship
Bill Hull
978-1-57683-897-6

The Complete Book of Discipleship is the definitive A-to-Z resource on discipleship for every Christian. This well-organized, indexed guide pulls together such topics as spiritual growth, transformation, spiritual disciplines, and discipleship in the local church and beyond.

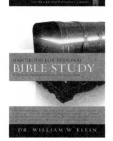

Handbook for Personal Bible Study
Dr. William W. Klein
978-1-60006-117-2

This well-organized handbook explains different aspects of Bible study. With a full index, *Handbook for Personal Bible Study* makes it easy for you to interpret the Bible and understand the history of it.

To order copies, call NavPress at 1-800-366-7788
or log on to www.navpress.com.